The 1879 Zulu War

Through the eyes of

The Illustrated London News

Compiled by Ron Lock & Peter Quantrill
Foreword by David Rattray

Q-Lock Publications
PO Box 402
Kloof 3640
kwaZulu-Natal
South Africa

ISBN 0-620308-99-0

Copyright © 2003

All rights reserved. No part of this publication may be reproduced, stored in a retrieval system, or transmitted in any form or by any means, electronic, photocopying or otherwise without express written consent of the compilers.

Printed and Bound by Pinetown Printers

FOREWORD

The Anglo-Zulu War of 1879 is arguably the most famous military campaign of the Victorian era.

This is with good reason; the Zulu victory at Isandlwana, days after the British invasion started, was for the British, simply incomprehensible.

At Rorke's Drift the Zulus, flushed with their success that morning at Isandlwana, and perhaps imbued with a similar arrogance that had bedevilled the British, failed to overrun that brave British garrison. Eleven Victoria Crosses were awarded for valour, and that battle continues to enjoy a disproportionately high profile.

No doubt the battles of Isandlwana and Rorke's Drift will continue to occupy the limelight, yet the campaign ran on for months. The British were involved in other defeats and disasters. The siege of Eshowe and the death of the Prince Imperial of France offer impossible twists to the tale, before that awful ritual Battle of Ulundi, which smashed the Old Zulu Order for ever.

This campaign was fought in a country, to paraphrase Alan Paton, "beautiful beyond any singing of it". Some of the finest artists in the world would bring this gorgeous geography into the hearths and homes of British people, in the pages of the *Illustrated London News*. The larger-than-life characters that occupied central stage in this extraordinary saga become household names in the homes of a nation at the zenith of her power.

While the *Illustrated London News* contained a wealth of fascinating domestic trivia, it was the reporting of the military campaigns abroad that caught the eye of the reader. For the subscription of a sixpence per week the British public would be mesmerised by the Zulu War of 1879, a campaign which attracts much attention to this day.

At times somewhat jingoistic and obviously one-sided, these skilful journalists provided some of the most evocative and eloquent copy ever to come of this country. Some would say they provided an exaggerated image of the "Noble Savage", but the British public were left in no doubt as to the calibre and quality of these fine Zulu people. Indeed, it was on the field of Isandlwana that the Zulus carved for themselves their place in history. They are amongst the most famous warrior nations in the world.

"S.B." Bourquin, that great gentleman, did us all a wonderful service when he privately published his compilation in 1971, meticulously extracting all the copy and some illustrations pertaining to the Zulu War.

Ron Lock and Peter Quantrill have established themselves in this field of military history. Their recently published *Zulu Victory, the Epic of Isandlwana and the Cover-Up* is a major contribution to the much debated saga of Isandlwana. It is thoroughly researched and beautifully written.

They have taken Bourquin's project a step further and produced this elegant publication which does fine justice to the heyday of illustrated newspapers.

Reading the faultless prosaic English will delight all who love language and give insight into an era of civilization now gone.

The provision of an index is a huge boon to those who will use this book for academic purposes.

125 years have now slipped by since that campaign which had such hideous consequences for the Zulu people. I would hope that in this period of commemoration our focus should rest on the upliftment and education of the descendants of those warriors who fought so bravely on these now famous battlefields so that they can participate in the prosperity of this new era.

All who visit these sites remark on the friendliness of these people, many of whom live in abject poverty. I believe their attitude brings upon us an awesome responsibility. It is incumbent on us too to see that the battlefields themselves are carefully preserved. They should always stand as monuments to the relationship of affection and respect that exists between two fine nations.

David Rattray

Fugitive's Drift, 2003

DEDICATION

Lieutenant-Colonel S. Bourquin and Tania M. Johnston were the original compilers of the Anglo-Zulu War as reported through the eyes of *The London Illustrated News* of 1879–that was over 30 years ago in an age of typewriters and Roneo machines.
Updated technology has now allowed us to scan the original two volumes of the ILN and to reproduce faithfully the quality of both text and illustrations.
However, "S.B." and Tania showed us the way. With their knowledge and support we affectionately dedicate this work to them.

Ron Lock and Peter Quantrill
Kwa-Zulu, Natal 2003

February 8, 1879

Reading the Ultimatum on the banks of the Tugela

THE ZULU WAR IN SOUTH AFRICA

War has actually commenced between the British Government in South Africa, represented by Sir Bartle Frere, with Lord Chelmsford commanding the military forces, and the King of the Zulus, whose name is usually written Cetewayo, but is pronounced Ketchwayo. His dominions are situated north of the British province of Natal, on the eastern seacoast and the adjacent mountains; the Transvaal province lies inland, west of the Zulu territory. There had long been a dispute about Zulu claims to the Utrecht district of the Transvaal, which till lately belonged to the Dutch Boers, but which has been annexed to the British dominions. It appears, moreover, that Cetewayo has, upon two or three occasions, caused refugees from his kingdom to be pursued and captured on our side of the frontier, and that some of his people have stolen cattle.

But the real cause of hostilities is the fear long entertained in Natal of the large military force maintained by Cetewayo. Sir Bartle Frere, as Governor-General of the British provinces and High Commissioner for all dealings with the native African races, has therefore sent an ultimatum to King Cetewayo, the terms of which embrace a partial disarmament, a rectification of the frontier, the appointment of a British Resident (with a voice in the great council of the Zulu nation), and the cession of St. Lucia Bay, on the ground that it is used as a landing place for arms and ammunition. The King had taken alarm at the British preparations for war, and sent two of his chief indunas into Utrecht to express his regret at the acts of some of his people in the disputed territory, promising their punishment and obedience in the future. He further expressed his surprise at the British forces hovering about his borders at seven different points, and was evidently uneasy at the erection of the Luneberg fort, which is situated on his flank and towards his rear.

The Intelligence Department has not been idle during the past three months. This is shown by the publication of a pamphlet entitled "The Zulu Army," for distribution to the columns in the field. It is compiled from trustworthy sources, and sets down the number of the Zulu forces at 42,000 warriors, as follows: - 20,000 from twenty to thirty years of age; 10,000 from thirty to forty; and the remaining 12,000 up to any age. The names, strength, residence, and distinguishing dress of each regiment are detailed, and the pamphlet is accompanied by a photographed sketch-map of Zululand, and a plan of the usual Zulu attack.

Our illustrations published this week are supplied by Mr James Lloyd, an artist and photographer of Durban, in Natal, who accompanied the Commissioners, Mr Brownlee, Mr J. Shepstone, Colonel Walker, and Mr H.F. Fynn, to meet the Zulu chiefs in a conference on the banks of the Tugela river, near Fort Pearson.

Her Majesty's ship Active, Captain Sullivan (Commodore Commanding Cape Station), lately returned from a trip up the coast to Delagoa Bay, where she is said to have made arrangements as to mutual assistance with the Portuguese during the war. On the home journey a surveying party were landed at St Lucia Bay, to examine its capacities for use as a landing station for troops. A few days afterwards she was anchored off the Tugela mouth to enable soundings to be taken, so that, in the event of having to shell the neighbouring heights, the position to be taken up might be known beforehand. The Tugela is the river which at one part separates Natal from the Zulu territory.

All this being satisfactorily concluded, H.M.S. Active returned to Durban and landed a naval brigade for service ashore, consisting of nearly 200 sailors and marines, under Captain Campbell. They are armed with two 7-pounder Armstrong guns, a Gatling gun, and several rocket apparatuses. They have proceeded to Stanger, from which they go to either of the nearest forts, Williamson or Pearson. The former is the first defensive position occupied by our forces inland. It is situated at the mouth of the Tugela on the Natal side, and, having been materially strengthened, is to be the headquarters dépôt for all the branches serving in the Lower District under Major Graves (the Buffs), Commandant of the Coast District.

Following the line of the river, farther up some thirty miles, at a place called the lower Drift, a new and powerful fort has been erected. Fort Pearson is on a high hill overlooking the river, and commands not only the Drift, but also a good deal of the country surrounding. It is almost inaccessible from the river, but easily approachable by a gradual slope on one side. One regiment, part of another, and a battery of artillery are to occupy this fort. Some way inland, and about two thirds of the way from the city of Durban to the Tugela, is Stanger, which is now rapidly becoming a large and important military centre, with which both the above-named forts will keep open their communications for supplies.

Fort Pearson, Lower Tugela, from the west

Fort Buckingham comes next, and is equally impregnable against any number of Zulus. This fort is strongly garrisoned, and obtains its supplies through Grey Town and Hermansburg. Both the latter places are occupied by troops, and are strong positions. From there up to Newcastle and Utrecht is very difficult country, thinly populated, and offering no inducement for bodies of the enemy to enter, even if there were any drifts except Rorke's Drift. The whole of the district is constantly patrolled by Natal Mounted Volunteer Corps, assisted by the Natal Mounted police having camps or dépôts at Helpmakaar, Estcourt, Weener, Colenso, and Ladysmith.

Newcastle has been turned into a large military camp, and, being almost halfway between the Natal coast and Pretoria, in Transvaal, also the junction of the roads to Utrecht and Lydenburg, is one of the largest dépôts for stores, supplies, and ammunition. Added to a large garrison regularly quartered there, troops are constantly passing backwards and forwards, requiring a large staff to attend to their requirements. About twenty miles to the north-east lies Utrecht, a town on the disputed territory, which it is of importance to have occupied by a large military force. It was from this place that the column under Colonel Wood started for Luneberg, still farther in the disputed territory, and now holding a large number of troops, which are shortly to be augmented by those parts of the 80th and 90th Regiments, the 13th, and the Frontier Light Horse, which have been withdrawn from Lydenburg. Utrecht is the key to the north-western gate of Zululand, and its value is apparently thoroughly understood and appreciated by the General.

The district between Natal and New Scotland is to be occupied by a large force of Swazi levies, raised under Commandant la Trobe Lonsdale. They consist of two regiments, and are officered by men chosen in the Cape colony by the Commandant, who have had great experience in the late war in leading native levies. The 'Swazis' are deadly antagonists of the Zulus, and the best fighting men in South Africa when properly led. Another Cape Colony corps has arrived in Natal; the Kaffrarian Riflemen, under Commandant Schermbrucker, about 450 strong. The Frontier Light Horse, also from the Cape, who have been engaged in Secocoeni's country, will join them there. Among the active preparations in Natal is the raising of a native contingent, to consist of ten battalions of 1000 men each. These men, carefully picked out by the magistrates from different native locations in the colony, will all be armed, equipped, officered, and trained, and then distributed along the whole border line, in company with forces of regulars and volunteers. Colonel Durnford, R.E., assisted by Captain Brunker, late 26th Regiment, has had this task to perform, aided by the Commandants. The officers and non-commissioned officers have been principally chosen from the Natal colony, and are a serviceable lot of fellows.

Another new and important position has been taken up at Helpmakaar, near Dundee. It is about twelve miles from Rorke's Drift at the junction of the Tugela and Buffalo Rivers. Three local volunteer corps, the Natal Carbineers, the Buffalo Border Guards, and the Newcastle Mounted Rifles, proceed there. The whole of the corps at Helpmakaar form part of Colonel Glyn's column, and act with the Natal Mounted Police, under Major Dartnell. These forces consist of the 1st battalion 24th, part of the Buffs, a battery of artillery, 520 of the Natal Mounted Police, the three volunteer corps, and two regiments of native levies, equalling 2000, making a total of about 3000 men. Three other corps – the Durham Mounted Rifles, the Alexandra Mounted Rifles, and Natal Hussars – proceed to Pots Sprint, beyond Grey Town and will join part of the column commanded by Colonel Pearson; but the act for the present under the immediate command of Captain Barrow, 19th Hussars.

The centre column is commanded by Colonel Pearson, 3rd Buffs, Commandant of Natal, a very able officer, who is assisted by Colonel Walker, Scots Guard, as chief of his staff. It consists of the Buffs, part of the second battalion 24th, under Colonel Degacher, two batteries of artillery, three volunteer corps, and two regiments of native levies, altogether about 3500. The headquarters of this column will be at Grey Town. The column at the coast is under the command of Major Graves, the Buffs, with headquarters in Stanger, and consists of the Naval Brigade, part of the Buffs, and second battalion 24th, two batteries of artillery, and two more mounted volunteer corps – namely, the Stanger Mounted Rifles, and Victoria Mounted Rifles – and two regiments of native levies, making over 3000 men.

When the rest of the native levies have been distributed, with the three regiments, the first battalion 13th, 80th, and 90th, between Rorke's Drift and New Scotland, we have nearly 15,000 men on the border. The 88th have also come round from the Cape. The colony has been divided into seven defensive districts, each under the charge of an officer appointed by the Lieutenant-Governor; town guards are also formed, and reserve volunteer forces. There are enormous stocks of provisions and ammunition, distributed all over the country; and the transport and commissariat services have proved themselves fully equal to the occasion.

THE ILLUSTRATED LONDON NEWS

February 15, 1879

THE ZULU WAR

BRITISH REVERSE

Telegrams of Cape news to Jan. 27, received by way of St. Vincent, bring news of a terrible disaster to the British troops in Zululand. In the first brush with the enemy, which took place on Jan. 12, and lasted an hour, the Zulu fled, leaving forty of their number dead, besides many who were taken prisoners; our troops having two killed and fourteen wounded. But on Jan. 22 a force of 20,000 Zulus attacked a British column consisting of a portion of the 24th Regiment and 600 natives, with one battery, and killed 500 men and thirty officers. The Zulus are said to have lost 5000 in killed and wounded, and the British force is reported to have been annihilated. A valuable convoy of supplies, including ammunition and commissariat stores, was captured, and the colours of the 24th Regiment fell into the hands of the enemy. The English army has recrossed the border, and a steamer has been sent to Mauritius to ask for reinforcements, and an appeal for additional troops has been sent to England. The position of Natal, the telegrams say, is serious.

The War Office has received from Lord Chelmsford the following telegraphic despatch: -

St. Vincent, Feb. 10, 6.40 p.m.
I regret to have to report a very disastrous engagement, which took place on Jan. 22, between the Zulus and a portion of No. 3 Column, left to guard the camp about ten miles in front of Rorke's Drift. The Zulus came down in overwhelming numbers; and, in spite of the gallant resistance made by five companies of the 1-24th and one company of the 2-24th, two guns, two rocket-tubes, 104 mounted men, and about 800 natives, they overwhelmed them. The camp, containing all the surplus ammunition and transport of No. 3 Column, was taken, and but few of its defenders escaped. Our loss, I fear, must be set down at thirty officers and about 500 non-commissioned officers, rank and file, of Imperial troops, and seventy non-commissioned officers, rank and file, of colonial troops. Court of inquiry ordered to assemble to collect evidence regarding this unfortunate affair, and will be forwarded to you as soon as received. Full particulars, as far as can be obtained, have been sent in my despatch, which will reach you by next mail.

It would seem that the troops were enticed away from their camp, as the action took place about one mile and a quarter outside it. The remainder of Colonel Glyn's column reoccupied the camp after dark the same night, having been with me twelve miles away all day. The following morning, the 23rd, we arrived at Rorke's Drift post, which for twelve hours had been attacked by 3000 to 4000 Zulus. The defence by some eighty men of the 24th, under Bromehead and a few others, most gallant. Lieutenant Chard, R.E., senior officer. 370 bodies lay close around the post. Complete Zulu loss at 1000 here alone.

At the camp where the disaster occurred the loss of the enemy is computed to be over 2000. Colonel Pearson, No. 1 Column, has been attacked, but repulsed the Zulus with success. List of killed and missing: - Royal Engineers – Colonel Durnford, Lieutenant Macdonald. Royal Artillery – Captain Russell, Captain Stuart Smith. First battalion, 24th Regiment – Colonel Pulleine, Major White, Captains Degacher, Wardell, Mostyn, and Younghusband; Lieutenants Hodson, Cavaye, Atkinson, Daly, Anstey, Dyson, Porteous, Melvill, Coghill; Quartermaster Pullen. Second battalion, Lieutenants Pope, Austin, Dyer, Griffith; Quartermaster Bloomfield; Surgeon-Major Shepherd.

At a meeting of the Cabinet held on Tuesday afternoon it was decided to despatch six battalions of infantry, two regiments of cavalry, two batteries of artillery, one company of engineers, three companies of the Army Service Corps, and one company of the Army Hospital Corps, as reinforcements to the Cape. The regiments are: - The second battalion of the 21st Foot, from the Curragh; the 58th Regiment, from Dover; the third battalion of the 60th Rifles, from Colchester; the 57th Foot, from Ceylon; the 91st Regiment, from Aldershot; the 94th Regiment, also from Aldershott; the 1st King's Dragoons, from Aldershott; the 17th Lancers, from Hounslow; the M and N Batteries, 6th Brigade, Royal Artillery; the 30th Company Royal Engineers, from Chatham.

The 24th (2nd Warwickshire) Regiment, which has suffered such terrible losses in engagement on the 21st ult., stands high among the most distinguished regiments in the British Army. Its record of service includes the following campaigns and battles: - Schellenberg, Blenheim, Neer-Hespen, Malplaquet, Germany, 1702-10; Carthagena, Minorca, Cherbourg, Guadaloupe, Corbach, Denkern, Wilhemstahl, Germany, 1760-2; Stillwater, America, Egypt, Cape of Good Hope, 1806; Talavera, Fuentes d'Onor, Salamanca, Vittoria, St. Sebastian, Pyrenees, Nivelle, Orthés, Peninsula, Punjaub, Chillianwallah, Goojerat, Indian Mutiny. At the battle of Chillianwallah the regiment lost even more heavily than on the present occasion, being literally cut to pieces by the Sikhs when entangled in the jungle. Its sobriquet is "Howard's Greens," from the name of a former Colonel and the colour of its facings.

The following are the names of the officers on the strength of the 24th Regiments, including both battalions. Those marked with an asterisk are reported among the casualties: -

Lieutenant-Colonels - R.T. Glyn, H.J. Degacher.
Majors – *H.B. Pulleine, W.M. Dunbar, W. Black, W.B. Logan.
Captains – W.R.B. Chamberlin, J.M.G. Tongue, J.F. Caldwell, W.M. Brander, H.A. Harrison, H.B. Church, *W. Degacher, G. Peyton, H.R. Farquhar, *W.E. Mostyn, R. Upcher, *G.V. Wardell, C.J. Bromehead, F. Glennie, W.T. Much, T. Rainforth, A.G. Godwin-Austen, *R. Younghusband, W.P. Symons, F. Carrington, H.B. Moffat, J.J. Harvey.
Lieutenants – H.M. Williams, *T. Melvill, L.H. Bennett, A.A. Morshead, *F.P. Porteous, W. Sugden, *C. D'A. Pope, G. Bromhead, G.S. Banister, S.T. Halliday, E.S. Browne, E.W. Curteis, *C.W. Cavaye, *M.J.A.Coghill, *E.O. Anstey, H.G. Mainwaring, *J.P. Daly, *G.F.J. Hodson, W. Heaton, R.A.P. Clements, *C.J. Atkinson, W.E.D. Spring, H.M.K. Logan, the Hon. U. de R.B. Roche, *H.J. Dyer, C.V. Trower, G.C. Palmes, *F. Godwin-Austen.
Sub-Lieutenant – *T.L.G. Griffiths. Second Lieutenants - *E.H. Dyson, A.W. Franklin, W. Weallens, W.W. Lloyd, L.G.L. Dobree, A.B. Phipps, C.E. Curll. Paymasters - *F.F. White, J. Mahony.
*Quartermasters – E. Bloomfield, *J. Pullen.
Surgeon-Major Shepherd, who is included in the list of killed and missing, left England only recently with the last batch of medical officers, and will be remembered as having taken an active interest in teaching the metropolitan police ambulance duties.

The following are some details of the services of the officers of the ill-fated 24th Regiment who have fallen: -

Major Henry Burmeister Pulleine, a Brevet Lieutenant-Colonel in the Army, and serving as Regimental Major in the first battalion of the 24th Regiment, entered the service as an Ensign on Nov. 16, 1855; became Lieutenant on June 4, 1858; Captain on Nov. 15, 1861; Major on Feb. 4, 1871; Brevet Lieutenant-Colonel on Oct 1, 1877. Captain William Degacher joined the Army as an Ensign on May 31, 1859; became a Lieutenant on Aug. 19, 1862; and Captain on Dec. 2, 1868. Captain George Vaughan Wardell joined as an Ensign on May 14, 1858; became Lieutenant on July 23, 1861, and Captain on Feb. 10, 1872. Captain Mostyn entered the Army as Ensign on July 29, 1862; was promoted to Lieutenant on March 23, 1866 and to Captain on Oct. 31, 1871. And, to conclude the list of Captains, Captain Reginald Younghusband entered the service as an Ensign on Aug. 20, 1862; became Lieutenant on Aug. 29, 1866; and Captain on March 14, 1876.

All these officers belonged to the first battalion of the 24th Regiment, as did also Lieutenant Charles Walter Cavaye, who entered the service as Lieutenant on Dec. 30, 1871; Lieutenant George Frederick John Hodson, Feb. 28, 1874; Lieutenant Atkinson, Feb. 28, 1875; Lieutenant Daly, Feb. 28, 1874; Lieutenant Anstey, March 9, 1873; Lieutenant Porteous, Ensign March 9, 1866, Lieutenant Dec. 22, 1869; Lieutenant Melvill, Ensign Oct. 20, 1865, and Lieutenant Dec. 2, 1868; and Second Lieutenant Dyson, May 1, 1878. Of the second battalion of the 24th Regiment three young officers are reported to have fallen – namely, Lieutenant Pope, who obtained his commission as Ensign on Jan. 8, 1868, and as Lieutenant on Feb. 4, 1871; Lieutenant Dyer, Lieutenant on Oct. 11, 1876; and Lieutenant Griffith, Sept 11, 1876.

Altogether, therefore, it will be seen from the above list that of the thirty officers belonging to the first battalion of the 24th Regiment fourteen, within one of half the whole number, are reported to have fallen in the terrible reverse suffered on Jan. 22 last.

We learn from a colonial newspaper that Lord Chelmsford's army comprised about 6600 Europeans and 7000 natives. Of these, about 1400 were mounted men, and there were twenty guns of different calibres attached to the columns. In addition, there were reserves of 1600 regulars and over 700 enrolled volunteers.
Sir Bartle Frere has published a memorandum on the causes which led to the conflict, which he maintains has not been provoked by the British Government, who have done their best to avoid war by every means consistent with honour.

February 22, 1879

The Zulu War in South Africa : Cetewayo, the Zulu King
Drawn from the life in June, 1877, by the late Mr Edward Tilt, during his visit to Zulu-Land

THE ZULU WAR

The momentous conflict which has finally broken out in South Africa between the British Imperial Government, on the Natal and Trans-Vaal borders and the savage tyranny of Cetewayo, King of the Zulus, is likely for several months to engross no small part of our serious attention. We do not feel called upon, in this and future notices of the subject as furnishing material for our Illustrations, to enter upon any discussion of the policy or morality of British dealings with the Kaffirs and other African nations. It is more than forty years since the territory of Natal, situated on the coast of the Indian Ocean, far remote and quite detached from the easterly provinces of the Cape Colony, was taken into British possession; but it was the annexation of the Trans-Vaal, not three years ago, that gave occasion to the present hostile relations with the neighbouring Zulu kingdom.

This remark is simply due to historical truth, and it is needful to avoid confounding the new emergency with the situation at the time of preceding Kaffir Wars, such as those of the Gaikas and Galekas in the Trans-Kei territory, the last of which was recently concluded. In those former conflicts, it is most important to observe, the Colonial Government of Cape Town was properly and directly involved by the endangered position of its own eastern frontier. But this is not apparently the case with a Zulu war to the north of Natal and to the east of the Trans-Vaal, since neither of those two isolated provinces has ever had any political connection with the Cape Colony, or has derived its European settlement from the Cape.

The Zulu War: Natal Mounted Police, under Major Dartnell, on their way to the front.
From a sketch by Mr. W. Nelson, Helpmakaar Camp, December 22.

It happens, indeed, that in the person of Sir Bartle Frere, her Majesty's representative in South Africa, the Governorship, or constitutional presidency of the self-governed colony in South-West Africa, is conjoined with the separate administration of Crown rule, through a Lieutenant-Governor of Natal, and a High Commissioner in the Trans-Vaal, as well as in West Griqua Land and several parts of South-East Africa; but this incidental association does not make the Cape colonists responsible for the acts of the Imperial Government, through Sir Bartle Frere, on the Zulu border nearly a thousand miles distant from their own quiet and secure capital city. We may, nevertheless, expect from the genuine public spirit, the British loyalty and patriotism, of the inhabitants of the Cape Colony, as well in its western as in its eastern districts, a spontaneous and voluntary exhibition of their readiness to co-operate with her Majesty's forces, to uphold the authority and dignity of her title, and to protect her subjects, both of native and of European race, on the banks of the Tugela and the Pongola. The same feelings would equally animate every other English community dwelling within reach of the scene of action in any quarter of the globe.

The Zulu nation is one of the two great races of Kaffirs, or South-east native Africans, inhabiting all the portion of that Continent which looks towards the Indian Ocean, from near the Great Kei River to near Delagoa Bay; the Amaxosa race, divided into many separate tribes, of which the Galekas and Gaikas are nearest to the colonial frontier, occupy the southern districts. The Zulus altogether may number, it is supposed, about six hundred thousand souls, half of them residing within the province of Natal, under British dominion, half of them remaining to the independent kingdom of Cetewayo, situated to the north of the Tugela, and extending almost to Delagoa Bay.

The Zulu War: Rourke's Drift, near the scene of the recent conflict.
From a sketch by Major North Crealock, 95th Regiment, Assistant Military Secretary.

This is not, indeed, a very large kingdom, but its absolute despotic constitution and singular military organisation, with the determined character of its ruler, make it the most formidable of all Native African Powers – more so, probably, than either the Ashantee monarchy at its full strength, or that of King Theodore in Abyssinia, when they defied the British arms to a decisive combat. The issue of this war, notwithstanding, is beyond all reasonable doubt, since the great resources of the British Empire will be used, so far as may prove needful, to obtain a complete victory, at whatever pecuniary cost.

Ever since the days of Chaka, whose reign extended from 1810 to 1828, the Zulus have been regarded as the military race of South Africa; and at the present time his nephew, Cetewayo, possesses a force of about 40,000 men, to a certain extent organised and fairly well equipped. The army is divided into several regiments, varying in strength from 400 to 2000, each commanded by an Induna or chief. Every male becomes a soldier at the age of fifteen, and continues to serve all his life. The regiments are composed of men of nearly the same age, new ones being formed from time to time by recruits, and distinguished from the veteran corps by the colour of their shields. In former years a bundle of light throwing assegais, a short and heavy one for stabbing, a shield, and "knobkerrie," or knobstick, were the arms of the Zulu soldier.

Now many regiments are armed with breech-loading rifles, in which case the stabbing assegai is still carried, the shield being discarded. In 1873 a small powder factory was established and a magazine built at the principal military kraal. This latter was called "Mainze-kanze" – i.e., "Let the enemy come now." Matrimony is forbidden to the soldier, though periodically the King orders a whole regiment to marry, selecting as their wives the daughters of men belonging to some specified regiment. Once during the year each regiment is called out for a month's training, which is said to consist principally in hunting and dancing. During this time the troops are quartered in one of twenty military kraals which are dotted throughout the country, the principal one being situated near the junction of the Black and White Umvolosi.

Strict discipline is enforced throughout the army, cowardice on all occasions being punished by death. To the women is intrusted the commissariat, and they perform long journeys on foot, often exceeding forty or fifty miles a day when carrying supplies to the army in the field. The Zulu has an innate love of fighting, and firmly believes in his own invincibility. Formerly his tactics were simple. Advancing in line, each man discharged his throwing assegais, then rushing in, armed with the stabbing assegai, he maintained a hand-to-hand fight against his enemy; but the introduction of firearms has modified this form of tactics. Unlike the Kaffirs of Cape Colony, the Zulus are said to prefer night attacks, and in order to be well prepared for such midnight alarms a uniform plan of encampment of a defensive nature is adopted for our army engaged against Cetewayo.

Such is the military character of the Zulu nation, against whom the British High Commissioner declared war, and ordered the British Army to cross the Tugela frontier river on the 11th ult.

We have described the plan of operations, and we reported last week the disastrous occurrence of Jan. 22, ten days after the beginning of actual hostilities by Lord Chelmsford's army. The left centre column, under the command of Colonel Glyn, with which was Lord Chelmsford's head-quarters as Commander-in-Chief, advanced from Helpmakaar through Rourke's Drift, just below the junction of the Blood River with the Buffalo River, which flows into the Tugela lower down. This place is nearly at the point of meeting of the frontier lines of the Natal and the Trans-Vaal provinces with that of the Zulu Kingdom; and a short distance across the last-mentioned frontier lies the kraal of Siwayo, the King's brother, whose fugitive wives, having escaped to the Natal side, were lately pursued and recaptured, and were stoned to death.

Lord Chelmsford seems to have divided the column of troops in Rourke's Drift, and taken half of them, with Colonel Glyn, on a reconnaissance in the direction of Colonel Wood, whom he met pushing forward. The remainder were left under command of Lieutenant-Colonel Pulleyne, to whose support Colonel Durnford moved northward with part of the right-centre column. Their camp was fixed about ten miles beyond Rourke's Drift to the eastward, where they had a hundred and two waggons of the transport service, with a thousand draught bullocks, and all the stores and surplus ammunition of Colonel Glyn's column. It is supposed that by some artifice of deception the Zulus contrived to lure Colonel Durnford into detaching a portion of his force from the sheltered encampment.

South African Warfare : Artillery passing through the bush.
From a sketch by Mr. Melton Prior in the late Kaffir War.

The details are still lacking, but we know that they were attacked by an overwhelming host of the enemy, reckoned at from fifteen to twenty thousand, and all the European troops were destroyed, with the officers and non-commissioned officers, except a few, of the native troops. Five companies of the first battalion of the 24th Regiment, and one company of its second battalion, with thirty officers of the regular army, and about seventy of the native force, altogether six hundred men, were killed in this terrible conflict. It took place a mile and a quarter from the camp, which was afterwards sacked by the enemy, and all the stores, bullocks, and waggons, besides the arms and ammunition of our soldiers, fell into their hands.

The Zulu War : Durban Mounted Volunteers, under the late Captain W. Shepstone, setting out for the front – from a photograph taken on November 30.

On the night of that day, the 22nd, the post in the rear, at Rourke's Drift, which had been left in charge of eighty men of the 24th, under Captain C.J. Bromhead, with Lieutenant Chard, R.E., as senior in command, was attacked by several thousand of the enemy, but withstood the assaults during twelve hours, till at daylight the Zulus, with great loss, were forced to retire. The names of the gallant officers who have fallen, with some additional particulars, were published in our last. Since then, we have learnt that the forces under Major Dartnell and Captain Lonsdale had a victorious engagement with the Zulus near Rourke's Drift, subsequent to the disaster of the 22nd; also that Colonel Pearson had safely established himself at Ekowe. The Zulus, in short, have not been able to force their way into Natal, though Lord Chelmsford's advance into Zululand has been checked for the time.

Great preparations have been made during the past week for the speedy dispatch of reinforcements from England, forming two brigades of infantry, under Major-General Hope Crealock, C.B., and Major-General E. Newdigate, respectively; also one brigade of cavalry, under Major-General Frederick Marshall; two batteries of Royal Artillery, and some companies of the Royal Engineers and Army Service Corps. About twenty steam-ships have been engaged by the Admiralty to embark the troops at Southampton and Portsmouth, and a few at Dublin and Queenstown. We reserve a detailed account of the forces to be employed until their arrangement is complete, but there has been an amount of military bustle seldom witnessed.

Our Illustrations of the subject published this week begin with the Portrait of Cetewayo, the Zulu King, which was drawn from the life, in July, 1877, by the late Mr. Edward Tilt, an artist who visited South Africa with his surviving brother, now in London. Mr. Edward Tilt proceeded from Natal to Zululand, and had an opportunity of drawing this portrait, at an audience or Court ceremony that he witnessed.

We are indebted to Major J. North Crealock, of the 95th Regiment, Assistant Military Secretary to Lord Chelmsford, for the sketches very recently taken of the Tugela, Helpmakaar, and Rourke's Drift, near the scene of the late disastrous conflict; likewise to Captain H.W. Maclear, of the Buffs, for the sketch of Colonel Pearson's first camp near the mouth of the Tugela; and to Mr W. Nelson for that of the Natal Mounted Police on their road to Helpmakaar. The photograph of the Durban Mounted Volunteers, by Mr. James Lloyd, which we have copied, has a melancholy interest from its containing the figure of Captain W. Shepstone, who is one of those killed on the 22nd. The page of Illustrations of Zulu and Kaffir people in their native costumes is supplied by the photographs of Mr. Kisch, of Durban. Our Special Artist, Mr. Melton Prior, who went through the last Kaffir War, is now on his voyage to South Africa for the service of this Journal.

REPULSE OF THE ZULUS

The following telegram, dated Capetown, Jan. 29, has been received through Reuter's agency, via Madeira:-

On Jan.24 Colonel Wood's columns (near Itambra Mountain) was attacked by a body of 4000 Zulus. The engagement resulted in a victory for the British troops, the enemy being completely scattered. The British sustained only trifling loss. The force under Colonel Wood is now falling back to cover Utrecht.

Several attacks on Colonel Pearson's and on the other columns have been repulsed.

A grand attack is expected daily from the Zulus, who are concentrating their forces in the direction of Ekowe, where Colonel Pearson's force occupies entrenched positions.

The gravity of the position of affairs is not exaggerated. It is expected that military operations will be confined to maintaining the *status quo* and guarding the strategical position on the border until the troops are strongly reinforced from England.

A body of 200 volunteers from Port Elizabeth will relieve the 88th Regiment at King William's Town.

Fuller details of the attack at Rorke's Drift confirm the extraordinary bravery displayed by the British troops.

Zulus And Kaffirs of South Africa

OUR ARMY

Professional and unprofessional readers may be expected to be almost equally interested in *The English Army*, by Major Arthur Griffiths (Cassell, Petter, and Galpin), and to derive almost equal gratification, if not equal profit and information, from a perusal of it. It is a large, sturdy volume, with covers of a colour appropriately suggestive of the "thin, red line;" and it is devoted to a consideration of the "past history, present condition and future prospects" of our military forces. The origin and growth of our

Army; its constitution and its machinery, both civil and military; the artillery, the cavalry, the engineers, and the infantry; the officers and the rank and file; the discipline, the numbers and organisation; the reserves and auxiliaries - such are the subjects of the several heads under which the volume is divided; and the last chapter is occupied chiefly with matters bearing upon the feasibility and probability of a foreign invasion of this country.

The author gives some excellent reasons why he is, on the whole, better qualified for the task he has undertaken than he would have been if he "were still on full pay;" and he then proceeds to attack his work with energy. One naturally turns eagerly to what he has to say about artillery, inasmuch as the late Russo-Turkish war is not generally considered to have borne out the expectations conceived by some enthusiastic, and probably partial, champions of that arm. He points out that the Russo-Turkish war "gave us few new lessons in the military art, and in many respects it was waged on principles strangely retrograde," so that it offered no very "strongly-marked results from the free employment of field artillery;" and he, therefore, is not at all shaken by the events of that war in his adhesion, on the whole, to the opinions of those who hold that artillery "constitutes now the true fate of nations and of armies."

He is somewhat cautious in his estimate of our efficiency in that branch, or, at any rate, he cannot be accused of a sanguine and a boastful spirit, when he affirms his belief that "our artillery, if it does not degenerate from its present high standard, but rather progresses steadily with the times, may fairly be expected to hold its own, when tested against the very best in the world." Now, as the excellence of artillery, more than of any other arm, must necessarily be to a considerable extent a question of expense, it would seem as if the richest country in the world ought to be able to make its supremacy in that respect a matter almost of certainty – other things, such as thews and sinews, skill, and smartness being, to say the least of it, equal. However, the author is undoubtedly right not to adopt the tone of a merely patriotic boaster.

And as to cavalry? We are told that "the British cavalry soldier is the direct representative of a long line of illustrious ancestors;" that "he can claim a not remote kinship with the knight-errant and the man-at-arms;" that he has always been more distinguished for his gallantry than for less brilliant but more useful qualities; and that he belongs to a service which needs considerable reformation. There is a particularly interesting chapter concerning "the corps of Royal Engineers," a body of men about whom the public know probably less than about any other, but who, nevertheless, have a very honourable record to show.

As for the infantry, the author naturally and justly speaks of them in the highest terms of eulogy, quoting, among other compliments paid to them, the well-known saying of a French Marshall – "The English infantry is the finest in the world; luckily, there is not much of it." He, however, is by no means blind to their deficiencies; and he regrets that no decision has yet been arrived at as to the way in which "the two principal needs of modern infantry," which are "(1) skill and promptitude in the use of entrenching tools," and "(2) thorough recognition of, and adequate instruction in, the only feasible method of attack," can be best supplied. And he does not hesitate, notwithstanding his admiration for our foot-soldiers, to assert that "if every soldier, or a large number in every battalion, may dig a hole to hide himself in at will, the consequences would be serious, even with the finest infantry in the world."

It is pertinent to ask whether during the American Civil War, when the process is believed to have been adopted to such an extent as to draw general attention to the advisability of it, the evil consequences apprehended were found to follow. Memory does not readily recall any flagrant instances. The author, discoursing about officers and soldiers, remarks of the former that their best points, "taken in the aggregate, are their courage and the care they take of their men," and that their worst "may be summed up in one" – namely, "want of interest in their profession;" and of the latter, the rank and file, whether English, Scotch, or Irish, that, for all their splendid achievements, they cannot be considered, on the whole, "the best material in the land."

He also offers some observations upon the abolition of purchase and upon the means of obtaining better and more numerous recruits. The subject of discipline is handled at great length, and many sickening details are given touching the military punishments which have been in vogue at various periods; a more humane and sensible system has prevailed in these later days; but there is still room for improvement and for the advent of some inventive genius who shall construct a perfect disciplinary code with a proper proportion of coercion on the one hand and encouragement on the other, if the latter alone be insufficient for the purpose. In treating of the "reserves and auxiliaries," the author takes a very wide range; he discusses not only our militia and volunteers at home, but also the forces at our disposal in India and in the colonies.

At the end of his volume he faces the bugbear of invasion, and does not feel at all easy in the presence of it. In fact, he devotes a good deal of space to proving that "the invasion of England, if improbable, is not impossible," a proposition which nobody is likely to dispute. However, it may be well to state what he considers to be the conditions indispensable for the success of a hostile expedition against us. They are five in number – first, "that we should be taken unprepared"; second, "that the enemy can command sufficient tonnage to permit him to ferry his troops across the Channel;" third, "that by stratagem, previously and at the time of action, he has evaded, out-manœuvred, or rendered our fleet powerless;" fourth, "that he has thus gained command of the sea for forty-eight hours;" fifth, "that he has been able to disembark a force sufficient to overthrow the troops hastily collected to oppose him, and can make a dash at the unprotected capital."

South African warfare: a halt of the 24th Regiment.
From a sketch made by Mr Melton Prior last year.

None of these conditions appears to him, on examination, "exaggerated or opposed to common-sense;" and he examines them all in detail. Of course, it is impossible to follow him here through his procedure; but it may seem to many persons that his second condition is entitled to the first place, seeing that if the enemy cannot get across the water we are evidently quite safe from him, whatever may be our state of preparation, and that the hostile programme would resemble one of "Hamlet" without a Prince of Denmark among the dramatic personages. Let the book, however, be read, and its arguments weighed; it certainly seems to deserve attention.

THE ILLUSTRATED LONDON NEWS

March 1, 1879

The information brought to Madeira by the Union steamship the Asiatic, and thence forwarded by telegraph to London, adds little of material importance to the knowledge of the state of affairs in South Africa we already possessed. No specially new light was thrown by it upon the "military disaster" in the neighbourhood of Rorke's Drift, which excited such a painful sensation among all classes last week. It is something to have learned, however, that apprehensions on the part of the Colonists at Natal have considerably subsided; that the Zulu Army has not followed up the advantage which it gained over the central invading column of British Troops by crossing the Tugela; that the measures taken for defence are generally regarded as adequate to stay the advance of the Zulus into Natal until the arrival of the reinforcements dispatched with such commendable promptitude by her Majesty's Government; that there has been no Native Insurrection in the Colony, nor any obvious signs of one; and that the tragical fate which befell a portion of Colonel Durnford's Column may now be viewed as an isolated reverse which, however accounted for, is not believed to indicate a general state of weakness dangerous to a continued hold by us upon our South African Possessions.

The Zulu War: Embarkation of the 91st Highlanders at Southampton

That the Zulu War will be a brief one it would be hazardous to predict. That it will cause heavy expenditure, be its issue what it may, or the time of its conclusion when it may, is already certain. But that its political consequences will be other than salutary to the European Settlers in Southern Africa can hardly, we think, be matter of doubt.

Lieutenant John Rouse Merriott Chard,
Royal Engineers

Lieutenant Gonville Bromhead,
24th Regiment

LIEUTENANT CHARLES D'AGUILAR POPE,
24TH REGIMENT.

LIEUTENANT NEVILLE J. AYLMER COGHILL,
24TH REGIMENT.

LIEUTENANT GEORGE FREDERICK J. HODSON,
24TH REGIMENT (AIDE-DE-CAMP).

LIEUTENANT FRANCIS PENDER PORTEOUS,
24TH REGIMENT.

LIEUT. -GENERAL LORD CHELMSFORD

The General commanding the forces in South Africa, who sat present charged with the arduous and anxious task of conducting the war against Cetewayo, King of the Zulus, has held his post scarcely a twelvemonth, having succeeded General Sir Arthur Cunynghame on Feb. 25 last year. He was then only Major-General the Hon. Frederick Augustus Thesiger, C.B., but succeeded to the Peerage on the death of his father, the late Lord Chelmsford, in the October following. He was born on May 31, 1827. He entered the Army in 1844, and was made Lieutenant and Captain of the Grenadier Guards in 1850.

He served at the siege of Sebastopol, for which he received the medal, with clasp; he also served in 1857 and 1858 against the Sepoy mutineers and other rebels in Central India. In 1858 he was Lieutenant-Colonel of the 95th Regiment, and obtained a Brevet-Colonelcy in 1863.

He was appointed, in 1861, on the Bombay staff, as acting Deputy-Adjutant-General. He accompanied the Abyssinian expedition of 1867 and 1868, under Lord Napier of Magdala, in the capacity of Adjutant-General, when he was favourably mentioned in the despatches to the War Office. From that time to the end of 1876, he held the appointment of Adjutant-General to the Commander-in-Chief in India. Having returned to England, he was promoted to the rank of Brigadier-General, and placed in command of the 1st Infantry Brigade at Aldershott. He married, in 1867, at Kurrachee, a daughter of Major-General Heath, and has four sons.

Our Portrait of Lord Chelmsford is from a photograph taken before he went to the Cape Colony, and it differs, we believe, from his present appearance in one particular, that of his now wearing the full beard. The photograph was taken by J. Weston and Son, of Folkestone.

Lieutenant-General Lord Chelmsford, K.C.B.,
Commander-in-Chief in South Africa

THE ZULU WAR

We had received, by the middle of this week, to which the present account of recent news is made up, intelligence, partly conveyed by the Madeira telegraph, from Capetown to the 4 ult. *The London Gazette* has published Lord Chelmsford's despatches of Jan. 9 and Jan. 14, which dates were two days before, and three days after, the commencement of active hostilities.

The Zulu War: Capture of Sirayo's stronghold, January 12.
From a sketch by Mr J.F. Marshall, of the Cape Civil Service.

Some further particulars have been reported of the lamentable disaster which befell the rear-guard of Colonel Glyn's column on the 22nd, with the destruction of a whole battalion of the 24th Regiment, ten miles from Rorke's Drift, at Isandula; also the successful defence of the Rorke's Drift post, on the same day, by Lieutenants Chard and Bromhead; and the victory of Colonel Evelyn Wood over another force of Zulus, at a place some twenty miles to the north.

We are enabled already to publish an Illustration from a sketch by Mr J.F. Marshall, Cape Civil Service, of the capture of Sirayo's fortified Kraal, on the banks of the Bashee under the Ngutu mountain range, east of Rorke's Drift, by a portion of Colonel Glyn's force on Jan. 12. This action is reported by Lord Chelmsford in his despatch of the 14th, and is minutely described by the Times' correspondent in a letter published on Friday of last week. But it is of secondary interest to the fatal conflict of Jan. 22 at Isandula, which place, sometimes named Insandusana will be found on the Map we present in the Supplement of this week. The following detailed account of the terrible disaster at Isandula is telegraphed from Madeira to the *Daily News*: -

Troops ships for the Zulu War reinforcements: The Spain ("National" Liverpool and New York line).

Troop ships for the Zulu War reinforcements: The Dublin Castle.

"The day before the action took place, Jan. 21, Colonel Glyn, in command of the third column, acting under the direct orders of Lord Chelmsford, sent away the advance guard, under the command of Major Dartnall, composed of a detachment of Carbineers, the Natal Mounted Police, Lonsdale's Native Contingent, and others. This advance guard sent to say it was engaged with the Zulus. Lord Chelmsford himself and Colonel Glyn pushed forward the main force, consisting of seven companies of the 2-24th, under Lieutenant-Colonel Degacher; Lonsdale's Native Contingent, under Major Black; 2-24th, and other troops; leaving behind as rear guard five companies of the 1-24th, under Lieutenant-Colonel Pulleine; one company of the 2-24th, under Lieutenant Pope; and a portion of the 1st Regiment of the Natal Native Contingent, under Lieutenant-Colonel Durnford, with the following cavalry: -

"About thirty Natal Carbineers, the Buffalo Border Guard, and about twenty-five Newcastle Mounted Riflemen. In addition, Colonel Durnford had Sikali's Horse and two guns, under Captain Russell, R.A. There were a few artillerymen. The Army Hospital Corps and the Commissariat, with a column of Lord Chelmsford's, moved forward with the main body either on the evening of the 21st or the morning of the 22nd. The rear guard had finished its usual morning march, and outspanned, when Zulu skirmishers were observed surrounding the hills. These skirmishers advanced towards the camp, keeping up a desultory fire. The camp was pitched in a broken country in a sort of valley, with distant surrounding hills.

"Colonel Pulleine sent skirmishers, who responded to the fire of the Zulus. It seems that the number of Zulus was not estimated, it being considered a slight demonstration of a few men. As the enemy's scouts were soon joined by bodies of considerable strength Colonel Pulleine's skirmishers were recalled, and the camp hastily put upon the defensive. The Zulu army then came on rapidly in regular battalions, eight deep, keeping up a heavy steady fire, until well within assegai distance. They then ceased their fire and hurled assegais. Our men kept up a very steady, telling fire, and great numbers of the enemy dropped, but without checking their progress. The places of the men who fell were constantly filled by comrades.

"While this attack was going on in the rear a double flank movement was executed, by which the horns of the Zulu army surrounded the camp. The disadvantage of the waggons not being packed in laager was now evident, and it led to the disaster. Our men had emptied their pouches, and found it impossible to replenish them, as the Zulus had obtained possession of the ammunition-waggons. The affair then became one of absolute butchery. Our officers and men were assegaied as they stood. They made no charges. The Zulu host came down with the weight of its battalions and literally crushed the small body, which could only defend itself with the bayonet, and very soon it had not even room to use that. The Zulus picked up the dead bodies of their comrades and hurled them on the bayonet points of our soldiers, thus simply beating down all defence. The work of destruction was complete.

"Within two hours from the time the Zulu skirmishers were seen there was not a living white man in the camp. The ammunition, the guns, the commissariat supplies, the waggons, the oxen, all the material of the column, fell into the hands of the enemy. Fortunately two cannons were spiked by Captain Smith, R.A., who was assegaied whilst in the act of spiking. As far as could be ascertained, the Zulus carried away all the ammunition and some waggons, and destroyed whatever was left behind. Mr Young, an officer belonging to Lonsdale's Contingent, who had been wounded in the skirmish with Sirayo's men some days previously, happened to be at the camp of Isandula, where his brother was superintending the return of the 23rd to Pietermaritzburg.

"Being invalided, and not connected with any regiment, he fired a rifle from the corner of a waggon until he had exhausted his ammunition. Being unable to obtain a further supply, and having no weapon whatever, he saw it was useless for him to remain any longer. Happily for him he had got a good horse, and a desperate dash carried him through a weak point in the enemy's cordon just in time. He was chased by the Zulus, who were swift runners, but could not get up with him. Looking back he saw our men, completely surrounded, firm as a rock, falling rapidly, but fighting to the last.

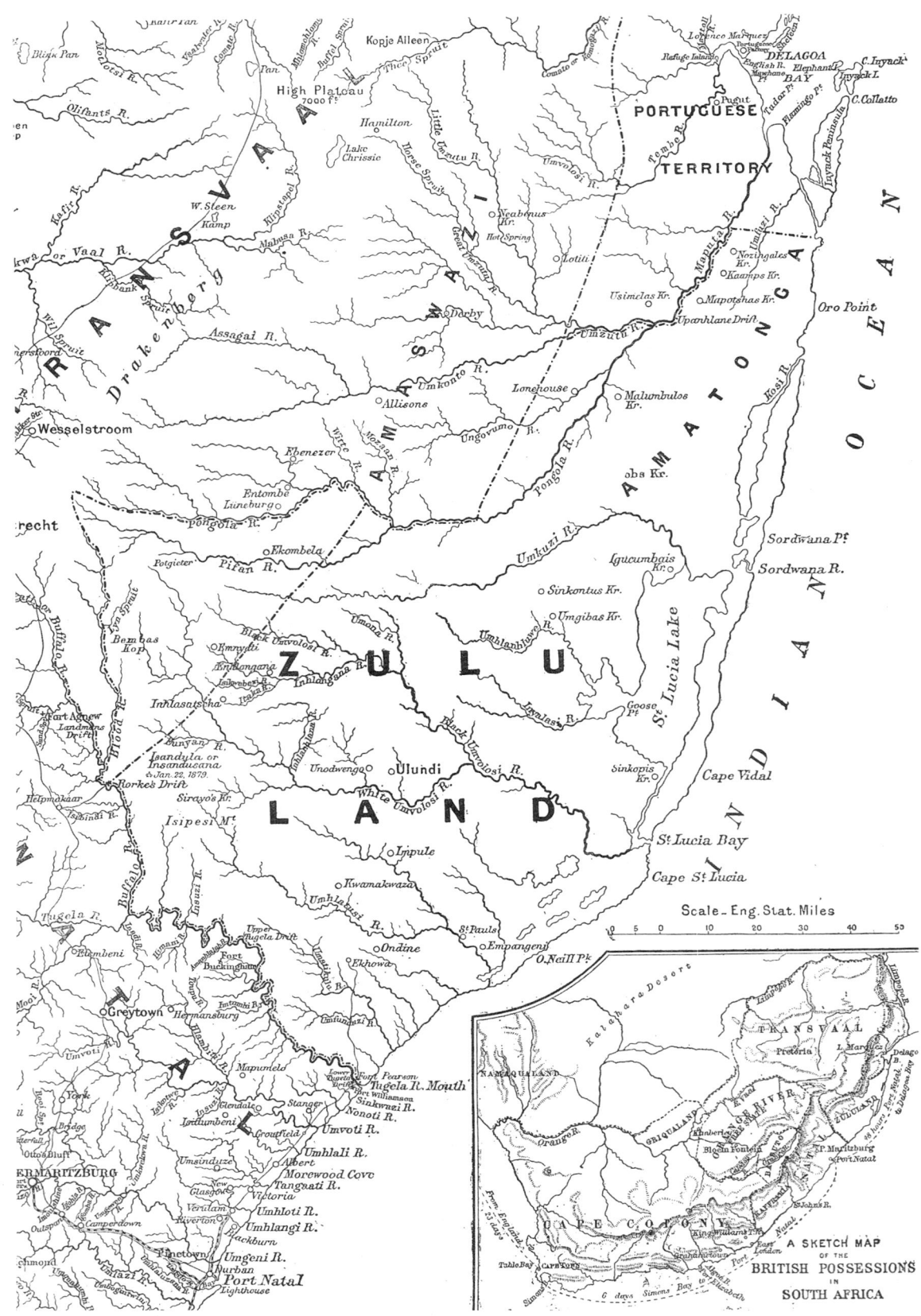

Map of Zululand with the adjoining frontiers

"The loud yells of the Zulus filled the air. There was no other noise except their demoniac shrieks, as the awful work was done with the short stabbing assegai. He saw Lieutenant Coghill trying to fight his way through, as also Adjutant Melville, who had seized the colours and was vainly trying to carry them through. It appears that Lieutenant Coghill was dispatched for assistance, as he was acting that day as staff officer to Colonel Pulleine. The place Young escaped through was, a minute after he passed it, completely blocked. He saw it was impossible to pierce the dense masses of Zulus between him and the Drift, so he made for a point on the river lower down, where he found no Zulus. He had, however, to jump the cliff, happily only ten feet high. If it had been a hundred he must have jumped it, as his pursuers were not far behind. His horse, having swam a few yards, was able to ford the rest of the river. He then rode to Helpmakaar. A few of the Natal Native Contingent and others were drowned in attempting to swim, but some were saved.

"It may be seen from this short narrative that the Zulu army was completely organised. It advanced, first throwing out skirmishers; then, as the battalions came down in mass, used their rifles whilst at long range with considerable effect. When near enough to use their own more familiar weapon, the assegai, they threw in two or three showers. All this time they were advancing steadily and rapidly, and the stabbing assegai was soon to work.

"The impression in Natal is that this engagement on the part of the Zulus is not attributable to generalship, but that the army of invasion was making for Natal and accidentally came across the rearguard of Colonel Glyn's column. Our troops were allowed to cross the river at various points. Colonel Glyn's main body was enticed by a feint advance away from its material. Then the main body of the enemy, supposed to be under Sirayo, the favourite Induna of Cetewayo, swept down on the baggage guard. Young and another, who were saved, speak in the highest terms of the way in which the gallant force sustained the assault of the overwhelming hordes of the enemy.

"Our native allies fought bravely, too, and if the camp had been formed in laager, and our men could have been furnished with the ammunition with which the camp was so generously supplied, it would have given a different account of the enemy. Mr Young says that the way in which the men were surrounded and crushed down by weight of numbers caused their utter annihilation. The great wonder was that so few men – for there were only about 600 men in the camp, excluding natives who ran, and not including Colonel Durnford's mounted men, under Captain Barton, who did fight well – were able in the open, and with no protection or cover, to keep off for four or five hours the large numbers of Kaffirs that must have attacked them.

"The line of Zulus which came down the hills to the left was nearly three miles long, and must have consisted of over 15,000 men, while a body of over 5000 remained on the top as a reserve, and took no part in the action, but simply drove off the captured cattle, waggons, and plunder.

"When these men moved they took most of their dead bodies with them in our waggons, mixed with the débris of the commissariat waggons, the contents of which, flour, sugar, tea, biscuits, mealies, and oats, were scattered about and wasted in pure wantonness. On the ground there were also dead horses, shot in every position, oxen mutilated, mules stabbed, while lying thick upon the ground in clumps were the bodies of the white men, with only their boots and shirts on, or perhaps an old pair of trousers, or part of their coats, with just enough showing to indicate to which branch they belonged. In many cases they lay with sixty or seventy rounds of empty cartridges alongside them, showing they had only died after doing their duty."

The defence of the commissariat post at Rorke's Drift, ten miles in the rear of the column which was intercepted at Isandula, in the manner above described, seems to have been a truly heroic action. In the afternoon of that day the two young officers, Lieutenant Gonville Bromhead, first battalion 24th Regiment, and Lieutenant Chard, R.E., left in charge of the Drift with a company of the 24th Regiment, first received intimation of the disaster from fugitives making for the Drift. Lieutenant Coghill had come from the fight at Isandula, by order of Colonel Pulleine, to summon reinforcements; and from Rorke's Drift he, with others, rode away to communicate with Helpmakaar, and was killed by Zulus in crossing the river.

Seeing an attack imminent, a barricade was hastily thrown up, under Lieutenant Chard's direction; the men using for this purpose a number of bags, biscuit-tins, and other matters belonging to the commissariat stores, part of the time being under fire. The attack took place soon after dark, by at least 3000 Zulus. The fight was kept up the great part of the night. The Zulus six times got inside the barricade, and were as often driven out at the point of the bayonet. In the meantime another body of Zulu troops passed to the rear of the military hospital and set fire to it, killing five patients and destroying all the medical stores. One man, a servant of Colonel Hassard, had a narrow escape. He succeeded in getting away from the hospital, and hid in the bush all night, exposed to the fire of the enemy on both sides.

At dawn the attacking force withdrew, for Lord Chelmsford's column was then seen approaching, and was enthusiastically hailed by the gallant defenders, who at first mistook it for another Zulu force. Three hundred and fifty-one dead Zulus were counted near the intrenchment and the number killed since that attack was estimated at 1000. The Zulus fought with infuriated zeal, even coming to the loopholes, and seizing the muzzles of the rifles. Assistant Commissary Byrne, who was killed, is said to have behaved nobly. It is hoped that all the men who have survived this engagement will be decorated with the Victoria Cross. They were, undoubtedly, the means of saving Grey Town and Helpmakaar, and also of securing time for effecting a retreat with the main column.

On the same night, Jan. 22, Colonel Pearson's column, south of Ekowe, forming the right wing of the whole army, having crossed the Lower Tugela into the enemy's country, was attacked by nearly 5000 Zulus; but these were repulsed and put to flight. Two days later, on the 24th, Colonel Evelyn Wood's column, to the north-east of Rorke's Drift, had a victorious engagement with 4000 of the enemy near the Inkanyana mountain, and defeated them, with trifling loss on our side.

The capture of Sirayo's kraal, on the 12th, of which Mr Marshall, an eyewitness, has sent us his pen-and-ink sketch, was not severely contested in fighting. But it was considered significant, at the outset of the war, because one of the immediate complaints against the Zulu King was that two women, the unfaithful and fugitive wives of Sirayo, who is Cetewayo's brother, had been pursued over the frontier into British territory, and had been carried back into Zululand to be put to death. Lord Chelmsford therefore thought it desirable to punish the family and clan of Sirayo at once by capturing their cattle. Accordingly Colonel Glyn directed three companies of 1-24th Regiment and the 1-3rd Regiment Natal Native Contingent to advance and capture the cattle, while Lieutenant-Colonel Russell, 12th Lancers, in command of the mounted portion of the force, was directed to continue along the waggon track to the high ground above.

By half-past eight in the morning the precipitous sides of the Ngutu mountain were occupied by the infantry, when fire was opened upon them by the Zulus, who were occupying very strong positions in the coves and rocks above. A fight ensued, which lasted about half an hour. The mountain side was cleared, the cattle and horses were captured; the Zulus left behind to defend the cattle made, however, a stubborn resistance, and ten dead bodies were counted in the rocks, and nine prisoners taken, three of whom were wounded. This probably does not represent their total loss. One man severely wounded was found next day. In the mean time, before the mounted men had quite reached the higher terrace of the mountain, they were fired upon by a force of Zulus concealed by rocks. These were attacked and dispersed with the loss of sixteen killed, among whom, it is said, was a son of Sirayo, Umkumbi-kaZulu. It is stated by a prisoner that another of the Chief's sons was also killed on this occasion.

Lieutenant Gonville Bromhead, who commanded the eighty men of the 24th Regiment in the heroic defence of the post at Rorke's Drift throughout the entire night, is twenty-three years of age, having been born in August, 1845. He is youngest son of the late Sir Edmund de Gonville Bromhead, Bart., of Thurlby Hall, Lincolnshire, who was a Waterloo veteran. Lieutenant Bromhead entered the Army in 1867, and served with his regiment in India till 1872, when the second battalion of the 24th returned to England. He afterwards went to the Cape with that regiment, which served through the late campaign in Kaffraria, and was thence moved to Natal. There is a Captain Charles Bromhead in the same regiment.

Lieutenant Neville Josiah Aylmer Coghill was born Jan. 25, 1852, and was heir to a baronetcy, as eldest son of Sir John Joscelyn Coghill, Bart., of Drumcondra, in the county of Dublin, and Castle Townsend, in the county of Cork. He was a nephew of the Right Rev. Lord Plunkett, Bishop of Meath. We and our readers were indebted to Lieutenant Coghill for some acceptable sketches of the war in the Trans-Kei, between the months of October, 1877, and January, 1878, before our Special Artist, Mr Melton Prior, arrived in South Africa.

Lieutenant Coghill was a young officer of great merit and promise. He was not among those killed in the fighting at Isandula with the entire second battalion of his regiment; but, acting as aide-de-camp to his superior in command, Colonel Pulleine, he was sent, during the conflict, to give the alarm at Rorke's Drift, with orders thence to ride on to Helpmakaar, and to call up reinforcements. In this service he reached the post at Rorke's Drift, and, by the intelligence which he brought there, enable Lieutenants Chard and Bromhead to put that post in a state of defence; but when he rode away from Rorke's Drift, to cross the river on his road to Helpmakaar, he was beset by a party of the enemy, and was there killed.

Lieutenant George Frederick John Hodson, one of the officers of the 24th killed at Isandula, was the second son of Sir G.F.J. Hodson, Bart., of Hollybrook House, Bray, in Wicklow, and of Green Park, Westmeath. He was born Nov. 26, 1854.

The portrait of Lieutenant Chard, R.E., is from a photograph of Mr J. Hawke, of Plymouth; and that of Lieutenant Gonville Bromhead, of the 24th Regiment, from one by Messrs Elliott and Fry, Baker-street; that of Lieutenant Charles Pope, by Lambert Weston and Son, of Dover; that of Lieutenant Pender Porteous, by M. Bowness, of Ambleside; that of Lieutenant Coghill, by L. Werner, of Dublin; and that of Lieutenant Hodson, by Werner, of Dublin.

We mentioned last week that Captain Shepstone, of Natal, a son of Sir Theophilus Shepstone, K.C.M.G., was among the killed. This was not, as we supposed, Captain William Shepstone, of the Durban Mounted Volunteers, but his younger brother George, of the Native Contingent, political assistant to Colonel Durnford.

The embarkation of troops sent out as reinforcement to Lord Chelmsford's army has been going on this fortnight past, at Gravesend and Tilbury Fort, in the Thames, as well as at Chatham, Woolwich, and Blackwall; at Southampton, Portsmouth, and Plymouth, at Kingstown (Dublin Bay) and Queenstown (Cork Harbour), and several other ports. Some of the first passenger, mail, and mercantile steamships of different lines have been engaged by the Admiralty for this transport service; those of the Union Steam-Ship Company, and likewise Messrs Donald Currie and Co., the ordinary employment of which is in the general traffic with the Cape; also, those of the "National" Liverpool and New York line, named the France, the Spain, the England, and the Egypt (for cavalry); the Inman Liverpool line, one of which is the City of Berlin, to convey the Scots Fusiliers; the Russia, China, and Olympus, of the Cunard or British North American line; the British India Company's ships Manora and others (for artillery); the Andean, belonging to the West of England and Pacific Company, of Liverpool; the City of Venice (for artillery, at Woolwich), and several more.

The following statement shows in detail the composition and strength of the relief force proceeding to the Cape: - 1st Dragoon Guards – 31 officers, 622 men, 91 officers' chargers, 480 troop horses; 17th Lancers – 31 officers, 622 men, 91 chargers, 480 troop horses; 17th Lancers – 31 officers, 622 men, 91 chargers, 480 troop horses; M and N Batteries of the 6th Brigade Royal Artillery – 10 officers, 536 men, 168 troop horses; 30th Company Royal Engineers – 6 officers, 196 men, 2 officers' chargers, and 44 troop horses; 21st Foot – 30 officers, 906 men, 7 chargers; 58th Foot – 30 officers, 906 men, 7 chargers; 3rd Battalion of 60th Rifles – 30 officers, 906 men, 7 chargers; 57th Foot, from Ceylon to consist (with draughts from England) of 30 officers, 906 men, and 7 chargers; 91st Foot – 30 officers, 906 men, 7 chargers; 94th Foot – 30 officers, 906 men, 7 chargers; 3rd, 4th, and 5th Companies of Army Service Corps (Transport Branch) – 19 officers, 550 men, and 480 horses; Army Hospital Corps – 4 officers, 140 men; Ordnance Store Branch of Army Service Corps – 1 officer and 32 men:

Totals (independent of miscellaneous draughts) – 282 officers, 8134 men, 226 officers' chargers, and 1652 troop horses. It was arranged that in no case an entire regiment should be taken in a single vessel. The Dublin Castle, which sailed on Wednesday week from the London Docks, received 700 of the 60th Rifles, and the Pretoria, departing on the same day from Southampton with the 91st Foot, 700 of that corps, were the first ships that started. The ships are furnished, by order of the Admiralty, with the boat-disengaging apparatus of Messrs Hill and Clark, Victoria-street, Westminster.

We give Illustrations of two of the transport ships employed on this occasion – namely, the Dublin Castle Royal Mail screw steam-ship, of Messrs Donald Currie and Co's fleet, in which the 60th Rifles embarked at Gravesend and Tilbury on Wednesday week; and the Spain, a sister ship of the France, in which the 17th Lancers and other cavalry go out. The Dublin Castle is a screw steam-ship of 2911 tons register, built in 1876, at Glasgow, by Messrs Robert Napier and Co. She has a length of 350 ft. a breadth of 39 ft., and a depth of hold of 29 ft. Her commander is Captain M.H. Penfold, an officer of the Royal Naval Reserve, and she has a picked crew of about one hundred men on board.

In order to turn the vessel into a comfortable transport, the fittings of the second-class saloon on the main deck had to be removed and replaced by tables for the men to eat at, with room for a mess of ten

Reinforcements for the Zulu War: Embarkation of the 60th Rifles at Tilbury

at each table, and hammock-hooks, rifle stands, and pegs for extra clothes had to be put up on this and the lower or orlop deck. Some saving is effected in a troop-ship in the space required for sleeping by dividing the men into three sections or watches, and then keeping one third of the number always on the upper deck. The forward part of the main deck has been converted into a hospital, with twenty-four spring cots for invalids, a bath, and so forth. The ship being divided by fireproof, massive iron bulkheads into distinct compartments, this part can be completely isolated from the rest of the ship.

For the ventilation of the orlop deck, Dr Edmund's patented system has been adopted. A rectangular wooden pipe, lined with metal, is carried round the sides of the ship high up between decks. Into this large, horizontal duct the foul air is admitted by smaller vertical wooden pipes, with slits in them, giving them some resemblance to organ pipes. The large air duct opens into an ordinary ventilating

The Zulu War: Embarkation of the 91st Highlanders at Southampton – "Good–by!"

cowl, within which is placed horizontally, a perforated tube, forming a circular wheel capable of revolving, and by driving steam through this a strong up-draught is established and the heated air from below is drawn out.

In addition to 1000 tons of coal, about 500 tons of cargo and stores had to be shipped, including oats for horses, of which five were taken out secured in wooden boxes placed on the upperdeck. About twenty-five tons of ice figure in the stores, and the men will be allowed as much water as they want, the water-tanks containing 34,000 gallons. To keep up this supply a condenser is carried capable of producing over eighty-five gallons per hour. An allowance of one pint of porter will also be served daily to each man. The soldiers will not have to cook for themselves.

The very large and commodious steam-ship Spain, of the "National" line from Liverpool to New York, took on board five or six hundred of the 1st Dragoon Guards (King's) at Southampton on Thursday last. This vessel is of the extraordinary length of 425 ft. 4 in., with 43 ft. 2 in. breadth; her tonnage is 4900 tons. She is four-masted, and has engines of 600-horse power nominal. The France, in which the 17th Lancers embarked at the Victoria Docks, Blackwall, on Tuesday last, is a fine vessel of 3500 tons, commanded by Captain Bragge.

We give two Illustrations of the departure of the 91st Highlanders (Princess Louise's) at Southampton, on board the Pretoria, on Wednesday week. The scene represented in our Extra Supplement shows the men waving a sign of farewell, and receiving the hearty "Good-by!" of their friends, as described in the London daily papers. The embarkation of the 60th Rifles on board the Dublin Castle at Tilbury on the same day, is the subject of our remaining Illustration. They were six companies of the third battalion of that regiment, from Colchester, making up their complement, 700, by a draught of 226 of the first battalion from the dépôt at Winchester. The second battalion is with Sir Samuel Browne's force in Afghanistan, and is now, we believe, at Jellalabad. The battalion just gone was, previously to embarkation, inspected by his Royal Highness the Duke of Cambridge, while Prince Edward of Saxe-Weimar inspected the 91st Highlanders at Southampton. The Pretoria arrived at Madeira on Monday evening, and proceeded, after a few hours' stay, on her voyage to the Cape.

The latest news, to last Wednesday evening, is dated Feb. 4, at which time, in Pietermaritzburg, for ten days past, no fighting had been reported. The British force now in the field, exclusive of reinforcements, is estimated at about two fifths of the number of men when the invasion commenced. The native contingents have been disbanded, and the disbanded volunteers are back again with the colony. The regular soldiers have been reduced, through various causes, 15 per cent from the original number.

Colonel Pearson, with 1200 men, consisting of the Buffs, the 89th, a company of Engineers, and a detachment of the Naval Brigade, is intrenched at Ekowe, thirty miles within the enemy's country. His communications have been interrupted for some days, and the bush surrounding the post is known to be infested with the enemy. He has, however, abundance of supplies for two months.

The second column, late under Colonel Durnford, consisting as it did almost entirely of native troops, has ceased to exist, and its removal has left Greytown, and other frontier districts, open to a raid of the enemy. The third column, consisting of Europeans, is being reorganised and newly equipped with all rapidity.

Colonel Evelyn Wood's column is declared to be capable of offensive operations. Ten days ago this column advanced to Tinta's Kraal, on the White Umvelosi, where it was contemplated to form an intrenched post. A court of inquiry is sitting on the disaster at Isandula.

The Queen has desired the Secretary of State for War to telegraph to Lord Chelmsford that she "sympathises most sincerely with him in the dreadful loss which has deprived her of so many gallant officers and men, and that her Majesty places entire confidence in him, and in her troops, to maintain our honour and our good name."

THE ILLUSTRATED LONDON NEWS

March 8, 1879

One might have imagined that the Army Estimates for the present year would have attracted special Parliamentary attention. It has not proved so, however. It cannot successfully compete with those habits of members which are best indicated by the words "dinner hour." Colonel Stanley, the Secretary for War, was unable, on Monday last, to get into Committee till after seven o'clock, and was therefore subject to the disadvantage of explaining the Estimates to a comparatively empty House.

Everyone will recall the promises he had made, during the Recess, of lightening the military burdens of the country by vigorous retrenchment. Most people will give him full credit for the desire and the expectation which he then expressed. The Zulu War, however, not then anticipated, has started up to

The Zulu War: Garrison of Fort Pearson, on the Lower Tugela, at Gatling gun practice.
From a photograph by Mr J. Lloyd of Durban, Natal.

defeat his good intentions. The result is that he has had, in part, to re-cast his Military Estimates, and, in part, to adapt them to the present position of affairs by Supplementary Estimates, of which, however, his speech gave little account. All that we know is that the number of men moved for in Committee is 135,625, and that the vote has been agreed to. This leaves us pretty well where we were. Assuming thus much, and acknowledging in general terms the disappointment of the Government that the reduction they had contemplated could not be carried out at present, the Right Hon. Secretary for War confined himself to such details of explanation as are rather interesting to the Army itself than to the Nation which maintains it.

Of course, the terrible disaster in Zululand, and the war into which Sir Bartle Frere has plunged with Cetewayo, King of the Zulus, accounts for much of the assumed impossibility, at the present critical moment, of reducing the number of our men and the expenses of their equipment. How far the determination of the High Commissioner at the Cape – for determination it may be gathered from his despatches to have been – may have been justified by local knowledge the British public have yet to learn. No explanation which he has yet given can be held to demonstrate the necessity of an immediate invasion of Zululand. He was cautioned more than once by the Government at home, who, however, left him to pursue his own course, on his own responsibility. Lord Chelmsford, the Commander of her Majesty's Forces in South Africa, must have acceded to Sir Bartle Frere's choice under a conviction that the invasion might be undertaken with the troops he had in hand with prospects of success.

It is needless to point out that the event has overridden both the political judgement of the High Commissioner and the military calculations of the Commander-in-Chief. The war seems to have been premature, even if it were ultimately inevitable. No such disaster as that at Isandula ought to have been possible in a well disciplined force. A Court of Inquiry is passing under review all the circumstances of the case, and until we have their report it would be unjust to indicate even by a bare supposition the Military Authorities with whom the blame really rested. But the effect of this disaster is that Natal is open to the incursion of the Zulus, which might possibly have been effected before now, but for the swollen state of the River Tugela. The latest despatches from the scene of operations are not by any means flattering. No Insurrection, however, of the Zulus living in Natal has been reported, although it has become clear that the Boers in the Transvaal are far more intent upon reasserting their claims to independence than upon stemming any inundation of the Zulus into Natal.

It will strike most readers of the recent Despatches from South Africa that the policy adopted by the Government of the Cape in reference to the Foreign tribes by which the European Settlements are surrounded, has been characterised, almost from beginning to end, by a mistaken view of what the relations of the two parties demand. That which may succeed in India may be very ill fitted to prevail in South Africa, and the experience of the High Commissioner, rich and various as it must be admitted to have been, may yet turn out but a doubtful qualification for dealing with the barbarous races with which his Government at the Cape has come in contact. The task before him is one requiring patience and forbearance far more than promptitude and impetuosity.

No doubt, British valour and British resources will prove themselves able, in the long run, to subjugate any number of South African antagonists; but is it needful to tax them to the utmost? Is the work they can accomplish such as may be best accomplished by such means? Can we hammer civilisation into savage minds by sheer force? Have we any proof that such policy has been largely successful? Will the conquest of Zululand, which is almost certain to be achieved, be followed by results of which modern civilisation can boast? Are we to fight our way through Africa, or shall we win it? And, in case the first plan be the shorter of the two, will it be the most productive of permanent advantage?

This is the most serious question involved in the present Zulu War. We shall stand by our kindred, as we ought; we shall assert, as we are now bound to do, our superiority in arms. We dare not retreat from the position to which we have advanced. But that does not necessarily imply that the extent and method of our advance shall always follow the precedent laid down for us by the High Commissioner Sir Bartle Frere.

On this occasion the country may be expected to sympathise with the Government. The promptitude with which they have dispatched reinforcements to Lord Chelmsford has won for them all but universal admiration. But it is evident from the declarations of the Colonial Minister that the Zulu War is not one of their seeking, and we would fain hope is not one which they will prolong beyond the absolute

LIEUTENANT-COLONEL H. B. PULLEINE.

CAPTAIN WILLIAM ECCLES MOSTYN.

LIEUTENANT HENRY JULIAN DYER.

LIEUTENANT T. L. G. GRIFFITH.

LIEUTENANT E. H. DYSON.

LIEUTENANT C. W. CAVAYE.

LIEUTENANT E. O. ANSTEY.

The Zulu War: Officers of the 24th Regiment killed at Isandula.

necessities of the occasion. The affair will prove extremely expensive, at best, and it may (although we do not think it likely) be disastrous to even more than one colony; but we have not ceased to hope that it will become memorable chiefly as a warning to self-willed Statesmen not to allow themselves to be carried away by ambitious projects which are more distinguished by romance than reason, and to

The Zulu War: Sketches at the Victoria docks on the departure of the 17th Lancers.

impress upon every representative of British honour, in whatever quarter of the Globe, the lesson that the dictates of justice should be conformed to, at any expense, in preference to the most inviting expediency which disregards it. It too often happens that civilians, when thwarted in their most benevolent enterprises, are more apt to use the sword to cut the knot of their difficulties than are soldiers themselves.

THE ZULU WAR

We are enabled this week again to present to our readers several authentic Illustrations, from sketches drawn on the spot by staff officers and others with Lord Chelmsford's army, showing the actual movements and engagements of Colonel Pearson's and Colonel Glyn's columns in Zulu Land; the scene of the disastrous conflict of Jan.22 at Isandula, where the 1st battalion of the 24th Regiment was utterly destroyed; the post at Rorke's Drift, so bravely defended by Lieutenants Chard and Gonville Bromhead during the night of that date; the march across the Buffalo valley, in the advance from Helpmakaar to Rorke's Drift; the crossing of the Lower Tugela by Colonel Pearson's column; and one or two scenes at the encampments of British troops, both on the Natal and the Transvaal frontier of Cetewayo's hostile kingdom.

Portraits are further given of some of the lamented young officers of the 24th, with Captain W. Eccles Mostyn, and the commander of the battalion, Lieutenant-Colonel H.B. Pulleine, who were killed in the desperate fight at Isandula; the portrait also of Major Dartnell, commanding the Natal Mounted Police, which bore part of the action of that fatal day.

We are, upon this as on former occasions, most especially indebted to Lieutenant-Colonel J. North Crealock, of the 95th Regiment, Military Secretary of the Commander-in-Chief, for the Sketches with which he has furnished us, by his own hand, of the scenes of those memorable conflicts, at Isandula (or Isandwana, as sometimes written) and at Rorke's Drift, on Jan. 22. It will be seen by reference to Lord Chelmsford's despatch relating the extraordinary events of that day, that the Commander-in Chief and his Staff, including Lieutenant-Colonel Crealock, with Colonel Glyn and the remainder of his force, arrived at those places some hours after the fighting was over; they halted, indeed, for the night at Isandula, surrounded by the dreadful proofs of recent slaughter, and pushed on before daylight next morning to relieve the heroic garrison of the post at Rorke's Drift. The sketches which supply our Illustrations for this week are those drawn by Lieutenant-Colonel Crealock at that time, and must be regarded as possessing the greatest possible interest, from their immediate connection with events never to be forgotten in British military history.

LORD CHELMSFORD'S DESPATCH

The despatch of Lieutenant-General Lord Chelmsford, dated five days afterwards, Jan.27, at Pietermaritzburg, gives an account of what the Commander-in-Chief saw and did on the 22nd, and how it came to pass that Colonel Glyn's column of troops was divided, to which circumstance, we suppose, the disaster may be fairly ascribed. At a very early hour in the morning Colonel Glyn, who had encamped on the 20th at Isandula, ten miles from Rorke's Drift, sent word that he had got a message from Major Dartnell, with the Mounted Police and Volunteers, on the north side of the Inhlatazye range, that the enemy were in great force there. Lord Chelmsford thereupon ordered Colonel Glyn to move on to Major Dartnell's assistance with the second battalion of the 24th Regiment, and with four guns and the mounted infantry. At the same time, an express was sent off to Lieut.-Colonel Durnford, R.E., who was at Rorke's Drift with 500 natives, half of them mounted and armed with breechloaders, to move up to strengthen the force which was left to guard the camp at Isandula.

The whole strength of this force was as follows: - Royal Artillery – two officers, 78 men, two guns; two rocket tubes; one officer, 10 men (Lieut.-Colonel Durnford's force); first battalion 24th Regiment – 15 officers, 334 men; second battalion 24th Regiment; - five officers, 90 men; Mounted European Corps – five officers, 204 men; Natal Native Contingent – 19 officers, 391 men; Natal Pioneers – one officer, 10 men. Lieut.-Colonel Durnford's force, 18 officers, 450 men. Total natives 851 men. Total Europeans (including officers), 772. With this force, Lieut.-Colonel Pulleine, first battalion 24th Regiment, was left in charge of the camp, and received strict instruction that he was left there to defend it.

We need not dwell upon Lord Chelmsford's account of his own movements in another direction that morning. He got a note, or rather Colonel Glyn, who was with him, got a note, from Colonel Pulleine, to say that "firing was heard to the left front of the camp" at Isandula. But no further message was received from Colonel Pulleine, and nothing could be seen by looking from the top of a high hill, with a powerful telescope, towards Isandula, which was about twelve miles distant.

The Zulu War: Departure of the 17th Lancers from Victoria Dock, Blackwall.

1. Cliff, 200 ft. high. 2. Waterfall. 3. Lieutenant-Colonel Russell's Mounted Infantry. 4. Major Dartnell's Natal Mounted Police and Volunteers.
5. The 2nd company, 1st battalion, of 24th Regiment. 6. N battery, 5th brigade, Royal Artillery (Lieutenant-Colonel Harness, R.A.).

The Zulu War: Colonel Glyn's force crossing the Buffalo River Valley, near Rorke's Drift, January 9.
From a sketch by the late Major Francis F. White, Paymaster of the 24th Regiment.

So, Lord Chelmsford spent the day in examining the country, and choosing a site for a new advanced camp, after a little skirmishing with a detached party of the enemy. His Lordship then proceeds as follows: -

"Having fixed upon the situation for the camp, and having ordered the troops then on the ground to bivouac there that night, I started to return to camp with the Mounted Infantry under Lieut.-Colonel Russell as my escort, when within about six miles of the camp I found the 1st Battalion Native Contingent halted, and shortly after Commandant Lonsdale rode up to report that he had ridden into camp and found it in possession of the Zulus. I at once sent word to Colonel Glyn to bring back all the troops, and I myself advanced with the Mounted Infantry and the Native Contingent battalion for about two miles, when I halted to await the arrival of the rest of the force. Lieut.-Colonel Russell went forward to reconnoitre the camp, and fully confirmed all that Commandant Lonsdale had reported.

Major Dartnell, commanding the Natal Mounted Police.

The Zulu War: Camp of 13th and 90th Regiments at Elands Nek, Transvaal border of Zululand.

"On the arrival of Colonel Glyn and his force, I at once formed them up into fighting order – guns in the centre, on the road, with three companies second battalion 24th Regiment on each flank in fours; Native Contingent battalions, one on each flank of the second battalion 24th Regiment in line, Europeans and natives, armed with guns, forming a third rank in front; Mounted Infantry on the extreme right, Natal Mounted Volunteers on the extreme left, Mounted Police in reserve. We advanced in this order across the plain with great speed and in excellent order, but could not reach the neighbourhood of our camp until after dark. The artillery came into action on the road and shelled the crest of the narrow neck over which our line of retreat lay, while the left wing, under Major Black, second battalion 24th Regiment, moved forward to seize a small stony hill on the left of this neck, the occupation of which would secure our left flank.

Major Black seized the position without opposition, and the right wing then advanced and occupied the neck in question, the right flank being protected by the precipitous sides of the Isandula Hill.

"The whole force lay down amid the debris of the plundered camp and the corpses of dead men, horses, and oxen, fully expecting to be attacked in front, and most probably in rear also. A few alarms occurred during the night, but it passed, however, without a shot being fired at us.

"At early dawn the following morning I ordered the troops to move off with all speed to Rorke's Drift, about which post I was in some anxiety. The troops had no spare ammunition and only a few biscuits; a large portion of them had had no other food for forty-eight hours. All had marched at least thirty miles the day before, and had passed an almost sleepless night on the stony ground. No one, therefore, was fit for any prolonged exertion, and it was certain that daylight would reveal a sight which could not but have a demoralising effect upon the whole force. I determined, therefore, to reach our nearest supply dépôt, at Rorke's Drift, as quickly as possible, and, as I have already said, moved off before it was fairly light.

"On sighting the post at Rorke's Drift heavy smoke was seen to be rising from the house, and the Zulus were seen retiring from it. It appeared as if our supplies at that post were lost to us; and I felt that those at Helpmakaar, some twelve miles further off, must have shared the same fate. To our intense relief, however, on nearing the Buffalo River the waving of hats was seen from the inside of a hastily-erected intrenchment, and information soon reached me that the gallant garrison of this post, some sixty of the 2nd Battalion 24th Regiment, under Lieutenant Bromhead, and a few volunteers and departmental officers, the whole under Lieutenant Chard, R.E., had for twelve hours made the most gallant resistance I have ever heard of against the determined attacks of some 3000 Zulus, 370 of those dead bodies surrounded the post. The loss of the garrison was thirteen killed and nine wounded.

"On reaching Rorke's Drift, I, for the first time, heard some particulars of the attack upon the Isandula camp, and am thus able to furnish the following narrative, the absolute accuracy of which, however, I cannot vouch for: -

"Shortly before the arrival of Lieutenant-Colonel Durnford in camp with his 450 natives information had reached Lieutenant-Colonel Pulleine from the left pickets that a number of Zulus had been seen on that flank. On receiving this information Lieutenant-Colonel Durnford asked Lieutenant-Colonel Pulleine to give him two companies of British infantry, in order that he might move up the heights on the left and attack them. Lieutenant-Colonel Pulleine at once stated that his orders were to defend the camp, and that, without a positive order, he would not allow the companies to leave. Lieutenant-Colonel Durnford then took his 450 natives up the heights, and went, so far as I can learn, about five miles from the camp, when he found himself in front of a very large army of Zulus. He at once sent back word to Lieutenant-Colonel Pulleine, and with his mounted Basutos retired slowly before the Zulus, who advanced to attack him.

"The mounted Basutos, I hear from many quarters, behaved remarkably well, and delayed the advance of the enemy for a considerable time. Their ammunition, however, began to grow short, and they were at last obliged to retire quickly on the camp. Being unable to find a fresh supply of ammunition, it appears they disbanded themselves and made the best of their way to the Buffalo, where they swam the river and recrossed into Natal, assisting, however, as far as they could, many of our fugitives from the camp to escape. As regards the proceedings of the six companies of British infantry, two guns, and two rocket tubes, the garrison of the camp, I can obtain but little information.

"One company went off to the extreme left, and has never been heard of since, and the other five, I understand, engaged the enemy about a mile to the left front of the camp, and made the most stubborn and gallant resistance. So long as they kept their faces to the enemy the Zulus were, I am told, quite unable to drive them back, and fell in heaps before the deadly fire poured into them. An officer who visited this part of the field of battle on the following morning reported that the loss of the Zulus in killed could not be less than 2000.

"When, however, the Zulus got round the left flank of these brave men they appear to have lost their presence of mind, and to have retired hastily through the tents, which had never been struck. Immediately the whole Zulu force surrounded them, they were overpowered by numbers, and the camp was lost. Those who were mounted ran the gauntlet, and some small portion managed to reach the river, which, however, at the point of crossing was deep and rapid. Many were shot or assegaied, and many were swept away by the current, and, it is presumed, have been drowned.

"Had the force in question but taken up a defensive position in the camp itself and utilised there the materials for a hasty entrenchment which lay near to hand, I feel absolutely confident that the whole Zulu army would not have been able to dislodge them. It appears that the oxen were yoked to the wagons three hours before the attack took place, so that there was ample time to construct that wagon-laager which the Dutch in former days understood so well. Had, however, even the tents been struck and the British troops placed with their backs to the precipitous Isandula hill, I feel sure that they could have made a successful resistance. Rumours reached me, however, that the troops were deceived by a simulated retreat, and in their eagerness to close with the enemy, allowed themselves to be drawn away from their line of defence.

"Our actual loss cannot as yet be correctly ascertained, but I fear that it cannot be less than thirty officers and about 500 non-commissioned officers, rank and file, belonging to the Imperial troops, and twenty-one officers and seventy non-commissioned officers, rank and file, of the colonial forces."

The above is Lord Chelmsford's account of this unhappy affair; and it seems rather feeble, not at all like the relation of Sir Garnet Wolseley's and Lord Napier of Magdala's operations in similar warfare. The famous despatch of Julius Caesar has often been quoted, "I came, I saw, I won a victory;" but Lord Chelmsford's might run thus, "I went, I did not see, I suffered a defeat."

NARRATIVE OF THE REV. "MR. WITT"

The Rev. Mr. Witt, a missionary who resided at Rorke's Drift, saw the battle of Isandula, and escaped with his life. He arrived in England on Tuesday night, and has given to the *Daily Telegraph* his account of the conflict, which runs as follows:

"It was on Jan. 22, 1879. Bright and warm rose the sun over my station, Oscarsburg, situate at the Buffalo River, on the Natal side. At the farm is a Drift into the Zulu country, known by the name of Rorke's Drift. Ten minutes' walk from the Drift were my houses, two large buildings, situate at the border of the Zulu country, and at the very place where the greatest resistance from the Zulus was expected. Those buildings were found very fit indeed for military purposes, and at the request of the General commanding the forces I left them at his disposal. A large outhouse, 80ft. by 20ft., which I used as a church, was turned into a commissariat store, and my dwelling-house, 60 ft. by 18 ft. was made an hospital, in consequence of which I had to send away my wife and three children. I myself stayed and acted as interpreter between the doctor in charge and the black people.

"Before the above-mentioned day all was quiet, wagons arriving constantly augmenting the store of provisions, and the only variation in this monotony was the reports of skirmishes taking place on this side of the river – but heavy storm is often proceeded by sudden calm.

1. The scene of the conflict. 2. Mounted infantry. 3. Native contingent. 4 and 6. Two companies of the 24th Regiment. 5. Four guns. 7. Company of 24th Regiment, under Major Black.

The Zulu War: Scene of the battle of Isandula, with Lord Chelmsford's advancing column.
Sketched on the spot by Lieutenant-Colonel J. North Crealock, on the evening of January 22.

Note by Lieutenant-Colonel Crealock: - *"Day waned, and the night hung over the hill, when we reached the last ridge, beyond which lay what had been our camp. To the hill on the left we sent off Major Black and three companies of the 24th, to seize it. The neck between it and the hill we must gain at all hazards. In silence we marched down into the gloom below, where lay, shrouded by a merciful pall, the horrors of the past day."* – [See also Lord Chelmsford's despatch]

"The 22nd came and witnessed the battle, in which the warriors on both sides showed, or perhaps were compelled to show, a courage that can be denied neither by contemporaries nor by posterity. Behold on the one side 1000 soldiers reinforced by equal their numbers of black ones, leaving their camp to attack an army more than ten times their number! Behold, on the other side this mass of Zulus, who, close together, walk straight against the mouth of the cannon! Look how thousands after thousands are killed, and nevertheless the mass prevails, without fear, over the dead bodies of the comrades against the destroying weapon! Behold on the one side a few dozen white troops, the only remainder of the thousand, look how they, after having shot away all their ammunition, keep close together, trying yet awhile, to fight for their lives with the bayonets. Behold, on the other side – the black ones- how they are fighting against the intruder and oppressor, fighting for liberty and independence, coming close to the bayonets and making them harmless by taking the corpses of their brethren and throwing them on them!

Isandula Hill – facsimile of sketch on the spot, by Lieutenant Newnham Davis of the 3rd Buffs

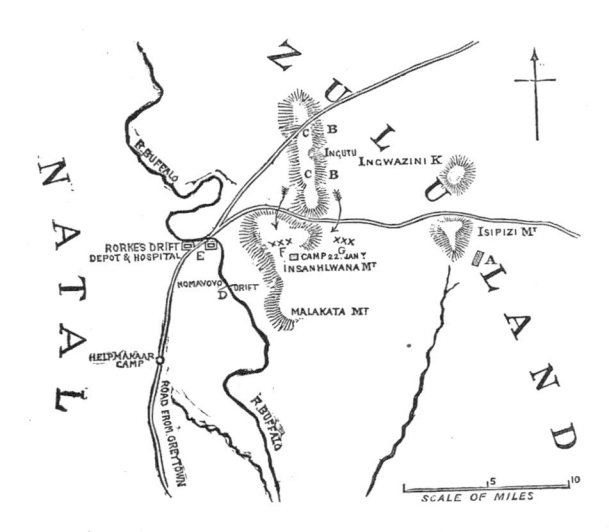

A. Position of General Lord Chelmsford in the afternoon of Jan. 22.
B. Supposed position of the Enemy in the morning of that day.
C. Enemy's position when first seen from the camp.   +Their line of advance.
D. Drift on Buffalo River by which the few survivors escaped.
E. Commissariat dèpôt and hospital. Rorke's Drift, held by Lieutenants Chard and Bromhead.
F. The first battalion of 24th Regiment advancing to meet the enemy.
G. Colonel Durnford's Native Contingent advancing.

Sketch of the positions of the forces engaged at Isandula, Jan. 22

"Who wins your warmest sympathy – the Captain, who, knowing that he is lost, stops a moment to spike the cannon and die; or the Zulu, who, in his excitement, leaves his fellow-soldiers behind, and alone makes the attack on the hospital at Rorke's Drift, resting his gun on the very barricade, and firing on those inside? Is your admiration greater for those ninety-five who entered the commissariat store at Oscarsburg and defended it against 5000 Zulus than those 5000 who fought outside the whole night, trying to overpower the whites, and who withdrew at daybreak, leaving 1000 dead, hundreds of whom were lying even on the very verandah of the house? Indeed your admiration ought to be as great for the one as for the other. Where did you find greater courage or contempt of death than theirs?

"Doctor R. and myself had in the morning made up our minds to pay a visit to a missionary in the neighbourhood. When about to start at noon we were told that a great fight was taking place over the river. In company with the Chaplain of the Forces we ascended a hill 500 feet high, between the station and the river, from which we had an excellent view of what was going on.

At a distance of three miles as the crow flies we saw the place where the camp was made. The whole spot was filled with black figures swarming about. Down below us, though very hilly and broken, there was a large flat between us and the camp, and on this flat we saw three lines drawn, the one end reaching the camp and the other the river. The whole of it was a shocking sight. The heavy firing from the rifles mixed with the rolling sound from the big guns and the movements of the lines, all this caused a nervous feeling that something terrifying was going on.

"My position was on a hill on the other side of the river from where the fight was raging. I watched the Zulus descend and draw themselves in long lines between the camp and the river. From where I stood I could also see the English forces advancing to the attack; but I could not see any hand-to-hand fighting. I observed that the Zulus were fighting heavily, and presently I saw that the English were surrounded in a kraal some little distance from the camp. What I was wroth to learn was the reason why the British troops left their camp to attack, instead of remaining on the defensive. In my opinion, they should never have thus advanced.

"As the fight progressed, and I saw that the English were being beaten, I prepared to fly, and had my horse saddled with that object in view. At length I noticed that the Zulus were crossing the river. It was not very deep. The water only reached up to their waists as they forded the stream. I saw that there was no time to be lost, and I dashed away on horseback as hard as I could go, chased by the Zulus, who did their best to catch me, but failed. So far as I have been able I have described the fighting which took place correctly. I could just discern that the Zulus were hurling the bodies of their comrades upon the bayonets of the English as they fought and endeavoured to defend themselves in the kraal, but that was all. The distance I stood from the fight prevented my observing events more closely.

"What struck us in the beginning was that a good many of the officers of the native contingent had one by one crossed the river some miles below the mission station, and came galloping towards it as fast as the horses could carry them; and, on the left hand side, we noticed some of the mounted natives crossing at the Drift, and driving some cattle before them. Although we could not clearly comprehend this movement, we did not pay much attention to it, our minds being far from dreaming of the real facts. In the meantime the three lines had drawn themselves more close together to one spot. Here was a large Kaffir kraal, which was gradually surrounded and fired at. How many men had entered it I do not know, and shall probably never learn, because what was inside there was certainly killed by Zulu bullets.

"After twenty minutes' heavy firing the resistance ceased, and the attacking ones divided themselves again. Half of them returned towards the camp, the other half, from 5000 to 6000, approaching the river, and the place where I was. Firing every now and then, they reached at last the river. There another skirmish took place. The spot where they crossed was half a mile below the Drift, and defended by a few Natal Kaffirs. A tolerably good force could easily have prevented their crossing. Having killed these few Natal Kaffirs, they crossed one by one. This done, they sat down for half an hour in order to get some rest, and to strengthen themselves from the snuffbox. Then they separated again, divided into two parties, the one following the course of the river, the other taking its way towards us.

"We now perceived that the house of a neighbouring farm on the Natal side was on fire; but we were so far from fancying that the Zulus would cross the river that we never had the slightest idea of the real

1. Rev. Mr Witt's house, with redoubt of mielie-bags and biscuit-boxes 2. Hospital burning.
3. Cattle kraal. 4. Tyana mountain. 5. Lieutenant-Colonel Russell riding up to the beleaguered garrison.

The Zulu War: The intrenched position at Rorke's Drift.
Sketched by Lieutenant-Colonel Crealock on January 23.

Note by Lieutenant-Colonel Crealock: - *"About 6.30 a.m. we reached Rorke's Drift, and saw the smoke rising from the Post. Too late! too late! But no – from amidst the smoke we saw some figures gesticulating; then a flag waved. Glasses out! They are red-coats! Russell and the mounted men are sent forward, plunge into the river, and scrambling out on the opposite side, gallop up. A moment's doubt if it be not a Zulu ruse. But no! The morning breeze now brings across the frontier river the glad sound of a British cheer. We are not too late. There were 351 dead bodies found lying around the house, and between it and the hill; and 60 around and in the burning hospital, which they had succeeded in firing."* [See also Lord far from fancying that the Zulus would cross the river that we never had the slightest idea of the real state of things, but were still thinking that the approaching black people were our own troops. They were now so close to us that their bullets could easily have reached us, and we saw that they were all naked. Reality, then, also stood naked for us. The thick mass that swarmed in the camp was the Zulus who had taken possession of it. The light lines firing at the kraal were Zulus, and finally, those who had crossed the river and were approaching were Zulus.

The few whites whom we had seen galloping now and then to the Natal side, perhaps, were the only surviving of all those who a week before had entered the Zulu country. Our eyes were opened, but why had they not been before? How had the idea of the possibility of a disaster on our side been so far from us that the clearest facts had been unable to make it enter our minds? The officers' flight, the burning farm, the immense masses (say 20,000) moving to and fro in light lines, why had not this long ago told us that the Lord's thoughts are not our thoughts nor our ways His? These ideas were crossing my mind while we speedily descended the hill, followed by the Zulus.

"Arrived at the houses, we saw at once a new proof of the sad truth to which our eyes had just been opened. The tents which surrounded the houses, and were used by a company left there under Major Spalding for the protection of the hospital and the commissariat stores, had been pulled down, and a temporary barricade of meal-sacks was made between the houses, which were a distance of twenty yards from one another. Here we were met by anxious questions from many lips, "Do the Zulus come here?" and compelled to answer "In five minutes they will be here.'

"In the same moment the fighting began in the neighbourhood. Though wishing to take part in the defence of my own house, and at the same time in the defence of an important place for the whole colony, yet my thoughts went to my wife and to my children, who were at a short distance from there, and did not know anything of what was going on.

"Having seen one part of the Zulus going in that direction I followed the desire of my heart, saddled my horse, and started to warn my family. But my poor family had had much to suffer before, in five days' journey to Maritzburg, chased by the Zulus, and frightened by all sorts of reports. I will pass over this of no interest for other people. The attack on Oscarsburg had been awful.

"Before I started I saw a Zulu alone at the barricade, kneeling and firing. The whole force drew nearer, and the battle drew on heavier. Soon the hospital was on fire. Our people found it impossible to defend themselves inside the barricade. They must retire within the walls, thus entering the commissariat store. The sick people were brought here, except five who could not be removed, and were stabbed by the Zulus and burnt. That the hospital was set on fire was certainly a great personal loss for me, as all my property was burnt; but it was of great importance for the whole colony, and especially for the people in the commissariat stores, as the flames of the burning house enabled them to aim properly on the Zulus and thus keep them at a fair distance. If the Zulus had known what they ought they should never have put fire to the house, and the heavy darkness of that dreadful night would have made our troops unable to defend themselves as they did."

The march of Colonel Glyn's column on Jan. 9 from Helpmakaar, in Natal, to cross the Buffalo river and advance through Rorke's Drift into the Zulu country, is illustrated by the sketch we have received from Major Francis White, Paymaster of the 24th Regiment. It shows the singular character of the scenery in the Buffalo valley, with a precipitous basaltic cliff, 200 ft. high, surmounting the steep downs, which are here grassy, and there overgrown with bush. There is a cataract or waterfall at the edge of the cliff, whence a stream pours down the slope, with a bending course, to join the Buffalo river, which at Rorke's Drift is eighty yards wide, and was greatly swollen by the rains.

The path or track by which the troops came on their route from Helpmakaar is seen ascending the hill obliquely, towards the left-hand part of the summit, as shown in this view, and crossing the stream about half way up. The valley is four miles wide at this place; but it must have been very near here that Lieutenant Coghill, orderly officer, and Lieutenant Teignmouth Melvill, Adjutant, were overtaken by the Zulus and slain, after crossing the river, while riding from the post at Rorke's Drift to convey news of the desperate encounter to Helpmakaar, fifteen miles distant, and to call up fresh reinforcements. The bodies of those two gallant officers have been found, together with the regimental colours of the 24th, which they were carrying off for safety.

PORTRAITS OF OFFICERS KILLED

We have now the melancholy task of briefly noticing those gallant officers of the 24th Regiment, whose lives were lost on that disastrous day. Lieutenant-Colonel Henry Burmeister Pulleine entered the Army, as ensign, in November 1855, obtained his Lieutenancy in June, 1858, became Captain in 1861, Major in February, 1871, and Brevet-Lieutenant-Colonel Oct. 1, 1877.

Captain Eccles Mostyn, of the 24th, was thirty-six years of age, and was the only son of the late Rev. G.T. Mostyn, formerly Incumbent of St. Thomas' Church, in the town of St. Helen's, Lancashire, and also of St. John's, Kilburn. He entered the service in July, 1862, and became Captain in October 1871.

Lieutenant Charles Walter Cavaye. who is the second surviving son of General Cavaye. now residing in Edinburgh, held his commission from December, 1871.

Lieutenant Edgar Oliphant Anstey was born at Highercombe, South Australia, March 18th, 1851, and was a son of Mr. G.A. Anstey, now residing in Harley-street, Cavendish-square; he had been in the regiment since 1873.

Sub-Lieutenant Thomas Llewellyn George Griffith was eldest son of the Rev. T.L. Griffith, Rector of Deal, Kent; he got his commission in September, 1877, but ante-dated 1876; and he was but a month or two over twenty-one years of age at the time of his death.

Lieutenant Henry Julian Dyer was eldest son of Mr. H.J. Dyer of Blackheath, and was in the twenty-fifth year of his age; he joined the 2nd battalion of the 24th Regiment in October, 1876.

Second-Lieutenant Edwards Hopton Dyson was a son of Major Dyson, of Denne Hill, Canterbury; his commission dated from last May.

The portrait of Lieut.-Colonel Pulleine is from a photograph by W.T. and R. Gowland, of York; that of Captain Mostyn, by Hills and Saunders, of Eton; that of Lieutenant Cavaye was taken at Capetown; that of Lieutenant Anstey, by Messrs. Elliot and Fry; that of Lieutenant Griffith, by Symonds, of Portsmouth; that of Lieutenant H.J. Dyer, on his eighteenth birthday, was taken at Nice; and that of Lieutenant Dyson, by H.P. Robinson, of Tunbridge Wells.

COLONEL PEARSON ON THE TUGELA

The operations of Colonel Pearson's column, which crossed the Lower Tugela from "Fort Pearson," seven or eight miles from the sea, on Jan. 12, have assumed considerable importance, as he has since advanced twenty or thirty miles northward into Zululand, and now occupies an intrenched position at Ekhowe, with sufficient stores, but is for the present shut up from communications. We have received, through Mr. J. Blair, Stoke Newington, a series of photographs taken by his brother at Colonel Pearson's head-quarters, to Jan. 13, representing the banks of the Tugela, the encampment of the 3rd Buffs, and that of the Victoria and Stanger Mounted Rifles, at Thring's Post, Fort Pearson, the Naval Brigade, formed of seamen of H.M.S. Active and H.M.S. Tenedos, and other subjects of interest. Two of these we have engraved for this weeks' publication.

The first shows the men of H.M.S. Tenedos, who now compose the garrison of Fort Pearson, practising with the Gatling gun, a weapon that has been described by us on former occasions. The second Illustration shows the crossing of the river Tugela, which is here of great width and depth, and at this season, being in heavy flood, is a swollen and rushing stream of extraordinary force and rapidity.

It is mentioned by Lord Chelmsford, in one of his despatches, that an anchor, with hawser attached to it, was, on the night of the 9th, torn up from the bottom of the river, and was carried away down stream and fixed in the opposite bank so firmly as to require five hundred men to haul it back. A seaman of H.M.S. Active was drowned in this operation, and Lieutenant Craigie, R.N., narrowly escaped the same fate, from the overturning of a boat or punt. This part of the Lower Tugela, it will be observed, is distant above ninety miles from Rorke's Drift, on the Buffalo; and we have next to speak of another place, Eland's Neck, on the Pongola, which is situated eighty miles farther up the country beyond Rorke's Drift.

Such is the extent of Lord Chelmsford's operations, with five detached columns, now practically reduced to four, or even to three, invading Zululand at points so distant from each other along a frontier line of two hundred miles.

The Zulu War: Colonel Pearson's column crossing the Tugela.
From a photograph by Mr J. Lloyd of Durban, Natal.

The north-west and north sides of Cetewayo's kingdom abut on the Transvaal British province; and here are stationed two columns, that of Colonel Evelyn Wood, V.C., from the Utrecht district, which has been acting in close conjunction with the head-quarters column of Colonel Glyn; and that of Colonel Rowlands, which is rather intended to prevent the enemy breaking into the Transvaal. A portion of Colonel Woods' forces, consisting of the first battalion of the 13th Regiment, two companies of the 90th Regiment, a battery of Royal Artillery, and Captain Carrington's Frontier Light Horse, with Native Contingent (Swazis), has been posted at Eland's Neck, on a branch of the Pongola, twenty miles from Luneburg, at the eastern boundary of the Transvaal.

It is situated on a plain 6000 ft. above the sea-level, with mountain ranges to the north and east, in which are veins of coal already worked by the inhabitants of the district.

We observe, in Wyld's Military Sketch-Map of Zululand and the Transvaal, among the settlements of this neighbourhood, the names of "Tiverton," "Silverton," and "Halberton," which will at once be recognised by those readers who are familiar with the English county of Devonshire. It is to be presumed that emigrants from that part of England have found their way to the most easterly region of the Transvaal, where we hope they will be allowed to dwell in safety.

The subject of our remaining Illustrations is the embarkation and departure of the 17th Lancers, which took place on Monday week, at the Victoria Dock, Blackwall, on board the steam-ship "France," a sister-ship to the "Spain," belonging to the "National" Liverpool and New York Line. The head-quarters of the regiment went out in the "England," from Southampton. The four troops embarked at Blackwall, numbering 280 men and 300 horses, were reviewed by the Duke of Cambridge before leaving their barracks at Hounslow and Hampton Court. His Royal Highness, with the Duke of Teck, visited the ship on the day of embarkation. The officers, non-commissioned officers, and band of the 18th Hussars, stationed at Woolwich, chartered one of the Thames steamboats, and came across the river, to bid a hearty farewell to the 17th Lancers, which was an act of fraternal kindness worthy of such gallant soldiers.

Since our last publication, there is but little fresh information from the Cape which has reached up by special telegram viâ Madeira. Lord Chelmsford has been reinforced by the 88th Regiment from King William's Town, a detachment of the King's Own from Capetown, and by small bodies of volunteers. No confirmation had been received of the reported attack on Colonel Pearson's position at Ekhowe. A reconnaissance has been made by Lieutenant-Colonel Buller of the military kraal at Bagulusine, which was burned and 400 cattle carried off. It was reported by spies that Cetewayo intends to invade Natal, but that the flooded state of the Tugela has thus far prevented him from doing so. Considerable anxiety was felt respecting the state of affairs in the Transvaal, and it was reported that the Boers positively decline to join in a war against the Zulus, except on condition of restoring the political independence of the Transvaal.

THE ZULU WAR

In addition to the other Illustrations of the Zulu War presented in this Number of our Journal, we are furnished with a rough outline Sketch, by Lieutenant Newnham Davis, of the Hill of Isandula, or, as he writes the name, Insanhlwana, with the remains of Colonel Pulleine's camp, burning tents and waggons, and hundreds of British soldiers and Zulus lying slain on the hill side. The Sketch Map, drawn by "W.J.J.W.," who was also there with Lord Chelmsford's force on its arrival, shows the positions of the different portions of the army that day.

March 15, 1879

BOOKS ON SOUTH AFRICA

At the present critical moment, when so many of our fellow-Englishmen are most anxiously expecting news of the war against the Zulus on the borders of Natal and the Transvaal, we can safely recommend the second edition of S.W. Silver and Co.'s *Handbook to South Africa*. It is an almost perfect compendium of colonial, topographical, statistical, and historical information; besides which, it contains brief and scientifically correct accounts of the physical features, the geology and mineralogy, the variations of climate, the vegetation, wild animals, and agricultural or pastoral resources of each district within or adjacent to the British dominions.

We cannot doubt that the political consequences of the present Zulu war, involving some very important questions of colonial policy, will make it needful to obtain the most complete and accurate knowledge of these subjects, however speedily we may hope to see the actual struggle on the Tugela and the Buffalo rivers victoriously finished. The Cape Colony, including its Eastern Provinces, which extend to seven hundred miles along the south coast of Africa, the Kaffir district beyond the Kei, which have recently been subjugated, the Diamond Fields or West Griqua-land, not long since placed under British Government, Basuto-land and Griqua-land East, owning a British protectorate, and the Orange River Dutch Republic, are indirectly concerned in these questions.

As for the province of Natal, and the Transvaal territory, which have had so many troubles to endure, it is but right that public opinion in England should be instructed by the best skill of authors and journalists upon their actual position, the different races of their inhabitants and of their savage neighbours, and all their internal affairs. We may here especially refer to the learned work on Natal, by Mr. Henry Brooks and Dr. R.J. Mann, with very beautiful illustrations, published by Mr. Lovell Reeve; and to Mr. Alfred Aylward's interesting volume, "The Transvaal of To-day," which is mentioned by itself more particularly. But the second edition of Messrs. Silver's "Handbook" is much cheaper and more convenient, and it is equally good for all the other provinces and settlements, British or Dutch in that region of the world, now so deeply sympathised with by all classes of people here at home.

The predecessor of Lord Chelmsford in the chief command of her Majesty's military forces in South Africa, who left that country but a twelvemonth ago, might be expected to give some useful information or advice upon the present alarming crisis. But General Sir Arthur Cunynghame's volume, printed in great haste and published by Messrs. Macmillan within a week after the news came of the disaster to the British arms on the Zulu frontier, might just as well have appeared six months ago. It contains not a single entire page that could not have been written at leisure during the five years of his residence and occasional tours of official visitation in different provinces of the British dominion there.

Five sixths of the book are filled with the common sort of personal anecdotes and observations, mixed with scraps cut out of old colonial papers, and with very crude political opinions, that have too often been retailed to us by travellers of a literary turn. These are not presented by Sir Arthur with the masterly talent and practised skill of Mr. Anthony Trollope, whose bright description of South Africa, we are pleased to notice, is about to be reissued by Messrs. Chapman and Hall in a cheap one-volume edition. General Cunynghame has really nothing to tell us that we have not heard and read several times before. He saw what everybody sees at Capetown and Grahamstown and on the roads hither and thither, visiting many of the colonists, inspecting their houses, farms, vineyards and ostrich-breeding yards, riding about the Karroo or the plains of the Orange and Vaal river country, and shooting various kinds of "bok."

It was not till the last six months of *My Command in South Africa*, as his book is entitled, that he was called upon to deal with hostile Kaffirs; and these were the Galekas, under their notable chief Kreli, in the Trans-kei district not very far beyond King William's Town. Our readers have not forgotten that last British and colonial war in Kaffraria, which broke out at the end of September 1877. It was latterly taken up by the Gaikas, under Sandilli, a cognate tribe dwelling still nearer to the white man's settlements, and was finally concluded by Lord Chelmsford, then General Thesiger, in the early part of last year.

General Cunynghame's operations would, no doubt, have been more successful if they had not been sadly hampered by the wrong-headed behaviour of the Ministry then in office in the Cape Colony, who have since been turned out.

Such was the view of Governor Sir Bartle Frere, and so we should think, from reading this portion of Sir Arthur's narrative, as well as from our recollection of the accounts current at the time. It is very natural that the gallant General should wish to offer his own explanation of those past military transactions, and to vindicate his reputation as a commander, which he may probably be able to do with results satisfactory to himself and his friends. But the Kaffir war of the Trans-Kei has nothing at all to do with the Zulu war beyond the Tugela, which is carried on in a different manner, with very dissimilar antagonists, and in a distant and different country.

General Cunynghame never went near any part of the frontiers of Zulu-land, and was only a few days in Natal, stopping at Durban and Pietermaritzburg, in 1875, and there he chanced to meet a few Zulus, but he does not seem to know much about them or their country. He made a three-month's tour in the Transvaal, soon after the annexation of that province in 1877, and was easily "crammed" by the partisans of that violent *coup d'état* with many preposterous tales of the misconduct of the Dutch Boers, and of the miserable state of their Republic. But we have learned now to regard the Transvaal business in quite another light. In any case, we should not be disposed to rely upon Sir Arthur Cunynghame's impartiality and freedom from prejudice; and it is to be regretted that he has not taken the trouble to search for evidence of the truth of these injurious allegations. He would find that nearly all of them have been proved to be false and calumnious, the mere inventions of party malice devised by obscure intriguers against the Transvaal Republic, who never came forward openly to substantiate their assertions.

But that question may or may not be revived, in consequence of the existing difficulty, through the refusal of the aggrieved Boers to lend active assistance to the British forces against Cetewayo. If anybody desires to know what is to be said on their side, and what was the actual condition of their independent commonwealth, after the unsuccessful attack on Secocoeni's mountain fortress in August, 1876, we recommend Mr. Alfred Aylward's interesting volume, *The Transvaal of To-Day*, recently published by Messrs. W. Blackwood and Co.

The author is a countryman of ours, who was at the Diamond-Fields of West Griqua-land when the Dutch Republic invited foreign volunteers to join in forming the Lydenburg Corps, under Captain von Schlieckmann, a young Prussian officer of the highest connections and character, nephew to General von Manteuffel. When he was killed in a skirmish near Fort Burgers, on the Steelport, Mr. Aylward took the command, and he relates how this small but well-equipped force, in which were many Englishmen, Germans and Americans, contrived to beleaguer Secocoeni until February, 1877, and compelled that troublesome enemy to sue for peace.

It has suited the purpose of some parties to conceal these facts, that they might represent the Transvaal people as helpless and shiftless, exposed to Kaffir incursions and perhaps to a Zulu army invading their country, though it is, and has always been, much safer from such dangers than the British colony of Natal. In many other respects, as Mr. Aylward shows, the character and position of the Dutch African settlers have been shamefully belied, upon several occasions, to create a pretext for robbing them of their recognised political independence. We can hardly wonder that they now resent such treatment and decline to fight our battles.

Some lively description of life and sport and the aspects of the country, in the Transvaal, as well as in Bamangwato, which is the land of the Bechuanas, to the north-west of that province, quite in the interior of Southern Africa, is given by a well-known writer, Mr. Parker Gillmore. His narrative, of which Messrs. Cassell, Petter, and Galpin have brought out a new edition, is called *The Great Thirst Land*; but that is only the name applied to the Kalahari Desert, the vast expanse of arid sandy wilderness beyond the Marico and Limpopo rivers. Before getting into that desolate region, where he went in pursuit of large and fierce game, he visited the remotest settlements of the Dutch boers, Jacobsdal, Zeerust, and Brackfontein, and found them dirty, churlish, and uncouth, as might be expected in that situation.

Among the backwoodsmen and prairie squatters of the Far West in North America, with which this author had previously gained some acquaintance, he might probably find not less disagreeable habits of life, though belonging to the English race. Delicacy and refinement are seldom permitted to flourish in the rude homes of a needy and laborious Border peasantry, distant many days' toilsome journey from any town, and out of the way of passing travellers.

The Boers, however, like every other nation, are to be estimated by the character of those met with in an ordinary position; and the Dutch citizens of Pretoria, or Potchefstrom, will bear comparison, we believe, with those of some English country towns and villages. Mr. Parker Gillmore was in the Transvaal shortly before the arbitrary annexation of that country to the British dominions. He met with Dutchmen who expressed grave apprehensions of the usurping and encroaching designs of England, at which they did not conceal their natural displeasure. But the author is a sportsman, not a politician, and it is scarcely to him that we should look for a just and considerate view of that question, which has now again come into importance through its effects in the present Zulu war.

The farther travels of Mr. Parker Gillmore extended to Soshong, a native town of the Bechuanas, the capital of King Kama, and thence he passed through Mashue to the capital of a neighbouring monarch, King Sechele, a hundred miles southward, near the old missionary station at Kolobeng. These places and people are familiar to the readers of narratives long since published relating to the evangelical labours of Dr. Moffat and Dr. Livingstone; and the whole region has been well explored in times past. Hunting adventures with lions, elephants, rhinoceros, leopards, and other formidable beasts, not to mention the antelopes of various kinds, fill a large part of this entertaining volume.

THE ZULU WAR

We shall resume next week the series of our Illustrations of the Zulu war. The despatch of Lieutenant Chard, R.E., relating to the extraordinary defence of the post at Rorke's Drift, has been published in the official *Gazette*. The Queen has conferred the Victoria Cross, for valour, upon him and Lieutenant Gonville Bromhead; and it is well deserved by them. Each of these officers will be also promoted to the brevet rank of Major, and will be made C.B. The news from Capetown, by telegraph from Madeira, is to the 18th ult., but there is little importance from Natal.

Colonel Pearson has been attacked by a large force of Zulus at Ekowe, but defeated them with enormous loss, pursuing them as far as Entamedi, one of the Zulu military kraals. Despatches from Colonel Wood report that he has captured a large quantity of cattle. He adds that the health of the British troops under his command is good. Sir Bartle Frere has received a communication from the President and people of the Orange Free State expressing sympathy with the British for the recent disaster at Isandula. The state of affairs in the Transvaal is disquieting, on account of the hostile attitude of the native tribes.

THE ILLUSTRATED LONDON NEWS

March 22, 1879

LIEUTENANT-COLONEL DURNFORD, R.E.

MAJOR FRANCIS WHITE.

CAPTAIN R. YOUNGHUSBAND.

CAPTAIN G. V. WARDELL.

CAPTAIN W. DEGACHER.

LIEUTENANT F. GODWIN-AUSTEN.

LIEUTENANT TEIGNMOUTH MELVILL.

THE HON. S. W. P. VEREKER, NATAL CONTINGENT.

LIEUTENANT J. P. DALY.

The Zulu War: Officers killed at Isanhlwana, January 22.

THE ILLUSTRATED LONDON NEWS — March 29th, 1879

The Zulu War: Recovery of the lost colours of the 24th Regiment. – A scene in the fort at Helpmakaar.
From a sketch by Lieutenant W.W. Lloyd.

THE ZULU WAR

We present the portraits of three more of the officers attached to Lord Chelmsford's army who lost their lives on Jan. 22, two of them in the disastrous conflict at Isanhlwana, and one, Assistant-Commissary Byrne, in the gallant and successful defence at Rorke's Drift. Lieutenant Charles John Atkinson, of the

1st battalion of the 24th Regiment, was in the twenty-fourth year of his age; he was the elder son and heir of the late Adam Atkinson, Esq., of Lorbottle, near Alnwick. He was educated at Eton, entered the Army in 1874, and obtained his commission as Lieutenant in 1878. Lieutenant Scott, of the Natal Carbineers, was brother to Mr. A.L. Scott, of Brasenose College, Oxford. Mr. Louis Alexander Byrne, Assistant-Commissary, was but twenty-two years of age; he was the fifth son of Mr. Richard Clarke Byrne, of Cardiff. He is said to have "behaved nobly" in the fight at Rorke's Drift.

We are indebted to Lieutenant W.W. Lloyd, of the 24th Regiment, for sending us the sketch from which we have engraved our Illustration of the retreat of the fugitives across the Buffalo River, which was drawn with the assistance of Lieutenant Smith-Dorrien, 95th Regiment. He sends those also of the interior of the new fort at Helpmakaar, and of the scene that took place there after the recovery of the lost regimental colours, when they were displayed and greeted with a military salute.

After the desperate combat at Isanhlwana, a scene of utter confusion seems to have occurred – horse and foot, black and white, English and Zulu, all in a struggling mass, making gradually through the camp towards the road, where the Zulus already closed the way of escape. Of what happened during that half-hour even those who lived to tell can remember but little. Every man who had a horse attempted to escape towards the river; those who had none died where they stood. One of the few saved was Lieutenant Smith-Dorrien, who was the transport officer with Colonel Glyn's column, and had been sent that morning by Lord Chelmsford with a despatch to Colonel Durnford at Rorke's Drift, ordering him to join Colonel Pulleine at the Isanhlwana camp.

He describes the fight and the subsequent flight to the Buffalo, of which he says:- "The ground there down to the river was so broken that the Zulus went as fast as the horses, and kept killing all the way. There were very few white men. They were nearly all mounted niggers of ours flying. This lasted till we came to a kind of precipice down to the river Buffalo. I jumped off and lead my horse down. There was a poor fellow of the mounted infantry (a private) struck through the arm, who said as I passed that if I could bind up his arm and stop the bleeding he would be all right. I accordingly took out my handkerchief and tied up his arm. Just as I had done it, Major Smith, of the Artillery, came down by me, wounded, saying, 'For God's sake, get on, man; the Zulus are on the top of us!' I had done all I could for the wounded man, and so turned to jump on my horse. Just as I was doing so the horse went with a bound to the bottom of the precipice being struck with an assegai. I gave up all hope, as the Zulus were all round me finishing off the wounded, the man I had helped and Major Smith among the number.

"However, with the strong hope that everybody clings to that some accident would turn up, I rushed off on foot and plunged into the river, which was little better than a roaring torrent. I was being carried down the stream at a tremendous pace when a loose horse came by me and I got hold of his tail, and he landed me safely on the other bank, but I was too tired to stick to him and get on his back. I got up again and rushed on, and was several times knocked over by our mounted niggers, who would not even get out of my way; then up a tremendous hill, with my wet clothes and boots full of water. About twenty Zulus got over the water and followed us up over the hill, but I am thankful to say they had not their firearms. Crossing the river, however, the Zulus kept firing at us as we went up the hill, and killed several of the niggers all round me. I was the only white man to be seen until I came to one who had been kicked by his horse and could not mount. I put him on his horse and lent him my knife. He said he would catch me a horse. Directly he was up he went clear away. I struggled into Helpmakaar, about twenty miles off, at nightfall, to find a few men who had escaped (about ten or twenty), with others who had been intrenched in a wagon laager."

Lieutenant Newnham Davis, of the 3rd Buffs, from whom we have also received a Sketch of the position at Isanhlwana, which was engraved by us two or three weeks ago, gives the following account of their escape:-

"When we saw that the camp was gone, and that our men began to try and get away by twos and threes, I said to Henderson, 'What are we going to do? Our only chance now is to make a run for it and dash through.' We started; he took to the right and I took to the left, and rode slap at the enemy. One fellow seized hold of my horse's bridle and I made a stab at him with my rifle (a foolish thing that has a 9-in. knife attachment); but the man caught hold of it and pulled it out of my hand, which at the same time made my horse rear and shy and cleared me of the man. I then had only my revolver, and I saw a Zulu right in my course, and rode at him and shot him in the neck. My horse got a stab, and many assegais were thrown at me; but as I was lying along my horse, they did not hit me. The ground was stony that I was going over, and I soon came to grief; but as there was no time to think, I was soon up and away again, and took the river in front of me.

"Many were then escaping, but, not being accustomed to take horses across rivers, they fell and rolled over, as the current was strong. I have had a good deal of experience in swimming horses, and I kept mine from falling, and directly he was in the water I threw myself off and caught hold of the stirrup. The Zulus followed us down and fired at us crossing. Some of the Zulus took the water after us, as our natives stabbed two Zulus just as they reached the Natal side. I never saw Colonel Durnford or George Shepstone after we left the gully or water-wash, and I did not see Henderson after we began our race until I met him next day at Helpmakaar."

Interior of the new fort at Helpmakaar.
From a sketch by Lieutenant W.W. Lloyd 24th Regiment.

Illustrations of the Zulu War.

LIEUTENANT C. J. ATKINSON, 24TH REGIMENT, KILLED AT ISANHLWANA.

ASSISTANT COMMISSARY L. A. BYRNE, KILLED AT RORKE'S DRIFT.

LIEUTENANT SCOTT, NATAL CARBINEERS. KILLED AT ISANHLWANA.

The Zulu War: Retreat of fugitives from Isanhlwana across the Buffalo River.
From a sketch by Lieutenant W.W. Lloyd, 24th Regiment, and Lieutenant Smith-Dorrien, 95th Regiment.

An account of the recovery of the colours of the 24th Regiment is furnished by a correspondent on the Zulu frontier, who writes as follows:-

"A party went from our little camp at Rorke's Drift, consisting of Major Black, of the 2-24th Regiment; the Rev. George Smith, chaplain of the forces; Captain Harford, nineteen men, the commandant of Lonsdale's corps, Captain Charles Raw; four men of the Native Mounted Contingent, and Brickhill, the interpreter to the staff. The downward course of the Buffalo River was followed until a crossing place at an almost impassable drift was reached, where many of our brave fellows, after the carnage of

Port Natal.

Durban, Port Natal, from the Bluff.

Isanhlwana camp, essayed to pass and perished in the attempt. The route was strewn with dead bodies, those of the natives composing the majority, these being either members of the Natal Native Contingent or loyal natives who believed in the supreme power of the Government or the magical effect of the boundary line even to the last. When the steep path leading down the precipitous rocks to the river was reached scouts were posted.

"A descent was made, and half way down, nearly half a mile from the river, lay the bodies of Adjutant Melvill and Lieutenant Coghill. These were decently interred, and service was performed by the chaplain. Lieutenant Coghill's ring, Adjutant Melvill's spurs, and other articles belonging to the brave fellows being carefully taken charge of by their comrades. The path thence to the river was strewn with dead Zulus and various paraphernalia of savage warfare. Arrived at the river, the dead horses, saddles, stirrups, spurs, leggings, charms, and articles of native dress, accidentally or purposely cast off, lying by the roaring stream, foaming over huge boulders, and passing between precipitous cliffs covered with bush and aloes, showed the spot where the rushing torrent and savage foe alike overwhelmed many brave men.

"About 500 yards below, at the crossing place, Mr. Harbour, of Commandant Lonsdale's corps, succeeded in finding the Queen's colours of the 1-24th Regiment, with the pole complete, injured by the action of the rapid stream, but otherwise untouched, the gilt lion and crown surmounting the poles, and the colour case were found by two other of Lonsdale's men a few yards lower down. These colours were borne back at the head of the little cavalcade in triumph, and when Rorke's Drift was reached the soldiers left their dinners or whatever occupation they were engaged upon, overjoyed at the sight of their lost colours regained, and gave their heartiest cheers for the old flag and for Major Black and the volunteers who had recovered them. The major, in a few well-chosen words, then handed the colours to Colonel Glyn amidst loud huzzahs, and the colonel with heartfelt emotion, on behalf of himself and his regiment, thanked the little band for the noble work they had voluntarily undertaken and successfully performed."

The fort at Helpmakaar is twelve miles from Rorke's Drift, and is now occupied by about 800 men, under Colonel Bray of the 4th Regiment. They have been suffering much from sickness, having to sleep on wet ground within the ramparts. They are 110 men of the first battalion of the 24th Regiment, and some mounted infantry. Many are clothed in all sorts of attire, one wearing an old sack, others having put on articles of apparel got from the Kaffirs, as their own kits were lost in the camp at Isanhlwana. The building of corrugated iron, shown in one of these Illustrations, is the dépôt storehouse at Helpmakaar.

The views of Natal Bay from the Bluff, and of the town of Durban, will be interesting to our readers. Natal Bay is by far the finest natural harbour on the East Coast of South Africa, or between Table Bay and Delagoa Bay, being a land-locked basin of very considerable area, which, although shallow in many places, could be improved immensely by dredging. But, unfortunately for us, a sand bar blocks the entrance, which during and after heavy weather is extremely troublesome and often dangerous. The now large and rapidly increasing importance of this port, the entrepot for an enormous territory behind and beyond the colony renders this bar an intolerable nuisance, and the Natal Legislature has taken the matter vigorously in hand, and, under Sir John Coode's directions, is spending large sums of money on harbour works, which, if even only partially successful will prove of immense benefit to all this portion of South Africa. The town of Durban is situated two miles further up the Bay, and is connected with the "point" or port and shipping by a short line of railway.

THE ILLUSTRATED LONDON NEWS

April 5, 1879

THE ZULU WAR

We are favoured again by Lieutenant-Colonel J. North Crealock, Military Secretary to Lord Chelmsford, with Sketches of some of the posts occupied by the British forces on the Lower Tugela, Fort Pearson and Fort Tenedos, and with one of Ekowe, the intrenched position still occupied by Colonel Pearson in Zululand, some twenty miles from the Tugela.

There is now intelligence of the war up to March 11, and though no great change is evident in the aspect of military affairs, the news is, on the whole, satisfactory. Lord Chelmsford has been reinforced by the 57th Foot from Ceylon, a seasoned regiment of old soldiers, as well as by the Shah's Naval Brigade, numbering close on 500 men. These forces are being pushed up to the Lower Tugela, the defence of Durban being intrusted to the Royal Marines.

In a despatch, dated Feb. 24, Lord Chelmsford, in discussing his arrangements for the relief of Ekowe, announced his intention of pushing forward a force under Lieutenant-Colonel Law, R.A., consisting of forty men from the Tenedos, two companies of the Buffs, four companies of the 88th, five of the 99th, one hundred native scouts, and a battalion of the Native Contingent.

The Zulu War: Colonel Pearson's intrenched position at Ekowe.

The arrival of the 57th and of the Shah would enable him greatly to strengthen this force, and, as Colonel Pearson officially reports that he has provisions to last until the end of March, no anxiety need be felt regarding the safety of the position at Ekowe. The field work surrounding the mission station is constructed on the most scientific principles; the ditch is a formidable obstacle, flanked by caponniéres and the usual defences; the ground within 800 yards of the fort has been cleared of all scrub and bush, and the ranges have been carefully marked up on all the most prominent objects; in fact, every care has been taken to render the position as wellnigh impregnable as possible.

The situation is healthy, and the hospitals are remarkably clear, only thirty-eight being sick out of a strength of upwards of 1400. It is highly improbable that Ekowe will be abandoned. The fortifications there are sufficiently strong, if held by a suitable garrison, to withstand any attack the Zulus might make on them, in whatever strength they might advance; so that in all probability Colonel Law will merely throw in provisions and ammunition to ensure the safety of the post until the arrival of the

The Zulu War: Fort Tenedos, on the Lower Tugela.

reinforcements from England, when Lord Chelmsford will be in a position to lay down a fresh plan of operations for the forthcoming campaign.

Formidable as the Zulus are, and good soldiers as they have undoubtedly proved themselves to be, early in April our forces in South Africa will be more than sufficient to warrant a reopening of the campaign with the certainty of success. By that time the 1st or King's Dragoon Guards, the 17th (Duke of Cambridge's Own) Lancers, five batteries of Artillery, 1st Battalion 3rd Buffs, 2nd Battalion 4th King's Own, 1st Battalion 13th Light Infantry, 1st and 2nd Battalions of the 24th, the 57th and 58th Foot, 3rd Battalion 60th Rifles, 80th Foot, 88th (Connaught Rangers), 90th Light Infantry, 91st Highlanders, 94th and 99th Foot, will all be in Natal. These, together with the Naval Brigade and colonial forces, will number about 1200 cavalry, 35 guns, and 14,000 infantry.

Fort Pearson, named after the Colonel of the 3rd Regiment (Buffs), commanding the column which has advanced upon Ekowe is situated upon an eminence which commands the lower drift of the Tugela river. It is a strong earth-work, with central citadel, and is armed with a 12-pounder Armstrong gun. The view from the fort is very fine, embracing the whole of the river to its mouth, and a sweep of about forty miles into the enemy's country. To the left, in our View, is Smith's Store, where Lieutenant-General Lord Chelmsford has taken up his abode for a day or two whilst making an inspection of the position.

Below Smith's store is seen the Pont, which has transported all the men and material across the river. On the right is the camp of the now disbanded Native Contingent, and farther on that of the 99th, on Euphorbia Hill, so called from a number of those trees which crown its summit. Here also is the burying-ground, tenanted by two of the Buffs, one seaman of the Active, one of the Tenedos, and an officer of the Natal Native Sappers. The rocky face of the hill on which the Fort stands is very abrupt down to the river, and thickly wooded in the crevices with small shrubs and trees. As shown in the Sketch, the river is very low, with mud banks visible, and the pontoon constructed by the Royal Engineers high and dry. The Tugela is the natural defence of Natal against the Zulus. Gun and signal departments at the Fort are in charge of a small party of men from the contingent supplied to the Naval Brigade by H.M.S. Tenedos.

That ship has given its name to Fort Tenedos, on the opposite shore of the Lower Tugela Drift. The column under Colonel Pearson crossed the Tugela on Jan.11, and at once proceeded to intrench itself in the event of any opposition. The spot selected for the prominent work was a farm-house and yard, late in the possession of a Dutch settler. The work commenced by Colonel Pearson has, since the departure of the main body of the troops, been strengthened and completed under the superintendence of the Commandant, Lieutenant Kingscote, R.N.

It would now task the capabilities of the whole Zulu army, or a very large force of a less savage character, for its reduction. The fort is situated on a gentle rise, about 300 yards from the river banks, and four miles from its mouth. The form is that of an irregular pentagon. It is protected by a strong earthwork ditch and abattis; while outside, and forming an almost complete cordon, is a line of "trous de loup," or deep pyramidal holes; these contain pointed sticks, which are made a more effective obstacle by the addition of wire drawn in all directions over them. Several mines, to be fired by electricity, have also been laid; broken glass is thickly strewn over the interior of the ditch and slopes.

Every precaution is taken, by means of spies, patrols, and vedettes, to guard against surprise by day or night. The fort is commanded by the guns of Fort Pearson, on the opposite bank of the river, which is here about 300 yards wide., twelve feet deep in some places, and with a strong current after heavy rains. The waters are dark and muddy; alligators are occasionally seen, but no accident has as yet befallen any of the numerous bathers, who have gone in for what is literally at times "a mud bath." All traces of the farm-house and offices have long since disappeared, and the tents and hospital marquee now occupy the entire available space.

The country in front extends in beautiful undulating, sloping hills, quite open, for about fifteen miles. This is now covered with the richest grass. In the distance is a missionary station, now, of course, deserted and wrecked; and between this and the Fort is the grazing ground for a large number of "trek," or draught oxen, waiting to convey stores and ammunition to the front. The road to the Drift or ford leads down to the right of the view. Here the passage of the river is effected by a large pont, or floating bridge, working on a steel hawser; the hauling from bank to bank being effected by spans of oxen. The pontoon and arrangement of the hawsers are the work of the Naval Brigade from H.M.S. Active, under Commander Campbell, R.N. and have answered their purpose admirably.

The garrison proper of the fort consists of sixty seamen and officers from H.M.S. Tenedos, a company of the 99th Regiment, a few mounted infantry, and an unknown number of Kaffirs, drivers, conductors, and others. The garrison, owing to the changes in the movement of troops, has varied in force from two

The Zulu War: The laager method of defence.

hundred to as many thousand. The armament is composed of three guns (a twelve, a nine, and a seven pounder), besides a Gatling and a rocket tube. It is extremely probable that this fort will be permanently held, or, at least, till the whole Zulu question is thoroughly and satisfactorily concluded.

As the question of laagers and the advisability of "laagering" camps is freely discussed in reference to the recent loss of Lord Chelmsford's camp at Isanhlwana, some details on this subject may prove of general interest. In Dutch, as in German, the word "laager" signifies "a camp," but in the colonial acceptation of the term essentially a defensible camp; any description of fortification, from a work accurately traced on the principles of Vauban to a simple barricade of waggons would be so called by the Dutch settlers of South Africa. Better to describe this form of defence, it will be well to take a particular example – viz., that adopted by Colonel Evelyn Wood. The ordinary waggon of the colony measures 18 ft. in length of body, the average height, not including the tilt, being 5 ft.

On arrival in camp the oxen are "outspanned," or unyoked, and the waggons drawn up lengthways, one in rear of the other, each "disselboom," or pole, resting underneath the waggon in front, so that the front wheels of the rear and rear wheels of the front waggon are touching. In this manner with fifty waggons a circle of about 300 yards in circumference is formed, and within this area the whole of the oxen, some 2500 in numbers, are herded every night, so that in case of attack they are in the safest place and at the same time out of the way of the defenders.

An outer circle of rather more than one hundred waggons forms the actual defensible line of the laager, the intervening space between the inner and outer circles containing the hospital, cavalry camp, and all horses belonging to the column. The tents of the artillery and infantry are arranged as close as possible outside the laager. In front of the centre are the guns of the artillery, a line of shelter-trenches covering the front of the infantry tents. In case of an alarm or a night attack the tents are immediately struck, the infantry occupying the shelter-trenches, the gunners standing to their guns, all mounted men to their horses.

The Zulu War: Fort Pearson, Lower Tugela River.

Brevet-Major Russell, killed at Isanhlwana.

Should it be found necessary to retreat within the laager, every man at once repairs to that waggon to which he has already been detailed, the guns being run back through a temporary opening in the outer circle of waggons. The strength of such a position is obvious. By distributing the men so that half of them lie under, the remainder in, the waggons, a double line of fire is brought to bear upon the enemy. We have already learnt by bitter experience what the Zulus can do. We know how on Jan 22. they hurled themselves in masses against the defenders of Isanhlwana, heedless of the murderous fire of our Martinis or the shrapnel which ploughed lanes through the columns. Yet we doubt, nay, more, we believe it to be absolutely impossible for the same enemy in equal numbers to force a position of such strength as we have endeavoured to describe. It is from the Boers that we have adopted the system of laagers.

In 1840, during the war waged by Dingaan, the then ruling Zulu King, against the Dutch settlers, 15,000 Zulus attacked 400 Boers in laager; the latter, without losing a single man, inflicted fearful losses on the enemy, though it should be stated that at this time the only weapon carried by the Zulus was the assegai, the Boers being armed with flint-locks.

Before dismissing the subject of camp defences, it should be added that, so far as concerns this particular column, in addition to the laager a strongly constructed redoubt in close proximity to the camp has been invariably thrown up in each successive position occupied by Colonel Wood. Whenever the main body leaves camp for the purpose of operating against the enemy, the hospital, stores, and ammunition, with a guard of from two to three companies of infantry and two guns, is temporarily established within this fort.

Our Illustration of the "Laager" is supplied by a Sketch drawn from a description, which was given on the spot by one of the Boers who had been engaged in the affair, of a fight with the Zulus in the early history of Natal, before that country was taken into British possession. The English and the Zulus have never been at war with each other till now, in the course of thirty-five years.

THE ILLUSTRATED LONDON NEWS

April 12, 1879

THE ZULU WAR

We have news from Capetown to the 18th ult. Our Special Artist, Mr. Melton Prior, arrived on the 6th, and has sent us the Sketches, engraved for this Number, of some incidents of his voyage on board the Union Company's mail steam-ship German. We learn the safe arrival at the Cape of several of the transport-vessels sent out in February with the reinforcements for Lord Chelmsford's army. The 3rd battalion of the 60th Rifles, in the Dublin Castle, the 91st Highlanders, in the Pretoria, and the M Battery, 6th Brigade Royal-Artillery, in the Manora, have reached their destination. Sr. Bartle Frere has left Natal for the Transvaal, to try and reconcile the malcontent Dutch citizens of the suppressed Republic.

From the seat of war, on the Zulu frontiers of Natal and the Transvaal, we have some news of interest. The Zulu King has sent messengers to Bishop Schreuder, of the Norwegian Missions, asking for peace. Mr J.E. Fannin, the Government Border Agent in Umvoti, on the Tugela, who also saw these messengers, reports as follows the substance of the message:- Cetewayo begs that the Bishop will explain to the Government that he never desired this war; he has never refused the terms proposed at the Lower Tugela; he had already collected 1000 head of cattle to pay the demand made on him. Sirayo's sons had escaped, and he was looking for them when he heard the English armies had crossed the Tugela; they attacked and killed many of Sirayo's people, but even then he did not despair of peace, for he then succeeded in arresting Sirayo's sons. He sent them bound with his army under Mavumgwana's charge, to be delivered up to the General at Rorke's Drift; three men were sent on to try and obtain a hearing, but they were fired at, and returned.

The fighting at Isanhlwana was brought about accidentally; the English horse attacked outlying parties of Zulus, who returned their fire; more came up and joined in the fray till the battle became general. The King protests that he never ordered his army to attack the English column, and his Induna Mavumgwana is now in disgrace for having permitted it. Cetewayo also says that Colonel Pearson provoked the attack made on him by burning kraals and committing other acts of hostility along the line of march. He now asks that both sides should put aside their arms and resume the negotiations with a view to a permanent settlement of all questions between himself and the Government. The King further states he would have sent in a message some time since, but was afraid; because the last time when he sent eight messengers to Lower Tugela they were detained, and he now begs they may be sent back. Mr. Fannin asked the messengers one question, whether the Zulu army was assembled. They say it is not; the men are all at their kraals.

The brother of the King Cetewayo, named Oham or Uhamu, who is head of an opposition party in Zululand, has crossed the northern frontier into the Swazi country, with a few hundred of his followers, and has joined the camp of Colonel Evelyn Wood. It is supposed that the main body of the Zulu army

The Zulu War: Dabulamanzi, brother of King Cetewayo, commander of the Zulu Army at Isanhlwana.

is preparing for an attack on Colonel Pearson's intrenched position at Ekowe, or Etshowe, as the name is written in Lord Chelmsford's despatches. Communications are still kept up with Colonel Pearson by signals with sunlight-flashing mirrors from the high ground on the banks of the Tugela near Fort Tenedos, of which we gave some Illustrations last week. The Ekowe garrison had provisions enough to last till the end of March with half rations. The road to that place is stopped by five thousand Zulus.

The following account of the present state of affairs in Natal is given by the *Daily News* correspondent there:-

"Maritzburg, March 9.

"News has been received by the Conway Castle of the dispatch of the reinforcements asked for, and at the same time a report has come in to the effect that the Zulu King is desirous of peace. The reinforcements were, of course, expected; as regards the other news, if it prove true, I shall be by no means surprised. The attitude of the Zulus since the day of Isanhlwana has been an increasing puzzle to all save those who from the first pointed out that the tremendous loss they sustained had disheartened them. There can be little doubt that Lord Chelmsford's camp was attacked with the chief, possibly the sole, object of plunder, and under the impression that no resistance would be encountered from the few men left in charge. These few men, however, and few they must have appeared, scattered as they were, to the advancing Zulu force, inflicted a loss as fearful as it was unexpected. Although the Zulus were left in possession of the camp, they saw their own dead and dying strewn on every side. Again, at Rorke's Drift the resistance experienced was wholly unlooked for.

"No one, indeed who knew the conditions beforehand could have expected that the post would be held, and it is worth while noticing that had it not been held the Zulu forces would have next passed over to the camp at Helpmakaar, which was practically undefended, and would thence again, in all probability, have descended upon the neighbouring villages. The check received and the loss experienced at Rorke's Drift staggered them, and heightened the effect produced by their losses at Isanhlwana. They went to their homes with their plunder, but the effect of the plunder was more than counterbalanced by the gaps in their ranks. The Zulu, notwithstanding his splendid fighting qualities, is a being possessed of strong domestic feelings. His home, his wife, and his cattle are objects of very high importance in his eyes and everything that breaks into his domestic relation is felt very keenly.

"The non-return of so many thousands – and the Zulu loss, it must be remembered, is equal to something like a sixth part of the whole adult male population – cannot but have had its effect on a people thus constituted. There had been a strong desire on the part of the Zulu nation to accept the terms offered them, and I have good reason to believe that the reason why the terms were not accepted was this:- That a subsequently published memorandum of the High Commissioner showed that the award in respect of the disputed territory was not intended to have the meaning which seemed to be on the face of it. There will, I have little doubt, be a good deal heard about this subsequent memorandum, and a strong case against the policy of Sir Bartle Frere will be based upon it. The Zulus might either have attacked Colonel Wood's column or Colonel Pearson's intrenchments, or invaded this colony any time during the last six weeks without encountering effectual resistance. Cetewayo is shrewd enough to know perfectly well that reinforcements have been sent for, and that they must soon arrive, and that but little time is left him before his overthrow.

"A desire for extermination is, I must confess, one of the most painful peculiarities of the present time, and if the arrival of reinforcements tends to heighten this inhuman outcry, better that those reinforcements had never been sent. The military feeling on the subject can be to some extent understood and excused, though it is painful to hear officers looking forward to wholesale destruction and doubting their ability to restrain their men. If the ideas at present prevailing in some circles were allowed to have free play, I do not think there would be many Zulus of any age or of either sex left alive this day twelvemonth. The feeling is less excusable in colonists who have lived side by side with the Zulu race for years, and who know better what they are worth. Our own natives are mostly of Zulu race, and their conduct during the present disturbed state of affairs have been beyond all praise and expectation.

It was commonly believed before the opening of the campaign that in the event of a reverse at the commencements, disaffection would manifest itself among the Natal natives. The campaign has

Sketches of the Zulu War

Interior, south-east front, looking towards Zululand.

North-east front.

Interior, north-east front. – On the watch.

Interior, west front.

The Fort at Helpmakaar

Troops on their way to the front. – Difficulties of transport.

completely collapsed, and circumstances have arisen of a nature calculated to try the temper of the most loyal, yet there has not been the smallest signs of disaffection. It is true that in the towns the native servants have left their work, but they have done this in order to protect their own property and families, to the safety of which, I am ashamed to say, this Government has shown itself indifferent.

"Natal colonists know this, and know also that our own Kaffirs are of the same stock as the Zulus, and yet they venture to join in the cry for extermination. I feel, however, bound to say that this temper is chiefly confined to new arrivals and to 'young Natal.' Old colonists are much more moderate and just in their notions, and this is particularly noticeable in respect to the Dutch families, who, living for the most part nearest to the border, might be supposed to be more interested in the Zulu question.

"Knowing as I do what a fearful stain will in future rest upon the cause of civilisation in South Africa if anything like a war of extermination is entered upon, I cannot but do my utmost to assure the public at home that with such a war the solid sense and experience of South African colonists will not be in sympathy. It is true that they have for years dreaded a Zulu invasion; but it is equally true that that invasion has never taken place, and it is, I am sure, likewise true that the dread of Zulu invasion has for years been made use of by the Natal Government in order to stave off colonial interference in native questions. My conviction is that, after what has occurred, a prolongation of the war for purposes of revenge or retribution will be the most dire mistake that could be made, and a mistake which will exercise a most prejudicial effect upon the interests of the colonists. If the Zulu King expresses his willingness to accept the terms originally offered to him, and to surrender the arms taken at the camp, peace ought to be made."

The portrait which appears on our front page is that of one of King Ketchwhyo's brothers, named Dabulamanzi, who is stated to be one of the three Zulu Generals commanding the Zulus, in the battle of Isanhlwana. This is a statement of a native, Ucadjana, of Seketwayo's tribe, whose account of the battle has been published; he says the other two commanders were Mavumgwana and Tyingwayo; and that the whole action was superintended by Untuswa, as "the King's eyes," watching its progress from a neighbouring high ground. The evidence of a Zulu deserter taken by Mr. Drummond, of the Headquarters Staff, mentions both Mavumgwana and Tyingwayo as commanding those regiments which formed a circle to inclose the small body of our troops; while other regiments, the Umcityu, Nokenke, and Nodwengu, to the right, and the Nkobamakosi and Umbonambi on the left hand, probably led by this brother of the King, Dabulamanzi, made their terrible final charge.

The Zulu War: Sketches at Rorke's Drift, by Lieutenant H.C. Harford, 99th Regiment.
The Rev. Otto de Witt's House.
Recovery of colours of 24th

The other statements of natives furnished by Mr. Drummond, and Mr. Longeast, interpreter, to the court-martial at Helpmakaar, do not say who was in command of the Zulu forces; but it may be concluded that the most active part in leading their direct attack was taken by Dabulamanzi. The portrait of him is copied from a photograph by Mr. Kisch of Durban, Natal.

The Sketches by Lieutenant H.C. Harford, of the 99th Regiment, staff officer to the commander of the 3rd Native Contingent, represent first a view of the Rev. Otto Witt's mission-house at Rorke's Drift, which had been converted into a dépôt and hospital of Colonel Glyn's head-quarter column of the army and which was so bravely defended by Lieutenant Chard and Gonville Bromhead, with scarcely a hundred men, against three thousand of the enemy, through-out the night of Jan. 22. The second of Lieutenant Harford's Sketches is that of the finding of the lost colours of the 24th Regiment in the Buffalo river, a few miles below Rorke's Drift, about five hundred yards lower down than the place where so many of the fugitives from the defeat at Isanhlwana were either overtaken and killed or were drowned in attempting to cross the river.

Another correspondent related this incident in our Journal of the 29th ult.; the party from Rorke's Drift who found the regimental colours and the bodies of Lieutenant Coghill and Teignmouth Melvill, consisted of Major Black, of the 24th, Lieutenant Harford, Captain C. Raw, commanding the detachment of Lonsdale's native corps, and the Rev. George Smith, chaplain, with about twenty men of the 24th and four or five mounted natives. It was Mr. Harbour, of Lonsdale's corps, who found the colours, with the pole surmounted by the gilt lion and crown, lying in the river, and the colour-case was a few yards below. The bodies of Coghill and Melvill were found half a mile from the river, on the side of a precipitous hill; they were at once decently interred, the chaplain repeating the usual form of Divine service for that occasion. This is the subject of Lieutenant Harford's third Sketch. The party then returned, with the rescued colours of the regiment, to the neighbouring post of Rorke's Drift.

The Zulu War: Sketches at Rorke's Drift, by Lieutenant H.C. Harford, 99th Regiment.
Graves of Lts Melville & Coghill.

Sketches from our Special Artist en route to the Zulu War.

The Zulu War: Zulus crossing a river.

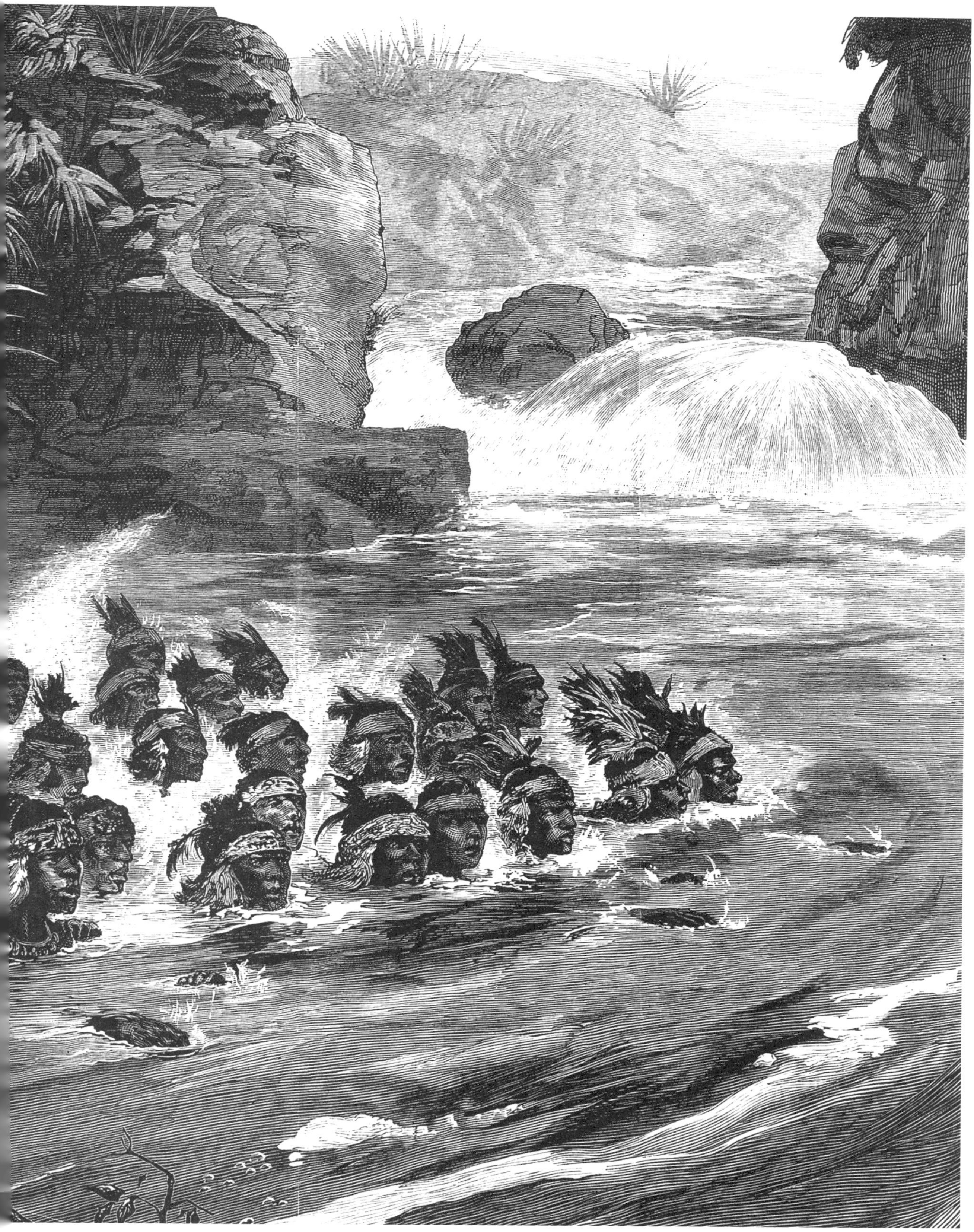

The fort at Helpmakaar, which is situated in Natal, twelve miles from Rorke's Drift, has been constructed, since the disaster of Jan.22, under the direction of Colonel Harness, C.B., R.A.., who is in command there. We are indebted to Captain H.B. Lawrence, of the second battalion 4th (King's Own) Regiment, for the four sketches of the interior of this fort at Helpmakaar. Another military correspondent, Lieutenant W.W. Lloyd, contributes the sketch of a detachment of the first battalion 24th Regiment crossing the Mooi River, in Natal, on their way to the front at the outset of this campaign. The wagon, being driven too quickly or carelessly, was upset in the river, and all its contents were thrown out; by the efforts of the soldiers during an hour and a half, with the aid of neighbouring Kaffirs, the vehicle was righted and got across the flooded river.

Our Illustration of Zulu troops crossing a river may find a suitable commentary in the following extract from the pamphlet which was lately compiled by order of Lord Chelmsford and published in Natal, giving an account of the enemy's military system:- "When a Zulu army on the line of march comes to a river in flood, and the breadth of the stream which is out of their depth does not exceed from ten to fifteen yards, they plunge in in a dense mass, holding on to one another, those behind forcing them forward, and thus succeed in crossing with the loss of a few of their number."

Our Special Artist's arrival at Capetown is recorded in the *Cape Times* of the 11th ult., which further mentions that, while on board the Union Company's mail steam-ship German, after passing Madeira, Mr. Melton Prior conceived the good idea of getting up a sale by auction, among his fellow-passengers, for the benefit of the widows and orphans of the soldiers of the 24th Regiment killed at Isanhlwana. The project was immediately taken up with great favour by the ladies and gentlemen on board, and by Captain Coxwell, the excellent commanding officer of the ship (the Commodore of the Company's fleet), who has been most kind and obliging to all under his care during the voyage. He cleverly officiated as auctioneer, so that the sale was a great success, realising an acceptable contribution to the relief fund, and our Special Artist had the gratification of handing over the money to Lady Frere at Capetown.

The voyage from Plymouth to Capetown occupied twenty days and eleven hours. The time-honoured ceremonial of a visit from "Neptune" on board the vessel was performed at crossing the Equatorial Line; this is the subject of one of Mr. Prior's sketches. There was a servant of Major Bromhead's who took fright at the summons to "be shaved" and tried to run off with a shriek, the "police" and others running after him. The German was passed by the American, another of the Union Company's ships, homeward bound from Capetown. News of the war being eagerly requested by signalling with flags, an interesting conversation went on in that manner.

While at press with our early edition news reaches us of a terrible affair which has occurred at Intombi Drift. One hundred and four men of the 80th Regiment, under Captain Moriarty, left Luneberg on the 7th ult., to meet waggons from Derby. They were delayed on the 8th, 9th, and 10th at the Drift by heavy rains. On the night of the 11th, in a dense mist, the laager was surprised by 4000 Zulus, under Umbelini. Captain Moriarty, Surgeon Cobbin, and forty men were killed. Twenty are missing, having probably been drowned. Forty-four escaped. The Zulus took the cattle but left the ammunition.

Much sickness and great scarcity are reported from Ekowe. The relieving column, 6000 strong, was to start on the 28th ult.

THE ILLUSTRATED LONDON NEWS

April 19, 1879

THE ZULU WAR

The news given in a portion of our last week's impression announced that another serious reverse has befallen the British troops. There has been again a surprise by the Zulus, and a serious loss of life is the result. On the 12th of last month, at daybreak, a convoy of one hundred men of the 80th Regiment, under the command of Captain Moriarty, in charge of twenty waggons from Derby to Luneberg, was surprised by a large body of the enemy. Captain D.B. Moriarty fell in the action, and sixty of his men

Camp of the 80th Regiment on the Zulu border.
From a sketch by Lieutenant Beverley Ussher.

are believed to have been lost. It is certain that over forty were killed, and over twenty are still missing. Lieutenant Harward, who escaped with forty-five men, says that he was with his men encamped on one side of the river Intombi, and that Captain Moriarty, with the remainder of the men, were on the other side of it. They were obliged to halt at night, the river being too full to enable the passage to be made.

Although some previous alarms had been given, they were surprised at daybreak by the sudden irruption of a body of over 4000 Zulus. The sentry only saw the enemy when they were fifteen paces off him. Only fifteen of Captain Moriarty's men got across the river to Lieutenant Harward, though his men poured a steady fire upon the enemy throughout. The Zulu loss was heavy, but it seemed to make no impression on their courage. The scene of the surprise is a spot down a hollow, with long grass sluits, and weeds around, so that the movements of the enemy were probably easily masked. It is considered to have been most imprudent for the waggons to have been brought up, and the men sleeping in them, within five miles of Umbeline. No shot was fired except by the sentry, and by the men with Lieutenant Harward, when the attack was discovered. Major Tucker, with some men of his regiment, has since visited the scene of the surprise, and read the Burial Service over the dead. The waggons, with the supplies, had been removed by the enemy, but some rockets and ammunition were recovered.

The Illustration presented on our front page this week is a view of the camp of the 80th Regiment at Derby, for which we are indebted to a sketch by Lieutenant Beverley W.R. Ussher, of that regiment. Derby is in the Transvaal territory, beyond the northern border of Zululand, and close to the Swazi country, over which Cetewayo has always claimed a sovereignty, disputed by the Transvaal Government. It is distant above a hundred miles from the Natal frontier, being situated quite on the opposite side of the Zulu kingdom.

Now that the reinforcements are arriving, no time will be lost in proceeding to the relief of Colonel Pearson, who is still cooped up at Ekowe. The Colonel has made good use of the time he has been beleaguered by the Zulus, having constructed a good road, which will materially facilitate future operations, and having also kept the enemy at a safe distance. Meanwhile the Zulus have not been idle, but have persistently harassed the British force, and have done their best to render the approaches from Natal impossible. It is known that Colonel Pearson's force is getting short of provisions, though from Kaffir accounts he seems to have made successful raids on the enemy's supplies.

Every exertion is being made on this side the Tugela to press forward a relieving force equal to any emergency which may arise, and the rapidly arriving transports have reassured the colonists as to their own safety, as well as to the relief of Colonel Pearson's column. An advance column, composed of local reliable native auxiliaries, besides 4000 British regular troops and a naval brigade, is already being organised to proceed towards Ekowe to cut through the Zulus who surround Colonel Pearson and his little force. This column for the relief of Colonel Pearson is composed of two companies of the Buffs, five companies of the 88th, four companies of the 99th, 57th, 60th, and 91st, the Naval Brigade, 500 of a native contingent, 2000 cavalry, and M battery of artillery. The relieving column is to cross the river Tugela on the 28th inst., and there is general confidence in the result of the enterprise; nevertheless, the military authorities expect and are prepared for heavy fighting.

The column altogether, which comprises some 6000 men, will march under the command of Major-General Crealock, who has come out with the reinforcements. Scouts who have come in report that the enemy are concentrated in large masses eleven miles to the north of the river. They are hidden in a dense jungle, and their numbers cannot be ascertained. Our troops are trying to get artillery up to the front, but the horses are out of condition. They are quite unfit for the rough work of the country. By heliograph signal we have received some news from Colonel Pearson, who says he can hold out for ten days longer. He is short of provisions only; his ammunition is abundant, as he has used it sparingly. Colonel Pearson has made a sally from his fortified position, driving off the enemy, destroying several kraals, and killing a large number of the Zulu army. Major Black, with twenty-seven volunteers, has visited the scene of the late battle of Isanhlwana, and recovered some private and regimental papers. One hundred waggons had been left by the Zulus, but the guns and ammunition had been removed.

The transports City of Paris, City of Venice, Lady Margaret, Olympus, and China, with reinforcements, had arrived at Capetown. A large and enthusiastic meeting was held there on the 24th, when resolutions were adopted endorsing the policy of the High Commissioner, and thanking the Home Government for so promptly dispatching reinforcements. By the arrival at Madeira of another steamer from the Cape we have later news from the seat of war in South Africa. The forces destined for the relief of Ekowe started on March 29, under the command of Lord Chelmsford. A severe engagement with the enemy was expected, and it was estimated that the strength of the Zulus was 35,000 men. Colonel Wood's column had been engaged in some severe fighting with the Zulus. On one day alone his camp was attacked, and the engagement which ensued lasted nearly four hours, but the British troops succeeded in driving away the enemy, in spite of their overwhelming numbers. Fighting had occurred in Basutoland on March 21 and 23. A meeting of Boers had been held, at which it was decided never to rest satisfied with less than independence.

THE ILLUSTRATED LONDON NEWS

April 26, 1879

The Zulu War: Fort Ekowe.

From a sketch by Mr T. Pearson, of Verulam, Natal.
THE HELIOGRAPH AT EKOWE

In the recent critical situation of Colonel Pearson's force shut up at Ekowe, till it was relieved by Lord Chelmsford's advance from the Tugela, on the 4th inst., messages were sent to and fro, across the enemy's country, a distance of twenty-five miles in a straight line, by means of the heliograph, or sun-flashing telegraph, which is the subject of one of our Illustrations. This apparatus has likewise been used for military purposes in the late campaign in Afghanistan, which was, to the best of our knowledge, the first example of its practical application to modern actual warfare.

But the idea has long been familiar to our military engineers; and at a meeting of the Royal United Service Institution, on June 14, 1875, when Admiral Sr. Henry Codrington presided, an interesting lecture upon this subject was delivered by Mr. Samuel Goode, which is printed in the quarterly Journal of that Institution, No. LXXXIII.

We take leave here to borrow from Mr. Goode's lecture so much as is needful for our readers to comprehend the nature and merits of this useful contrivance. The inventor is Mr. Henry C. Mance, of the Government Persian Gulf Telegraph Department, who in 1869, being then on the service in the Bombay Presidency, submitted it to the consideration of the General Government of India. It was referred to the Commander-in-Chief in India, and a report from the Quartermaster-General, in 1873, bore testimony to its great utility, stating that the signals conveyed by such means, using Morse's telegraphic combination of dots and dashes to represent the different letters of the alphabet, were found "perfectly clear, and could easily be read, in ordinary weather, at a distance of fifty miles, without a telescope."

The heliograph consists of a mirror mounted on a suitable stand, with adjustments to revolve and incline it so that the sun's rays can be reflected with ease and precision in any required direction. The horizontal movement is obtained by a tangent-screw in contact with a wheel, on the axle of which is also a revolving plate carrying the mirror; the vertical inclination is altered by screwing a steel-rod through a nut attached to the top of the mirror. Both adjustments are so constructed as to admit of the reflection being thrown at first approximately true, then absolutely so, and so kept, notwithstanding the ever-changing position of the sun.

By pressing the tangent-screw outwards it is removed from contact with the wheel; the plate is then revolved freely by the hand to the required place. The rod attached to the top of the mirror slides into a cylindrical handle at the back until the desired elevation is attained; it is then clamped, and by a slight movement of the tangent-screw or the rod the lateral or vertical inclination of the mirror can be adjusted with the utmost nicety. The cylindrical handle is connected by a ball-socket-joint with a lever attached to the revolving plate, so that the lever handle and rod together form a finger key. The depression of this key slightly alters the inclination of the mirror, which is restored on the pressure being removed by a spring beneath the lever. Thus by the action of the finger-key the reflection of the mirror can be thrown on and off any given spot, and by varying the duration of the pressure the flashes are made long or short.

By combining these long and short flashes, which are equivalent to the dashes and dots of the Morse Code, the letters of the alphabet are indicated, and the transmission of verbal messages is made possible. Good signallers can send them at the rate of twelve or fifteen words per minute. In order to ensure the flash being directed truly, a small portion of quicksilver is removed from the centre of the mirror, giving it the appearance of having a hole in it. Through this a signaller looks towards the station with which he wishes to communicate, while a sighting-rod is set up about ten yards before him in a true line with it.

A metal stud, answering to the sight of a rifle, is then slid upwards or downwards on the rod until the centre of the mirror, the stud, and the distant station are truly aligned. This done, however much the mirror is revolved, the alignment is never disturbed, inasmuch as the centre, being the axis on which it moves, is stationary. It follows, as a matter of course, that when the flash from the mirror is thrown on the stud it is in a right line with, and is visible from, the station beyond at which it is directed. The signaller has therefore only to take care that the flash rises to the stud every time the finger-key is depressed.

The observer has merely to look towards the signalling station, when a succession of bright starlike appearances meets his gaze, which he can readily interpret into words. On the sighting-rod slides also a short cross bar. It is placed at the same distance beneath the stud as the pressure of the finger-key rises the flash on the rod, and so that, when the mirror is at rest, the flash falls on the bar, its centre coinciding with the point of intersection. As the position of the sun alters, the flash would gradually move from this central position, to which it must be preserved by a slight turn at intervals of the tangent-screw and vertical adjustments. The rod thus serves as an object on which to throw the flash, and thus for ascertaining its whereabouts; it also affords a means of directing the flash truly. Both rod and bar are usually made of white wood, the reflection being more visible on a white than on a dark substance.

It is evident that if it were required to send the flash in a direction precisely opposite to the sun, a difficulty would arise, but this is easily obviated by employing a second instrument, its function being to reflect the rays back into the first, which then flashes them to the required spot with as much ease as if no intermediary had been employed. Another apparent difficulty - that of making a true alignment with a station twenty or fifty miles off - has in reality no existence. It is easy to attract the attention of a lookout, however distant; he responds with a rightly-directed flash from his instrument and at that starlike appearance the original signaller aims with as much ease as he would at the moon.

It may be added that, as the vertical adjustment forms part of the finger-key, the movement necessary to obviate the changing position of the sun can be made while in the act of signalling, one hand being also at liberty to control the tangent-screw.

The heliostat, which has been in use more than half a century for the trigonometrical survey of the United Kingdom by the Ordnance Department, is an apparatus by which a plain mirror, employed as a reflector, may be adjusted to any position with the utmost nicety; and, by the aid of a theodolite, in expert hands, or of a certain arrangement of telescopes, its reflected flash of light can be directed with the utmost precision, and with complete steadiness, to a point sixty or even a hundred miles distant. In the triangle of survey measurements formed between Scawfell in Cumberland, Slievedonard in Ireland, and Snowdon in Wales, the three sides are respectively 111 miles, 108 miles and 102 miles in length.

Before this application of sun-flashes to connect distant points of survey, for the purpose of fixing their relative bearings, which was introduced by Colonel Colby, R.E., in 1823, the lime-light had been used by Captain Drummond, R.E., and had been found tolerably efficacious, in one instance as far as sixty-six miles, from a mountain in Donegal to a height near Belfast. The heliostat, of which an improved modification was produced by Captain Drummond, and another by Professor Gauss, in Hanover, is an instrument of much greater power.

It is not, however, a talking instrument; and it had been in use nearly half a century when the happy thought occurred to Mr. Mance of converting rays of light, which had preciously been regarded in a signalling sense as entirely passive, into active speaking agents. This he did by adapting to a mirror, mounted somewhat similarly to the old heliostat, a means of imparting to the reflections the character of pulsations of varied duration, in accordance with the Morse code. In fact, by furnishing his instrument with a finger-key, he gave it a tongue capable of distinct and effective utterance; he also found it a language in which to speak the Morse code.

The telegraphic system of signals for expressing the alphabetic letters, and thereby spelling words, employed with the electric telegraph according to Mr. Morse's system has often been described. A short stroke, usually called a "dot" though its shape is really oblong, and a long stroke, or "dash," combined in various order of succession, like the few counters used for marking at whist, will indicate every letter, without using in any case more than four signals; as, for example, *k* is represented by dash, dot, dash; *l*, by dot, dash, dot, dot; *m*, by two dashes; *n*, by dash, dot; *o*, by three dashes; *p*. by dot, dash, dash, dot; also *e*, by a single dot; and *t*, by a single dash.

This is common and familiar telegraphic shorthand writing; and it can be executed as readily by Mance's heliographic reflector of light, as by the transmission and regulated interruption of the electric current through a wire. Apart from the communication of alphabetic symbols – that is to say, for spelling words instead of speaking – there is reason to believe that the use of sun-flashed signals is very ancient. It is even said that, when Alexander the Great invaded India, more than 2000 years ago, his fleet, coasting along the shores of the Persian Gulf and Beloochistan, was guided by mirrors displayed on the shore. Mr Galton, in his "Notes on Travel," speaks of the use of a similar contrivance by some North American Indians on the Rocky Mountains.

The Zulu War: The heliograph at work, flashing messages to a beleaguered force.

A signalling apparatus was erected by the Russians during the siege of Sebastopol, to direct convoys of stores and provisions approaching the fortress. The use of an "occulting system of lights" for such purposes was long since recommended by Mr. Charles Babbage, who contributed a paper on this subject, about 1861 or 1863, to the Transactions of the Society of Engineers. But Mr. Mance is entitled to the credit of having first constructed the complete-speaking heliograph. It may admit of considerable improvements, and Captain Begbie, of the Madras Engineers, has invented an apparatus, which was described in the discussion at the United Service Institution, and which seems to have some advantages. One of our correspondents with the army in Afghanistan has heard a favourable report of the performance of the heliograph in that campaign.

THE ZULU WAR

We are happy to announce the relief of Colonel Pearson's force which had been shut up in the fortified missionary station of Ekowe since the last week in January. Lord Chelmsford has succeeded in fighting his way through the enemy from the Lower Tugela to that place, defeating an attack made on his camp by 1000 Zulus on the morning of the 3rd inst., under the leadership of Dabulamanzi, the Zulu general who commanded at Isanhlwana and whose portrait we gave a fortnight ago.

The column under Lord Chelmsford's immediate command numbered about 5700 fighting men, of whom 3400 were Europeans and 2300 natives. It consisted of the 99th, 91st, 57th, 3d –60th Regiments, a portion of the Buffs, and the Naval Brigade, with 200 cavalry, and two battalions, each 800 strong, of the Native Contingent. The force was divided into two columns, the advance commanded by Colonel Law, the rear commanded by Major Pemberton. Lord Chelmsford in person commanded the whole.

The Naval Brigade, consisting of the men of the Shah and the Tenedos, with two nine-pounders and three Gatling guns, had the honour of leading the advance. They were followed by five companies of the 99th Regiment, the 91st Regiment, and two companies of the 3rd Buffs. With them were 150 waggons, by which marched a battalion of the Native Contingent, and two troops of mounted men.

After these came the rearguard, composed of the 57th Regiment, 200 men of the Naval Brigade (the Boadicea's contingent) the 3rd Battalion of the 60th Regiment, a regiment of the Native Contingent, and two troops of mounted men. The troops marched on the 29th ult. The column extended over a considerable distance.

No difficulties were met with on the road, which wound over a slightly undulating country. The native horse scouted on both sides, but although a few Zulus were seen on the distant hills, evidently watching the progress of the column, these in no case ventured within gunshot. In the afternoon of the 29th the head of the column reached Inyoni. As the other troops arrived they closed up, and a camp was formed with the waggons in the centre, and the troops in a hollow square around them. The men were set to work at once, and before nightfall had thrown up intrenchments which would have been capable of withstanding an attack should the enemy have ventured upon it. Inyoni lies some nine miles north of the Tugela, and is situated on rising ground near the stream. The next halting-place was the Amatikulu.

No attack was expected until the 1st inst., as the Zulus were reported by Colonel Pearson to be massing in a strength estimated by him at 35,000 men at a point not far distant from Ekowe. The following account of the battle on the 2nd inst., and the subsequent relief of Ekowe, is telegraphed by the *Standard* special correspondent:-

Gingihlovo, April 4.

On the 1st, at daybreak, we broke up our camp on the right bank of the Amatikulu, and marched seven miles to this place. Here we formed a laager, and threw up strong intrenchments round the camp. It is situated on slightly rising ground, and the tower at Ekowe is visible from here. Soon after we had encamped, Colonel Pearson flashed some signals to us that a large force of the enemy was on the march towards the Inyezane, and that it would not be safe for us to let our cattle graze outside the laager.

The night passed without alarms; but at half-past five in the morning large masses of the enemy were sighted coming down from the north-east. They crossed the river Inyezane, and as they came on they seemed to cover the hills all round. They formed for attack in a sort of crescent shape. The 60th Rifles covered the front of camp sheltered behind intrenchments. To their right was the Naval Brigade of the Shah, with Gatlings placed in the corner of the intrenchment. Next came the 57th, under Clarke. At the second corner were two 9-pounders; the 91st held the rear line. At the next corner were again some Gatlings, then came two companies of the 91st, three companies of the 3rd Buffs, and the 99th. Placed near the left rear was the rocket battery under Lieutenant Cane, of the Shah.

The enemy pressed forward to the front at great speed, but were received by a tremendous fire from the 60th Rifles. In half an hour the onward rush was checked at this point, and by 6.30 the 60th ceased firing, the enemy being here beaten back. Sweeping round to our right, the enemy then made a determined effort to force their way in on that side, but were met and checked by a tremendous fire from the 57th and 91st. Nothing could be finer than the manner in which these masses of Zulus, with their white shields, their head-dresses of leopard-skin and feathers, and the wild ox tails hanging from their necks, advanced, assegais in hand, against our intrenchments. A few fired a shot now and then, but as a rule they advanced at a steady rush, keeping a sort of dancing step with each other, upon our line of intrenchments. Notwithstanding the tremendous musketry fire that they encountered, they pressed forward in the most gallant manner right up to our intrenchments, and it looked for some time as if, in spite of the hail of fire from our breechloaders, they would force their way to the intrenchments, and bring the matter to a hand-to-hand fight. After a few minutes, however, the fire proved too much for them, and they wavered and began to fall back.

At 6.40 Barrow's cavalry sallied from the camp in front, and most gallantly charged the enemy, who, hidden in the bush were keeping up a scattered fire upon the intrenchments. At ten minutes past seven, the flank attack being repulsed, the Native Contingent left the laager and fell upon the rear of the enemy, who were now flying in all directions. At half-past seven all was over, and one of the fiercest little fights that has ever been witnessed came to an end. Among our casualties are Colonel Northey, of the 60th Rifles, badly wounded, but doing well; Lieutenant Johnson, of the 99th, dangerously; Dr. Longfield of the Shah, badly, but doing well; Captain Hinxman, of the 57th, and Major Barrow, of the 19th Hussars, wounded. Five soldiers were killed and twenty-one wounded, and five sailors were wounded.

A large number of the enemy who fell within a range of 500 yards have been buried. Great numbers were killed by the Native Contingent and by the cavalry in pursuit, and great numbers must have been wounded and escaped. All the troops, native as well as Europeans, behaved well. The attack was very fierce while it lasted, and the dead were found lying in masses within thirty yards of our trenches. The Zulu army is supposed to have numbered about 7000. It was composed of picked men of five of the favourite regiments of the King, under his brother Dabulamanzi, assisted by several thousand of the native tribes. The prisoners say that the old men are, for the most part, with the King at Inhlatyze. The women and cattle are in laager, at Umhlatusi and Ingogo.

The victory was a complete one. Barrow's cavalry pursued the enemy as far as Inyezane. Large numbers threw away their arms, among which are many Martini-Henry rifles, no doubt part of those taken from the 1-24th at Isandula. At daybreak next morning a flying column, composed of the 91st, the 60th, and 57th Regiments, and some Marines, left the camp, leaving behind them the 99th, the Naval Brigade, and the Native Contingent to defend the camp. The relieving column met Colonel Pearson at twenty minutes past five, and found the garrison extremely reduced by sickness.

The whole of the garrison returned with General Chelmsford's force the following night, entirely evacuating Ekowe, which was evidently unhealthy, and to which access by any future relieving force would have been difficult. The arrangements during the march and at the camping-grounds were excellent, and great credit is due to Lord Chelmsford and his staff for their excellent management.

Upon the day after the battle a flag of truce came in from the King's brother proposing as surrender. At present it is not known whether the offer was a sincere one, or was only a feint to delay our probable advance upon Ulundi. Lord Chelmsford replied that the only terms he could grant would be that all the chiefs and their men should come in and surrender themselves as prisoners.

Lord Chelmsford and the main body of the force returned at once to the Tugela. This place will be strongly intrenched and will be held by a regiment. At three o'clock this morning, while some of the troops were encamped in an intrenched position near the Inyezane river, one of the pickets, thinking that he saw the enemy, fired. Dunn's scouts, who were lying immediately behind him, taking the alarm, rushed back on the pickets of the 60th, carrying them with them. The men of the 60th in camp, taking them for enemies, fired without orders upon them, wounding five of the 60th pickets and killing one, and wounding ten of Dunn's men.

The following is the official return of the wounded at Gingihlovo on the 2nd inst.:- General

Chelmsford's Column: Staff, Colonel Crealock, 60th, slightly wounded; Colonel Northey, dangerously. Mounted Infantry, Major Barrow, 57th, and Captain Hinxman, slightly. 99th, Lieutenant Johnson, dangerously.

Royal Navy, Dr. Longfield, dangerously. 3rd Private, Private Flannery, dangerously. 57th, Private Perkins, dangerously; Deacon and Haines, slightly. 60th, Sergeant Dallard, slightly; Privates Aylett and Franey, slightly; Jolled and Lassieff, dangerously. 91st, Privates Wedenas, Sutton, and Gillespie, severely; Stendre, slightly; Brednard, Balley, and McIntyre, dangerously. 99th, Privates Blackwell and Braer, slightly; Drew and Armstrong, dangerously. 88th, Private Brigan, dangerously. 90th, Private Hartley, severely. Shah, Seamen Bird and Bulger, severely. Boadicea, Cordy, slightly; Henchley, dangerously. Marine Artillery, Bombadier Parnise, dangerously. Tenedos, Petty Officer Porteous, slightly.

The Ekowe relief force crossing a stream.

We have also details of the engagements between Colonel Wood and the enemy. On the 28th ult. Colonel Buller, with all the mounted forces, started for the strong plateau of Mhlobani, on which Umbelini kept the greater part of his herds. The opposition was but slight, and it is supposed that the greater part of the defenders were away.

The plateau was gained; great herds of cattle were collected; and the homeward march began. When fairly in the plain the Zulus came up in immense force. This body of troops is said to have been dispatched by Cetewayo to the assistance of Umbelini. Our cavalry, being greatly scattered among the herds, were unable either to unite or to offer any effectual resistance. The Zulus, rushing among the cattle, drove them in all directions, and this added greatly to the confusion, so that the battle was rather a series of isolated fights than a general engagement.

Captain Barton's frontier horse and Colonel Weatherley's troop suffered most heavily, being completely separated from the rest of the corps. Altogether our loss is eighty-six men and twelve officers killed. The officers who fell were Colonel Weatherly, Captain Hamilton, of the Connaught Rangers, Lieutenants Croneys, Weatherley, Poole, Sarmenter, Von Steiten, Piet Uys, and Mr. Llewellyn Lloyd, and Captains Campbell and Barton, of the Coldstream Guards. After four hours' fighting the rest of the cavalry extricated themselves, and fell back upon the camp. The Native Infantry, for the most part, bolted early in the fight.

Next day, the 29th ult., Colonel Wood's camp at Kambulaka was attacked early in the afternoon by four Zulu regiments, under Mnyamana. Colonels Buller and Russell were soon engaged with them, on the north side of the camp. The Zulus were, however, too strong and determined to be resisted, and Colonel Buller fell back inside the laager. The enemy came on in great force until within 300 yards of the intrenchment, when a heavy fire was opened upon them by the men of the 13th Regiment. This checked their advance upon the front. Major Hackett, of the 90th, with two companies, moved to the rear of the cattle laager, which the enemy were now threatening by a flanking movement. The Zulus then made an attack round the whole circuit of the camp, their efforts being mainly directed against the right front and rear.

A party of the enemy occupied a hill at a short distance from the camp, and kept up a very galling fire with Martini rifles. The attack was continued with great fierceness and resolution until half-past five, when the Zulus, who had suffered terribly from the fire of our breechloaders, began to fall back. The retreat, once commenced, was converted into a rout by our cavalry, under Colonel Buller, which sallied out and fell upon them. The pursuit lasted seven miles, great numbers of the enemy being killed, they being too exhausted to rally or offer any effectual resistance to the cavalry. Three hundred fire-arms which they had thrown away – including many Martini-Henrys – were collected. In the fight we lost about a hundred men killed and wounded, including seven officers.

Lieutenant Nicholson, R.A. worked two mule guns with great effect until mortally wounded, when Major Vaughan, of the Transport Corps, replaced him in his command. Major Hackett was dangerously wounded. Lieutenant Bright, of the 90th, was killed; and Lieutenant Smith, of the 70th, severely wounded. Colonel Wood, in his report, mentions Colonels Gilbert and Buller, Captains Gatewood and Maude, and Lieutenants Smith and Lyson, as having rendered excellent service. This is considered to have been one of the bloodiest engagements that has ever been fought in the colony. It is reported that Cetewayo himself had come from Ulundi with his troops, and that he witnessed the engagement, which would account for the determination and fury of the Zulu attacks. Their loss is estimated at three thousand men.

The safe arrival of most of the troop-ships and transports lately dispatched from England to South Africa has already been reported; but one of those vessels, the Clyde, which took out 550 officers and men, drafted from different regiments, to supply the lost battalion of the 24th killed at Isanhlwana, has not been fortunate. We learn that, on the 3rd inst., this ship was wrecked on a reef inside Dyer's Island, near the Cape, but all the troops and the crew were saved and were landed in Simon's Bay. Only one day was lost in sending the troops on to Durban. The stores on board the Clyde were lost.

Our Illustrations of the Zulu War presented this week comprise two Sketches by our Special Artist, Mr. Melton Prior – namely, one of the 91st (Princess Louise's) Highlanders leaving the troop-ship Pretoria, at Durban, to be conveyed to shore by a smaller vessel; and one of a scene on board during the passage of that ship round from Capetown to Durban, when some of the officers and men amused themselves by firing with pistols at the sea-fowl, which was called "practising for the Zulus". The 91st Highlanders mustered 940 strong, who disembarked in good order, and marched into garrison headed by the band playing national airs. The Pretoria had made the passage from England in twenty-four days.

Illustrations of the Zulu War:

Colonel C.K. Pearson.
Late commanding the garrison at Ekowe.

Mr John Dunn.
Late guide to the Ekowe relief force.

Practising for the Zulus on board the Pretoria on the voyage to Natal.

From a sketch by our Special Artist.

We present in our first page engraving a view of Colonel Pearson's fortified post at Ekowe (pronounced Etchowe) the old Norwegian missionary station of Bishop Schreuder in Zululand, with its conspicuous church tower. This drawing, for which we are indebted to Mr. T. Pearson, of Verulam, Natal, may be compared with the plan of Fort Ekowe, annexed to Captain Macgregor's Map of the route thither from the frontier on the Lower Tugela, lithographed by the Intelligence Branch of the Quartermaster-General's Department, and recently issued by the War Office.

The buildings of the missionary station at Ekowe consist of three brick houses, thatched with straw, and the church, also built of brick, with a galvanised iron roof, and with a small tower 40 feet high. These buildings are still standing, inclosed in the fort, the houses forming stores, the church an hospital, and the tower a look-out place, from which heliograph signals were made to Fort Tenedos, on the Tugela, distant twenty-five miles as the crow flies. Besides these buildings, at some distance outside the fort were three other houses, now pulled down to prevent giving cover. The fort is an irregular hexagon, surrounded by a ditch 10 feet deep and 10 feet wide.

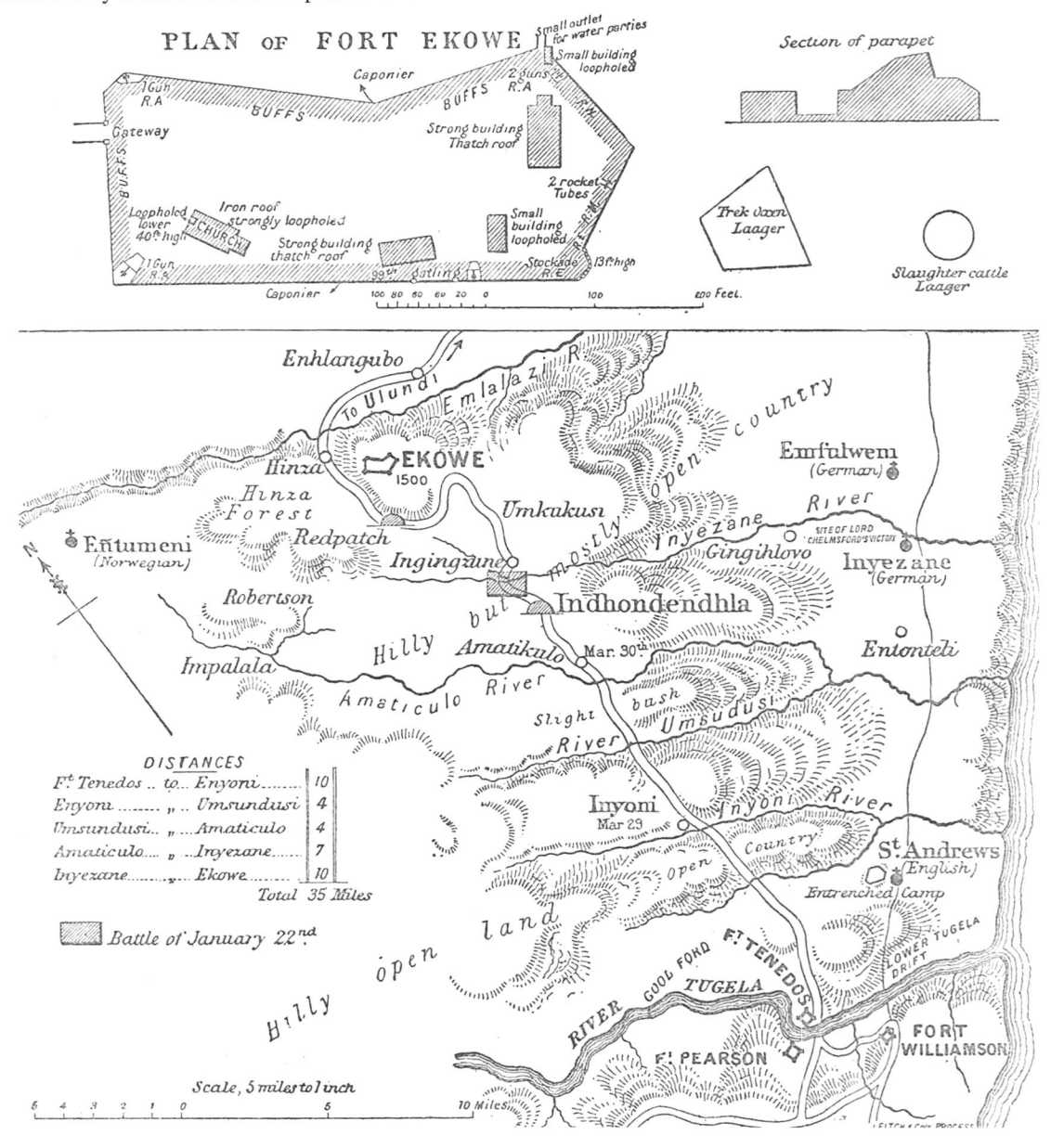

Map of Lord Chelmsford's route to the relief of Ekowe, and plan of the fort.

Drawn by Captain H.G. MacGregor, of the 29th Regiment, for the Intelligence branch of the Quartermaster-General's department.

The ground here rises about 2000 feet above the level of the sea, but the fort was commanded on almost all faces. To the south-east, 1400 yards off, is a hill about 500 feet higher, from which, as from all the high points around, magnificent views can be obtained. The sea glitters on one side about twenty miles off; the view on the other sides was over green rolling ground, dotted here and there with Kaffir kraals, the slopes covered with a dark bush, which stretches in green waves till they surge into a chain of hills 300 ft. high. The church was loopholed for defence; and the fort had 450 yards of parapet for the use of musketry, with batteries for one Gatling gun, two 12-pounders, two 7-pounders, and two rocket tubes. On those faces of the fort which were unflanked were caponieres, and the salients were rendered impracticable to a sudden rush by all sorts of cunning obstacles. The cattle were kept outside in two pens, or stockaded inclosures, called "laagers". The garrison consisted of six companies of the Buffs, three companies of the 99th, one company of Royal Engineers, one subdivision of Royal Artillery, the Naval Brigade, and Native Pioneers – in all about 1250 men, with Colonel Pearson in command.

The route from Fort Tenedos and the Lower Tugela Drift, as shown by Captain Macgregor's sketch map, which is copied in our Engraving, crosses the rivers Inyoni, Umsundusi, Amatikulu, and Inyezane, successively, at intervals varying from four to seven miles from each other. The direction is almost due north. Lord Chelmsford preferred keeping to the eastward, approaching the missionary station near the sea-coast, and so reached the Inyezane River at Gingihlovo, where he formed his intrenched camp on the night of the 1st inst., and won his important victory next morning.

The site of this hard-fought battle is indicated in the map as engraved for our Journal. It was higher up the same river, at Ingungzane, on the upper main road to Ekowe, that Colonel Pearson fought his engagement of Jan. 22, immediately before his occupation of Ekowe. The road there passes into rugged and thickly-covered land, after lying comparatively open from the Tugela to the Amatikulu, and not very hilly, but of undulating ground. Lord Chelmsford has, for this reason, decided not to hold the fort at Ekowe, but to construct one at Gingihlovo.

Our Portrait of Colonel E.K. Pearson, formerly of the 3rd (Buffs) regiment of infantry, and latterly commanding the No. 1 column of the army for the invasion of Zululand, will be regarded with peculiar interest at a time when public anxiety for his fate, and that of his comrades, beleaguered during eight weeks in the fort at Ekowe, has been at length happily relieved. The portrait is from a photograph taken at Gibraltar in 1864, and his personal appearance may have changed to a certain extent, but it was a fair likeness at that time.

We also give the portrait of Mr. John Dunn, an English resident among the Zulus, who acted as guide to Lord Chelmsford's relieving force, riding ahead of the staff with about one hundred of his own armed servants. Mr Dunn is the son of a medical gentleman formerly practising in the colony of Natal, but is about forty years of age. He seems to have a fondness for wild adventures, and about twenty years since went into Zululand, where he took an active part in the Zulu civil war between Cetewayo and Umbulazi, rival sons of the old King Panda and competitors for the throne. Umbulazi, on whose side Mr. Dunn chose to fight, was defeated and slain; whereupon Mr. Dunn made friends with Cetewayo, and has enjoyed the King's confidences till within the last few months.

He was at one time employed by the Natal Government, with a salary of £300 a year, to superintend the passage of Tonga labourers, from the northern coast country, through Zululand, on their way to service in Natal. But it was found that, under cover of this immigration system, there was a great importation of fire-arms from Delagoa Bay for the use of the Zulus. The British Government did not approve of it, and Mr. Dunn was deprived of his salary two or three years ago. He is, nevertheless, reputed to be a wealthy man, keeping up a large domestic establishment in the Zulu style; but when he visits the neighbouring colony, he appears in the ordinary fashion of an Englishman. In Zululand, he holds the rank of an Induna, or State Councillor and General, and his diplomatic services may yet be rendered useful.

The Zulu War: The 91st (Princess Louise's) Highlanders leaving the Pretoria at Durban.

From a sketch by Mr Melton Prior, our Special Artist.
THE ILLUSTRATED LONDON NEWS

May 3rd, 1879

The Zulu War: Sailors of H.M.S. Shah crossing the river for the relief of Ekowe.
From a sketch by Sub-Lieutenant Smith-Dorrien, R.N.

THE ZULU WAR

Our Special Artist, Mr. Melton Prior, sends us an Illustration of the 91st (Princess Louise's) Highlanders, at Durban on March 19, two days after landing from the steam-ship Pretoria, starting from the camp to join Lord Chelmsford's army on the Tugela, for the advance to the relief of Ekowe. It was between ten and eleven in the morning when they left the camp, with their band playing a lively tune, all in the highest spirits, and encouraged with hearty cheers from the blue-jackets of the Naval Brigade, who were shortly to follow and join them in their march through Zululand, as well as from the assembled crowd of

The Zulu War: The 91st+ Regiment leaving camp at Durban for the front.
From a sketch by our Special Artist.

The regimental colours were carried by two of the officers. An address of welcome had been prepared by the Scottish residents at Durban, and was presented to the 91st in the camp there. Major Bruce had the men drawn up in order for the reception of those who came as a deputation from their fellow-country-men of North Britain. He responded to the address with a brief and soldier-like speech, thanking the Scotchmen of Natal, and expressing a hope that the 91st would do their duty. So in fact they did, in the fight of April 3rd at Gingihlovo, which we related last week, and by which the safety of Colonel Pearson and the garrison of Ekowe was secured.

The Zulu War: Luneberg and the Pongola River.

The Naval Brigade also under Commander Brackenbury, performed its part valiantly in that conflict, after having been the object of much grateful attention in the seaport town of Natal. We are indebted to Sub-Lieutenant Smith-Dorrien, R.N., for a Sketch of the sailors from H.M.S. Shah crossing the Tugela river on their way to the front with the force under Lord Chelmsford. The men were dressed in blue serge jackets (or "jumpers" as they prefer calling them) and trousers, with canvas shoes, and straw hats, each carrying a Martini-Henry rifle, and brought with them two 9-pounder guns, one Gatling gun, and two rocket-tubes. The whole brigade was under Commander Brackenbury, and the other officers were Lieutenants Lindsay, Drummond, Henderson, Abbott, Sub-Lieutenants Hamilton, and Smith-Dorrien, Drs. Shields, Sebbold and Connell, Mr Cooke and Mr. O'Neil (gunners), and Mr. Chapple (clerk). The Royal Marine Light Infantry were under Captain Phillips, and the Royal Marine Artillery under Captain Burrows.

A view of Luneberg and the Pongola River, with the neighbouring bush country, on the northern frontier of Zululand, is contributed by Lieutenant N. Newnham Davis, of the Buffs. We have, by the way, to correct a small particular in reference to the quotation we gave, on March 29, from a letter describing the disastrous affair at Isanhlwana, that letter was not written, as we supposed, by Lieutenant Newnham Davis, but by Mr. Davis, of the Native Contingent. Lieutenant Newnham Davis was, indeed, with Lord Chelmsford on that fatal day, Jan 22, and accompanied him next day to Helpmakaar, and we received from him a sketch of the site of the destroyed camp at Isanhlwana, which appeared in this Journal nearly two months ago. But the letter we quoted on March 29, which related the actual flight from Isanhlwana, was not one of his writing.

With regard to Luneberg, it is a small border village of German settlers on the banks of the Pongola, in a district of the Transvaal province which has lately been invaded by Umbelini, the Swazi chief under the patronage of King Cetewayo, who claims it is part of his dominion. It was near this place that the recent disaster to Captain Moriarty and a detachment of the 80th Regiment took place, on their road with a convoy between Luneberg and Derby. But Luneberg is now strongly garrisoned, and there can be no fear of Cetewayo doing much damage that way.

The Kaffrarian Rangers, one hundred in number, have been turned into a mounted corps, and have joined the irregular cavalry, which, with the mounted infantry, now form a very large force, as follows, all under the command of Lieutenant-Colonel Russell, 12th Lancers:- Frontier Light Horse, Lieutenant-Colonel Buller, 60th Rifles, about 250; Raaf's corps, 150; Weatherley's Horse, Lieutenant-Colonel Weatherley (late 6th Inniskillings), 70; Kaffir Mounted Rifles, Commandant Schermbrucker, 100; mounted infantry, various corps, Lieutenant-Colonel Russell, about 120; Basutos (black), about 150; Baker's Horse, expected, about 200 – total, 1040 cavalry, belonging to the column under the command of Colonel Evelyn Wood, V.C., C.B., whose head-quarters are at Utrecht, in the Transvaal.

The last Illustration of the Zulu war to be noticed in this week's publication, is a Sketch by our Special Artist on board the Pretoria, during the passage of the 91st Highlanders from Capetown to Natal. The mess piper of that regiment was accustomed daily to sound a loud musical summons at the officers' dinner-time; but whether it was the "Roast Beef of Old England", or "Cauld Kail at Aberdeen," we are not precisely informed.

The latest news is, from Cape Town, to the 8th ult., but does not add very much to our intelligence of last week. Colonel Pearson and the troops relieved from the garrison of Ekowe have arrived at the Tugela. Colonel Northey has died of the wound he received in the fight at Gingihlovo; and Lieutenant Mason and one or two more have died of fever. The Zulus have burnt the houses at Ekowe. It is reported that Cetewayo has withdrawn beyond the Umvolosi. The British advanced position is not to be at Gingihlovo, but at the Amatikula, and no further movement is expected just yet.

En route to the Zulu War: The mess-piper of the 91st on board the Pretoria.

THE ILLUSTRATED LONDON NEWS

May 10, 1879

The Zulu War: Attack on an escort of the 80th Regiment at the Intombi River.
From a sketch by Lieutenant Beverley W.R. Ussher, 80th Regiment.

THE ZULU WAR

The following rather gloomy description of the present situation of affairs in South Africa is given by the Capetown correspondent of the *Daily News:*

"Capetown, April 15.

"Since the successful relief of the garrison of Ekowe, and since the victorious repulse by Wood of the great attack on his camp, no shot has been exchanged with the enemy, who is reported by some to have retired, baffled and disheartened, beyond the Umvolosi River. Great preparations in men and material are being made for the final advance into Zululand, for which, as usual, our plans and intentions have been published to the world, and therefore to the enemy, some weeks before the operations can begin.

"This time – unless a fresh change in the plan takes place – the invading army will proceed in two columns, one starting from Doornberg between Helpmakaar and Utrecht, and the other along the coast, following roughly the original track of Pearson's column. General Crealock will command the coast column, having under him Pearson, who has been gazetted brigadier. General Clifford has been appointed to the staff, and General Marshall to the command of the cavalry brigade, which will advance from the north, supported by the force under Wood, who is also appointed a brigadier. The force now under Glyn, near Helpmakaar, will move to Doornberg to strengthen the column. It is said that the advance cannot take place for a fortnight, and when we consider the enormous amount of transport and stores which a force numbering some 20,000 men will require, it is more than doubtful whether the time will admit of even so speedy a beginning of the actual work of the war.

"For up to the present it must be remembered that literally nothing has been done towards the original object of hostilities. Several Zulu attacks have been repulsed with much slaughter, and we have discovered that as long as we remain carefully intrenched nothing can hurt us; but, on the other hand, all our attempts at anything like active operations have led to disaster; and it is only too evident that in the future we shall have to rely on something like a regular campaign to reduce a foe who can choose his own time for attack, and who can unless he chooses remain practically unmolested.

"The latest news from Zululand tells us that the people are building kraals in the bush country, where they have sent their women and cattle, and that they have been joined by several Amatongas. The latter are a tribe to the immediate north of Cetewayo, bordering on Delagoa Bay, and are not formidable as warriors; but the news, if true, shows that any rate a retreat is open for the Zulu army, and that they do not intend to give up without another final struggle for life and land.

"Great apprehensions are expressed as to the danger of a raid into Natal being made by the desperate army of Cetewayo when our advance – which, of course, they can easily elude – takes place; but it is hard to believe that even the blind, unquestioning courage of the Zulu regiments will prompt them to stake their all on such a hazardous course. It is far more likely that they will now confine themselves to the defence of their country, and to those unexpected and overwhelming attacks on small parties which have already caused so much mischief.

"Every day makes it more apparent that the expenditure on account of this war will be something enormous. South Africa is being ransacked for horses and mules, and two steamers are being dispatched to Monte Video to bring across 800 of the latter animals. Upwards of 300 ox wagons, each of which carries three tons, are in regular employment, at the high rate of £80 a month. Men are being enlisted and equipped wherever possible, at the rate of five shillings per diem and everything found, and there must be some 1200 of this expensive cavalry now serving with the army in the field.

"The waste of commissariat stores is very great, and one of the principal causes of the bad health of the troops is said to be the smell arising from the bags of rotting grain which have been put on the ground at infinite trouble and expense. Altogether the original estimate for the war – viz. ten millions, is already spoken of as too small, and those well qualified to judge speak now of a possible twelve millions to be expended on the reduction of a tribe numbering at most 60,000 men, or, in fact, at the rate of £200 per Zulu; and the most melancholy part of the business is that all this gigantic waste of money, to say nothing of the valuable lives, will leave the country ten times worse off than it was before.

"One tenth of this sum spent in immigration, in defensive works, in railways, or even in intriguing with the Zulu tribe, would have done some good to the colony, and in a few years would have peacefully disposed of the bugbear which Sir Bartle Frere has so carefully raised. But now, after destroying a tribe, and after wasting a country at such infinite cost, we shall find ourselves face to face with a difficulty which will go far to ruin the prospects of South-Eastern Africa forever. On every side lie doubt and danger."

Our Special Artist, Mr. Melton Prior, sends us the two Sketches which are engraved for this week's publication, representing, first, General Lord Chelmsford reviewing the Native Contingent at Ford Tenedos, on the left bank of the Tugela, a few days before his force marched to the relief of Ekowe;

and secondly, the troops crossing that river, from Fort Pearson to Ford Tenedos, under the personal superintendence of Lord Chelmsford. Our Artist has gone up the country, by way of Helpmakaar and Rorke's Drift, to join the force under Brigadier-General Evelyn Wood; and the Commander-in-Chief is now expected to move his head-quarters in the same direction, from which is to be drawn the principal line of advance into Zululand in the operations about to be commenced.

It is stated, however, in a telegram of the 22nd ult., that Lord Chelmsford has asked for additional reinforcements, to the amount of another full brigade of infantry. Those which were sent out from England have all arrived in Natal. The 21st, 58th, and 94th Regiments of Infantry, a regiment of Lancers, and the Dragoons, have marched to Doornberg, under the command of Major-General Newdigate.

We are indebted to Lieutenant Beverley Ussher, of the 80th (Staffordshire volunteers) Regiment, for a Sketch of the disastrous affair of March 12 on the Intombi river, between Luneberg and Derby on the Transvaal frontier north of Zululand, with the following brief account of it:-

"I send a sketch of an engagement between an overpowering force of Zulus and a convoy of our men, which took place about five o'clock on the morning of the 12th inst. Our party, which was commanded by Captain D.B. Moriarty, consisted of Lieutenant Harward, Dr. Cobbin, and 105 men, 35 being on the Luneberg side of the river, the remainder, under Captain Moriarty, on the opposite side. The convoy was detained on the banks of the Itombi, as it was impossible for them to proceed, because of the late heavy rains had rendered the fords impassable. This was a very bad position for a camp, as it is closely surrounded by hills inhabited by the enemy.

"The morning on which our men were attacked was misty, enabling the enemy to approach and take up their position without being seen. When the mist lifted, the sentry on this side of the river gave the alarm, as he saw the enemy close to the "laager" on the opposite side. However, this was of very little use, as the Zulus, on gaining the rise, fired a volley, then, dropping their rifles, rushed by thousands on our men, and in a few minutes surrounded the camp. Some of our men attempted to cross, but they were nearly all assegaied in the water. The men on this side poured in volley after volley, by that means enabling a few of their comrades to join them; but they had to make their retreat, as the enemy were crossing in great numbers.

"Directly the news was brought into camp, Major Tucker, commanding the 80th Regiment at Luneberg, accompanied by Lieutenants Johnson and Sherrard, Dr. Wardrop, and myself, with two mounted orderlies, proceeded to the scene of the attack, which is about five miles distant from Luneberg. On approaching the river, he saw an immense swarm of the enemy, estimated at between 6000 and 7000 retiring in a dense column about two miles away. It may well be imagined with what rage and chagrin our men saw the enemy almost within range, while at the same time, for want of cavalry, we had to allow them to retire unmolested.

"Major Tucker, observing that the enemy were retiring from the laager, sent an orderly back to the camp for Lieutenant Potts and 150 men, for the purpose of burying our dead. Our losses are Captain Moriarty, Surgeon Cobbin, and sixty rank and file killed or drowned, and two wounded. The loss of the enemy is estimated at 200 and two prisoners taken."

May 10, 1879

BRIGADIER EVELYN WOOD, V.C., C.B.

The recent engagements of that division of the army on the frontiers of Zululand which is commanded by this distinguished officer has been scarcely less remarkable than those of the force immediately directed by Lord Chelmsford for the relief of Colonel Pearson at Ekowe. Colonel Wood had under his command the 90th and 13th Regiments of Light infantry, several batteries of Royal Horse Artillery, the Frontier Light Horse under Lieutenant-Colonel Redvers Buller, C.B., the Mounted Infantry under Major Russell, different Corps of Mounted Colonial Volunteers, under Colonel Weatherley, Captain Raaf, and Captain Schermbrucker, and a company of Boers from the Transvaal, under Mr Piet Uys. He had formed an intrenched camp near the Transvaal frontier at Kambula-hill, a spot on the watershed dividing the rivers which fall into Delagoa Bay and those having a more southerly course through Zululand.

The Zulu War: General Lord Chelmsford reviewing the Native Contingent on the banks of the Tugela: Natives shouting, "H-H-OOO!"
From a sketch by our Special Artist, Mr Melton Prior.

101

The position had been well selected. It covers Utrecht and the Transvaal, is situated so as to give confidence to the Amaswazi, and commands three lines of road – viz., that leading, viâ Derby, to Pretoria or Swaziland; that entering Natal at Rorke's Drift; and the main Utrecht-Zululand road by which Colonel Wood originally advanced. The movements of this column were at first practically confined to its mounted men and natives, under the command of Lieutenant-Colonel Buller, ably assisted by the Dutch leader, Commandant Uys. The surrender of Oham, a brother of the Zulu King, seemed an important success. But since the disaster of March 12 on the Intombi, where an escort of the 80th Regiment, under Captain Moriarty, with a train of waggons from Derby to Luneberg, was cut off by the enemy, Colonel Wood has had to fight more considerable battles, employing his main force.

On the 28th, having sent his cavalry to drive in a large herd of Zulu cattle on the Tlobane mountain, fifteen miles from the camp at Kambula, and, having afterwards joined them with his staff, he witnessed a skirmish in which the enemy were apparently repulsed, and he then returned to camp, leaving the mounted troops to follow with the cattle they had taken. But at the foot of the mountain they were met by a large Zulu army, consisting of three bodies estimated at 7000 each, which completely overwhelmed the small British force, caught as it was among precipitous ravines impassable for horses. About fifty were killed, amongst whom were Colonel Weatherley and his son, Captain Ronald Campbell, Lieutenant Williams, Baron von Stettencrom, Mr Lloyd the interpreter, and Commandant Uys.

Brigadier Evelyn Wood, V.C., C.B.
Lately killed in action.

Lieutenant Nicholson, R.A.
Commanding the Utrecht Division.

On the next day, the 29th, the camp of Colonel Wood at Kambula was attacked by the whole force of the enemy, and a series of desperate assaults continued from half-past one to half-past five in the afternoon, till the Zulus were finally repulsed, with a loss of above two thousand men. The British loss was but twenty-five killed, including Major R.H. Hackett, of the 90th, and Lieutenant Nicholson, R.A.

Brigadier-General Evelyn Wood, whose portrait we have now the pleasure of giving, was formerly in the Royal Navy. He entered that service in April, 1852, but served on land, in Captain Sir William Peel's Naval Brigade at the siege of Sebastopol, acting as aide-de-camp, from October, 1854, to June, 1855, when he was severely wounded, in carrying the scaling-ladders for the unsuccessful assault on the Redan, on June 18; and was mentioned with praise in Lord Raglan's despatches. He received the Crimean medal with two clasps, the 5th class of the Medjidieh and the Turkish medal, and was made a Knight of the French Legion of Honour.

He soon afterwards entered the Army, and served in the Indian campaign of 1858 as Brigade Major; he was present at the actions of Rajghur, Sindwaho, Kharee, and Baroda, was twice mentioned in despatches, and obtained a medal. In 1859 and 1860 he commanded the first regiment of Beatson's

The Zulu War: Troops crossing the Tugela under the inspection of Lord Chelmsford. From a sketch by our Special Artist, Mr Melton Prior

Irregular Horse, employed in hunting down rebels in the jungles of Seronge; he was thanked by the Indian Government for his attack upon a band of these desperate foes, and his valour was further rewarded with the Victoria Cross. Colonel Wood also raised the second regiment of Central India Horse.

In September, 1873, he accompanied General Sir Garnet Wolseley to the Gold Coast, and took part in the Ashantee War, for which he organised a native force. He commanded these and others in the attack upon the Ashantees at Essaman, and on the road from Mansu to the River Prah, following the enemy's retreat, before the arrival of the European troops. He afterwards commanded the right column of the army at the battle of Amoaful, and took part in the subsequent battle of Ordahsu, and at the capture of Coomassie. For these services he was several times mentioned with approbation in the official despatches, and received the medal with clasp, with the brevet rank of Colonel, and the Companionship of the Bath. He is Lieutenant-Colonel of the 90th, or Perthshire regiment of Light Infantry. We learn, by the latest news from the Cape, that both Colonel Wood and Colonel Pearson have been appointed Brigadiers.

Our Portrait of Brigadier-General Evelyn Wood is from a photograph by Mr A. Campbell, of Murray-place, Stirling.

LIEUTENANT NICHOLSON, R.A.

Among the officers who fell in the defence of Brigadier Evelyn Wood's intrenched camp at Kambula hill on March 29 was Lieutenant Frederick Nicholson, of the 10th Brigade of Royal Artillery, by whom, it is stated in the Brigadier's despatch, "The two mule guns were admirably worked in the redoubt, till he was mortally wounded." Major Hackett, who was also killed, with Captain Woodgate, Captain Gatewood and other officers are mentioned as having shown a fine example of courage in this conflict.
The portrait of Lieutenant Nicholson is from a photograph by Mr W. Cobb, of Woolwich.

THE ILLUSTRATED LONDON NEWS

May 17, 1879

THE ZULU WAR

Our Special Artist, Mr. Melton Prior, furnishes the illustration which constitutes our two-page Engraving. This represents the column of troops conducted by Lord Chelmsford from the Tugela to the relief of Colonel Pearson at Ekowe, with the train of laden ox-waggons for conveying stores, descending to cross a "drift," or ford, over a river in Zululand. The force numbered altogether above six thousand men, consisting of twenty-six hundred infantry, six hundred and forty of the Naval Brigade, and fifty mounted Europeans, one hundred and fifty mounted natives, two 9-pounder guns, four 24-pounder rockets and Gatlings, and twenty-one hundred and fifty of the Native Contingent.

The column set out from Fort Tenedos, on the Zulu bank of the Tugela, on March 29. Colonel Law, R.A., commanded the advanced guard, composed of the brigades brought by the Shah and Tenedos, two companies of the Buffs, five of the 99th Regiment, and the whole of the 91st Regiment. Two Companies of Mounted Natives and a Battalion of Native Foot marched on either side of the waggons. Major Pemberton commanded the rear guard, which was composed of the Naval Brigade (two hundred men), brought by the corvette Boadicea, the 57th Regiment, the third battalion of the 60th Rifles, and a squadron of mounted natives; also Lord Chelmsford, Commodore Richards, R.N., and staff.

The waggons, of which there were about one hundred, and some pack mules, with their escort of native troops, both mounted and on foot, guarding the convoy on each side, the horsemen in advance of both flanks, are most conspicuous in our Artist's Sketch. They carried twelve days' store of provisions for the moving column of troops, and a month's store for those in garrison at Ekowe.

We are indebted to Captain Laurence, of the 4th (King's Own) Regiment, second battalion, attached to Brigadier-General Evelyn Wood's column of troops on the Transvaal frontier of Zululand, for two or three sketches, one of which appears in this Number. It represents two of the Frontier Light Horse, under command of Lieutenant-Colonel Redvers Buller, V.C., C.B., of the 60th Rifles, forming part of

Brigadier-General Evelyn Wood's force at Kambula Kop, and here acting as videttes or scouts to descry the approaching enemy.

These frontier light cavalry are mounted on small but hardy horses about fourteen hands in height; and the distance they will go is simply incredible – fifty to eighty miles in a day is no unfrequent occurrence. They have only two paces, cantering and walking, and very little of the latter. The men's uniform is picturesque – a patrol jacket, and pantaloons of yellow cord bound with black braid, long boots, in which they stick a short sword-bayonet for their rifles, and a soft wideawake hat, sometimes of huge dimensions with a red puggeree, completing a very serviceable dress. Their ammunition they carry on a belt worn over their shoulder, and resembling the cartridge-belts used in England, but worn round one's waist. As the men are mostly colonists, and know something of the country and habits of the natives, they do most of the outpost duty, for which they are invaluable.

THE WRECK OF THE CLYDE

The steam-transport Clyde, the loss of which was lately reported in the news from the Cape, left the Royal Arsenal, Woolwich, on Saturday, March 1, with 550 officers and men, who were sent out to Natal to fill up the gap in the unfortunate 24th Regiment. Several of the officers belonged to the Brigade of Guards, who were attached to the 24th for service during the campaign, and the Duke of Connaught was one of the many friends who was present on the pier to bid the troops goodbye.

The Clyde was hired by Government from her owners, Messrs. Temperley, Darke, and Carter, of London, and was in command of Captain Luckhurst, an officer of considerable experience. She was built in 1870 by Messrs. Connell, of Glasgow, and was first named the City of Poonah. She was a screw-barque of 2283 tons, built of iron, with three decks and five iron bulkheads. Her length was 325 ft., her breadth of beam 36 ft., and her depth of hold 27 ft. Her engines were of 240–horse power. Her stores included about 120 tons of ammunition, in which is reckoned some 7-pounder shells and a considerable quantity of small-arm cartridges. The bulk of the cargo consisted of provisions, principally preserved meats in sealed tins, packed in wooden cases.

Having safely and speedily made the voyage from England to Capetown, the Clyde proceeded on Wednesday, April 2, at half-past four in the afternoon, to leave Capetown for Natal, with the troops on board under the command of Colonel Davis, of the Grenadier Guards. After being twelve hours from port, she was enveloped in a fog; but, as the officer on duty supposed, quite clear of the coast, when suddenly rocks and breakers appeared out of the fog before her. The ship was then but a few lengths from the breakers. The only thing to do was to reverse the engines, and this was done on the instant.

Wreck of the Clyde transport at the Cape of Good Hope.

The Zulu War: The march to Ekowe – the relief column crossing a drift.
From a sketch by our Special Artist, Mr Melton Prior

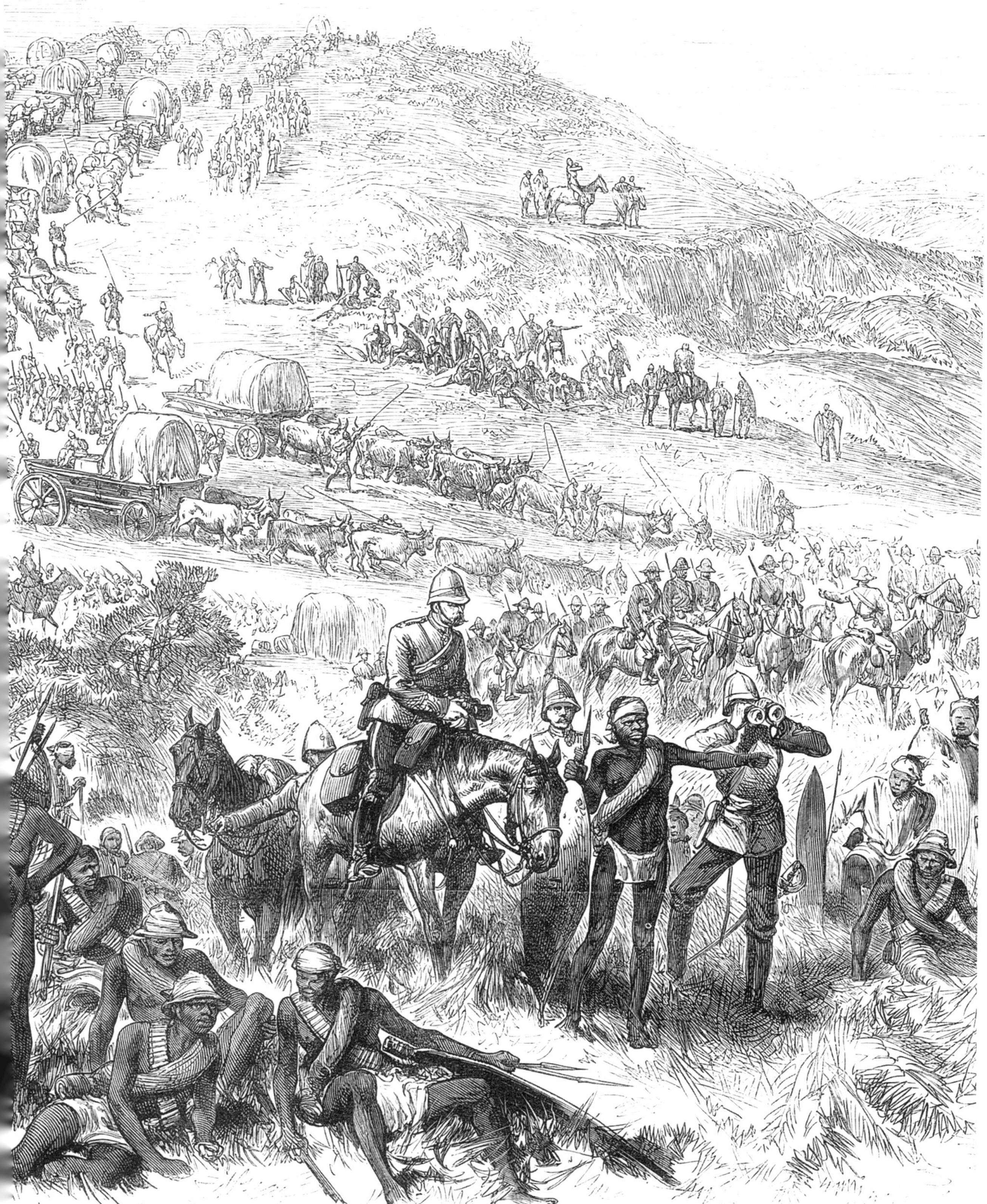

She was then going at from ten to eleven knots an hour, and before way was stopped a grinding sound was heard under the bows and extended amidships, when she stuck fast upon what was believed to be a bar of sand.

The men on board behaved coolly, and steps were taken to land them at once. They were put ashore in boats on the mainland, the ship having struck about a mile inside Dyer's Island, in Walker's Bay, about seventy miles to the south-east of Capetown. At the same time it was decided also to send one of the boats to endeavour to reach Simon's Bay, in order to procure assistance. The first officer volunteered to perform this work, and, when about two thirds of the troops had been landed, started with four seamen in a small, light craft, only about 20 ft. long. Happily there was no sea or wind at the time, and this enabled the troops to land safely.

The Duke of Cambridge, in his speech at the Royal Academy dinner, remarked how well they behaved. "Such was" said his Royal Highness, "the admirable discipline and devotion evinced by the young soldiers, commanded by officers of the Guards, that the result was that, the vessel having struck at five in the morning, by eight o'clock every man was landed, and even the horses were swum ashore without a single accident of any description. That was simply the result of discipline. If there had been the slightest confusion, the slightest irregularity – if there had been any forgetfulness on the part of the officers concerned, or any want of attention on the part of the non-commissioned officers and men, the chances are that very few of the men would have been saved; but such was the devotion to duty and discipline that the result was as I have described. I firmly believe that the English soldier is ready to do anything he can be called on to do."

The boat's crew sent off to summons help reached Simon's Bay about ten o'clock, having come a distance of seventy miles in about seventeen hours. They boarded the Tenedos, then lying at anchor, and conveyed their unfortunate news. The Active and the Tenedos were immediately sent off to the assistance of the Clyde, and the Tamar, happening to reach Capetown shortly afterwards, was also dispatched, and it was determined that she should re-embark the troops, and convey them to their destination. This was accomplished with very little loss of time. The Clyde sank not long after the troops and crew left. A valuable cargo of arms and ammunition and other stores was thereby lost.

The Zulu War: Frontier Light Horse on vidette duty discovering the Zulus near Colonel Wood's camp.
From a sketch by Captain H. B. Laurence, 4th (King's Own)

Our Illustration, from a sketch made at the time, shows the Clyde sunk near the shore of Dyer's Island, with three feet of water over her upper deck. The Tenedos and the Tamar are shown in the distant part of this view, and the boats are seen conveying soldiers from the Clyde to the Tamar.

THE ILLUSTRATED LONDON NEWS

May 24, 1879

The Zulu War: Men of H.M.S. Shah at Ginghilovo.
From a sketch by Lieutenant Smith-Dorrien, R.N.

THE ZULU WAR

Our special Artist, Mr. Melton Prior, furnishes an Illustration of the important battle of March, 30, fought by Brigadier-General Evelyn Wood, V.C. C.B., in defending his fortified camp at Kambula Hill, on the Transvaal frontier of Zululand, against a very large attacking force. This was two days after the disaster which a portion of his force, chiefly the irregular cavalry, had experience on the Zlobane mountain.

On the 29th, which was the very next day, Brigadier Wood received information that he was about to be attacked, and he accordingly took steps to ensure the safety of his camp, which consisted of a square waggon laager surrounded by an intrenchment of a strong profile, thus giving a double tier of fire on all sides. A short distance above, to the north-west, a small redoubt had been thrown up, in which two mountain-guns were placed. At 1.30 p.m. on the 30th the attack commenced, and was continued with great pertinacity until 5.30, when the enemy fell back in confusion. The course of this hard-fought fight was thus described in Colonel Wood's own despatch next day:-

"The mounted riflemen, under Colonel Buller and Major Russell, engaged an enormous crowd of men on the north side of the camp. Being unable to check them, the men retired inside the laager, followed by the Zulus, until they were within 300 yards, when the advance was checked by the 13th Regiment, at the right rear of the laager. The front of the cattle laager was meantime stoutly held by a company of the 13th Regiment. They could not, however, see the right rear; and the Zulus coming on boldly, I ordered Major Hackett, of the 90th Light Infantry, with two companies, to advance over the slope. The companies moved down to the rear of the cattle laager. By the accurate firing of the 90th Light Infantry on the Zulus spread out to front and rear of the camp, the attack on our left had slackened.

"At 2.15 p.m. heavy masses attacked our right front, and rear. The enemy, well supplied with Martini-Henry rifles and ammunition, occupied a hill where they were not seen from the laager, and opened such an accurate fire, though at long range, that I was obliged to withdraw. A company, commanded by Captain Woodgate, was well led by Major Hackett, who, with Captain Woodgate, was standing in the open under a heavy fire, and showed a fine example to the men, as did Lieutenant Strong, who, sword in hand, was well in front of his company. The Zulus retired in their immediate front, but the companies being heavily flanked, I ordered them back.

"Whilst bringing them in Major Hackett was dangerously wounded, and he will be a heavy loss to the regiment. The two mule guns were admirably worked by Lieutenant Nicholson, R.A., in the redoubt, until he was mortally wounded. Major Vaughan, R.A., Director of Transports, replaced him, and did good service. The horses of the other four guns, under Lieutenants Biggs and Slade, were sent under the laager until the Zulus came within one thousand yards of them; but still these officers, with their men, and Major Tremlett, R.A. to all of whom great credit is due, remained in the open during the whole of the engagement.

"In Major Hackett's counter-attack Lieutenant Bright, 90th Light Infantry, an accomplished draughtsman and a most promising officer, was wounded and died here during the night. At 5.30 p.m., seeing the attack slackening, I ordered out a company at the 13th Regiment to the right rear of the laager, and Captains Laye and Cox, of the 90th Light Infantry, to the edge of the krantzes, on the right front of the cattle laager, and they did great execution amongst a mass of retiring Zulus. Commandant Ross at the same time ran in with some of the men to the rear of the camp, and did similar execution. The mounted men, under colonel Buller, pursued for seven miles the flying Zulus retreating on our left front, killing great numbers, the enemy being too much exhausted to fire. We are still burying Zulus, of whom fifty are close to our camp. I cannot estimate their entire loss, which is, however, very heavy. Three hundred fire-arms have already been picked up close to the camp, several Martini-Henry rifles being amongst them."

It has been mentioned that Brigadier Wood's camp at Kambula was strongly fortified. The following detailed account, in a private letter, gives some additional particulars.

The writer says:- "We are in a very strong position up here; on a high narrow ridge on one side of the camp is a precipice, the other side is very steep; in front there is a long narrow open stretch of ground, and immediately in rear of our camp about two hundred and fifty yards off, perched on a small isolated eminence, about a hundred feet above us, is a fort with a deep ditch mounting two guns. The camp consists of two laagers, an outside square one composed of about ninety waggons, end to end, and an inner circle of about fifty waggons, where the oxen are kept at night. In addition to this the camp is intrenched on three sides. The Hospital Frontier Light Horse and R.A. horses are inside the first or square laager, the Frontier Light horses are tied to the waggons comprising the inner circle or ox laager. The tents of the 13th, the 90th Royal Artillery and staff are outside.

"On the alarm being given, tents are struck at once, by the poles being pulled away, and the men line the shelter trenches, and get on and underneath the waggons if hard pressed; nearly all the waggon-drivers are armed with Martini-Henrys and assegais, and would make short work of any Zulus getting inside. My hammock-bearers are instructed to line the inside of the waggons at the hospital corner of the laager, and it is rather amusing to see them practising how to fight with their assegais any Zulus that might creep under or over the waggons." It was this position that the Zulu army ventured to attack in broad daylight, and from which they were only repulsed after four hours' hard fighting, with a loss which will more than make up for their former victory.

We have been favoured by Lieutenant-Colonel J. North Crealock, 95th Regiment, Military Secretary to the Commander-in-Chief in South Africa, with Sketches illustrating the battle of April 2 at Ginghilovo, when Lord Chelmsford's intrenched camp on the road to Ekowe (Etshowe) for the relief of Colonel Pearson and the garrison there, was attacked by a very large force of the enemy. The following is Lord Chelmsford's account of the battle of Ginghilovo:-

"On April 1 the column marched six miles to the Ginghilovo stream. About one mile from the Inyezane river a laager was formed in a favourable position. From this point the road at Etshowe, after crossing swampy ground, winds through a bushy and difficult country for some fifteen miles, the last eight or nine being a steady ascent. The whole country is covered with high grass, and even what appears to be open plain is really sufficiently undulating to afford easy cover to considerable bodies of natives. Etshowe could be plainly seen from the laager, and flash-signalling was at once established.

"Before the laager was completed a heavy thunderstorm came on; rain again at nightfall, and lasted during the night. The laager defences were, however, satisfactorily completed after dark. The north or front face was held by the 60th Rifles, the right flank face by the 57th Regiment, left flank face by the 99th Regiment and the Buffs, and rear face by the 91st Regiment; and each angle was manned by the Naval Brigade, Bluejackets, and Marines, the Gatling of the Boadicea being on the north-east corner; two rocket-tubes on the north-west, under Lieutenant Kerr; two 9-pounder guns, under Lieutenant Kingscote, on the south-west; and one Gatling gun and two rocket-tubes on the south-east, under Commander Brackenbury. The night passed without any alarm.

"On April 2, according to our invariable rule, the troops stood to their arms at four a.m. A heavy mist shrouded the country; the sun rose about 6.15 a.m.; our mounted men, as usual, were at the earliest dawn scouting around. At 5.45 reports came in from them simultaneously with the pickets of the 60th and 99th Regiments, that the enemy were advancing to the attack. No preparation was necessary, and no orders had to be given beyond saddling up of the horses of the officers of the staff. The troops were already at their posts, and the cattle had not been let out to graze. At six a.m. the attack commenced on the north front; the Zulus advanced with great rapidity and courage, taking advantage of the cover afforded by the undulations of the ground and the long grass. The enemy, however, did not succeed in approaching nearer than twenty yards.

"Several casualties took place here at this time, among them Lieutenant-Colonel Northey, 3-60th, who, I regret to say, received a bullet wound from which he eventually died two days ago. Lieutenant Courtenay's horse was shot as he stood beside him, Captain Burrow and Lieutenant-Colonel Crealock being slightly wounded at the same time, and Captain Molyneux's horse was shot under him.

"The Gatling gun was of considerable value at this period of the defence. The attack, checked here, rolled round to the west, or left face; here Lieutenant G.C.J. Johnson, 99th Regiment, was killed. Whilst this was being developed, a fresh force came round to the rear, probably from the Umisi Hill anticipating (so prisoners state) that our force would prove insufficient to defend, at the same time, all the faces of the laager; here they obstinately held their ground, finding cover in long grass and undulations.

The Zulu War: Inside the laager at Ginghilovo during the Zulu attack.
From sketches by Lieutenant Smith-Dorrien, R.N.

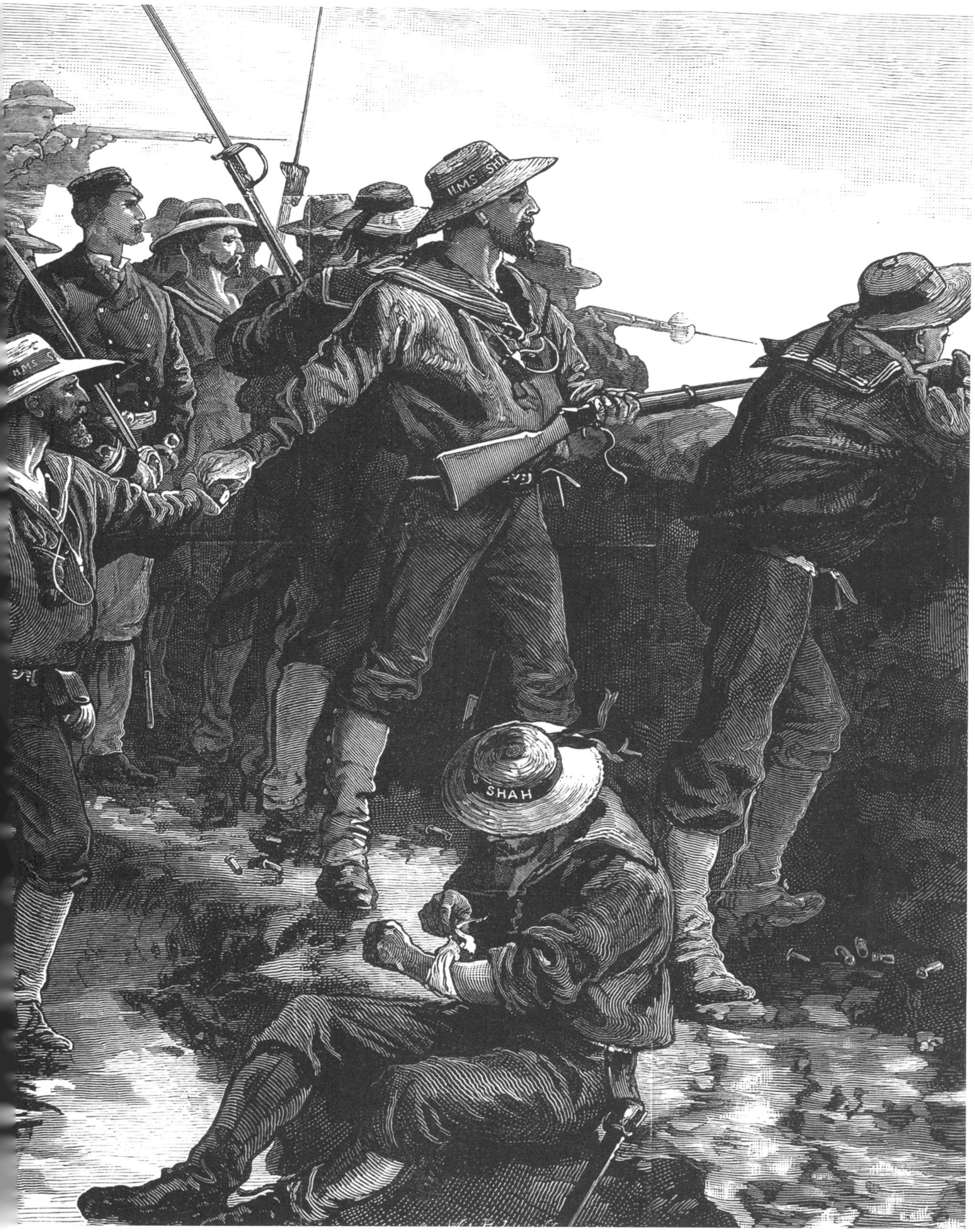
H.M.S. SHAH
SHAH
H.M.S.

"The Mounted Infantry and Volunteers meantime, having left the laager, had been engaged in clearing its front face, I now directed Captain Barrow to advance across the right or east face and attack the enemy's right flank. It was now 7.30 a.m., and during one hour and a half the Zulus had obstinately attacked three sides of the laager. Even previous to the mounted men appearing on their flank, the Zulus had, I believed, realised the hopelessness of attempting to pass through the zone of heavy rifle fire which met them on their attempting to charge up against the rear face; but on their appearance, the Zulu retreat commenced. On seeing this the Natal Native Contingent, who were formed within the intrenchment on the rear face, clearing the ditch, rushed forward with loud cheers in pursuit.

"Led by Captain Barrow's horsemen, the pursuit was carried on several miles. This officer reports the sabres of the Mounted Infantry to have proved of the greatest service, some fifty or sixty men having been sabred. At eight a.m. Colonel Pearson, who, through a glass, had witnessed the fight from Etshowe, telegraphed his congratulations to us. Bodies of Zulus were to be seen hurrying away towards the Indulinda, making a stand nowhere, and throwing away their arms to assist their flight. Within a short time I directed officers and burying parties to count the enemy's loss within 1000 yards of the intrenchment. 471 were buried; 200 have been since found near the scene. But, from the chance wounded men we have found five miles away, and the execution done at long ranges by the artillery, I have no hesitation in estimating the enemy's loss at 1000 men.

"It appears from the statements of the prisoners taken that about 180 companies were engaged either in the attack or in reserve, which, estimated at sixty men per company (less than half their strength), would give about 11,000 men. This, I am inclined to think, may be the number of the force that was ordered to attack us; but this is far less than that given by the prisoners taken. Our casualties are small considering the easy mark the laager afforded the assailants; and had it not been for the cover afforded the troops by the broad shelter-trench, I should have had to report a much heavier loss."

"We are indebted also to a young naval officer, Sub-Lieutenant Smith-Dorrien, R.N., for sketches of the fighting at Ginghilovo, in which the Naval Brigade took a leading part. In fact, the seamen of H.M.S. Boadicea, with the Marines of H.M.S Shah, with the 60th Rifles, were the first engaged, opening a steady fire on the enemy as soon as they were well within range. Later on in the engagement the Boadicea's Gatling gun did great execution. Six Zulu warriors were found dead in a cluster thirty yards from it. Next to the 60th, another party of the Shah's men, with one rocket tube and the 99th Regiment facing due west, were called upon to use their rifles. It was from this front and bearing to its left (where the Tenedos Bluejackets were intrenched) that the hottest attack developed itself.

"The latest news is from Capetown to the 29th ult., but is of little importance. Lord Chelmsford and his staff had left Natal for Utrecht in the Transvaal, and would join the head-quarters of Brigadier-General Wood at Kambula. The greatest difficulty of an advance was the transport of stores, and it was expected that the Zulus would burn the grass of their country. Zulu raids in the Utrecht district were becoming frequent. The French Prince Imperial was unable to accompany Lord Chelmsford from indisposition."

THE LATE CAPTAIN HON. R. CAMPBELL

Among the officers who were attached to the staff of Brigadier-General Evelyn Wood, V.C., C.B., commanding the column of troops on the Transvaal frontier of Zululand, was Captain the Hon. Ronald Campbell, of the Coldstream Guards, sometime Adjutant of that regiment. We have learned with much regret the death of this brave officer, on March 28, in the conflict with the Zulus on the Zlobane mountain, which also proved fatal to Colonel Weatherley, Mr. Lloyd, the interpreter, Captain Barton, of the Coldstream Guards, Lieutenant Williams, of the 58th Regiment, and Mr. Piet Uys, commandant of the Dutch Volunteers.

The following passage of Brigadier Wood's despatch to Lord Chelmsford, relating the action of that day, shows the manner in which Captain Ronald Campbell met his death:- "We soon came under fire from an unseen enemy on our right. Ascending more rapidly than most of the Border Horse, who had got off the track, with my staff and escort, I passed to the front; and, with half a dozen of the Border Horse, when within a hundred feet of the summit, came under a well-directed fire from our front and both flanks, poured in from behind huge boulders of rocks. Mr. Lloyd fell mortally wounded at my side, and as

Captain Campbell and one of the escorts were carrying him on to a ledge rather lower, my horse was killed, falling on me.

"I directed Colonel Weatherley to dislodge one or two Zulus who were causing us most of the loss; but, as his men did not advance rapidly, Captain Campbell and Lieutenant Lysons and three men of the 90th, jumping over a low wall, ran forward and charged into a cave, when Captain Campbell, leading in the most determined and gallant manner, was shot dead; Lieutenant Lysons and Private Fowler followed closely on his footsteps, and one of them – for each fired – killed one Zulu; they dislodged another, who crawled away by a subterranean passage, reappearing higher up the mountain. At this time we were assisted by the fire of some of Colonel Buller's men on the summit. Mr. Lloyd was now dead, and we brought his body, and that of Captain Campbell, about half way down the hill, where we buried them, still being under fire, which, however, did us no damage."

In another part of his official despatches, Brigadier Wood says of Captain Campbell, his orderly officer, that "he was an excellent staff officer both in the field and as regards office work, and having showed the most brilliant courage, lost his life in performing a gallant feat." Again, in a private letter of the 29th, the General says, "I never saw a man play a more heroic part than he did yesterday."

The Hon. Ronald George Elidor Campbell, who was second son of the present Earl of Cawdor, was born in 1848, and entered the Army in 1867 as Ensign in the Coldstream Guards. He became Lieutenant and Captain in May, 1871, and Adjutant the same year. He married, in 1872, a daughter of Bishop Claughton, now the Bishop of St. Albans.

Officers killed in the Zulu War:

CAPTAIN THE HON. RONALD CAMPBELL.   LIEUT.-COL. WEATHERLEY, TRANSVAAL BORDER HORSE.   LIEUTENANT G. C. J. JOHNSON, 99TH REGIMENT.

THE LATE COL. WEATHERLEY

The sad and tragic death of Colonel Weatherley in the recent engagement at Zlobane, on the Transvaal frontier of Zululand, is deeply felt by all his friends and old brother officers. They will recognise their old comrade in the touching account given by the correspondent of one of the daily papers. He is there described as surrounded by hundreds of Zulus, fighting desperately to the last, with one arm round his brave young son, a subaltern in his troop, whom he vainly endeavoured to protect from the fate which was from the first inevitable. It was truly a gallant death; but none the less to be deplored by those who knew and loved him.

Frederick Weatherley's career was an eventful one. He was the son of the late Ilderton Weatherley, Esq., and grandson of John Weatherley, of Willington House, near Newcastle-on-Tyne. At an early age he was appointed to a distinguished regiment of Austrian Dragoons. In March 1855, he received his commission in the 4th Light Dragoons, then serving in the Crimea. With this regiment he was present at

1. Laager of waggons, behind an intrenchment.   2. Cattle laager.   3. Tents struck lying on the ground.
Redoubt with guns on the summit.

The Zulu War: Battle of Kambula Hill, March 29th.
From a sketch by our Special Artist, Mr Melton Prior.

117

The Final Repulse of the Zulus at Ginghilovo
From sketches supplied by Lieutenant-Colonel J. North Crealock

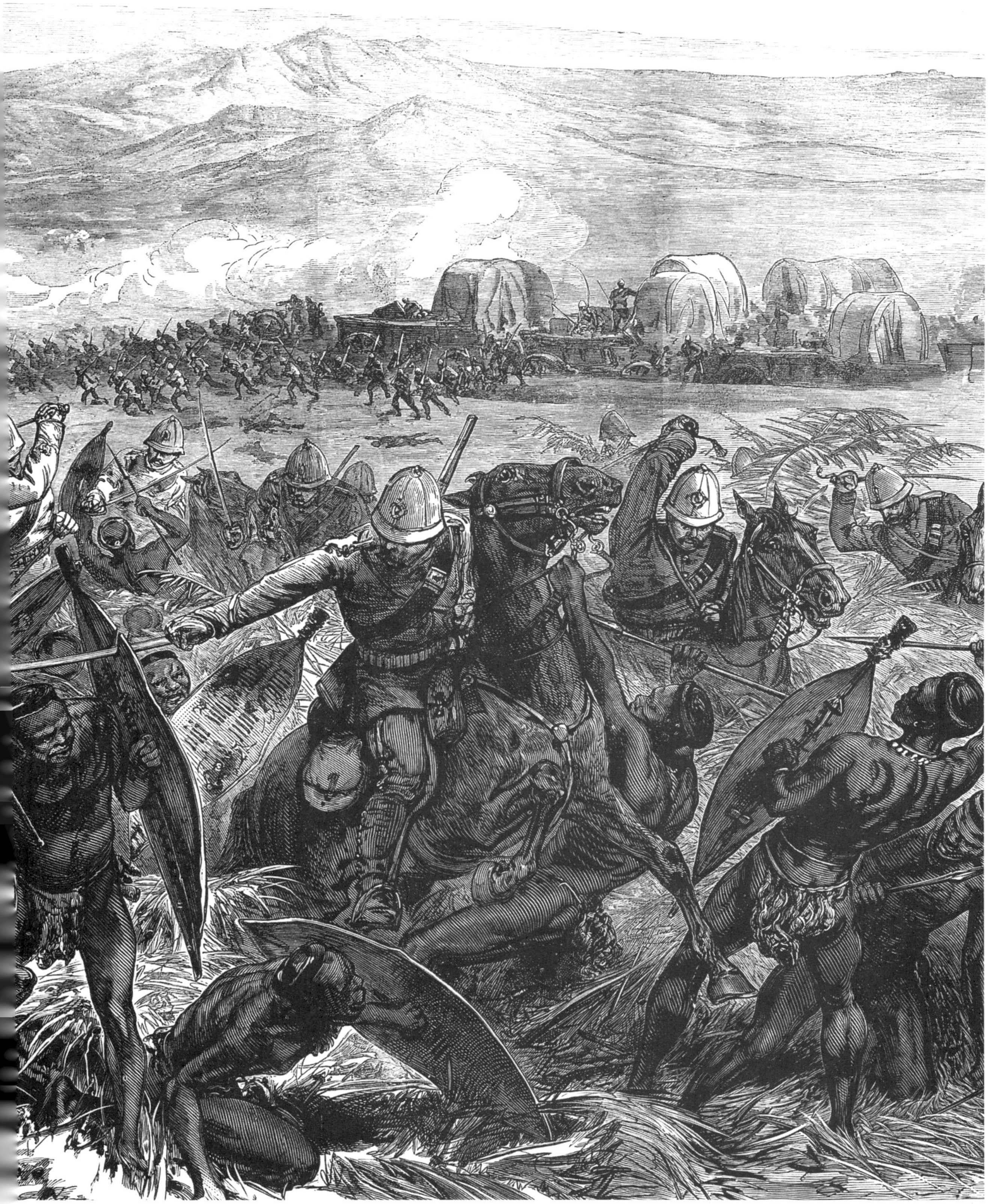

the battle of the Tchernaya, and took part in the field operations of the allied brigade of Light Cavalry, under General D'Allonville, at Eupatoria, and in all the subsequent operations in the Crimea, up to the conclusion of peace.

On the return of the 4th Light Dragoons to England, in 1856, he exchanged into the Carbineers, as Lieutenant, and with that regiment served with much distinction throughout the Indian Mutiny. He was present at the operations in Rohileund; the affair of Kukrowlie, and the capture of Bareilly; the relief of Shajeanpore, and the two subsequent attacks; the affairs of Mohundee and Shahabad; the operations in Oude, and the action at Buxarghat, in the Trans-Gogra; the actions of Musjedia, Churdal, and Bankee. He received the Crimean medal and clasp, the Turkish, and the Indian Medal. He again exchanged into the Inniskilling Dragoons, from which regiment he retired with the rank of Captain. He subsequently accepted the command of the 1st Sussex Administrative Battalion of Artillery Volunteers, which appointment he resigned in 1877.

Possessing considerable property in the Diamond Fields and in the Transvaal, he had found it imperative, for his own interest, that he should personally superintend it, and had for the past few years resided at Pretoria, where his conspicuous abilities soon obtained for him a prominent position. Utterly opposed to the policy of annexation, he, nevertheless, rendered the most loyal help to General Sir Arthur Cunynghame, and in a great measure prevented the outbreak of any disturbance on the proclamation of her Majesty's Government there. His services were considered worthy of public and special commendation by the Commander-in-Chief.

His latest act was the raising of a troop of seventy horsemen, to assist Colonel Wood. This troop, from causes as yet unexplained, appears to have been surrounded and almost annihilated, leaving their gallant chief and his son dead upon the ground. As a warm and chivalrous friend, a gentleman in the truest sense of the word, and the beau ideal of a cavalry soldier, his loss will long be mourned by those who knew him and appreciated his worth. He married a daughter of the late Colonel Mountjoy Martyn, by whom he had two sons and one daughter, and one of the sons, a boy of fourteen, shared his fate in the recent action.

THE LATE LIEUT. JOHNSON

The correspondent of the *Cape Argus*, who narrated the battle of April 2 at Ginghilovo, speaks of the deaths of Colonel Northey and Lieutenant Johnson, as much regretted incidents of that fierce engagement. He says, "Among the officers killed was Lieutenant George C.J. Johnson, instructor of musketry in the 99th Regiment. The loss of this gallant young officer is universally deplored. He was the life and soul of his regiment, which, as one of his superior officers declares, could have better spared many an older man. He was shot through the heart, death being almost instantaneous, and he fell with one of those merry jests upon his lips which had done not a little to make him the friend and the favourite of all ranks among his comrades in arms."

He was twenty-eight years of age, and was the second son of William Johnson, Esq., D.L. of Vosterburgh, near Cork, who belongs to very old Cork family resident there for many generations past. The account of his son's death has created a feeling of the deepest regret in the city and county of Cork, where the father is much respected. Lieutenant Johnson's grand-uncle, Lieutenant-Colonel Noble Johnson, of the 87th Royal Irish Fusilliers, was killed in action at Monte Video, in 1805.

THE ILLUSTRATED LONDON NEWS

May 31, 1879

The announcement made in both Houses of Parliament as to the measures taken by her Majesty's Government in regard to the state of affairs in South Africa is also of a satisfactory character. Sir Garnet Wolseley has been appointed to the supreme Civil and Military Command in Natal, the Transvaal, and the adjacent Native Territories, and will exercise, within those limits, the same ample powers as those of Sir Bartle Frere. The present High Commissioner will still act as such in the Cape Colony and all the settlements immediately dependent upon it. Lord Chelmsford will cease to have the command-in-chief of the Forces operating in Zululand. Neither the one nor the other is authoritatively superseded, but in the district now the seat of war Sir Garnet Wolseley is placed above them.

Does this change signify a change of policy? Of that of the Government we may, perhaps, confidently say "No" – of that of Sir Bartle Frere, "Yes." The action of the former was evidently brought about by the conflict of opinion between the High Commissioner and his superior at home. Between him and the Government there has been a difference which the latter has not attempted to conceal. The public despatches furnish abundant evidences of it. Sir Michael Hicks-Beach has expressed in his elaborate instructions views which could not possibly be reconciled with those of Sir Bartle Frere – views to which he would not consent to submit, nor would he resign the trust committed to his charge.

The country is now assured that the Government desire no extension of territory in South Africa on any conditions whatever; that they have in Sir Garnet Wolseley an officer fully cognisant of the policy and objects of Her Majesty's advisers, who, having secured the safety of what we already possess, will hold himself ready to receive any bonâ fide overtures for peace which may be made to him by the Zulu King. Notwithstanding the reticence of Ministers in both Houses, we suspect that they will be as pleased as any of the Queen's subjects to withdraw from a war undertaken in opposition to their own advice, attended with several disasters, prosecuted at an immense expense, and likely, under no circumstances, to bring honour to the kingdom.

It seems certain that Cetewayo is anxious to make peace; that he has more than once attempted to open negotiations for that purpose; that reasonable terms are not likely to be refused by him; and that there needs no extermination of the Zulu people to place the adjacent Colonies in complete security. It is not probable that England will consent to maintain in South Africa an army of 20,000 men, at least, to operate for the sole advantage of the comparatively few colonists of European blood. She has been most unwillingly dragged into the war, and although she will neglect no obligations which the situation imposes on her, she will rejoice exceedingly to come to moderate terms with her foe.

We hope there is now some valid prospect of this. It may not be settled before the close of the present Session. It may not, perhaps, precede the opening of a second campaign. But it will not be considered unlikely that, before Parliament meets again after its prorogation in August the country will receive satisfactory assurance that peace everywhere prevails. We need hardly pray that it may be so.

THE ZULU WAR

It was announced by her Majesty's Ministers this week, in both Houses of Parliament, that Lieutenant-General Sir Garnet Wolseley is to be sent immediately to take the supreme military command in South Africa, and to direct the civil government both of Natal and of the Transvaal, having the authority of High Commissioner for dealing with Cetewayo and all other native chiefs and tribes to the northward on the frontiers of those eastern provinces. Sir Bartle Frere is to remain Governor of the Cape Colony, but is to act as High Commissioner only for native affairs, such as those of Kaffraria, Griqualand, and the Basutos, concerning the southern and western portion of the British dominions.

Sir Henry Bulwer, as Lieutenant-Governor of Natal, and Colonel Lanyon, as Administrator of the Transvaal, will continue in office, but will be subordinate henceforth to Governor Sir Garnet Wolseley, instead of to Sir Bartle Frere. Lord Chelmsford may also remain, but in subordinate military command. These arrangements have been hailed with entire approval by every section of politicians, both in Parliament and in the Press; and still greater satisfaction is felt that our Government has declared its intention not to annex any portion of Zulu territory; and that Sir Garnet Wolseley is instructed to make peace with Cetewayo as soon as pacific overtures come from the Zulu King, upon secure and reasonable terms.

The new Governor and Commander-in-Chief has already started from England for the scene of his arduous and important task. He will be assisted by a Staff of his own selection, the chief being Colonel Pomeroy Colley, C.B., who was with him in the Ashantee War, and who is now Private Secretary to the Viceroy of India.

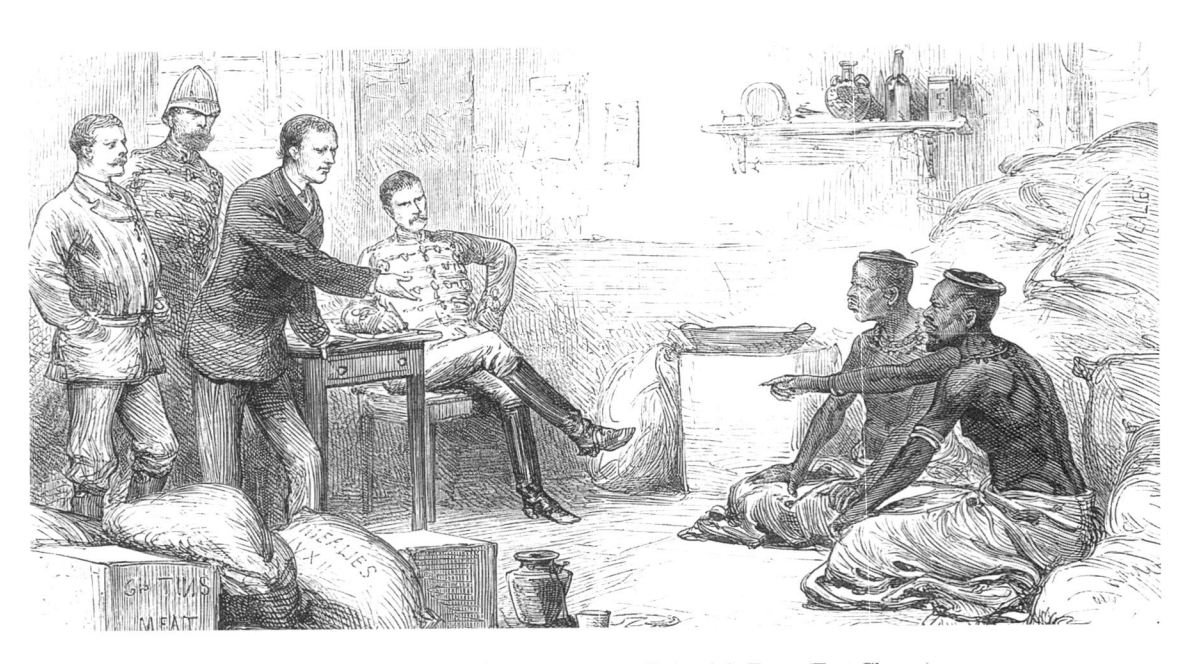

Interrogating Cetewayo's messengers at Dalmain's Farm (Fort Cherry)

General Marshall and staff going to the front : Post cart travelling in Natal.
Sketches by our Special Artist, Mr Melton Prior.

The recent news from South Africa has been rather discouraging. It is rumoured that Lord Chelmsford has asked Government to send him three more battalions of troops; and the *Daily News'* military correspondent speaks of an entire change, for the second time, in the Commander-in-Chief's plans of the projected advance into Zululand. Instead of two widely separated columns, there would be one massive column, preceded by the flying column of Brigadier-General Wood, and moving slowly forward, with strongly fortified positions at short intervals; but this would require the accumulation of large quantities of stores, and, with the great difficulty in obtaining means of transport, there would be much delay in preparing for active operations.

A second campaign would probably be needful, and the cost of the war must exceed all former calculations. Lord Chelmsford has arrived at Brigadier-General Wood's headquarters, at Kambula Hill, with his staff, accompanied by the French Prince Imperial. The whole camp, on the 4th inst., was about to be moved towards the Blood river, on the frontier of Zululand. There had been no further serious engagement with the enemy, and Cetewayo was reported to have sent messages of peace.

The proposed line of advance is from Dornberg, in the Transvaal, west of Zululand. Newdigate will move down the White Umvaloosi towards Ulundi, Wood's column will keep near the Black Umvaloosi. The nature of the ground on the right bank of the White Umvaloosi is well suited for cavalry, being somewhat hilly, but open and without bush. As these columns move over the ground striking south-east, Crealock's column will push its two divisions, one along the coast, leaving the Inyezane River and making for Point Durnford, skirting the seashore and coming up in rear of Cetewayo's kraal. The other, making straight for Ungoyawi, will endeavour to clear out the women and cattle now in that bush, and will then form a junction with the right brigade at Empangi, and from there move on to the White Umvaloosi. The three columns – viz., Crealock's, Newdigate's, and Wood's Flying Force – will arrive about the end of June within striking distance of each other, within thirty miles north-east, south-east, and east respectively of Ulundi.

The great difficulty about the successful carrying out of this programme is that there is no communication between the columns, neither are there any reserves; and should the forces of the Zulu King be concentrated upon one particular point any check sustained by one column could not be assisted by help from the others. It is thought improbable that the Zulu army will attempt to pass through our lines on to Natal, but if they should do so there are absolutely no means of defence whatever that could stay their progress.

The latest accounts show that the following troops belonging to General Crealock's column are now upon the Lower Tugela:- The Naval Brigade, four batteries of Artillery; the 3rd Buffs, 57th, 60th, 88th, 91st, and 99th; and the Royal Engineers, a Hospital Corps, Lonsdale and Crook's squadrons of Horse, with Colonial and Native forces – in all 9215 men.

Newdigate's command at Doornfontein comprises the Dragoons and Lancers, four batteries of Artillery, both battalions of the 24th, portions of the 13th, the 21st, 58th, 80th, and 94th, the Royal Engineers, a Hospital Corps, and volunteers – in all 10,238 men.

Wood's command comprises a portion of the 13th and the 90th, the Royal Engineers, the Army Service Corps, the Frontier Light Horse, Baker's Horse, the Transvaal Rangers, Wood's Irregulars, and the Natal Native Horse: total, 3092 men.

Thus the force which will invade Zululand, irrespective of any reinforcements which may be on the way, is 22,545 men.

The loss during the campaign has already been heavy; 107 officers in all have already fallen in battle or by disease. Many more are very sick. The men are exposed, without tents, to a burning sun by day, and to cold dews by night; and a large proportion of the soldiers are mere boys, whose constitution is not strong enough to resist these unwholesome influences.

Large parties of Zulus have burned the grass between Ingenia and the Black Umvaloosi. This is exceedingly bad news, as now that the grass is dry enough to fire there is no saying to what extent the Zulus may clear the country of all forage. The fires on the Umvaloosi may be considered as putting a stop to all forward movements of the cavalry, which will probably be kept in the Transvaal to overawe the Boers.

Our Special Artist, Mr Melton Prior, furnishes the two Illustrations of the Zulu War engraved for this week's publication. One represents the mode of travelling by post-cart, with six horses driven at full gallop, between Durban or Pinetown and Pietermaritzburg, the capital of Natal. General Marshall and his staff came on by this conveyance, which does thirty-four miles in less than three hours, changing horses every eight or ten miles, and keeping up a mad speed over hill and dale throughout the journey.

The other Illustration is that of the Chief of the Intelligence Department of Lord Chelmsford's Staff examining two of Cetewayo's messengers at Dalmain's farm-house, which is now occupied as an army store-house, and has been fortified under the name of Fort Cherry. The Hon. A Burke, the *Daily Telegraph* correspondent, and Captain Cherry, were present at this interview. It appears that the messengers could not give satisfactory proof of their being duly accredited by the Zulu King.

OFFICERS KILLED IN THE ZULU WAR

The portraits of Colonel Weatherley, late commanding a troop of Border Horse raised by himself in the Transvaal, and of Captain the Hon. Ronald Campbell, of the Coldstream Guards, on the staff of Brigadier-General Evelyn Wood, appeared in our last publication. They were killed in the conflict with the Zulus of Umbelini's following on the Inhlobane mountain, on March 28, the day before the Zulus made their great attack on Brigadier Wood's fortified camp at Kambula hill. We now present the portraits of two other officers who were killed in the same action – namely, Captain George Williams, of the 6th West York Militia, who was serving in this campaign as Lieutenant of the Frontier Light Horse; and Lieutenant James Pool, who held the first post of that rank under Colonel Weatherley in his corps of volunteer cavalry.

The circumstances of their lamented death have partly been related in our former notices of the affair of March 28; but a private letter from Captain H. Vaughan, R.A., written next day, addressed to Mr Morgan Williams, of Aberpengwern, Neath, brother of the deceased Captain George Williams, gives the following account of it:-

"An expedition started on the 27th, consisting of the Frontier Light Horse and two other volunteer corps of mounted men, with a few artillery and a number of friendly Kaffirs, altogether one thousand men, under command of Colonel Redvers Buller, V.C. Another column started about six hours later, under Colonel Russell, the whole being under the immediate command of Colonel Evelyn Wood, V.C., C.B. The object of this expedition was to storm the Inhlobane mountain, a great Zulu stronghold, where they had collected all their cattle. I send a rough sketch of the place.

Colonel Buller, with his men, had to go round to the back of the mountain coming up from Zululand, as this was the only accessible place for mounted men. On the side nearest the camp Colonel Russell had to go up and meet Colonel Buller on the top. On his arrival at a certain height it was found he could not go up the slope to the top, as it was full of immense boulders and stones, and there was a wall built across by the Kaffirs. Some of his men got up on foot, but came down again. Meanwhile Colonel Buller had reached the place he was to go up, and sent Lieutenant George William's troop to hold a small hillock on the left, to keep the fire down and cover his advance.

The place was in the shape of a horseshoe, and there was a ridge running up the centre. The whole of this horseshoe space was filled with Kaffirs, under the cover of rocks, firing away. Colonel Buller and his force, by keeping on the left side of the ridge, were protected from the fire coming from the right of the horseshoe; but there was the fire from the left-hand side to be put down. So Lieutenant George Williams and his men were told off; and, while he was in the act of placing them, a bullet that nearly struck Colonel Buller hit Lieutenant George Williams in the head and knocked him over. His death must have been instantaneous; he could not have suffered any pain.

His body for the time was left where it was; but afterwards Captain Barton, of the Coldstream Guards, with twenty-five men, went down to the spot, tied the body on a spare horse, and was coming back to camp, when they fell in with a large force of Kaffirs and were dispersed. Captain Barton was killed. Colonel Buller's force had by this time reached the top, captured the cattle, and were coming back again when they encountered an immense number of the enemy, who came up the same way as they did, and there was a regular scramble to get down to where Colonel Russell should have been at the time. The place, however, was quite impracticable for horses. How any got down was a mystery, with the horses plunging madly, while the Kaffirs were shooting and assegaing the poor fellows. It was a disastrous day."

OFFICERS KILLED IN THE ZULU WAR

| Captain G. Williams, Frontier Light Horse. | Captain D.B. Moriarty, 80th Regiment. | Lieutenant J. Pool, Transvaal Border Horse. |

Another officer of the same surname, Lieutenant Charles Ellis Williams, of the 58th Regiment, was killed in this day's fighting on the Inhlobane Mountain. Lieutenant James Pool, who shared the fate of his superior officer, Colonel Weatherley, was a brother of Mr John Pool, of Blenheim-street, Newcastle-on-Tyne, and had many friends in the North of England. Eleven officers fell in this unlucky business, and there were some remarkable escapes. The bravery and generous self-devotion of Major W. Knox Leet, of the 13th Light Infantry, in saving the lives of his comrades in the retreat, did not pass unnoticed. Brigadier-General Wood has recommended him for the Victoria Cross. The following letter from Lieutenant Metcalfe Smith, of the Frontier Light Horse, relates this praiseworthy exploit:-

Kambula Camp, March 31

"I am most anxious to bring to notice that, in the retreat from the Inhlobane Mountain on the 28th inst., Major Leet, of the 13th Light Infantry, who was quite a stranger to me, saved my life, with almost the certainty of losing his own life by doing so. We were going along the top of the mountain, pursued by the Zulus, when Major Leet said to Colonel Buller that the best way to get the men down was by the right side; and the Colonel said it was, and called out so to the men. However, everyone but Major Leet, myself, and one other man, kept on to the front of the mountain; while we began to descend the on right side. Major Leet and the other man were on horseback, but I was on foot, my horse having been shot.

When we had got down a little way, a great many Zulus rushed after us, and were catching us up very quickly. The side of the mountain was dreadfully steep and rugged, and there was no pathway at all. They were firing and throwing their assegais at us while they rushed upon us. The third man, whose name is unknown to me, was killed about halfway down. While I was running by myself and trying to

Zulu method of advancing to the attack.

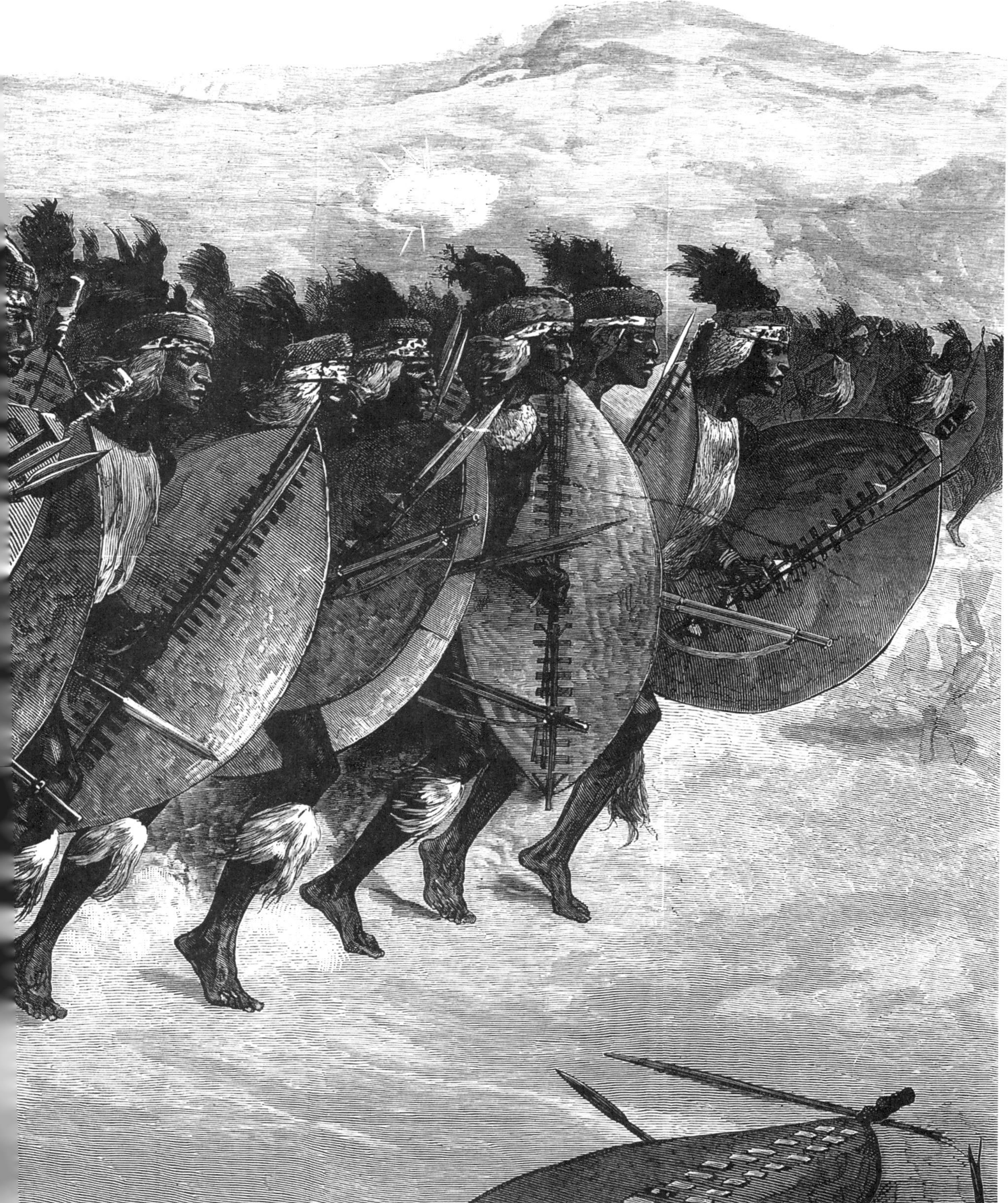

get away from the Zulus, who were rapidly catching me up, I turned round and shot one with my revolver. I was then quite exhausted and out of breath, and intended to sit down and give up all chance of saving my life, as the Zulus were within a few yards of me; but Major Leet persisted in waiting for me, and called to me to catch hold of the pack-saddle he was riding, which I did.

Major Leet then, finding that I could not keep beside the horse, I was so done up and the hill so steep and rugged, insisted, though I told him it was of no use, on stopping and dragging me up behind him on the horse, which was also greatly exhausted. By the greatest good luck, he escaped from the bullets and assegais of the Zulus and got near the Colonel's men, coming down the end of the mountain. Had it not been for Major Leet, nothing could have saved me, and I owe him the deepest gratitude, which I shall feel as long as I live."

The writer of the above letter, Lieutenant A. Metcalfe Smith, belongs to the 5th West York Militia, but is serving, like the late Captain George Williams, as a volunteer, with the rank of Lieutenant in the Colonial Corps of Light Horse. The unfortunate comrade of whom he speaks as having followed himself and Major Leet down the right side of the mountain, but who was overtaken by the Zulus and killed, was Lieutenant Duncombe, of Wood's Irregulars, but likewise of the Yorkshire Militia.

Colonel Redvers Buller, in his official despatch concerning the action of March 28, says:- "The Zulus pursued us in force, and with so many dismounted men we experienced great difficulty in descending the mountain, and but for the exertions of a few our retreat would have been a rout; as it was we got down with a loss of those men who were too badly wounded to be kept on horses. As specially distinguishing themselves in the retreat, I wish to mention Commandant Raaff, Transvaal Rangers, and Captain Gardner, my staff officer, both of whom were also conspicuous in the assault in the morning.

Major Leet, 13th Light Infantry, as well as Captain Darcy, Frontier Light Horse, although himself dismounted, rallied the men, saving the lives of many footmen – Lieutenants Blaine and Smith, Frontier Light Horse; Lieutenant Wilson, Baker's Horse; Captain Loraine White and Adjutant Brecher, Wood's Irregulars; Sergeants Crampton and Ellis, Troopers Landsill, Whitecross, Duffy, Pietersen, Hewitt, and Vinnicombe, Frontier Light Horse."

Major William Knox Leet entered the Army, as an Ensign of the 13th Light Infantry, during the war with Russia in 1854 or 1855; he served as Adjutant of that regiment during the Indian Mutiny War, in which he was actively engaged, and was frequently mentioned in despatches. He was promoted to the rank of Captain in November, 1864, became Musketry Instructor of his regiment, and subsequently served on the staff in that capacity during several years, till he was appointed in July, 1872, Deputy-Assistant-Adjutant-General of the Cork Military District. He held that appointment five years, and was then promoted to the brevet rank of Major, and joined his regiment in South Africa, under the command of Colonel Redvers Buller, V.C., C.B. His brother is Captain J.H. Leet, of the Royal Navy. We are glad to observe that Major Leet's behaviour is to have its due recognition by the award of the Victoria Cross.

The disaster of March 12 on the Intombi River, four miles from Luneburg on the Transvaal frontier, where a detachment of the 80th Regiment, under Captain D.B. Moriarty, were surprised in their camp, and nearly sixty were killed out of a hundred, will not have been forgotten by our readers. The portrait of Captain Moriarty is given in this week's paper. He was forty years of age.

The portrait of Captain Moriarty is from a photograph by Mr Abel Lewis, of Douglas, Isle of Man; that of Lieutenant Pool by Messrs W. and D. Downey; and that of Captain George Williams by Messrs Elliott and Fry, London.

THE ILLUSTRATED LONDON NEWS

June 7, 1879

The Zulu War : Waiting. – A sketch in a fortified camp in Zululand.

THE ZULU WAR

Our Special Artist, Mr. Melton Prior, sends a sketch of the King's Dragoon Guards halting at Pinetown, near Durban, previously to marching up the country in Natal; and a view of the mouth of the Tugela, the river forming the boundary of Zululand, as beheld from Fort Pearson.

Among other Illustrations given this week are that of a sentinel on guard in one of the fortified encampments which were occupied by Lord Chelmsford's force on the march to relieve the garrison of Ekowe; and the servants of the Zulu Royal Household employed in preparing King Cetewayo's dinner. With reference to this last-mentioned subject, there is a curious point of ceremonial etiquette, observed by Mr. J.A. Farrar in his little book, "Zululand and the Zulus," which is not precisely explained. He states that "the Royal cook may never tell the King, or any of his family, that the meat is cooked; he must convey the intelligence by saying that he is tired of roasting."

Probably, however, the cook always takes care to do complete justice to the culinary preparation of the meat before presuming to announce his own indisposition to continue his appointed task; but it seems a whimsical and unaccountable scruple to avoid making any direct report of the condition of the meat itself. The national superstition of witchcraft is doubtless at the bottom of this and many other peculiar Zulu customs.

We also present four portraits of Zulu chiefs who have visited Natal, and who were photographed there, attired in the most fashionable modes of hair-dressing peculiar to their nation.

The hair is stiffened with a kind of gum, which enables it to retain the shapes artistically moulded according to the wearer's fancy, or prescribed as an indication of his rank in life. Married men are distinguished by having their hair formed into a circular ridge, which may or may not be developed into one or two peaks at the front or back of the head. Pieces of horn and bone, the hollow of which sometimes does duty as a snuffbox, are frequently stuck in this elaborate head-gear.

The latest news from the seat of war is to May 12, and we are again told that an important change is impending in the disposition of the campaign. The main advance will now be from the lower Tugela base. The flying column of Brigadier Wood, operating as a diversion, will invade from the north-western flank; and from the forces now gathering about Dundee, reinforcements both of cavalry and infantry will be sent to the Lower Tugela column.

This change, if made, will necessarily involve considerable additional delay. The Dragoon Guards will probably go to the Transvaal. Lord Chelmsford and his staff are at Utrecht. He has sent orders for three months food, forage, and rations to be stored at a place called Conference Hill, for Wood's column; but if Wood's column is to be a flying one it cannot require stores for so long a time at a place so great a distance from the scene of operations, especially when two month's provisions both for Newdigate's and Wood's columns are already deposited at Dundee, Ladysmith, and Balte's Spruit.

The Commander-in-Chief meanwhile, has telegraphed home to the effect that his operations are delayed through commissariat and transport difficulties. We learn that Brigadier Wood has broken up his camp at Kambula and has formed a new one at Queen's Kraal, on the White Imvolosi, in order that he may be able the better to co-operate with General Newdigate.

The *Natal Times* states that the general British advance has been postponed for the present, owing to difficulties of transport; but that a force consisting of two cavalry regiments and six guns will make a rapid march to Ulundi. No official information on this subject has, however, been made known.

Much sickness prevails at Fort Chelmsford, and 173 men have been sent back thence invalided to the Tugela. General Crealock is at Fort Pearson, and has been seriously ill from typhoid fever. A new camp has been formed on the Amatikulu, named Fort Crealock. Frequent convoys pass between the forts and the Tugela, but few Zulus being seen on each occasion.

It is rumoured that Cetewayo has burnt his kraal at Ulundi, and has retired in a north-westerly direction. His brother Dabulamanzi has not yet surrendered, and his intentions are suspected.

King's Dragoon Guards on the march : Halting for the night at Pinetown.
From a sketch by our Special Artist, Mr. Melton Prior.

King Cetewayo's cooks.

131

Zulu dandies, showing the modes of wearing the hair.

The Zulu War : Mouth of the river Tugela, from Fort Pearson.
Sketch by our Special Artist, Mr. Melton Prior.

THE ILLUSTRATED LONDON NEWS

June 14, 1879

THE ZULU WAR

The news from South Africa, to the 20th ult., gives a very uncertain prospect and contradictory rumours about the continuance of the military campaign lately recommenced by Lord Chelmsford. Two or three Zulu messengers had come in at Fort Chelmsford, on the road to Ekowe, ostensibly to sue for peace on behalf of King Cetewayo; but their credentials were not deemed sufficient. Mr John Dunn had been commissioned, however, by General Crealock to confer with these messengers. If their reports might be trusted, Cetewayo had expressed surprise at the treatment to which he had been subjected, had again expressed his unwillingness to fight, and had desired to live in peace as the White Man's Son. Referring to his coronation, he asked, "Why do they make me King in the morning and kill me in the afternoon. What have I done?"

The reply was given that he must show by deeds, not words, the sincerity of his wishes; and that if he and his chief men submitted they would not be harshly dealt with. The messengers were also told that any further representations must be made to the General at Utrecht. The next step was that Cetewayo dispatched an envoy to Major-General Crealock on the 16th, desiring him to send a European to discuss terms of peace. John Dunn was accordingly sent to Cetewayo's kraal, and has since returned. It is believed that the negotiations failed in consequence of the refusal on the British side of any terms but unconditional surrender. Cetewayo's good faith in making proposals for peace is doubted.

The contemplated rapid march upon the Zulu King's kraal at Ulundi has been abandoned. The principal Zulu chiefs, including Dabulamanzi, whom rumour has so often slain, were at the King's kraal, and the regiments dispersed. John Dunn gives it as his opinion that General Crealock's column could not under favourable circumstances get beyond Fort Lord Chelmsford before next September.

1. Spur of Oscarberg
2. Ridge where the waggons are.
3. Isandhlwana Hill.
4. Bashee Valley.
5. Sirayo's Krantz.
6. Road from the Ponts.
7. Road to fort.
8. Buffalo River.
9. The Waggon Drift over the River.

The Zulu War : Fort Melvill, near Isandhlwana.
From a sketch by Private Mellsop, 24th Regiment.

The military situation in Natal is not encouraging. The grass is fast drying up, and ready to be burnt by the Zulus, which will deprive the draught cattle of food on the march. The transport and Commissariat difficulties are causing increased anxiety, and the movement of the troops is delayed in consequence. A committee has been formed by the Lieutenant-Governor to inquire into the question. It is said that many are holding back wagons and oxen, with the view of forcing the Government to give them higher prices. Two to three pounds a day are being given for the hire of a wagon and a span of oxen. When it is known that 1600 waggons are employed, and that this is quite inadequate, the cost and the difficulties will be realised.

The Commissariat stores at Greytown have been destroyed by fire. About two months' supplies, valued at £5000, are totally lost. The cause of the fire is at present unknown. Greytown is a small post, on the road from Pietermaritzburg to the north, and garrisoned by two companies of the 94th Regiment.

Spies report the presence of four Zulu impis in the eastern angle of Cetewayo's country. One is now behind Isandhlwana, and is expected to cross into Natal at Fugitive Drift, near Rorke's Drift. The second is to cross at the junction of the Tugela and Buffalo Rivers. The third, which is to cross into the Newcastle district, shows itself on the Blood River, opposite our position, to divert attention. The patrols have seen mounted Zulus about Sirayo's country, a sign of the proximity of an impi. The Zulus have visited and ransacked the Kambula camp since our abandonment of the river and the Bashee river, in the south-western corner of Zululand.

Colonel Buller was to conduct a mounted reconnaissance along the line of invasion, accompanied by Colonel Harrison, to select a post for the next advanced dépôt and camp. With them goes Prince Louis Napoleon.

Lord Chelmsford telegraphs that there is to be a reconnaissance by Crealock's division, and the naval authorities give hope that stores may be landed at the mouth of the Umldlazi. This will be a great assistance. Colonel Lanyon hopes to bring down five hundred mounted burghers for defence of the Transvaal frontier under Pretorius. The reconnaissance ought to decide the best line for advance for Newdigate; and Wood's advance should commence in ten days. General Clifford, Maritzburg, adds:- "Lord Chelmsford requires two months' supplies with force advancing, and one month's at advance dépôt,

Conference-hill. No date can be fixed for completion. Want of transport drivers is the cause of delay."

Sir Bartle Frere is making a triumphal progress though the colony. He is now at the Diamond-Fields, receiving fêtes and congratulations.

The Free State Volksrad has carried a resolution expressing sympathy with the Transvaal, and a wish for its independence. The President opposed this motion without avail.

We have been favoured by Lieut-Colonel H.J. Degacher, commanding the second battalion of the 24th Regiment, with a sketch of the last resting-place of those lamented officers, Lieutenants Melvill and Coghill. Our readers will bear in memory their gallant attempt to carry off the Queen's colour of their battalion from Isandhlwana, and how it was washed away from them whilst crossing the swollen torrent of the Buffalo river, they themselves narrowly escaping drowning, but only to fall whilst climbing the steep cliff which here forms the right bank of the river. They fell about five yards from the spot where they are buried. The corpses of Zulus found round them showed that they had fought to the last.

The last resting-place of Lieutenants Melvill and Coghill.
From a sketch by Colonel Degacher, 24th Regiment.

We ought to add that their gallant attempt proved successful, as the colour was afterwards found in the bed of the river by Major Black, and returned to the first battalion of that regiment. The cross is the gift of his Excellency Sir Bartle Frere, the inscription on it being as follows:- "In memory of Lieut. and Adjutant Teignmouth Melvill and Lieut. Nevill J.A. Coghill, 1st Battalion 24th Regiment, who died on this spot 22nd January, 1879, to save the Queen's Colour of their regiment. " And, on the reverse side, "Jesu, Mercy," "For Queen and Country."

Another sketch by Private Mellsop, of the 24th, shows in the foreground "Fort Melvill," named after the late Lieutenant Melvill, on which the little garrison of Rorke's Drift have been now engaged for many weeks past. It is an oblong fort with flanking towers, built partly in masonry, partly with dry wall, loopholed throughout, and surrounded by a ditch, with an obstacle formed of aloes planted on the glacis. It is constructed on a height 150 yards from, and overlooking and commanding, the ponts by which the invading army crossed on Jan. 11 last.

Lieutenant R. da Costa Porter, R.E., has superintended its erection; and, manned with 200 Europeans, it may be considered impregnable against any number of Zulus. A large stone store, roofed with galvanised iron, has been built inside, to hold commissariat supplies. The Isandhlwana hill stands up boldly in the distance, and the wagons of the ill-fated column may still be seen with a good glass standing and lying about on the ridge marked 2 in the sketch. It is distant quite seven miles and a half as the crow flies, and the camp was pitched on the far side. "Sirayo's" krantzes and caves are four miles and a half from the fort.

The remaining sketch, also by Private Mellsop, represents the little cemetery at Rorke's Drift, where lie the remains of the brave men who were killed in the defence of the post of Jan.22 and of those who have succumbed to fever or other disease. It is situated half way between the now famous "store" and the hill at the back called "Oscarberg." The monument consists of an obelisk standing on a massive square base, and these on two solid stone steps, all of the hardest white freestone, and is 10 ft. high.

The whole work has been done by the men of the second battalion 24th Regiment, under the superintendence of Lieutenant Gonville Bromhead, and is to replace a rustic wooden cross previously erected by Lieutenant Chard, R.E. The design and ornamental inscriptions, as well as the sketch, are the work of Private Mellsop. On one face is a wreath of laurel inclosing the number of the regiment (XXIV.), who furnish the greater part of the graves; on the other side are the names of the dead, twenty-seven in number.

The cemetery at Rorke's Drift.
From a sketch by Private Mellsop, 24th Regiment.

The portraits of two more officers who have met their death in this war are presented on another page – namely, Captain Warren R.C. Wynne, of the Royal Engineers, and Sub-Lieutenant Arthur Tyndal Bright, of the 90th (Perthshire) Regiment of Infantry, commanded by Colonel Evelyn Wood, V.C., C.B. Captain Wynne had been attached to Colonel Pearson's force in the beleaguered fort of Ekowe, after commanding the right wing in the battle of Inyezane, on Jan 22, and his engineering skill had greatly contributed to the defence of the fort till it was relieved by Lord Chelmsford. He has previously laid out and superintended the construction of Fort Tenedos, on the left bank of the Tugela river.

He was seized with fever at Ekowe, and died a few days after leaving that place, having got no farther than Fort Pearson. His superior officer, Colonel Pearson, has borne full testimony to the value of his services, and has stated that his fatal illness was "entirely due to over-exertion at a time when he was in very indifferent health." He was just thirty-six years of age on the day of his death; he was the eldest son of Captain John Wynne, R.H.A., of Wynnstay, near Dublin, his mother being a daughter of Admiral Sir Samuel Warren. The portrait is from a photograph by A. Bassano, of Piccadilly and Old Bond-street. Sub-Lieutenant Arthur Tyndal Bright was killed on March 29, in the defence of Brigadier-General Wood's fortified camp at Kambula Hill against a very large attacking force of Zulus, when Major Hackett also received his death-wound. The photograph of this young officer is one by Browne, Barnes, and Bell, of Liverpool.

The late Lieutenant A.T. Bright, 90th Regiment

The late Captain W.R.C. Wynne, R.E.

THE ILLUSTRATED LONDON NEWS

June 21, 1879

THE ZULU WAR

Our Special Artist, Mr. Melton Prior, furnishes a Sketch of the graves of soldiers of the 99th Regiment at Fort Pearson, on the banks of the Tugela. We gave the portraits of Lieutenant-Colonel Francis V. Northey, late commanding the third battalion of the 60th Rifles, who was mortally wounded in the battle of April 2 at Gingihilovo, and died a few days later, much regretted by the whole army. He was the son of E.R. Northey, Esq., of Epsom, and grandson of Admiral Sir George Anson; he was born in 1836, was educated at Eton, where he was captain of the cricket eleven, and entered the service in 1855. He served with his regiment in the Oude campaign of 1858, and in the Red River Expedition, under Sir Garnet Wolseley, in 1870. He was married to a daughter of Lieutenant-Colonel G.C. Gzowski, of Canada.

The other portrait is that of General Sr. Garnet Wolseley's chosen and very efficient Chief of Staff, Colonel George Pomeroy Colley, C.B., C.M.G., of the 2nd (Queen's Royal) Infantry, who has been holding the post of private military secretary to the Viceroy of India. Colonel Colley entered the service in 1852; he obtained the rank of Lieutenant in 1854, Captain in 1860, Brevet-Major in 1863, and Brevet-Colonel in 1874.

Colonel G.P. Colley, C.B., C.M.G.,
Chief of the Staff to Sir Garnet Wolseley.

The late Lieut.-Colonel Northey, 60th Rifles
Killed in the Zulu War.

He was employed on special service in the Kaffir wars of 1858 to 1860, then served in the China war, at the capture of the Taku forts and in the advance on Pekin; afterwards, under Sir Garnet Wolseley, in the Ashantee war of 1873, commanding the transport and line of communications, and at the battle of Amoaful and taking of Coomassie. He has been repeatedly mentioned in despatches and thanked by Government, besides receiving promotions and war medals with clasps. His ability as a military administrator is generally recognised. Our portrait of Lieutenant-Colonel Northey is from a photograph by Mr.Crawford Barnes, of Colchester; that of Colonel Colley, from one by Messrs. Maull and Co., of London.

The Zulu war news of the past week is not very important. It is a tardy consolation to learn that the battle-field of Isandlwana has been revisited, and some of our dead soldiers there have at last been decently buried. This was done on May 21, exactly four months after the terrible disaster which attended the commencement of the war. The following extract of a letter from Rorke's Drift gives an account of the mournful excursion:-

"A strong reconnaissance was made from here to-day. Five hundred of Sirayo's men were reported to be mealie-reaping at the head of the Bashee Valley, and 200 Zulu scouts were said to be behind Isandlwana. General Marshall, with the Dragoons, the left wing of the Lancers, and Bengough's natives from Dundee, were joined a few miles from here by the right wing of the Lancers, two guns, four companies of the second battalion of the 24th Regiment, and seventy-five pair of transport-service horses.

The right wing of the Lancers, under Colonel Drury-Lowe, started for the head of the Bashee Valley, Bengough's men turned to the left, and beat up the valley further on. The men of the 24th Regiment remained watching Sirayo's Kraal. As we proceeded a lovely sunrise revealed the fatal Isandlwana still in the distance. We had a picturesque march – the Lancers with their pennons, and the red-coated Dragoons – through mountainous scenery and misty valleys. Smart trotting brought us to Isandlwana Neck, where we saw the first dead bodies. Hundreds were only partially clothed. On the other side of the Neck, behind Isandlwana, lay the camp in a line extending over half a mile. Most of the deserted wagons there were uninjured, mealies growing round and under them from the scattered seed.

The majority of the men had evidently been killed outside the camp. Among the wagons there were comparatively few bodies, and they were equally scattered. The body of Captain Shepstone was discovered and buried. Colonel Durnford's body with those of Lord, Downe, and Vereker, all of the Artillery, was also buried. At the express request of the officers of the 24th Regiment, none of their dead were buried. Colonel Glyn proposed to bring his entire regiment to witness the final interment of their comrades. Several note-books and papers were found untouched. The native dead were extremely scarce. We harnessed the transport horses to thirty-seven of the best wagons and two water-carts, and then returned."

The Queen's message to Lord Chelmsford, thanking him and the troops for their services at Kambula and Ginghilovo, has been received at Fort Pearson, producing intense satisfaction among the troops. The 1st of June was the day fixed for the forward movement of the troops into Zululand. A number of wagons were arriving daily at Dundee, Landsman's Drift, and Conference Hill, to fill up the dépôts. Forage for the thirty-five days, bread-stuffs for three months, and other supplies had already been collected A report from Newcastle says that the Prince Imperial, on the 21st, while riding out from the camp, with several officers, was surrounded by the enemy. Three of our Zulus were killed. The Prince put his horse at a krantz (a rocky descent), and had a narrow escape.

SKETCHES IN SOUTH AFRICA.

The readers of Captain Lucas's pleasant book, "Camp Life and Sport in South Africa," will at once recognise the different types of native character, with their features and costume, which are shown in our page of Sketches by Mr. Doyle Glanville, a Colonial Government medical officer, formerly of the Union Steam-Ship Company's service.

They are selected from a variety of races and nationalities, in several parts of the British dominions; from Capetown, from Port Elizabeth, from King William's Town, from Kaffraria, from the Dutch provinces of the upland interior, and from the half-tamed Zulus of Natal. The Malays, also, who have long been settled at Capetown, and find employment about the docks and harbour there, figure in one of these Illustrations, with the singular broad straw hat, of a conical form, worn by the man, and the ample skirts and kerchiefs of the women.

At King William's Town, as our own Special Artist, Mr. Melton Prior, showed by the Sketches there a twelvemonth ago, the "School Kaffirs," or those who have been educated by European teachers, are fond of dressing with an exaggerated imitation of English fashions, like the Negroes and negresses of the West Indies and the United States. These may be compared with the simple attire of a Chief at home in British Kaffraria, in the act of putting on his "kaross," or loose coverlet of sewn jackal-skins with the ornamental tails; while the young Zulu from Natal goes almost naked, only with a very small apron and bands on his arms and ankles, and with his hair stiffened by gum and raised into a sort of bonnet.

The scene of a grass hut, and the family lounging in front of it, was sketched in a kraal of British Kaffraria. A Fingo labourer at Port Elizabeth, wading through the surf with a bale of goods to be carried from the ship's boat to the shore, is an example of the inconveniences of that harbour, to which frequent reference has been made by visitors to South Africa, The pastoral occupations of the Dutch Boers, and especially the new business of ostrich-farming, which has been taken up in different parts of the country with more or less success, have also been made a theme of comment upon former occasions.

Sketches in South Africa.

1. Young Zulu Chief, Natal.
2. Kaffir Chief, robed in a kaross of jackal skin.
3. Dutch Boer, with an ostrich.
4. Kaffir kraal and domestic life.
5. Malays at Capetown.
6. Civilised Kaffir belle in King William's Town.
7. Civilised Kaffir going to church or chapel.
8. Fingo landing ship's cargo, Port Elizabeth.

The late Prince Imperial.

DEATH OF THE PRINCE IMPERIAL

The War in South Africa seems doomed to be fertile of disaster, of which, perhaps, the last that has been brought to our knowledge is not the least. The tragical death of the Prince Imperial in an insignificant foray has excited deep regret throughout Europe, of which no inconsiderable share is due to the commiseration felt for the Empress Eugénie in the loss of her only Son.

The circumstances under which Prince Louis Napoleon met his fate are not yet wholly known in detail to the English public. It is, however, satisfactory to be assured, on the highest authority, that the ill-starred expedition to Zululand undertaken by the Imperial youth did not involve, to any extent, the responsibility of either the War Office or the Horse Guards.

The Duke of Cambridge's statement in the House of Lords on Monday afternoon put this matter beyond all doubt. The Prince went out not in the service of the English Army, to which project her Majesty's advisers felt themselves unable to yield their assent, but simply "on his own account," and in his individual capacity, to witness the campaign which his comrades at Woolwich had been ordered to attend.

Letters of introduction from his Royal Highness Commanding-in-Chief had been written in his behalf to Sr. Bartle Frere and to Lord Chelmsford, requesting them to give him such assistance as they could in the fulfilment of his purpose. He was, in fact, a visitor to the British Army in South Africa, commended to the good offices of the High Commissioner and the Commander, but left very much to his own discretion. How he came to accompany the small reconnoitring party which encountered the attack in which he was killed, to whom the mismanagement is to be attributed owing to which he lost his life, and what explanation can be given of his having been left behind by his comrades as soon as danger declared itself, we have yet to learn, and the information will be awaited with general anxiety. Happily, the body of the Prince has been recovered, and will be forwarded with due respect by the earliest means of conveyance to this country.

The death of the Prince, sincerely as it is lamented, is not, perhaps, more impressive than the bereavement sustained by the Empress, his mother. For her, sympathy is universal. Her Majesty the Queen, who returned from Balmoral only on Saturday morning last, paid a visit of condolence on Monday afternoon to her Imperial sister. We know from other sources how much her Majesty was charmed with, and attached to, the Empress Eugénie before the terrible catastrophe at Sedan that precipitated her husband from his throne.

We have, one and all, observed the dignified, unobtrusive, and gentle demeanour of that lady ever since her arrival in this country, both before and after the death of Napoleon III. We have been made to appreciate her passionate fondness for her only son, and her wise uprearing of him, in the interval of her exile. What hopes she entertained of him it would be impertinence to inquire.

He was born Heir to the French Empire, he might, of course, have become its Head, though events of late have not favoured the cause of Imperialism in France. But his education was so conducted as to qualify him for the post if he should ever attain to it, and it is quite probable that his Imperial Mother had faith in his eventual exaltation to it. All such prospects, however, as may have heretofore partially brightened her widowed life have been ruthlessly effaced. The future can only be to her one of resignation. Many a woman left in humble life whose hearth has been left desolate has felt, and still feels, the same bitterness of woe, the same consciousness of solitude, the same transference of her cares and her affections from this world to the next.

We all sympathise with the mournful situation, whenever and wherever our attention is called to it. The difference in the case of the Empress is that she has filled so wide a space in the sight of Society that her outlook has been upon so much more extensive a scale. She has, however, certain compensations, if compensations they can be considered, in her adverse fortune. The Monarchs and the great ones of Europe have been prompt to condole with her. Her political friends naturally share her grief, and would, if possible, by sharing, lessen it. She is not left altogether alone, although, doubtless she has been riven from the object which gave special significance and value to the esteem of those who now offer her their sympathy. The tears which are shed for her and with her cannot but, in some measure, exert a healing influence, and soothe her sorrows during the remainder of her days.

Of the lessons which are taught to us by this sad event we refrain from repeating what will occur to every reflective mind. The instability of human greatness is one of them, which has been so often witnessed in this generation that it scarcely needs to be emphasised. We are reminded of it almost yearly. Ambition, successful for a while, suddenly cut short by death, or by deposition, is now a familiar story in the world's annals. The wonder is that it seems to be read with so little profit, and that the objects upon which the heart sets itself with intensest desire and most earnest effort are still so frequently of so little real worth.

In this respect, nevertheless, we think there is progressive improvement. Men are more disposed than they were to choose for themselves ends which are not at the mercy of the merest and, possibly, the most inglorious casualty. They are more apt, perhaps, to recognise the fact that happiness and honour in the present life are more surely associated with good done to others than with benefits sought chiefly for their own glorification.

Politically, the death of the Prince Imperial will make itself felt chiefly in France. To the Bonapartist party it is almost equivalent to "the crack of doom." That party, it is true, has been dwindling for some time past. Its chief men have lost the respect of society. Its virtues, such as they were, have fallen into desuetude. It is now represented by persons whose character inspires no confidence.

Prince Jerome is little liked in France. Even if he were trusted, he is deeply pledged against Imperialism both in Church and State. The Republic has consequently been strengthened by an event which most Republicans, as well as others, will personally deplore. Its dangers henceforward will arise chiefly from itself. It has no external foe of which it need stand in fear. But the position abounds with temptations, Lack of caution is too commonly the fruit of unusual prosperity. "Festina lente," as it has been for some years past, so now as much as ever it needs to be, the motto of the French Republic.

But it is not in a political so much as in a personal sense that the untimely end of the Prince Imperial will be viewed by the world at large. So much promise nipped in the bud! Such manliness, modesty, gentleness, and high-trained intelligence snatched from this life by the hands of a few barbarians! Such a cruel contrast of what is with what might have been! This will be the direction in which men's thoughts will chiefly run, and as they run will read the moral which it teaches.

THE WAR IN SOUTH AFRICA

On the road to the front – "Curry's Post."
From a sketch by our Special Artist, Mr. Melton Prior.

Our Special Artist, Mr Melton Prior, furnishes a sketch of "Curry's Post" on the road up the country in Natal towards the actual scene of warfare. Another correspondent supplies us with an Illustration of the "laager," or fortified defensive position at Verulam, on the coast road between Durban and the Lower Tugela. The sketch of a vidette, or outlook post, in the neighbourhood of one of the laagers, will also contribute to make our readers acquainted with the aspect of military activity on the frontier.

Vidette outside a laager.

The main road from Pietermaritzburg, the capital of Natal, proceeds northward to Newcastle, a distance of nearly two hundred miles, passing the villages of Estcourt and Ladysmith. Except the rude sheds or huts that are called hotels, at the places where the post-cart changes horses, the country presents no evidence of human occupation. At rare intervals a clump of trees in a dell of the far-stretching veldt is pointed out as marking the residence of a farmer. But the house itself in most instances has been abandoned. The line followed by the post-cart is a considerable distance from the Zulu frontier, but the dwellers along it have not considered themselves safe. At every halting-place one finds a laager of more or less formidable character.

The laager at Ladysmith is quite massive, and at Newcastle a permanent laager includes all the public institutions of the place, from the post-office to the law courts. Newcastle is in the second line of defence, covered by the first line and by the posts at Dundee, Doornberg, and Conference Hill. But Newcastle has little interest as a military position. There is a fort on a bluff overhanging the village, with a few huts around it, furnished with accommodation for one company of the 4th Foot. It is used also as a convalescent station for General Wood's column.

Fort Cherry, of which we had to speak the other day, is sixty-three miles from Pietermaritzburg. It stands to the left of the road from Greytown to Kranzkop, about four miles and a half from the latter place, and nine miles from the Tugela River. It was built entirely by the first and third battalions of the Natal Native Contingent and a company of the Natal Native pioneers. The news of Isandhlwana reached their camp two days after the disaster, and found the frontier at this point lying open to raids at the pleasure of the Zulus.

Captain Cherry set his men to work at once, and a sufficient temporary intrenchment was thrown up before nightfall. This has now developed into a fortress, which is impregnable by Zulus. By nature the position was a strong one, the fort crowning the crest of a gradually sloping hill, perfectly open, and commanding a distant prospect on every side. The fort has 350 yards of parapet, and incloses an area of 8800 yards. From the bottom of the ditch, which runs all round and is thickly planted with sharpened stakes, to the crest of the parapet, is 20 ft., the wall rising sheer from the ditch, which, again, is 10 ft. wide. To take such a position with a rush seems beyond even Zulu numbers and courage.

Pietermaritzburg is a town which might be very easily defended. It retains exactly the same form of arrangement that it had when first laid out by its Dutch founders. It consists of eight parallel thoroughfares, about 180 yards asunder and a mile and a half long, these crossed at convenient intervals by transverse streets of similar character, something more than a mile in length. The laager which has been formed in the heart of the city is about 400 yards square, and includes the public buildings, the gaol, several churches, a bank, and some of the principal stores. The doors and windows on all sides of the laager have been secured by barricades, and the open spaces covered with wooden boardings, carefully loopholed, but subject to perforation by the bullet of a Martini-Henry at any distance under fifty yards. The entire front of the position can be raked from a couple of bastions placed at two opposing angles; but the laager is not yet provided with any sort of artillery.

Stores of provisions have been laid in, wells sunk, and instructions issued to the inhabitants regarding what must be done in case of an emergency. The ordinary European male population above eighteen years of age is returned in the Census of about 1800; but the city contains at the present moment a great number of strangers. The defence of the city will be conceded wholly to the inhabitants, the military confining their exertions to Ford Napier, which has been rendered a practicably impregnable post. It mounts ten or a dozen guns of various date, shape and calibre; but apparently there are more guns than gunners. However, if the Zulus are well advised they will certainly give Fort Napier a wide berth, and they will do well to be almost equally cautious in their approach to the city laager.

Our correspondent's sketch of the laager at Verulam shows a rather elaborate structure; the base of the wall is of stone masonry, white-washed; the upper part is of brick, likewise white-washed, and perforated with loopholes for the rifles of the garrison. The top of the wall is surmounted with broken bottle-glass which the naked Zulus would find it painful to climb over. The building behind this wall is the Verulam Court-house, with a zinc roof and a bamboo verandah.

Interior of Verulam laager, on the road to the Lower Tugela.
From our Special Correspondent.

The following is an extract from the letter of our Correspondent at Verulam, on the 11th ult:-

"After the exciting events of the last few weeks there is a great dearth of news. Our troops still hold their respective encampments, and are chafing at the delay consequent on the difficulties of transport, but very shortly a general advance into Zululand may be expected; for at the different dépôts large accumulations of provisions have been stored. All the main roads to Durban are protected by fortified laagers, so that in case of need it may afford protection to the surrounding inhabitants.

During the late scare after the disaster at Isandhlwana, Murray's hotel at Pinetown, a small village twelve miles from Durban, was speedily turned into an impregnable fortress in a very simple way. The modus faciendi was thus – a trench about 3 feet deep was dug, as to encircle all the outbuildings; iron rails were then placed on each side of the trench at regular intervals, and sleepers heaped up between them to the height of 10 ft; the exposed side of this wooden wall was then plastered over with mud, in order to frustrate any attempt of the savages to burn the garrison out.

Great hopes are now being entertained of saving 90 miles of carriage to the Lower Tugela by erecting a landing-place near Fort Durnford. H.M.S. Forester has been surveying the coast, and has reported favourably on the project. If this scheme could be effected it would greatly facilitate the movements of the troops at the Lower Tugela, besides saving the Government a large item of expenditure, for the freightage of goods from Durban to the Lower Tugela has reached the exorbitant demand of 20s. a cwt.

Many opinions are hazarded about the issue of the Zulu War, and I need scarcely say that very few of them point to the same conclusion. One thing is clear – that our troops have to contend with a more powerful destroyer than the Zulu. Invalid soldiers are being daily sent to Durban from the front; and a sergeant in the Engineers told me that now our men are beginning to feel the effects of the privations which they endured while they were cooped up at Ekhowe.

Sometimes only rotten biscuits were served out; and the men, being sheltered only by wagons, were often exposed to the rain. General Crealock has now seen the necessity of putting the soldiers under canvas, and a large number are now on their way to the Lower Tugela from Durban. Most of the fighting will take place near the sea-coast, as the Zulus are reported to be swarming in the bush, and the cold of the higher country will drive them down. In my next letter I hope to be able to speak of a brilliant victory achieved by our gallant troops, and a speedy termination of this ill-starred campaign."

Some later news from the Lower Tugela is given in the following letter from our own Correspondent, dated May 24:-

"A convoy returned from Fort Chelmsford this afternoon, but there is little to narrate of comparative importance from that quarter. Here are some items of news which may be interesting. Major Barrow has made a survey of the River Umhlatosi, and a drift has been selected as suitable for a temporary bridge. The Zulus at present command this crossing from a neighbouring hill, as was plainly demonstrated by one Zulu, who was surmised, by his correct aim from that vantage point, to be the happy possessor of a Martini-Henry.

A small body of the enemy was also seen in the distance on the top of a neighbouring hill. These little incidents tend to confirm the conviction that beyond the Umhlatosi River a firm resistance will be made to our onward march. The Engineers are taking advantage of the red clay on which the fort stands to construct an underground magazine, with galleries. They are at present mining below the centre fort. A marked improvement in the health of the troops is apparent by the decrease in the number of the sick conveyed in this return convoy as compared with former ones – there were only thirty-seven considered unfit. Of course, the hygiene might be better. Some hopes are now entertained that a favourable change has taken place; for the wind, which formerly blew from the St. Lucia swamps, and consequently conveyed malarious particles, has suddenly shifted to a more healthy quarter.

Captain Murray, of the Intelligence Department, has been absent two days on a reconnaissance, and a survey of the surrounding country almost up to Ekhowe was made. The bush was reported to be free from Zulus, but small fires were distinctly seen against the sky-line; no doubt small kraals were in close proximity. It helps to confirm the opinion that the Zulus are busily employed in gathering their crops, and that the peace negotiations made by Cetewayo are only a ruse to allow sufficient time for them to accomplish this purpose.

The tangible result of this reconnaissance was the capturing of five horses and sixty oxen; most likely they were stray cattle from our camps. A general advance movement will shortly be made by this column. Transport by oxen is slow and tedious, besides being a most expensive mode of locomotion, for the slightest amount of extra fatigue renders them unfit. They are then unyoked and left to die on the road side. It is said that the effluvia on the road to Fort Chelmsford is sickening. There is a bullock at about every 400 yards lying in a state of putrefaction; and, to make matters worse, the best part of the hides has been stripped by the natives for the purpose of making shields.

The sickness that was so prevalent while the troops were penned up at Ekhowe has been traced to the poisoning of the water used by the troops.

This was caused by animal matter silting through the clayey soil and impregnating the water. That the Zulus are no novices about the advantages of good health among our troops has been clearly proved by the finding of fifty dead Zulus heaped up in the river Inyezane for the evident intention of poisoning the water. All our soldiers are now under canvas. Formerly, before Major Crealock was appointed to the command, they were exposed to the night dews, and many cases of illness occurred solely through exposure.

The General immediately recognised the necessity of a reform in this respect, and many valuable lives have been saved through his promptness and foresight, for tents were rapidly sent up from Durban, and the exigencies and emergencies were dealt with so expeditiously that a favourable change in the health of the troops was the immediate consequence. Even the Natal Native Pioneers have tents. They are encamped close to Fort Pearson, on Euphorbia Hill; they are a fine body of men. The bravery of one of their number was conspicuously shown by his being the only man who volunteered to run the gauntlet from Ekhowe after two months' isolation of the garrison from the outward world. This daring feat he successfully accomplished on no less than three separate occasions.

There has been great dissatisfaction at the way which patients have been treated at the hospital at Hirwin; perhaps they arise from the insufficiency of accommodation there. An improvement is confidently expected when the wooden huts are completed; they are being built close to Fort Pearson, under the direction of Mr. Fynney. When our troops leave for the front the fears of the Natal colonists will greatly increase. All the practicable drifts of the Tugela will be strongly guarded, and no raid on the part of Zulus into Natal need be feared expect in large masses; of course this again is an unlikely contingency, for the savages have a peculiar dread of a hostile force in their rear.

The undermentioned officers under Major-General Crealock are all well known for their ability and energy, and the General may be congratulated in securing the services of so many valuable and experienced officers.

Major Walker, 99th Regiment, is Assistant-Adjutant-General; Captain Carden, 82nd, is Deputy-Assistant Quartermaster General; Lieut.-Colonel Law is commanding the Royal Artillery, Captain B. Lord commands the Engineers, Captain Murray, 13th Foot, is Deputy-Assistant-Quartermaster-General for the Intelligence Department, and Deputy-Commissary W.G. Gordon is the Commissary-General of Ordinance, while Assistant-Commissary-General Hasley is Commissary of Supplies.

The Aides-de-Camp are Captain Byng, Late Coldstream Guards; Lieutenant Hutton, 3rd Battalion 60th Rifles; Lieutenant Coleworth, R.N. Little reliance may be placed upon the reports of a cavalry raid up to the King's kraal; an expedition of this kind against such a powerful foe would be of a too hazardous nature. The volunteers stationed at Krantz-Kop made a raid into Zululand last Tuesday; their spoils consisted of 140 head of cattle, only one Zulu was killed fighting. These small raids are of little material value; it only shows the Zulus that we are not to be caught napping, and are prepared to meet any attack from their side."

The date of our latest news is to the 3rd inst. besides the lamentable death of the Prince Imperial, which is related and commented upon in a separate article, there is some additional military intelligence. But it seems uncertain whether the Zulus were prepared to resist Lord Chelmsford's advance into their country. The head-quarters of the Commander-in-Chief had been at Landman's Drift, on the Buffalo River, with those of General Newdigate's division, which had been joined by our Special Artist on the 19th ult. On the 28th ult. Lord Chelmsford and staff, with the remainder of Newdigate's column, left that place for Koppie Allein, on the Blood River.

The forces there, when the concentration is complete, will be the Lancers, Dragoons, six companies of the 21st, 58th, and first battalion 24th Regiment; seven companies 94th; Batteries G, E, and six Royal Artillery; Companies 2 and 5 Engineers; 1300 natives; 70 volunteers; together with the Military Train: Total 5670. Two companies of the 24th remain at Landman's Drift, and three at Dundee. The flying column of Brigadier-General Evelyn Wood was encamped at Munhla, but was about to move on to a point fourteen miles distant, on the Umpungina River. The following is a statement of Lord Chelmsford's plan for the advance, which would take place in the first days of June:-

"The dépôt at Conference Hill moves to Koppie Allein, and the column with one month's provisions and 300 waggons, will pass, if a reconnaissance proves the route to be practicable south of the Itelezi Hill. If not, north, passing the Incotu Mountains and Inlhabaumkosi on the right, and meeting Wood twenty miles from Ibabanago; then, together with Wood, moving in advance to Ibabanago, where the column will entrench and wait, riding and reconnoitring, while the wagons, with a strong convoy, return for fresh supplies.

When supplies arrive a force, the strength of which is hereafter to be determined, abandoning tents, and advancing in light order with six week's provisions, will make a dash at Ulundi and destroy five large military kraals there, the usual rendezvous of over 30,000 men during the feast of first fruits and other occasions. Further movements depend partly on the lower column.

At night on the march each column will form two laagers echeloned, the cattle between them and the cavalry outside. The troops will always be under arms an hour and a half before daylight. The Dragoons will be employed in reconnoitring. One wing goes to Rorke's Drift and will remain reconnoitring toward Isipezi Hill and northward to prevent an impi from assembling on the right flank of the column.

The other wing will perform the same office on the left flank. The two companies of the 94th stay at Conference Hill, and keep the road to Utrecht open, as on the north natives make daring raids. Three companies of the 21st go to Koppie Allein. After the middle of this month it will be impossible to forward more forage to the columns, the Free State supplies ceasing. The cavalry must then work down to the coast. At present there are two months' supplies at the front. The commissariat has latterly been very vigorous. After the advance Landman's Drift will be the head dépôt."

Brigadier Wood reports that a chief twenty-three miles off has sent to say that he wishes to surrender, but is afraid unless our soldiers are near. He states that Cetewayo does not want peace, and has ordered the Zulus to assemble between Zlobane and Inyezane. Sirayo's and Nikandi's men, and the Mageni, Mkobamatosi, and Amakandah regiments have left Ulundi to attack the British army on its march.

Mr Moodie, magistrate of Ladysmith, collecting native hut tax.
From a sketch by our Special Artist, Mr. Melton Prior.

THE HUT TAX IN NATAL

One of our Special Artist's sketches in Natal, on his way to the front, in order to join the army of Lord Chelmsford for the advance into Zululand, represents a scene which belongs to the ordinary civil administration of the British Government in that South African province.

Mr. Moodie, the resident official magistrate at Ladysmith, was sitting day after day for more than a fortnight, with his clerks at a table under the tree in front of his abode, to receive payment of the hut tax yearly due from all the Zulu and other native householders of every kraal or village in his district. The tax is fourteen shillings upon each hut, and every Zulu or Kaffir husband, who possesses a number of wives, is obliged to keep each of them, with her children, in a separate hut, so that a polygamist has to pay rather heavily to the British Government for his extravagant indulgence in such multiplied matrimony. But this system is a very bad one, and it has long been complained of by the missionaries and others who feel a sincere interest in the moral and social welfare of the native African people. The female sex are terribly oppressed by their domestic tyrants, even under British rule.

DEATH OF THE PRINCE IMPERIAL

The unhappy and inglorious warfare in South Africa, begun last January without the authority of her Majesty's Government, has already cost the lives of many young Englishmen, officers of the ill-fated 24th and other regiments whose portraits have been given in this Journal with such brief notices as were acceptable to the feelings of their bereaved parents and private friends.

It has been our willing task in each of these mournful instances, with the permission, or more frequently at the express request of the afflicted relatives, to minister such poor consolation as might be afforded by the publicity thus bestowed upon the memory of a lost son or brother; and we have not, as is the ordinary practice in time of war, restricted it to the cases of distinguished men in the higher military commands.

The same kind and degree of public condolence must now be accorded by us to the French Imperial family, and especially to the widowed Empress residing at Chiselhurst, upon the sad fate of a youthful Prince who had been educated with English comrades of his own age at the Royal Military Academy of Woolwich, and who was personally known to the members of our own Royal family, as well as to many other people of rank and station in this country.

It was on Friday, yesterday week, that the news which had arrived on the night before, and which had been communicated by the Secretary of State for War to the House of Commons at a late hour, spread through the whole kingdom and all over Europe. There was but one feeling of regretful sympathy, upon the merely personal ground of a great sorrow having befallen those of an illustrious household by the sudden termination of an interesting and promising life in the early years of manhood; and with the grief of a mother deprived of her only child, after losing her husband, the late Emperor Napoleon III, since they came to dwell amongst us.

No consideration of the political consequences, which might or might not possibly accrue hereafter from his premature decease, to the future state of parties in France, or to the relative prospects of the Imperialist and Republican forms of government there, has been permitted to enter the English public mind. We can regard such questions, which Frenchmen alone have a right to decide for themselves, with comparative indifference to the result, only desiring that France may enjoy secure peace and prosperity, and may long possess and improve the institutions most agreeable to her own people.

The Prince Imperial – Napoleon Eugène Louis Jean Joseph Bonapart, sometimes called Prince Louis Napoleon – was born at the Palace of the Tuileries, in Paris, on March 16, 1856. It was during the sittings of the Congress of Paris for the conclusion of peace between Russia and the Western Powers. The French and English courts and reigning families were at that time in the habit of corresponding with each other upon terms of intimate friendship. In the third volume of the "Life of the Prince Consort," edited by Mr. Theodore Martin, under her Majesty's direction, we find messages to our Queen from the Emperor, reporting the condition of the Empress in a difficult and dangerous childbirth, followed by a letter to the Prince Consort, in which he says:-

"Let me thank your Royal Highness for the congratulations you have been so kind as to send me. I received your letter and that of the Queen an hour after I had written to her; so that I do not venture again to weary her with my letters, but I beg you will once more express to her all my gratitude. I have been greatly touched to learn that all your family have shared my joy; and all my hope is that my son may resemble dear little Prince Arthur, and that he may have the rare qualities of your children. The sympathy shown on this last occasion by the English people is another bond between the two countries; and I hope my son will inherit my feelings of sincere friendship for the Royal Family of England, and of affectionate esteem for the great English nation."

The Emperor Napoleon III. was at that date approaching his forty-eighth birthday, and the Empress Eugénie, born May 5, 1826, was nearly thirty years of age. They never had any other child. The infant Prince Imperial was brought up in France, usually at St. Cloud, under the constant supervision of his parents, till the overthrow of the Empire, by the defeat of the French armies in the war of 1870, when the Empress and her son came to England, and were afterwards here rejoined by her husband.

The Empress of the French and the infant Prince Imperial.

We venture to reproduce, in this week's Number of our Journal, two pleasing little memorials of the infancy of the Prince Imperial, which appeared in the *Illustrated London News*, respectively, on Aug. 28. 1858, and on Sept 3, 1859. Every little boy in the world has ridden a toy horse and has played at soldiering; the child of the Emperor Napoleon III was sure to inherit a taste for such amusements, and to be allowed its full gratification.

In his fourth year, a Grenadier of the Guard.

At the age of two and half, on a toy horse.

Aged eighteen, a cadet of Woolwich.

In accordance with the usual custom for princes of the Continental reigning families, his name was inscribed, in the first days of his baby-hood, on the list of soldiers in a crack regiment, the Grenadiers of the Imperial Guard; and he was promoted to the rank of Corporal at six years old. General Frossard was charged with the superintendence of his education when he passed from under the care of an English governess. His companion at lessons and play was a boy of the same age, a son of Dr. Conneau, the physician and attached friend of Napoleon III., by whose assistance, in 1846, the future Emperor was enabled to escape from his prison at Ham.

The literary studies of the Prince Imperial were directed by a competent private tutor. He was, of course, perfectly instructed in the physical accomplishments and exercises befitting his position, riding, fencing, and gymnastics, to which much attention is devoted in the training of French youth of the upper class. He sometimes accompanied the Emperor's hunting parties in the Forest of Fontainebleau, attired in a huntsman's dress of green, with a silver horn, in chase of stag or deer.

As he grew older he was permitted, with Louis Conneau, to enjoy one or two summer excursions in different provinces; rambling through Lorraine upon one occasion, in 1866 quite innocent and unsuspicious of the tremendous events that were to change the political destiny of that fine country; and in 1868 they visited Corsica, the historic cradle of the Bonaparte family, attending the centenary festival of the annexation of that island to France.

So passed the juvenile years of the Prince Imperial, till the commencement of the great war between France and Germany, in July, 1870. The Emperor, when he started from Paris to join the army between Metz and Saarbrück, took with him the Prince his son, then aged fourteen, with the rank of Sub-Lieutenant in the Guards. He was present at the battle of Spicheren, on the hills above Saarbrück, early in August, when, as the Emperor informed the Empress in a despatch published immediately afterwards, "Louis a fait son baptême de feu" – that is to say, in plain unaffected language, he had an opportunity, for the first time, of standing the fire of an enemy's guns. The Prince, however, was not long allowed to partake with his father the experiences of that unfortunate campaign, but was sent back to Paris when the French army began to retreat.

The disastrous battle of Sedan, on Sept.2, with the surrender of Napoleon III., as a prisoner of war, caused the speedy over-throw of the French Empire, and the Empress, with the Prince Imperial, betook herself to England for refuge. The Emperor, being soon released from his captivity at Wilhelmshöhe by the termination of the war, came to live with his family at Camden Place, Chiselhurst. But his health was greatly impaired, and in January, 1873, he died there, surrounded with many tokens of public and private respect, leaving the widowed Empress and the young Prince, not yet seventeen years of age, to inherit the regard of those who approved some parts of the Emperor's conduct, and who did justice to the better features of his character.

The Prince Imperial, as we have observed, became an Artillery Cadet, and a pupil of the royal Military Academy at Woolwich, continuing to reside with his mother at Chiselhurst, which is but a few miles distant. His behaviour as a student, and the assiduity with which he applied himself to the scientific and practical lessons of that establishment, have been attested by those well acquainted with its discipline, and by the figure he has made in official examinations.

He had exhibited a degree of proficiency that fairly entitled him to be rewarded with a Commission in the Artillery; but he was advised not to enter the regular service of the British Government, probably in consideration of the views of French political partisans, who looked upon him as de jure Emperor, and who had, upon his twenty-first birthday, formally renewed their expressions of allegiance to the heir of Napoleon III. It is scarcely worth while to inquire, what may have been the expectations or the wishes of the Prince himself, or how far his outward attitude, in this respect, may have been determined by a not unbecoming deference to the opinions of his elders, and especially to the example of his illustrious father, whose memory would be associated with the maintenance of his claim to rule over the French nation, as representative of the Bonaparte dynasty.

The young prince was certainly not deficient in courage of any kind; he had much spirit and love of enterprise, and was not averse to win his share of distinction in the world, but he does not seem to have been engrossed by visions of political ambition, such as haunted the youth of the late Emperor. It is doubtful whether he would ever have been tempted to risk any wild adventures like those of Strasbourg and Boulogne, or to solicit the votes of a democratic National Assembly, as in 1848, for the post of

In Memoriam – the late Prince Imperial.

AT CHISELHURST

ZULULAND

EN ROUTE TO ZULULAND.

President of the Republic, with the possession of administrative power, and a stepping-stone to the Empire of 1852.

This Prince might some day have been made Emperor by the contrivance of others, but would hardly, in any combination of circumstances, have raised himself to the throne by his own exertions. He was not the less favourably regarded, on that account, by the majority of our own countrymen, who have been averse to look forward to more French Revolutions, desiring a permanent and tranquil settlement of affairs in the government of that nation.

The Prince went through a two years' course of studies, as a gentleman cadet, in the Royal Military Academy, entering that institution on Nov.18, 1872, and remaining till the close of 1874. His studies were continued without intermission, except for a short period, in January and February, 1873, when he was kept at home by the death of his father. He was prevented, by the same cause, from attending the periodical examination held about that time. He afterwards joined the first class of students preparing for the competitive examination to gain commissions in the Royal Engineers and the Royal Artillery. With this class he was associated during the remainder of his career at the Royal Military Academy.

He was at first under a considerable disadvantage, from his imperfect knowledge of the English language, in which instruction was conveyed to the students. But he succeeded in over-coming this difficulty by his unremitting diligence and industry, and in every subsequent examination he obtained a higher place. The final result was, at the examination in February, 1875, that he stood seventh in a class of thirty-four, which entitled him to a commission either in the Royal Artillery or the Royal Engineers, if he had chosen to enter the British Army. The total number of marks he obtained in the general examination was 31,615; he passed sixth in mechanics and mathematics, seventh in fortifications and artillery, first in horsemanship, and fifth in gymnastics.

The Governor of the Royal Military Academy, General Sir Lintorn Simmons, in his report to the Duke of Cambridge, Commander-in-Chief, stated that "the Prince Imperial, by his invariable punctuality and exactitude in the performance of his duties, by his perfect respect for authority and submission to discipline, has set an example which deserves honourable mention among his comrades of the commission class, who are commended in high terms for their excellent conduct and sense of duty."

We may also quote the remark of Dean Stanley, preaching in Westminster last Sunday morning, when he spoke of the late lamented Prince, of the circumstances of his life and death, and of the character he had earned during his residence among us, "We also know of him," said Dean Stanley, "as he passed as a student in our own renowned Academy at Woolwich, winning the friendship of his companions, and achieving his first honours without fear or favour in that branch of the profession which had attracted the studies of his father and his uncle. He, young as he was, has left a stainless name behind him, honoured and respected even by his adversaries.

To his comrades; to you, English young men; to you, English boys, as I have been told by many who knew him best, to you, I say, he has left the best legacy possible – the example of a faithful and earnest friend, the example of a pure life and clean lips. To the country who had sheltered his fallen family he gave what he could, his service and his life. He won for himself the sympathy, he won for himself something at least of the soldier's glory, which in his case was so dear, without the dark shadow of slaughter and bloodshed."

This was Dean Stanley's pulpit testimony last Sunday in favour of the Prince Imperial's brief yet distinguished career. With regard to his occupations at Woolwich, it may be added that he held the rank of Corporal in the Cadet Battalion there, and was highly commended, at the field-day manoeuvres on Feb. 16, 1875, for the manner in which he put the battalion through its manual and platoon exercise. One of the Portraits we have engraved represents him in the full uniform of that corps; another shows him in undress uniform as a Woolwich Cadet.

The Prince left England four months ago to join the army in South Africa under command of Lord Chelmsford. His motive was probably no other than the natural inclination of a young man, who had been brought up with ideas of soldier-ship, to take part in some active field operations. He did not belong to the Army, and could not, therefore, expect to obtain any military rank. His position would be simply that of a volunteer, nominally placed on the Staff of the Commander-in-Chief, and really the guest of Lord Chelmsford at headquarters.

The two private letters of introduction with which he was furnished by the Duke of Cambridge on Feb.25, the day before his departure from this country, were read in the House of Lords on Monday last. They may here be quoted as showing precisely the manner in which the young Prince was unofficially assisted to gratify his own personal desire.

In writing to Lord Chelmsford, the Duke of Cambridge said of the Prince Imperial that "he is going out on his own account to see as much as he can of the coming campaign in Zululand. He is extremely anxious to go out and wanted to be employed in our army; but the Government did not consider that this could be sanctioned, but have sanctioned my writing to you and to Sir Bartle Frere to say that if you can show him kindness and render him assistance to see as much as he can with the columns in the field I hope you will do so. He is a fine young fellow, full or spirit and pluck, and having many old cadet friends in the Artillery, he will doubtless find no difficulty in getting on, and if you can help him in any other way, pray do so. My only anxiety on his account would be that he is too plucky and go-ahead."

In the letter to Sir Bartle Frere his Royal Highness stated that the Prince was going out "to see as much as he can of the coming campaign in Zululand in the capacity of a spectator. He was anxious to serve in our army, having been a cadet at Woolwich; but the Government did not think that this could be sanctioned. But no objection is made to his going out on his own account, and I am permitted to introduce him to you and to Lord Chelmsford in the hope and with my personal request that you will give him every help in your power to enable him to see what he can. I have written to Chelmsford to the same effect. He is a charming young man, full of spirit and energy, speaking English admirably, and the more you see of him the more you will like him. He has many young friends in the Artillery, and so I doubt not with your and Chelmsford's kind assistance he will get on well enough."

These letters plainly show that the Government and military authorities at home did not intend to accept the services of the Prince Imperial as a military officer. He was not to be placed under Lord Chelmsford's command, but was received by his Lordship simply as a visitor.

Upon his arrival at Capetown, in the absence of Sir Bartle Frere, he was entertained by Lady Frere at Government House, but lost no time in going on to Natal. There he became the guest, at Pietermaritzburg, successively of Sr. Bartle Frere and of Lieutenant-Governor Sir Henry Bulwer, till he reached the head-quarters of General Lord Chelmsford, whom he first met at Durban on April 9. There are but scanty notices of what he did and experienced in the months of April and May; he was ill with a slight fever during two or three weeks of that time. In the latter part of May, being on the general staff, he was attached to the cavalry corps of Colonel Redvers Buller, V.C., C.B., operating on the northern frontier of Zululand.

The following account of a reconnaissance in which the Prince Imperial took part, before the one in which he met his death, is taken from the *Natal Witness*, the correspondent of which was with Brigadier Wood's Flying Column:-

"May 16

"I returned this afternoon from a three days' patrol, in which little was done, little was seen, and many were disappointed. The force numbered about sixty of the Frontier Light Horse, under Captain D'Arcy and Lieutenant Blaine; forty of the Basutos, under Captain Cockerell and Lieutenants Henderson and Raw, and about eighty of Baker's Horse, the whole being under the direct command of Colonel Buller. This active commander was accompanied by the Prince Imperial, Lord W. Beresford, A.D.C. (who has already made himself familiar with the country) and Mr. Drummond.

We first went to Conference Hill, where the tents of the 94th are now pitched; and a more uninteresting, bare, and stony spot to pitch tents on could not be discovered elsewhere outside the Kalahara. The forts are, it must be said, really good. They are firm, square, grim, and fixed. From Conference Hill we went afterwards to a farmer's house about five miles off, and here we bivouacked while our horses fed contentedly in the mealie-fields. At dawn next morning the troops took a slightly southerly course, crossing the Blood River and passing on to a hill from which one could see Rorke's Drift some four miles distant.

The country from Conference Hill is open, and a good road might easily be made between the two camps. We off-saddled at a kraal where the Zulus had been overnight – in fact, a few of their number had been there that morning, but did not wait for us. I saw them making off up Sirayo's Hill, just opposite, and they did not stop until they reached the top, when they took instant proceedings to call a gathering of the clan.

The town-crier, on a grey horse, gave due notice to all citizens living in kraals; and very soon we beheld, from our halting-place below, a respectable assembly of blackskins on the ridge above. The man on the grey horse acted as general as well as town-crier, and divided his forces judiciously. He posted his infantry on the left and the cavalry on the right of the pass. The infantry I should say, numbered fifty, while the horsemen could only muster eight. Opposed to this army was Colonel Buller's Irregular Horse. Some of the young hands thought a bloody conflict was about to be fought out on the hill-side; the older hands calculated that the Zulus would disappear as soon as we move upwards.

The older hands were right. When Lieutenant Raw, who had been sent on ahead with six of his Basutos, reached the summit, he found himself in undisputed occupation of the field. After galloping about from point to point, the Prince espied a Zulu on a distant kopje, and made after him. Off went Lieutenant Raw and the six Basutos after the impatient Prince, and on came Baker's Horse in the wake of the Basutos. The kopje was reached in time for them to see a few scared Zulus making off across country, far down on the plains below. In the hope that one bullet out of fifty might find a billet in a black man's body, Baker's Horse opened fire upon the flying specks beneath. There were no casualties.

On our right was Isandhlwana, about us the valleys in which the Zulu army concealed themselves before making that terrible onslaught on the unsuspecting troops. Away on the left rose the flat-headed Mhlazatze. Round the base of the hill, on which we were Colonel Buller noticed four large kraals, and at once decided upon burning them. Baker's Troop and the Frontier Light Horse went away down the north-west slope of the mountain, and burnt the kraals there, while Colonel Buller, with the Basutos, descended on the south-east slope, coming out upon a kraal where the Zulus had been recently engaged in shelling mealies. When the horses had had their fill these were destroyed, and we proceeded to another kraal, where we were joined by the other mounted men.

After this we proceeded homewards. The wind blew cold, most bitterly so; and for those who had no blankets there was no sleep that night. The Prince was among the forlorn and coverless ones, and he wandered up and down disconsolately. Next day nothing occurred. We breakfasted, we dined; we saw no Zulus, killed nothing; met with no accidents, and got into camp as quiet as you like. Those who know the Zulus say the patrol has done great good in burning the kraals as such acts teach the natives that we mean to thoroughly suppress them. One thing has been ascertained, and that is that there are no Zulus in any number in the north-east corner of Zululand."

The fatal occurrence which we have now to deplore took place on the 1st inst., between four and six miles from the camp of Brigadier-General Wood at Itelezi, east of the Blood river on the frontier of the Transvaal territory bordering Zululand. It seems that the Prince was there, apparently not under Brigadier Wood's command, but acting with the staff of General Newdigate, whose head-quarters were not far removed, and who was sending out reconnoitring parties in this direction. His Imperial Highness was associated with the Deputy-Assistant-Quartermaster-General, Lieutenant J. Brenton Carey, of the 98th Regiment, and was making his skill as a draughtsman available to furnish topographical sketches of the neighbouring positions.

For this purpose, on the morning of June 1, his Imperial Highness rode out with Lieutenant Carey, and with an escort of six white men of Berrington's Horse and one Zulu guide, in order to survey and sketch the next proposed camping-ground, which was about eight miles distant. Their day's work had been undertaken, for the Intelligence Department, by orders of the Assistant-Quartermaster-General; but Lord Chelmsford, who was not then at the advanced head-quarters, did not know, as he says, that the Prince had been detailed for this particular duty.

We have, as yet, no direct report of what happened from Lieutenant Carey, nor any despatch from his immediate commander relating to this affair; but the facts seem to be generally agreed upon. The party rode over the ground they had intended to survey, and it is believed that the Prince made some sketches; they came to a Zulu kraal, or village of huts, which seemed to be deserted and empty. It was two miles from the Inshallami mountain. Near this kraal, the name of which is Edutu, they halted for brief repose in a field of maize or "mealies" where they probably ate a hasty lunch or breakfast.

The saddles were taken off their horses, and they were all quite at ease, not suspecting the near approach of their concealed foe through the tall stalks of the maize-plants. It is said that Lieutenant Carey first perceived a dark face grinning at them amidst the thick growth of corn, and that, when he gave the alarm the Prince exclaimed, "I see them too." The whole party at once started to their feet, saddled their horses in great haste, and endeavoured to mount and ride away, not being able to guess the number of Zulus by whom they were surrounded.

The enemy, or some of them at least, had muskets or rifles, with which they fired a volley close at hand; killing or wounding, as it seems, two of the troopers, who were afterwards found dead on the spot. The Zulus then rushed forth to attack them. The Prince attempted to mount his horse as the others did; but in so doing he took hold of the leather flap supporting the wallet attached to the saddle; this flap tore away in his hand. His foot slipped, and he fell, letting go the reins, so that the horse took fright and galloped away.

The Prince ran after his horse; and not being able to catch it, tried to escape on foot. There was a "donga" or gulley in the field, two or three hundred yards distant. Towards this, in the meantime, Lieutenant Carey and the four mounted troopers who got off had ridden at full speed. Having crossed it, on emerging from the long corn or grass, Lieutenant Carey bethought himself of the Prince. He looked back, and saw the Prince's riderless horse but not the Prince himself.

This seems to have been the first knowledge that Lieutenant Carey had of what had happened to the Prince in attempting to mount with his companions. However, it did not appear to Lieutenant Carey, who had only one or two of the troopers with him, that he ought to return and look for the Prince or attempt a rescue. They all rode away towards the camp at Itelezi; but, on the way, they met Brigadier-General Wood and Colonel Buller, with an escort of three men, coming to look for them.

Lieutenant Carey reported what had taken place, and the commanding officers went back to the camp, where orders were given for a strong patrol force to go out next morning and to recover the Prince's dead body if it could be found. Accordingly, on the 2nd inst., at an early hour, six troops of cavalry, under General Marshall, were conducted to the scene of this disaster. No Zulus were now met with, and it is stated that only twenty or thirty had been seen the day before.

An assegai, the weapon which slew the Prince Imperial.

The body of the unfortunate Prince Imperial was found lying in the gulley, a hundred and fifty yards from the Zulu kraal. It had been stripped naked and thrown in there; only a necklace was left, upon which were suspended a locket with medallion portraits and hair, and a scapulary, with an "Agnus Dei" or medal of the Virgin Mary, both of these probably the gifts of his mother. The Zulus had regarded them as magical charms or talismans, and had been deterred by superstitious fears from touching them. There were eighteen wounds on the Prince's body, none of them from bullets, but all from the stabbing assegai, or short spear, an Illustration of which deadly weapon is shown in one of our Engravings.

Two of the stabs had pierced his body quite through from the chest to the back; two had gone through the sides, and one had destroyed the right eye. The bodies of the two troopers of Berrington's Horse, likewise bearing marks of the assegai, were found at a few yards' distance. It only remained for General Marshall and the other British officers to remove the mangled remains of the unfortunate young Prince to the camp at Itelezi. A stretcher or bier was formed of blankets laid upon lances; and the corpse was laid upon this, after sending to the camp a message that it had been found, and that an ambulance should be provided to receive it. The bier was then lifted by the officers present who were highest in rank – General Marshall, Colonel Drury Lowe, R.A., Major Stewart, and several officers of the 17th Lancers.

They carried it towards the camp, to meet the ambulance, in which it was deposited, and there was a funeral parade at the camp that afternoon. The ambulance containing the Prince's body was then sent to the rear, and the body was to be taken to Durban, for embarkation at that port, and for conveyance to England, probably on board H.M.S. Tenedos, which lay under orders to return home. This is all we have yet learnt of the sad affair in South Africa, which has caused such deep affliction at the English residence of the bereaved Empress, and so much general regret amongst the people of this country, as well as in France.

Napoleon Eugene Louis, Prince Imperial.
Born at Paris, March 16, 1856. Killed in Zululand, June 1, 1879.

An incident of the Prince Imperial's visit to Scotland in the January of last year is recalled by the circumstances above related. So far as our present information goes, it would appear that it was his failure to mount his horse that led to his death. Yet the Prince was not only a bold but a most skilful rider. This was illustrated in a remarkable manner when he was the guest, along with the Prince of Wales, of the Duke of Hamilton, in January 1878.

On the Sunday on which the party at Hamilton Palace visited Merryton, for the purpose of inspecting the famous stud of Clydesdales belonging to Mr. Drew, the Prince Imperial leaped on the back of Lord Harry, a horse which had never been ridden before. The bystanders looked on with amazement, not unmingled with alarm, as he scampered round the yard, hardly knowing whether to admire or reprove the wildness of the feat.

THE EMPRESS, BEREAVED OF HER SON

At Chiselhurst, on the morning of yesterday week, the sad news was not allowed to come suddenly and unexpectedly on the Empress. Precautions were taken to prevent the newspapers being sent to Camden Place, and the servants were enjoined, in case they heard anything, to keep their lips closed.

Lord Sydney, who is the lord of the manor at Chiselhurst, arrived at Camden Place at ten o'clock, by special direction of the Queen, to break the news. The Empress, who had been looking forward to receiving a letter by this mail, could not at first believe the intelligence; but Lord Sydney had brought with him the official telegrams received at the War and Colonial Offices, and with these a message of condolence from Lade Frere.

The Empress was greatly afflicted, but she bore her truly inexpressible grief with much fortitude. Lord Sydney was the bearer of expressions of condolence from the Queen, the Prince and Princess of Wales, the Duke and Duchess of Edinburgh, the Duke and Duchess of Connaught, Prince Leopold, Prince and Princess Christian, and the Duke and Duchess of Tek.

The Queen also telegraphed to the Empress, expressing her deep sorrow and her heartfelt sympathy. The Prince and Princess of Wales did the same. The members of the French Embassy, where many messages of condolence have been received from Paris and other places – some from prominent members of the Republic – transmitted expressions of the deepest sympathy. In the afternoon many visitors arrived from London. Most of them were French subjects, who called at the Lodge and left their cards.

Major-General Sir Dighton Probyn came specially to represent the Prince of Wales, and at once drove to the house. There came also Prince Lucien Bonaparte, Lady Burdett-Coutts, the Marchioness of Lansdowne, the Belgian, Danish, and Swedish Ministers, Sr. John and Lady Lubbock, Lord and Lady Abinger, the Marquis and Marchioness of Ailesbury, the Duc de Frias, Prince Jacques Pignatelli d'Avignon, the First Lord of the Admiralty and Mrs Smith, Sr. W. Knollys, Colonel Kingscote, M.P., the Duc de Marino, the Marquis de Caux, the Marquis de Griell, General de Bülow, Count de Sponneck, secretary to the Danish Legation, Count Steenbock, and others.

The Empress on Saturday afternoon recovered considerably, particularly after visits paid her by the Duke of Cambridge and the Duchess of Sutherland. Her Majesty's principal physician, Baron Corvisart, issued a bulletin on Saturday morning announcing that the Empress has slept a little during the night, but that depression arising from great grief continued.

The visitors to Camden Place on Saturday were very numerous, amongst them being the Duke of Cambridge, the Duchess of Sutherland, the Turkish Ambassador, Mdlle. Musurus, the Austro-Hungarian Ambassador and Countess Karolyi, the Portuguese Chargè-d'Affaires, Sir Michael Hicks-Beach, Bart., M.P. (Secretary for the Colonies), the Chargè-d'Affaires of Japan, the Portuguese Naval Attachè, the Secretaries of the Austrian and Portuguese Legations, the Earl and Countess of Derby, Lady Inglis (sister of Lord Chelmsford), Lord and Lady Augustus Paget, Viscount Hinchingbrook, M.P., Lord and Lady Colville of Culross, Lady Foley, Lady Adeliza Manners, Lady Molesworth, Viscount Torrington, and General Sr. Hastings Doyle.

By the first train on Sunday morning arrived M. Rouher and Madame Rouher, and Lord Sydney. The latter had been specially ordered by her Majesty to call on the Empress and inform the Queen of her condition. The noble Lord was soon after enabled to telegraph to her Majesty the news of the improvements in the Empress's health. The Empress directed that the room which the late Prince occupied should have a temporary altar erected in it, so that her Majesty might hear mass.

The service was conducted by Monsignor Goddard, in the presence, besides the Empress, of the Duchess de Mouchy, Madame Breton Bourbaki, Madame d'Arcos, the Duc de Bassano, and Baron Corvisart. Though greatly affected, her Majesty displayed wonderful self-possession, and on the Duc de Bassano leading her to her apartment she observed to him, "I didn't think I could be so strong;" and Monsignor Goddard observed, "She bears her grief as a brave, noble, and Christian lady could only bear it." The father added that immense consolation had been derived by the Empress from the telegrams which had reached her from every part of the world. The Pope, through Cardinal Bonaparte, who is now in Rome, sent the Papal benediction and his condolence with the Empress in her great sorrow.

The visitors on Sunday were very numerous. Amongst those who entered their names were - Earl and Countess Tankerville, Earl and Countess Granville, the Marquis and Marchioness of Lansdowne; Vice-Admiral Sr. W.H. Stewart, Comptroller of the Navy, and Lady Steward; Viscount Holmesdale, M.P., Mr Childers, M.P. and Mrs Childers, Lord and Lady Odo Russell, Earl and Countess Stanhope, General and Lady Emily Hankey, Lord and Lady Rendlesham, the Hon. A. Yorke (Equerry to Prince Leopold), the Marchioness of Tweeddale, and Lady Stanley of Alderley.

In the village of Chiselhurst all the tradesmen showed their respect for the Prince by closing their shutters on Saturday. The interior of the little Roman Catholic church, in which are interred the remains of the late Emperor was draped in mourning, the walls being covered with black cloth. The altar was similarly draped, and on the cross was placed a wreath of immortelles.

Here, at an early hour on a Sunday morning, mass was said, and at the usual eleven o'clock service the church was crowded. The persons composing the congregation were without exception attired in deep mourning, and many of them had evidently travelled from distant places.

The sacred edifice presented its ordinary appearance, save the fact that the chair and prie-Dieu where the lamented young Prince used to kneel, were draped in black. For years past the Empress and her son have worshipped side by side, separated only by the vacant seat of him who was the husband of the one and the father of the other; and it is impossible to conceive the painful thoughts which must force themselves on the bereaved wife and mother, whenever she may next occupy her customary place in the church, and feel the absence of those who once filled the chairs beside her.

At the conclusion of the mass, which had been celebrated by Father Weale, Monsignor Goddard ascended the pulpit, and delivered a short address touching the sad event on which the mind of every person present was dwelling. The reverend gentleman was visibly overcome by his emotion. He took for his text 1 Peter, chap. v., verses 6,7,8, "Humble yourselves, therefore under the mighty hand of God, that He may exalt you in due time, casting all your care upon Him, for He careth for you," and speaking with considerable feeling, said:-

"It will be easily understood by all this morning that my duty is to ask you to pray earnestly for the Prince and the Empress – the dead son, the childless widow. The words of the Epistle from which the text is taken are wondrously appropriate – 'be humble under the mighty hand of God, and cast your care on him, for he careth for you.' It is utterly impossible for me to tell you forcibly enough of the grief I feel in losing one so generous and so brave.

We loved him so well that, as far as our judgement can go, he was so necessary for us. It seemed to us in our hearts that upon him rested the happiness of the country and glory to the Church of God. We trusted he would return to us; but God is wisdom, and his blow shows that no man is necessary. How unsearchable are His ways! The beloved Prince was taken away from us lest wickedness should guide his soul, but his lifeless remains will be brought here and laid beside his father's tomb.

Previous to his starting I wrote him a letter, reminding him that it was the season when all true Catholics approached the altar, and did their duty to the Church, lest amidst the hurried preparations for his

departure he should overlook this. The Prince had replied – and probably it was one of his last letters:-
'My beloved Curé, - I thank you for the letter you have written; it proves to me all the love you bear me; but I am anxious that the hour of my departure should not make me forgot my duties as a Christian. I will be present to-morrow, and receive for the last time the communion in the church of Chiselhurst, where I desire to be placed if I die. – Your most affectionate, Napoleon.'

The next morning he came and did the solemn duties. He knelt at his father's tomb and kissed it, left the church and went to the station – for the last time – but will be brought back here. We must pray for him; for although he was so good, so generous, and so wise – although he was a Christian in life, a Christian soldier in death – yet we must pray for him. He was taken so suddenly, and may, therefore, need our prayers. Let us, therefore, pray for him, earnestly and continuously – the only son of his mother, and she a widow. Her sorrow is too great. What is there left for her in this world but to die? All is lost! Pray for her. It will be a consolation for you to know that at half-past nine this morning I said mass at the house, and the Empress assisted. She is seeking consolation from above, and I ask that your prayers may be for comfort for the childless widow."

At the close of the service several of the congregation repaired to the Emperor's tomb, and spent some moments in devotion. There was another service in the afternoon, and mass celebrated in the chapel of Napoleon III.

THE QUEEN'S VISIT TO THE EMPRESS

The Queen, accompanied by Princess Beatrice and Prince Leopold, and attended by Lieutenant-General Sir H. Ponsonby and the Marchioness of Ely, left Windsor Castle at five o'clock on Monday afternoon on a visit of condolence to the Empress Eugénie at Chiselhurst. The Royal party on quitting the palace drove to the Windsor Station of the South-Western Railway, where the special Great Western train used by her Majesty in her journeys to and from the metropolis and about the suburbs of London was stationed in readiness opposite the Queen's private waiting-room, near the Datchet-road. Her Majesty was in very deep mourning, and the Princess was in black, as were likewise the suite in attendance upon the Queen and Royal family. Colonel Campbell, deputy-chairman of the South-Western Railway, Mr A. Guest, and Mr Govatt, directors, and Mr E.W. Verrinder, were present to receive the Queen.

The train left the station at 5.5, and proceeded past Richmond to Waterloo Junction, where the control of the train was transferred to Mr John Shaw, manager and secretary of the South-Eastern Railway. There was a large assemblage of spectators at Waterloo, who raised a ringing cheer as her Majesty passed slowly by the platform on to the Charing-cross section of the South-Eastern line, by which the Royal train proceeded on its way viâ London Bridge and New-Cross. Chiselhurst was reached at ten minutes past six o'clock. Outside the railway station, and on the road leading to the villas and the common, the highway was lined with spectators, among whom the best of order prevailed, while opposite the door leading to the platform was an open carriage and four bays.

Her Majesty, upon alighting from the saloon was received by Lord and Lady Sydney and Sir Edward Watkin, M.P., chairman of the South-Eastern Railway, who were in attendance upon the platform. General Sir H. Ponsonby escorted the Queen, Princess, and Prince to their carriage, Lord Sydney preceding the Royal party in his brougham, and a few minutes later her Majesty, amidst the loyal salutations of the bystanders, drove from the station.

There was a large gathering of people about the entrance to Camden Place waiting to see the Queen arrive. Her Majesty was received by the Duke de Bassano and the Duchess de Mouchy. Too weak to descend from her own room, for she has eaten little food for the last few days, the Empress Eugènie received the Queen in her boudoir alone, and without Princess Beatrice and Prince Leopold, who remained in another room. Her Majesty stayed with the Empress for upwards of half an hour. That the interview was painful in the highest degree may well be imagined, as the Queen appeared deeply touched and affected. Towards the close of the visit, and just as the Queen was leaving, Prince Leopold and Princess Beatrice proceeded to the chamber of mourning, where they remained for a few minutes before their departure from the mansion.

Her Majesty and the Prince and Princess returned from Chiselhurst shortly after seven o'clock, nearly half an hour later than had been arranged, visibly affected by what had passed. The Queen appeared to be in the deepest grief and shedding tears as she entered the saloon, while Princess Beatrice and Prince Leopold were evidently also overcome by emotion. Her Majesty remained standing in the carriage weeping till the train quitted the platform at ten minutes past seven o'clock on the return journey. The train arrived at Windsor about eight o'clock, the Queen and Royal family driving at once to the Castle.

The remains of the late Prince Imperial, it is believed, will arrive in England in about three weeks' time. It is expected that the garrison of Woolwich, at which the late Prince received his military training, will furnish the troops who will undoubtedly attend the funeral; but, as the body can hardly reach England before the second week in July, and the last duty will probably be deferred until a week later, no orders have yet been given on the subject, nor any arrangements made for the interment.

The funeral of the late Emperor was not attended with military honours, because his Majesty was residing in England simply as a private individual; but in the case of his ill-fated son it is felt that, although by law a foreign citizen, his connection with the British army, and the circumstance that he fell in the service of this nation, render it imperative that the honours invariably paid to a departed comrade shall not be omitted. The gentlemen cadets at the Royal Military Academy, amongst whom the Prince Imperial ranked as a distinguished senior, have a strong desire to attend his obsequies, and it is possible that they may head the procession and form the firing party. On its arrival in England the body will be taken directly to Chiselhurst, and it is understood that it will lie in state at Camden Place.

THE ILLUSTRATED LONDON NEWS

July 5, 1879

THE ZULU WAR

Evening promenade with the Royal Scots Fusilier at Landman's Drift.
A sketch by our Special Artist, Mr. Melton Prior.

Our Special Artist, Mr Melton Prior, contributes two Sketches of the camp of Major-General Newdigate at Landman's Drift, where the division commanded by that General, and accompanied by Lord Chelmsford with his head-quarters Staff, remained till May 28, removing on that day to Kopje Allein. These two places, with Conference Hill, which was at the same time occupied by Brigadier-General Evelyn Wood, form a triangle in the Utrecht district of the Transvaal territory, bordering on the western frontier of Zululand, and separated from it by the Blood River, a tributary of the Buffalo, their junction being at Rorke's Drift.

The isolated rocky hill named the Kopje Allein, which commands a drift or ford over the Blood River, on the main road from Utrecht into the Zulu country, is the most advanced position yet held, preparatory to the invasion of Cetewayo's kingdom. Major-General Newdigate's division consists of the 2nd Battalions of the 21st Fusiliers and 24th Foot, the 58th, and the 94th; the Cavalry Brigade, under Major-General F. Marshall, composed of the King's Dragoon Guards, 17th Lancers, and Lonsdale's Horse; the Artillery, under Colonel Reilly, C.B., M and N Batteries, 6th Brigade R.A., a Gatling Battery, and two companies of Sappers, under Lieutenant-Colonel Harrison, Acting Quartermaster-General.

One of our Artist's Sketches in camp shows the evening promenade in front of the tents of the Royal Scots Fusiliers (21st Regiment of the Line) to the rousing strains of their kilted "pipe major." This takes place almost daily before the officers' dinner-time, when friendly visits are exchanged from tent to tent, and there is an hour of social relaxation. It is to be hoped that bag-pipe music is equally agreeable to the Englishmen and to the Scotchmen in that part of the camp. It is the only music in the division.

The second Illustration is that of troops practising the manoeuvres which belong to the defence of this fortified camp against a possible attack. Every morning, an hour before daybreak, they are exercised in striking the tents and occupying their allotted positions on the parapet, which is lined by half the men, in single rank, while the other half stand in support; each company having its own allotted position.

Graves of men of the 99th Regiment at Fort Pearson.

The second battalion of the 21st, and the 58th Regiment, can strike their tents and occupy their positions in less than two minutes after the order being given. They are constantly practised also in volley-firing by sections. Lieutenant-Colonel W. Pole Collingwood, commanding the 21st or Royal Scots Fusiliers, has been placed in command of the 2nd Infantry Brigade, consisting of the 24th and 94th Regiments.

While at Fort Pearson, on the Lower Tugela river, soon after his arrival in Natal, our Special Artist made a Sketch of the graveyard in which are buried a few soldiers of the 99th Regiment, who died there in March last. This furnishes another Illustration of the Zulu War.

With reference to the war against the insurgent Basuto chief Morosi, in the mountain region west of Natal, around the sources of the Orange river, an Illustration of his formidable natural stronghold appeared in our last. It was from a Sketch by Mr Watermeyer, of Graaf Reinet, in the Cape Colony.

THE DEATH OF THE PRINCE IMPERIAL

We have the details of this lamentable event by the arrival of news from the Cape to the 10th ult. The report of Lieutenant J. Brenton Carey, 98th Regiment, Assistant Deputy-Quartermaster-General, who accompanied the Prince Imperial on the reconnaissance which led to his melancholy death, is as follows:-

"Having learnt that his Imperial Highness would proceed on June 1 to reconnoitre the country in advance of the column and choose a site for the camp of the following day, I suggested that, as I had already ridden over the same ground, I should accompany him. My request was granted; but at the same time, Colonel Harrison, Acting Quartermaster-General stated that I was not in any way to interfere with the Prince, as he wished him to have the entire credit of choosing the camp. Shortly before starting, I found that no escort was prepared, and applied to the Brigade-Major of Cavalry.

I received the necessary orders, and at 9.15 six men of Bettington's Horse paraded before head-quarters. With these and a friendly Zulu, provided by the Hon. Mr Drummond, we started. Six Basutos of Captain Shepstone's Corps were also under orders to proceed with us, and before crossing the Blood river I sent on to him to ask for them. The messenger returned to say that they would meet us on the ridge between the Incenzi and Itelezi Hills. I again sent the man with orders to bring the escort back with him. On our right and left flanks I saw large bodies of Basutos scouting. Arrived upon the ridge, we dismounted, wishing to fix the position of some hills with our compasses. Colonel Harrison then rode up and told us that General Marshall's cavalry was coming up.

When he had left I suggested to the Prince to wait for the remainder of the escort. 'Oh no; we are quite strong enough.' At a mile and a half we ascended a commanding and rocky range of hills beyond Ilyotozi River. I proposed that we should here off-saddle, but the Prince said that he preferred to off-saddle near the river. We remained for half an hour sketching and surveying the country with our telescopes. Seeing no one, we descended to a kraal in a valley below and off-saddled. No precautions were taken, as no Zulus were expected to be in the neighbourhood. The Prince was tired, and lay down beside a hut. The men made coffee, and I reconnoitred with my telescope.

At 3.35 I suggested saddling up. His Imperial Highness said, 'Wait another ten minutes;' but in five minutes gave me the necessary order. I repeated it, and then went to fetch my horse from the mealie-fields. I had saddled and mounted on the home side of the kraal when I heard his Imperial Highness give the order, 'Prepare to mount.' I looked round and saw his foot in the stirrup. At the same time I said, 'Mount,' and as the men vaulted into the saddles I saw the black faces of Zulus about twenty yards off, rushing towards us through the mealie-fields. They shouted and fired upon us as we rode off. I thought that all were mounted, and, knowing that the men's carbines were unloaded, I judged it better to clear the long grass before making a stand.

Knowing from experience the bad shooting of the Zulus, I did not expect that anyone was injured. I therefore shouted as we neared the donga, 'We must form up on the other side. See to the retreat of everyone.' On looking back I saw one party following us, while another on our left was attempting to cut off our retreat across the ridge. Meanwhile we were under a heavy fire, and after we had crossed the donga a man said to me, 'I fear the Prince is killed, Sir.' I paused, looked back, and, seeing the Prince's horse galloping on the other side of the donga, asked if it was any use returning. The Zulus had already passed over the ground where he must have fallen, and he pointed out the men creeping round our left. I paused for our men to come up, and then galloped on to find a drift over the Tomboeto River."

The evidence of the surviving members of the escort may be compared with the report of Lieutenant Carey. The names of the men were Sergeant Willis, Corporal Grubb, and Troopers Letocq, Cochrane, Abel, and Rogers. Abel and Rogers were killed.

The first witness, Sergeant Willis, said:- "We descended a hill to a kraal about a hundred yards from the Imbanani River. The kraal contained four or five huts. There was clear ground in front, but high grass and standing crops all round the other sides. We were ordered by the Prince to off-saddle, and, after knee-haltering, turned our horses into the grass. We lay down outside the huts and took some cooked coffee, while the Kaffir looked after the watering of the horses. At ten minutes to four the Prince gave the time, saying, 'Let the horses have ten minutes more.' The Kaffir drove up our horses, and at four we were ordered to saddle. The Kaffir said he had seen a Zulu across the river, going up the hill opposite.

We saddled as quickly as we could. The Prince then gave the order to mount, and all of us did so, except Trooper Rogers, who was trying to catch his led horse. A sudden volley was at that instant fired, and we all made our way out at once, except Rogers, and I saw him lying against the hut.

"Did you see the Prince? – I cannot say. I saw two men fall from their horses, but cannot say who they were, because I was galloping hard. About fifty yards in front was a deep donga, and when we caught up to Lieutenant Carey I was told the order was to make for Colonel Wood's camp. The Zulus continued firing after us as we galloped for 200 yards, and yelling. We got back to camp about seven o'clock, all together.

"How far do you think you went to the kraal? – About twelve or fifteen miles from the Blood river.

"How many Zulus do you think there were? – From the shots, I should say fifty. Corporal Grubb caught the Prince's horse and rode him in, leading his own. I never saw the Prince again. "

The second witness, Corporal Grubb, after a repetition of the first part, deposed: "We went, as near as I can guess, twenty miles from Blood River to a kraal. Before we got there the Prince told us to loosen girths, and went sketching with Lieutenant Carey to the brow of a hill. When he came back we mounted, and we went down to another kraal. The Prince came up, saying, 'You can water your horses at the river and cook your coffee.' We off-saddled there for an hour. The kraal had five huts, with a stone cattle-inclosure; two or three dogs were about, and there were traces of Zulus having gone away only shortly before we arrived. Tambookie grass six feet high, with Kaffir corn and mealies growing amongst it, was standing all round it except in front of the way by which we escaped. Here there was twenty yards of open ground.

We had our coffee while the native looked after the horses. The Prince said, 'It is ten minutes to four; we will saddle at four.' The Kaffir came up saying something which no one understood till I interpreted. It was that he had seen a Zulu at the river on the other side. We lost no time in saddling, fetching our own horses. The Prince gave the order, 'Prepare to mount.' I took the time from him. He took hold of his horse, and said, 'Mount.' The Prince mounted; but before we had time to get our right feet into the stirrups a volley was fired from the mealies. We were all seated except Rogers, who was trying to catch his led horse. The volley was fired from about twenty yards. The Zulus shouted 'Usutu,' and 'Here are the English cowards.' I turned round, saw the Zulus, and put spurs to my horse. As I went I saw Rogers behind a hut, to the shelter of which he had run, and I shouted out, 'Come along.' I saw him level his rifle at a Zulu. I rode on with Abel full gallop.'

"Who was leading then? – Lieutenant Carey and Cochrane. When we had got a few yards from the kraals a bullet struck Abel full in the back about an inch below his bandolier. He was half a length in front of me. I saw they were firing high, and so lay along my horse. Letocq passed me saying, 'Put spurs to your horse, boy; the Prince is down.' I looked back, and saw the Prince was clinging to the stirrup-leather and saddle underneath his horse for a few lengths, and he then fell. His horse, as far as I could make out, trampled on him. I unslung my carbine to have a shot at the Zulus, but the horse just then plunged into the donga, and I fell forward on his neck and lost my loaded carbine.

The Zulu War: "Ready !" At General Newdigate's head-quarters, Landmans' Drift.

When I recovered my seat I found the Prince's horse close beside me. I could not catch it, so I got behind it and drove it along till I caught up to Lieutenant Carey. He then said, 'Some one must catch the Prince's horse; and I replied, 'As my horse is fagged, I will catch it and ride it into camp.' I dismounted and caught the horse and rode it into camp. The Zulus made one rush at us, but we were too quick, and they continued independent firing till we were out of range. We rode on till we fell in with General Wood, Colonel Buller, and two mounted infantry. We made our report, and they, looking through their glasses, saw six Zulus leading away our horses. I saw no more of the Prince.

"What was the last order given? – The Prince said, 'Mount.' I heard no order after that, but at the sound of the volley I watched Lieutenant Carey. We all of us put spurs to our horses and galloped.

"How many Zulus were there? – I should say forty or fifty.

"What were the Zulus firing with? – From the whiz of the bullet that struck Abel, I know they had Martini-Henrys.

"Before you mounted, how were you standing? – We were in line, the Prince being in front of us. Our backs were to the kraal. "

The third witness, Trooper Cochrane, after some repetition of the preliminary evidence, stated: "We rode, I think, twenty miles from the river, meeting General Wood's column coming down the hill, about ten o'clock. We then went to a kraal between the hill and the river. The Prince there ordered us to off-saddle. We stopped an hour, when the Prince ordered us to saddle up again. When we had done so Lieutenant Carey said it was half-past three, and the Prince gave the word 'Prepare to mount,' and afterwards, 'Mount.' I was next to him. We mounted, but I did not see him do so. He was, I think, doing something to his bit.

All of a sudden a volley was fired at us, the Zulus giving a tremendous shout. The horses were frightened, and we could hardly hold them. Some broke away, and the rest bolted with us. When I got across the donga, or about fifty yards from the kraal, I saw the Prince on foot, closely pursued by Zulus. His horse was then galloping off in another direction. I saw no more of the Prince. I followed Lieutenant Carey. He gave no orders. About a quarter of an hour afterwards Grubb and Willis caught us up and told us that Abel, Rogers, and the Kaffir were killed.

"In what direction was the Prince running? – He was running after us.

"How many Zulus were pursuing him? – I think about a dozen.

"How far off were they? – About three yards from him. They had all guns and assegais.

"Was any effort made to rally or halt, or any attempt made to save the Prince? – No; we had only three rifles with us.

"How far did you gallop? – About two miles without stopping.

"Did anyone ask about the Prince? – No; we were separated."

Trooper Letocq gave evidence as follows:- "The kraal we came to last was about fifty yards above the river. Here the Prince told us to off-saddle, and then the Kaffir was sent into the hut to see if anyone was there. He went down afterwards to the river for some water, and we had coffee. After an hour the Prince ordered us to saddle up. When we had all saddled up he asked, 'Are you all ready?' and we said, 'Yes.' He then said, 'Mount,' and, just as we were springing to our saddles, the volley was fired from the mealies at fifteen or seventeen yards. We had gone to that very place to catch our horses.

When we were saddling up the Kaffir, who had been to the river to water the horses, said he had seen a Zulu going up the river away from where the volley was fired. I dropped my carbine and had to dismount for it. In remounting I was unable to get my feet into the stirrups: my horse was galloping so hard from fright. I lay across the saddle. I passed the Prince, but was unable to stop for him, having no power over the reins.

As I got clear away from the kraal I passed the Prince. He then had hold of the stirrup-leather and the cantle of the saddle, and was trying to get his foot into the stirrup, but his horse was going too fast. I said to him, 'Dépêchez vous, s'il vous plaît, Monsieur, et montez votre cheval.' He made no reply. He had not caught hold of the bridle; he could not keep up with the horse, and I saw it tread on him, and the Prince fell down. The Zulus were firing all the time, but I could not see them. I saw no more of the Prince. I followed Lieutenant Carey. He was leading at first, but some of us passed him.

We galloped two or three miles, the Zulus trying to surround us. I saw Grubb and Willis could not catch up to us, and asked Lieutenant Carey to wait for them. He said, 'We will cross the spruit and wait for them on the rise on the other side.' Grubb and Willis were 300 yards behind us, for their horses were knocked up.

"Were any orders given to stop or rally, or try to save the Prince? – No.

"Did any of you mention the Prince, or did Lieutenant Carey say anything about him? – No; all that I heard Lieutenant Carey say all the time was, 'Let us make haste, and go quickly.'"

The above evidence was taken by Captain Bettington on the return of the survivors. The testimony as thus given was signed by each witness as correct. The Prince's horse, a grey charger, was brought into the camp; and it was observed that the holster of the saddle was partly torn off. A military court of inquiry has been held, over which Major-General Marshall presided, but the result is not known.

The finding of the Prince's body on the day after he was killed, by a strong force of cavalry under Major-General Marshall, which brought it back to the camp at Itelezi, was described in our last. The body was found quite naked, and pierced with nineteen assegai wounds, lying in the donga or ditch. The necklace or chain, to which a locket was suspended, had been left with the body; also the Prince's watch and rings, and other trinkets, with a small reliquary, which the Zulus probably feared to touch, supposing them to be magic charms.

Interior of the lodge at Camden House, Chiselhurst : Signing the visitors' book.

There was a religious service performed by a Roman Catholic chaplain at the camp, and the body was subsequently removed to Pietermaritzburg, where it was received by the Lieutenant-Governor, the Colonial Secretary, and the officers of the garrison, and placed in the Roman Catholic church, where it lay in state. The remains were to arrive on the 11th ult. at Durban, whence they would be conveyed, escorted by the garrison, on board her Majesty's ship Boadicea, which would proceed immediately to Simon's Bay. There the body would be transferred on board her Majesty's troop-ship Orontes, in charge of Colonel Pemberton. The Orontes will be met by part of the Channel Fleet, as an escort of honour, and may be expected to arrive at Sheerness one day next week.

Sympathy : A sketch at the Lodge gate, Camden Place, Chiselhurst.

Another of her Majesty's ships will then convey the Prince's body from Sheerness to Woolwich. The officers and men of the Royal Artillery at Woolwich, as well as the cadets of the Royal Military Academy there, under General Sir Lintorn Simmons, will march with the coffin to Chiselhurst, where a solemn funeral will take place in the Memorial Chapel, at the tomb already occupied by the mortal remains of the late Emperor Napoleon III. We shall publish ample Illustrations of all these proceedings, besides the Sketches we expect to receive from Mr Melton Prior, our Special Artist in South Africa, showing the manner in which the remains of the Prince were conveyed from the head-quarters of the army to the capital of Natal, and to the port of embarkation, with the public honours that were bestowed upon it.

At Paris, on Thursday week, there was a funeral mass performed in the Church of St Augustin, which was attended by many persons of high rank, Queen Isabella of Spain and her husband, Lord Lyons and the other Ambassadors, Marshal M'Mahon, the Princes of the Bonaparte family, and many senators and deputies. In London, on Sunday last, and again on Monday and Tuesday, there were special services at the Roman Catholic Cathedral of Southwark, at the Pro-Cathedral in Kensington, and at the Church of St John of Jerusalem, in Great Ormond-street.

The residence of the Empress, Camden Place, Chiselhurst, has been daily visited by numbers of the aristocracy and upper class of society, who came to inquire about her Majesty's health and to leave messages of personal sympathy. Two of our Illustrations, one representing the scene outside, at the lodge gate, and the other that of visitors writing their names in the book kept at the lodge, show what has been witnessed there from day to day since the disastrous news reached England. We also give an Illustration of the interior of the room at Camden Place, which was used by the Prince for his private study; and his favourite riding hack, which bears the name of Stag, is the subject of one of our Engravings.

The death of the Prince Imperial was alluded to by the Prince of Wales in his speech last week at the dinner of the West London hospital. He spoke of him as "a brave young man, who was the guest of this country; and personally, " his Royal Highness added, "I can only say that a more charming or more excellent young man could never have existed, and if it had been the will of Providence that he should have been called to succeed his father as Sovereign of the great neighbouring country, I have every reason to believe that he would have been an admirable Sovereign, and that, like his father, he would have been a true and great ally of this country."

In like manner, the Duke of Cambridge, at the dinner of the Trinity House Corporation on Saturday, stated that the Prince Imperial was bent upon going to South Africa, from an intense anxiety to show his gratitude to the Queen and the country for the manner in which he had been treated while living in this country. "As to his conduct, I think there can be no doubt, he was a thoroughly good, high-minded, high-principled young man.

As to his courage, singularly enough I had observed on several occasions the intense dash in his character, and in a letter I have from him he thanks me for having given him a hint on that very subject. I had said to him that he should not run unnecessary risk or expose himself unnecessarily; I gave him that hint; but so strong was his desire to see service, and to show the noble spirit which dwelt within him, that he could not restrain his feelings in any way, and if the opportunity occurred he would only be anxious to go the front. The result is deplorable; but there can be no question that the feelings were noble and generous, and I am only grieved that a life so valuable should have been so unhappily cut off."

With the approval of his Royal Highness the Commander-in-Chief, a general subscription throughout the Army has been commenced to erect a memorial of the late Prince Imperial. The Prince of Wales and the Duke of Connaught, Field-Marshals Lord Strathnairn and Sir Charles Yorke, Lord Napier of Magdala, and the other officers of high rank, are on the committee. The subscription is not to exceed £1 from any individual contributor.

Our Portrait of the Prince Imperial, given as the Extra Supplement last week, is from a photograph by the London Stereoscopic Company.

THE ILLUSTRATED LONDON NEWS **July 12, 1879**

THE LATE PRINCE IMPERIAL

The late Prince Imperial : Mortuary chapel at St. Mary's Roman Catholic Church, Chiselhurst.

The recent death of this youthful member of an illustrious family, who, after receiving his education in England since the death of his father, the late Emperor Napoleon III., an exile amongst us, has fallen by a disastrous incident of South African warfare, continues to occupy a large share of public attention.

The mortal remains of the late Prince Imperial have already reached England, and the funeral is appointed to be performed on the day of this publication (Saturday), at eleven o'clock, at St. Mary's Roman Catholic Church, Chiselhurst. The following account of the proposed arrangements was made up on Thursday afternoon:-

Her Majesty's troop-ship Orontes, Captain G.R. Kinahan, from Simon's Bay, at the Cape, bringing the body of the Prince Imperial, was signalled off Plymouth on Wednesday. Having communicated with the authorities on shore, the Orontes proceeded up Channel to meet the Admiralty yacht Enchantress, either at the Spithead anchorage or at Portsmouth. The Enchantress was to receive the coffin from the Orontes on Thursday, and was to bring it on to Woolwich. It is expected that the Enchantress will arrive at Woolwich about four o'clock on Friday afternoon. The coffin will then be landed, and will be taken into the place for the ceremony of identification, as arranged by Major-General Turner and Major-General Younghusband, the senior officers of the Royal Arsenal.

At first the Guard-Room, not far from the entrance, was selected, but subsequently a more suitable place was found nearer the pier, being an isolated octagonal building at the western end of the wharf, formerly the Watergate Guard-room, but now used as an armoury by the 26th Kent (Royal Arsenal) Rifle Volunteers. The building is only about 24 feet in diameter, and contains but one room; but in shape and size, and in its dome-like appearance, external and internal, it will form an appropriate resting-place for the deceased Prince. The interior of this building will be draped with black. The coffin will be opened immediately and the official document of identification signed, and then the coffin will be again and finally closed; for the proposed inspection of the remains at Camden House, Chiselhurst, has been abandoned.

The removal of the coffin from Woolwich to Chiselhurst will take place on Friday evening, instead of Saturday morning, as at first arranged. It will be escorted by three squadrons of Royal Horse Artillery, and by the 5th Lancers. The Prince of Wales, the Duke of Connaught, and the Duke of Cambridge are expected to be present at Woolwich, as well as next day at the funeral.

It had been intended to have a simple religious ceremony during the transhipment of the remains from the Orontes to the Enchantress. The Rev. Father Ballard, the Naval Roman Catholic Chaplain at Portsmouth, and the Rev. W. Legrave, one of the military chaplains, were to be on board the Enchantress, and these clergymen, with Father Rooney, who comes by the Orontes, were to incense and sprinkle the coffin, and repeat a short service for the dead, the act of transhipment being announced on shore by the firing of twenty-three minute guns from the flag-ship Duke of Wellington and the lowering of the ensigns by the squadron.

These proposed arrangements were altered on account of the rough weather. Lieutenant-General the Hon. A.E. Hardinge, C.B., one of her Majesty's Equerries, with Prince Edward of Saxe-Weimar, Prince Joachim Murat, Comte Davilliers, Vicomte Aguado, Baron de Bourgorny, Marquis de Bassano, and Comte de Turenne were on board the Enchantress. The saloon on the after-deck has been transformed into a mortuary chapel.

On arriving at Camden House the body will be borne into the hall by officers of the Royal Artillery, where it will remain until the time appointed for the funeral, this (Saturday) morning at eleven o'clock, when the same officers or others belonging to the same corps will replace it upon the bier and the funeral procession will be formed. The gentlemen cadets from the Royal Military Academy, Woolwich, will lead the way with arms reversed, and the mounted band of the Royal Artillery will precede the gun-carriage. Among those who will immediately follow the remains as chief mourners may be expected the Prince of Wales, the Duke of Connaught, and the Duke of Cambridge. In anticipation of an immense crowd of spectators, ample arrangements have been made for keeping the ground. From Camden House to the little Church of St. Mary's, on the opposite side of the Common, is barely half a mile, and part of the direct route is along a narrow lane.

The most difficult parts of the way were avoided at the funeral of the late Emperor by a slight détour, and in the present instance those who will have charge of the proceedings have decided, after careful examination of the neighbourhood, upon a still more circuitous course, which will afford both a more convenient approach to the church and a longer line of observation for the spectators. The 5th Lancers have arrived at Woolwich from Brighton, and will be of service in keeping the line of march, in which duty other regiments will assist. Colonel Sir E.Y. Henderson, Chief Commissioner of Metropolitan Police, has been engaged at Chiselhurst in making his dispositions, which will be locally in charge of Inspector Wilson, of the R Division.

Three batteries of the Royal Artillery will be stationed on the Common, and fire minute guns from the time the procession starts from Camden House until the body enters the church. The Gentlemen Cadets will fire three volleys from their rifles as the body enters the sacred edifice, having previously formed a lane for it to pass through, and the officers who carry it into the church will file out at the side door, leaving the rest of the duties to the friends of the deceased Prince. A short mass and religious service will follow, and the ceremony will probably be concluded by twelve o'clock.

There have been during the week several changes made in the religious portion of the programme for the funeral this day, at St. Mary's Catholic Church, Chiselhurst. The changes have been made in deference to the wishes of the Empress, and sanctioned by the ecclesiastical authorities. It will be a Low Mass which will be offered for the repose of the soul of the Prince – not a grand High Requiem Mass, as at first intended. Bishop Danell, of Southwark, will say the Mass, which will be accompanied by the Rev. Dr. Crookall's music – the simple responsories of the matins – the choir also singing the "Introit," the "Kyrie Eleison," and other portions of the Gregorian Dead Mass. Madame Christine Nilsson has volunteered her services to sing some of the solos in the service, and the local choir will be supplemented by the treble singers from the choir of St. George's Cathedral, Southwark.

According to the Roman Catholic ritual, the "officiating priest" should meet and receive the remains at the door of the church. The Bishop of Southwark will perform that duty, sprinkling the coffin with holy water, and reciting the prayers proper to the occasion. A procession will then be formed, and the coffin will be placed on the catafalque in front of the alter, which, as well as most other parts of the church, will be heavily draped with black cloth. When the chief mourners, the members of the Imperial Household, and other prominent personages present are conducted to their seats, the Bishop will immediately vest at a side altar, and commence the Low Mass.

At the conclusion of the Mass the ablutions will be given with prayer, incense, and holy water, by Monsignor Goddard, Canon Bamber, Canon Drinkwater, Canon Doyle, and the Bishop respectively. The choir will be under the direction of the Rev. Dr. Crookall. As the church can only accommodate 250 persons, the attendance of the clergy, which would otherwise be very large, must on this occasion be limited. The inquiries for tickets of admission have been out of all proportion to the accommodation the church affords.

An Illustration of the mortuary or memorial chapel attached to St Mary's Roman Catholic Church at Chiselhurst, is presented on our front page. This chapel was erected by the Empress Eugénie, at her private cost, for the temporary resting place of her husband, the late Emperor Napoleon III. She laid the foundation-stone on June 7, 1873, five months after his death, the Prince Imperial taking part in the ceremony. The architect was Mr H. Clutton, and Messrs. Brass were the builders. The chapel is a small building, only 24 ft. long, 12 ft. wide, and 18 ft. high in the interior, but the exterior has an elevation of 40 ft., surmounted by two Imperial eagles and a cross. It communicates with the south-west corner of the adjacent church, and it has a private entrance for the sole use of the Empress.

The building is in the Gothic style of architecture. The exterior walls are of Bath stone, those inside of Caen stone, with a vaulted ceiling and polished marble columns. On the tesselated pavement are the Imperial crown and the letter "N" and "E" alternately. The sarcophagus, which was a gift of Queen Victoria, is placed in the centre, and the altar at the west end, to accord with the position of the holy table of St. Mary's Church, which is similarly placed. The chapel is lighted by three windows at the side, and one large rose window.

By the latest news from the Cape, which is to the 17th ult., we have accounts of the reception there afforded to the body of the Prince Imperial, which was sent from Natal on board H.M.S. Boadicea, and arrived in Simon's Bay on Sunday, the 15th. The coffin was at once transferred to her Majesty's ship Orontes, being conveyed upon a pinnace towed by the steam-launch of the Boadicea through a line of men-of-war boats, the crews of which stood with their oars peaked and their heads uncovered. Arrived at the Orontes, the coffin was lifted from the yard-arm and lowered on the shoulders of British sailors to the deck, where Dr Leonard, the Roman Catholic Bishop of Cape Town, with assistant priests, performed the usual service for the dead, while her Majesty's ship Active fired minute guns. The officers of the Active and the Boadicea, as well as of the Dutch men-of-war Van Galen and Silveren Cruis, which arrived on the previous day, took part in the solemn ceremony.

Sir Bartle Frere, Lady Frere, the Hon. W. Littleton, Captain Hallam Parr, Colonel Hassard, R.E., Mr G. Sprigg, and members of the cabinet, as well as many other visitors from Cape Town, were present and evinced marked respect, the deep grief of the Governor and Lady Frere being particularly noticeable. When the coffin was placed in the mortuary chapel, Lady Frere laid upon it a handsome cross of palm-leaves and immortelles; and the Misses Frere and Mrs Wright covered the steps with camellias and other beautiful flowers.

The Military Court of Inquiry which investigated the circumstances attending the death of the late Prince Imperial has concluded its sittings and has handed in a report. In this Lieutenant Carey is censured for his conduct on June 1, and regret is expressed at the inadequacy of the escort accompanying the Prince. The result is that a court-martial has been held on Lieutenant Carey. This was inevitable. As the indictment now stands, that officer is charged with misbehaviour in presence of the enemy when in command of the escort in attendance on the Prince Imperial. Lieutenant Carey contends that he was not in command of the escort – that at his own request he was permitted to accompany the Prince, but was specially ordered not to interfere with him in any way.

In this there is a direct conflict of opinion between the subaltern under trial and the Assistant-Quartermaster-General, Lieutenant-Colonel Harrison, R.E. Pending the trial, and until we have fuller details of the unfortunate occurrence, it is difficult to form an opinion as to the extent of culpability of either officer. As matters stand at present, Lieutenant Carey's indictment reads, "for having misbehaved before the enemy on June 1, when in command of an escort in attendance on the Prince Imperial, who was making a reconnaissance in Zululand; in having, when the said Prince and escort were attacked by the enemy, galloped away, and in not having attempted to rally the said escort or in other ways defend the said Prince." Colonel Harrison, replying to questions in court, says that in the matter of escort he was not ordered to treat the Prince as a Royal personage, but as an ordinary officer, using, however, due precaution.

The following is given by the *Daily News* as the finding of the Court of Inquiry:-

"The Court is of opinion that Lieutenant Carey did not understand the position in which he stood to the Prince, and in consequence failed to estimate aright the responsibility which fell to his lot. Quartermaster-General Harrison states in evidence that Lieutenant Carey was in charge of the escort; while Lieutenant Carey, alluding to the escort, says, 'I do not consider that I had any authority over it.' After the precise and careful instructions of Lord Chelmsford, stating, as he did, the position the Prince held, and that he was invariably to be accompanied by an escort in charge of an officer, the Court considers that such difference of opinion should not have existed between officers of the same department.

Secondly, the Court is of opinion that Lieutenant Carey is much to blame in having proceeded on duty with part of the escort detailed by the Quartermaster-General. The Court cannot admit the plea of irresponsibility on Lieutenant Carey's part, inasmuch as he himself took steps to obtain the escort, and failed; moreover, the fact that the Quartermaster-General was present on Itelezi Ridge gave Lieutenant Carey the opportunity of consulting him on the matter, of which he failed to avail himself.

Thirdly, the Court is of opinion that the selection of the kraal where the halt was made, surrounded as it was by cover for the enemy, and the adjacent difficult ground, showed lamentable want of military prudence. Fourthly, the Court deeply regrets that no effort was made to rally the escort and show a front to the enemy, whereby the possibility of aiding those who had failed to make good their retreat might have been ascertained."

Lieutenant Jahleel Brenton Carey, of the 98th (Prince of Wales's) Regiment of Infantry, lately holding the office of Deputy-Assistant-Quartermaster-General on the staff of General Newdigate, in the Zulu War, is a son of the Rev. Adolphus Carey, Vicar of Brixham, in South Devon. He was educated at the Staff College, and entered the Army as an Ensign in January, 1865, and became Lieutenant in March,

1868. The record in Hart's "Army List" is that he served with the Expeditionary force, under Brigadier-General Harley, in British Honduras, in February and March, 1867, and was mentioned in the despatches. The *Daily Telegraph*, in a leading article of last Tuesday, gives the following account of his family connections and of his own personal antecedents:-

"The maternal grandfather of Lieutenant Carey was that able and courageous sailor of Nelson's time, Sir Jahleel Brenton, who on board the Ceasar at Gibraltar, in 1801, and in command of the Spartan frigate at Cerigo, Pesaro, and elsewhere, not only did splendid service, but was also the brilliant commemorator of naval glories, and received a baronetcy for his blameless career. Mr Carey's brother, now Gunnery Lieutenant of the Triumph, wears the medal of the Royal Humane Society, for saving life on three several occasions. The unfortunate officer himself bears a most creditable record down to the late deplorable occurrence, and the details of his services, if we may rely on what has publicly appeared from those who are friends, almost exclude the possibility that he can be considered lacking in natural courage, understanding, or self devotion.

Educated at a French Lycée Impériale, he was of all officers at the front the best fitted to accompany the Prince, and to understand how precious that life was in view of possible contingencies. He passed from Sandhurst to a free commission in the 3rd West India Regiment in 1865, and was in sole command of the fort of Accra on the African coast at the early age of eighteen. Returning to Jamaica with his regiment, he volunteered for the Honduras War while still enfeebled by fever, and, indeed, bravely affected to be in good health lest he should be debarred from joining the expedition. Here he was favourably mentioned in despatches, especially for his skill and fearlessness in reconnoitring and drawing maps of the hostile country.

His regiment being disbanded, and he himself put on half-pay, he came to Hythe, and obtained a first-class certificate there; afterwards volunteering for the English ambulance in the Franco-German War, where he was thrice taken as a prisoner on the field while engaged in duty. The Société de Secours aux Blessés presented him with a diploma of thanks, as well as a cross and ribbon, in gratitude for his faithful services to the French wounded. His ability is answered for by the fact that he passed the Staff College with high testimonials; and his zeal for duty by his having volunteered 'for any capacity' in the Zulu War immediately after hearing of the Isandula disaster.

Sailing from England in the Clyde on March 1 last, he was thanked by his commanding officer for having spent the whole night at Capetown urging on the coaling of the ship, so that the reinforcements which she carried might arrive without delay at Durban. On the next day, when the ship was wrecked, he was again commended for his zeal and ability; while on the march up country to Dundee it was he who preceded the draughts of the 24th Regiment, surveying the road and marking out camping-grounds; and he, again, who, for his cool-headedness and skill, was placed on Lord Chelmsford's staff, and was appointed to survey and map the road of advance to Ulundi."

We learn by the latest news from Rorke's Drift, dated the 23rd ult., that the decision of the court-martial on Lieutenant Carey has been sent to England for confirmation. Lieutenant Carey returns to England at the first opportunity.

THE ZULU WAR

Our news from Capetown is to the 24th ult. Sir Garnet Wolseley arrived the night before, in the Edinburgh Castle, to take up his new office as Governor of Natal and the Transvaal and as High Commissioner for native and foreign affairs in territories north and east thereof, including the seat of war, with supreme military command. The remains of the slain at Isandhlwana were buried on the 22nd ult.

The plan of campaign as it at present stands is simple. General Clifford commands the base and line of communication from Durban to Utrecht. The line of the Tugela and Buffalo rivers from Fort Pearson to Rorke's Drift is held by battalions of natives commanded by British officers, and supported by detachments of the 24th Foot and King's Dragoon Guards. The army of invasion consists of three columns. No. 1, under Major-General Crealock, C.B., with its head strongly intrenched on the Umlalezi river, is being massed at Fort Chelmsford, and will shortly throw forward an advanced brigade to St. Paul's, an English mission station midway between its present position and Ulundi.

This force consists of Barrow's Mounted Infantry, Lonsdale's Colonial Horse, a battery of Royal Artillery, the Buffs, 57th, 3rd Battalion of the 60th, the 88th, 91st, and 99th Regiments, with a Naval Brigade and Barton's and Nettleton's Native Contingents. The 2nd Division, which is under Major-General Newdigate, C.B., is encamped about twenty miles east of Koppie Allein, and it has reconnoitred and cleared the country as far as Ababamengo, distant about fifty miles from Ulundi. This force consists of the 17th Lancers, a squadron of the King's Dragoon Guards, two batteries of Artillery, a Gatling battery, the 21st Fusiliers, the 1st Battalion 24th Regiment, the 58th, and 94th, with native contingents.

The northern column, under Brigadier-General Sir Evelyn Wood, V.C., K.C.B., is advancing in a south-easterly direction from its old camp at Kambula Kop, viâ Munhla Hill, on Ababamengo, where it will effect a junction with Newdigate's column, and then lead the advance on Ulundi.

It consists of Tremlett's battery, of Royal Artillery, the first battalion 13th Light Infantry, the 90th Light Infantry, and a wing of the 80th Foot, together with Buller's Horse. Lord Chelmsford's plan seems to be to move on to Ulundi with Wood's and Newdigate's columns from the westward, and then, sweeping round to the south-east, effect a junction with Crealock's advanced force at St. Paul's, and so drive Cetewayo into the north-east corner of Zululand. His rear in the direction of the Transvaal and Secocoeni's territory is well guarded by the 4th King's Own and the 80th Foot. When once Ababamengo is passed, General Marshall, with the Cavalry Brigade, will be intrusted with the task of patrolling the lines of communication and conveying the transport trains which must be pushed up from the base to the heads of columns.

Our Special Artist, Mr Melton Prior, besides his Sketches of the battlefield of January 22, at Isandhlwana, which he visited, and saw the unburied dead of the British Army, on May 21, contributes a view of the Fort and Camp at Dundee, in Natal, which is about thirty miles distant from the Zulu frontier at Rorke's Drift.

The Zulu War : Fort and camp at Dundee, Natal.
From a sketch by our Special Artist, Mr. Melton Prior.

ISANDHLWANA REVISITED

Our Special Artist with the British Army in Zululand, Mr Melton Prior, sends us the sketches we present in this week's Number of our Journal, the Engraving in one instance being a facsimile of his original Sketch, showing the hideous traces and relics of past slaughter on the disastrous battle-field of Isandhlwana, with the abandoned waggons and wreck of the camp, as found on May 21, when Isandhlwana was revisited, four months after the terrible event which cost nearly a thousand English lives.

It was on that day, as we have already reported, that General Marshall, with a strong detached force consisting of the 17th Lancers, one wing of the King's Dragoon Guards, two guns of the Royal Artillery, and five companies of the 2nd battalion 24th Regiment, with some Natal Volunteers and Natives, set out from Rorke's Drift for a reconnaissance in the direction of Isandhlwana. The distance is eleven miles, and the infantry troops did not go on all the way.

Our Artist writes as follows:- "The sight I saw at Isandhlwana is one I shall never forget. In all the seven campaigns I have been in – the Ashantee war, the Carlist war in Spain, the campaigns of Bulgaria and the Balkan and Roumelia between the Russians and Turks, and that of the preceding year in Herzegovina, and the Kaffir war of 1878 – I have not witnessed a scene more horrible. I have seen the dead and dying on a battle-field by hundreds and thousands; but to come suddenly on the spot where the slaughtered battalion of the 24th Regiment and others were lying at Isandhlwana, was far more appalling. Here I saw not the bodies, but the skeletons, of men whom I had known in life and health, some of whom I had known well, mixed up with the skeletons of oxen and horses, and with waggons thrown on their side, all in the greatest confusion, showing how furious had been the onslaught of the enemy.

Amidst the various articles belonging to them which were scattered over the field of carnage, were letters from wives at home to their husbands, from English fathers and mothers to their sons, portraits of those dear to them, and other homely little things, remembrances of the dearest associations. Skeletons of men lay on the open ground, bleaching under a tropical sun, along miles of country. The individuals could only be recognised by such things as a patched boot, a ring on the finger-bone, a particular button, or coloured shirt, or pair of socks, in a few known instances. And this could be done with much difficulty, for either the hands of the enemy, or the beaks and claws of vultures tearing up the corpses, had in numberless cases so mixed up the bones of the dead that the skull of one man, or bones of a leg or arm, now lay with parts of the skeleton of another.

The Lancers went about all over the field, often here and there quietly lifting the clothes off the skeletons, or gently pushing them on one side with their lances, to see what regiment they belonged to. I almost regretted to see this done, for it seemed like sacrilege. But this is a time of war."

The following extract from a letter of the Daily News' correspondent is likewise a correct description of the scene, and will serve as a further commentary upon our Artist's Sketches made that day on the spot:-

At the top of the ascent beyond the Bashee, which the Dragoon Guards crowned in dashing style, we saw on our left front, rising above the surrounding country, the steep, isolated, and almost inaccessible hill, or rather crag, of Isandhlwana, the contour of its rugged crest strangely resembling a side view of a couchant lion. On the lower neck of the high ground on its right were clearly visible up against the sky line the abandoned waggons of the destroyed column.

No Zulus were seen. Flanking parties covered the hills on each side of the track, along which the head of the column pressed at trot, with small detachments of Natal Carbineers in front of the Dragoon Guards. Now we were down in the last dip, had crossed the rocky bed of the little stream, and were cantering up the slope that stretched up to the crest on which were the waggons. Already tokens of the combat and bootless flight were apparent. The line of retreat towards Fugitives' Drift, along which, through a chink in the Zulu environment, our unfortunate comrades who thus far survived tried to escape, lay athwart a rocky slope to our right front, with a precipitous ravine at its base.

The Zulu War : The field of Isandhlwana revisited.
Facsimile of a sketch by our Special Artist, Mr. Melton Prior.

In this ravine dead men lay thick – mere bones, with toughened, discoloured skin like leather covering them, and clinging tight to them, the flesh all wasted away. Some were almost wholly dismembered, heaps of clammy yellow bones. I forbear to describe the faces, with their blackened features and beards blanched by rain and sun. Every man had been disembowelled. Some were scalped, and others subjected to yet ghastlier mutilation. The clothes had lasted better than the poor bodies they covered, and helped to keep the skeletons together.

All the way up the slope, I traced, by the ghastly token of dead men, the fitful line of flight. Most of the men hereabouts were infantry of the 24th. It was like a long string with knots in it, the string formed of single corpses, the knots of clusters of dead, where, as it seemed, little groups might have gathered to make a hopeless, gallant stand and die. I came on a gully with a gun limber jammed on its edge, and the horses, their hides scored with assegai stabs, hanging in their harness down the steep face of the ravine. A little further on was a broken and battered ambulance waggon, with its team of mules mouldering in their harness, and around lay the corpses of soldiers, poor helpless wretches, dragged out of an intercepted vehicle, and done to death without a chance for life.

Still following the trail of bodies through long rankgrass and among stones, I approached the crest. Here the slaughtered ones lay very thick, so that the string became a broad belt. Many hereabouts wore the uniform of the Natal police. On the bare ground, on the crest itself, among the waggons, the dead were less thick; but on the slope beyond, on which from the crest we looked down, the scene was the saddest, and more full of weird desolation than any I had yet gazed upon. There was none of the stark, blood-curdling horror of a recent battle-field, no pool of yet wet blood, no raw gaping wounds, no torn red flesh that seems yet quivering – nothing of all that makes the scene of yesterday's battle so rampantly ghastly – shocked the senses.

A strange dead calm reigned in this solitude of nature. Grain had grown luxuriantly round the waggons, sprouting from the seed that dropped from the loads, falling in soil fertilised by the life-blood of gallant men. So long in most places had grown the grass, that it mercifully shrouded the dead, whom four long months to-morrow we have left unburied.

As one strayed aimlessly about, one stumbled in the grass over skeletons that rattle to the touch. Here lay a corpse with a bayonet jammed into the mouth up to the socket, transfixing the head and mouth a foot into the ground. There lay a form that seemed cosily curled in calm sleep, turned almost on its face, but seven assegais stabs have pierced the back. Most, however, lay flat on the back, with the arms stretched widely out, and the hands clenched. I noticed one dead man under a waggon, with his head on a saddle for a pillow and a tarpaulin drawn over him, as if he had gone to sleep, and died so.

In a patch of long grass, near the right flank of the camp, lay Durnford's body, the long moustache still clinging to the withered skin of the face. Captain Shepstone recognised him at once, and identified him yet further by rings on the finger and a knife with the name on it in the pocket, which relics were brought away. Durnford had died hard – a central figure of a knot of brave men who had fought it out around their chief to the bitter end. A stalwart Zulu, covered by his shield, lay at the Colonel's feet. Around him, almost in a ring, lay about a dozen dead men, half being Natal carbineers, riddled by assegai stabs.

These gallant fellows were easily identified by their comrades who accompanied the column. Poor Lieutenant Scott was hardly at all decayed. Clearly they had rallied round Durnford in a last despairing attempt to cover the flank of the camp, and had stood fast from choice when they might have essayed to fly for their horses. Close beside the dead, at the picquet line, a gulley traverses the ground in front of the camp.

About 400 paces beyond this was the ground of the battle before the troops broke from their formation, and on both sides this gulley the dead lie very thickly. In one place nearly fifty of the 24th lie almost touching, as if they had fallen in rallying square. The line of straggling rush back to camp is clearly marked by the skeletons all along the front. Durnford's body was wrapped in a tarpaulin and buried under a heap of stones. The Natal Carbineers buried their dead comrades roughly. The gunners did the same by theirs. Efforts were made, at least, to conceal all the bodies of the men who had not belonged to the 24th Regiment. These were left untouched by special orders from General Newdigate.

The Zulu War : Isandhlwana revisited – fetching away the waggons, May 21.
From a sketch by our Special Artist, Mr. Melton Prior.

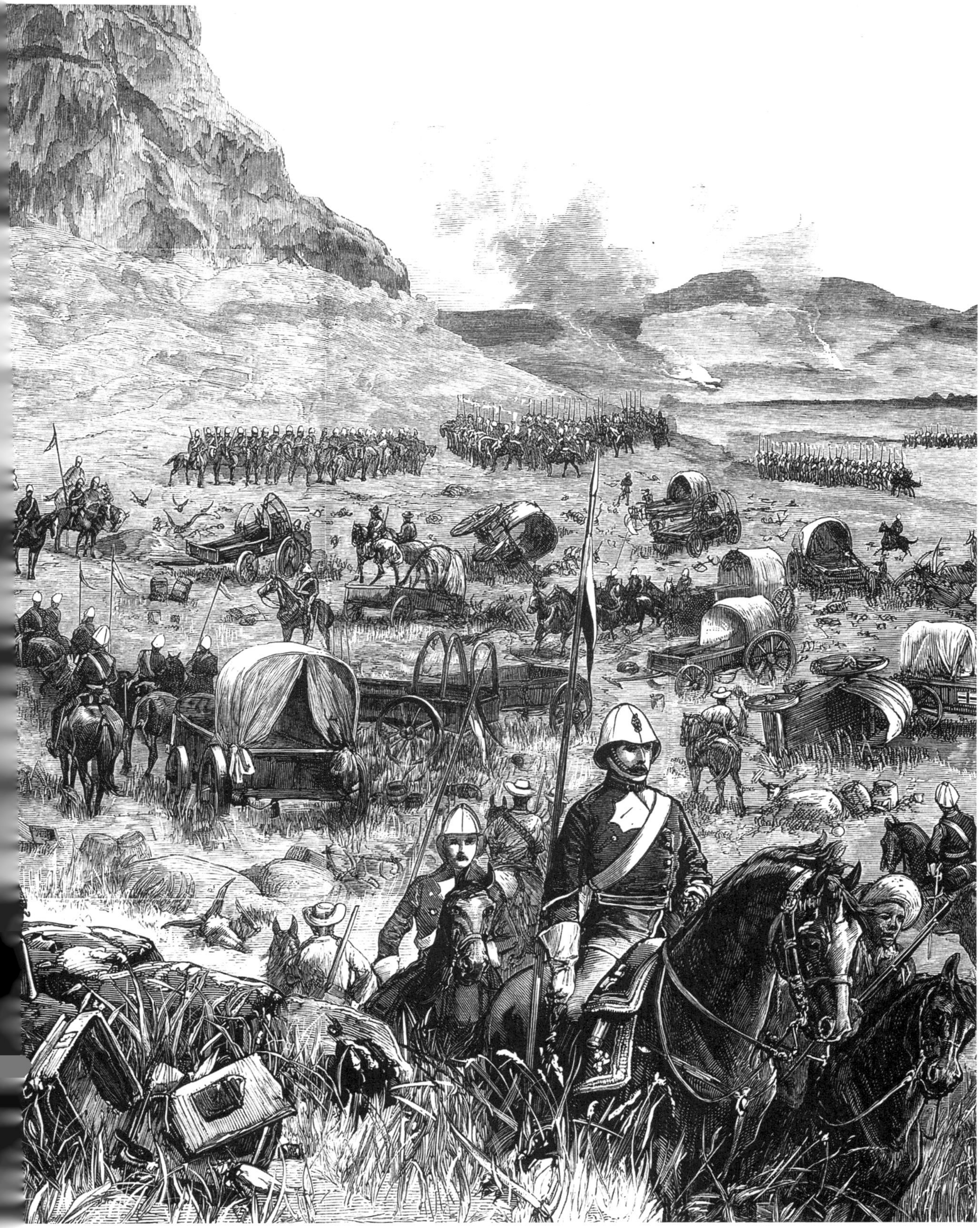

General Marshall had nourished a natural and seemly wish to give interment to all our dead who so long have lain bleaching at Isandhlwana but it appears that the 24th wish to perform this office themselves, thinking it right that both battalions should be represented, and that the ceremony should be postponed till the end of the campaign. In vain Marshall offered to convey a burial party of the regiments with tools from Rorke's Drift in waggons. One has some sympathy with the claim of the regiment to bury its own dead; but why postpone the interment till only a few loose bones can be gathered. As the matter stands, the Zulus, who have carefully buried their own dead, who do not appear to have been very numerous, will come back tomorrow to find that we visited the place not to bury our dead, but to remove a batch of waggons.

Wandering about the desolate camp, amid the sour odour of stale death, was sickening. I chanced on many sad relics – letters from home, photographs, journals, blood-stained books, packs of cards. Lord Chelmsford's copying book, containing an impression of his correspondence with the Horse Guards, was found in one of his portmanteaus, and identified, in a kraal two miles off. Colonel Harness was busily engaged collecting his own belongings. Colonel Glyn found a letter from himself to Lieutenant Melvill, dated the day before the fight.

The ground was strewn with brushes, toilet bags, pickle bottles, and unbroken tins of preserved meats and milk. Forges and bellows remained standing ready for the recommencement of work. The waggons in every case had been emptied, and the contents rifled. Bran lay spilt in heaps. Scarcely any arms were found, and no ammunition. There were a few stray bayonets and assegais, rusted with blood. No firearms.

All this time teams of horses were being hitched somehow on to the soundest of the waggons, till about forty fit to travel had been collected on the crest. Scouting parties had been firing the Zulu kraals around, which were blazing brilliantly. A report came in that some of these had been occupied the previous night, and had been hurriedly abandoned, the shields and assegais being left behind. Smouldering ashes were found in one, but not a single Zulu was visible; not even the old women. All had cleared off, and Lowe's detachment joined from the burning movement without having fired a shot or struck a blow. By twelve at noon the recovered waggons had started under escort for Rorke's Drift, and soon after the return march commenced, and was finished without incident.

THE ILLUSTRATED LONDON NEWS
July 19, 1879

Amid accessories of the most profoundly impressive character, the body of Louis Napoleon, the Prince Imperial, was on Saturday last committed to the tomb. England, in association with whose military service he fell, paid to his mortal remains, since transported hither with vigilant and tender care, such homage, as may well express her own sorrow for the melancholy event, but which can do but little, of course, to lighten the burden of woe which oppresses the bosom of the Imperial lady who is now, not merely a widow, but childless.

A public but not an officially State funeral served to draw together at Chiselhurst a representation of all classes of English people, from her Majesty the Queen to her humblest subjects, for the purpose of testifying respect for the departed and feeling commiseration for the bereaved Empress. Necessarily, in this act of devotion there was a personal intermingling of the Royal House and what yet remains of the Bonapartist family.

The Funeral was significant of every sentiment befitting so solemn an occasion, save such as might have indicated a political purpose and it was, perhaps, all the more stirring to the tenderer emotions of humanity, inasmuch as it was strictly and purely personal in its meaning. We have gone to the grave to weep with no other view than to express the affectionate regret we feel in the untimely loss of the honoured guest whom we had taught the profession of Arms, and who was cut off in voluntary service with our own Army.

Considered merely as a spectacle, the Funeral of the Prince was sufficiently striking. But it is not in this light that most people will regard it, nor is this the characteristic of which will be best remembered. Every incident of it betokened the sincerity and depth of the mental and moral feelings which it excited. The tears were real. The distressful commiseration for the loss which the Empress Eugénie has sustained was but feebly illustrated by the sights and sounds, "the pomp and circumstance" of the occasion. Mind rather than matter was pre-eminent in giving voice to the public sorrow.

Funeral of the Prince Imperial : The soldiers' last homage to the dead.

Death of the Prince Imperial.
From sketches by our Special Artist, Mr. Melton Prior.

1. Spot where the Prince's body was found.
2. Where the bodies of the two slain troops were found.
3. Kraal where the party off-saddled and rested.
4. Brigadier-General Woods' Camp, three miles distant.

From beginning to end of what may be called the melancholy pageant, a genuine pathos pervaded its every feature. Especially was this the case in connection with the movements of our own Royal Family. In this respect, what must be described as a public funeral presented characteristics seldom seen except at private interments of the dead. There was no theatrical display – none, at least, inappropriate to the solemnity – but a real outburst of manly and womanly emotion.

The tragic elements which prevailed at the death of the Prince, the inexpressible desolation of the Imperial Mother, the lessons of mutability in human affairs which the case enforced upon the mind, the remembrance of the virtues of the departed young man, and the tale of broken hopes, baffled aspirations, and defeated purposes which the circumstances so rudely told, preoccupied the thoughts and feelings of the mourners, and shut off for the time being all interest in the mere external traits of the scene. The realities to which it pointed stood out so clearly from the outward semblances in which they were pictured that the latter were forgotten, and the over-powering force of the former was exclusively recognised. Seldom in recent times has any public ceremonial so closely touched the hearts of those who took part in it.

We are in hopes that, after a brief interval of reflection, even the most ardent supporters of the French Republic will admire, rather than resent, the deep personal interest which has been displayed in this country in association with the Burial of the Prince Imperial. It will, no doubt, be remembered that

5. Where the body of a slain Basuto was found.
6. General Newdigate's Camp, half a mile distant.
7. Vidette Post of Lancers.
8. A span of oxen.

Louis Napoleon was the guest of the Nation; that, together with his parents, he cast in his lot with us when yet in his boyhood; that he received instruction and submitted to discipline in our Military Schools; that in his going in and out amongst us he engaged the sympathies of all with whom he came in contact; that he voluntarily and persistently elected to join his comrades when they were ordered out to South Africa; that he met his death in a manner which, even as Englishmen, we could not but deplore; that, in some sort, we felt ourselves responsible for his cruel "taking off;" and that, without the smallest reference to political susceptibilities or antipathies we were, whether we chose it or not, practically guardians of his welfare.

Of the sense which these considerations excited in our minds we have given unaffected expression at his Funeral. No generous people could have done less. We have treated him as one belonging to ourselves, while we have held ourselves completely aloof from any tendencies he may have betrayed, or any thoughts he may have entertained, touching the political future of his country. He was a genuine Frenchman, but we have mourned over him as we should have done over an Englishman of like position, character, and promise.

We have never discovered even in the highest walks of our society any special interest in impeding the progress of the Republic of France. On the contrary, we have noted the self-restrained attitude which it has assumed with satisfaction, and that satisfaction has been almost unanimously and loudly expressed. We have not changed our attitude in this regard. To bewail a friend does not necessarily imply a participation in all the expectations which his friends have cherished of him. France need not fear the outbreak of Imperialism in this country – at least so far as she is concerned. Any attempt to turn late events to political account against the established Government of France, or against the Constitution which she has thought fit to adopt, would instantly provoke an opposition as general and irresistible as to demonstrate its futility.

No! Our sorrow at the tomb of the Prince Imperial forebodes no danger to the settled institutions of our neighbour. Neither our Queen, nor our Court, nor our Parliament, nor our Army, is ignorant of the true foundations upon which international friendship must rest for security. It is not for us to dictate to others the form of Government under which they shall live. Our history, from time immemorial, has exhibited no love of Cæsarism in the British Race. But we are mindful of the duties of hospitality, and the personal affections which we form either for Princes or for Leaders of the people, we do not readily surrender to suspicions or susceptibilities not grounded upon facts.

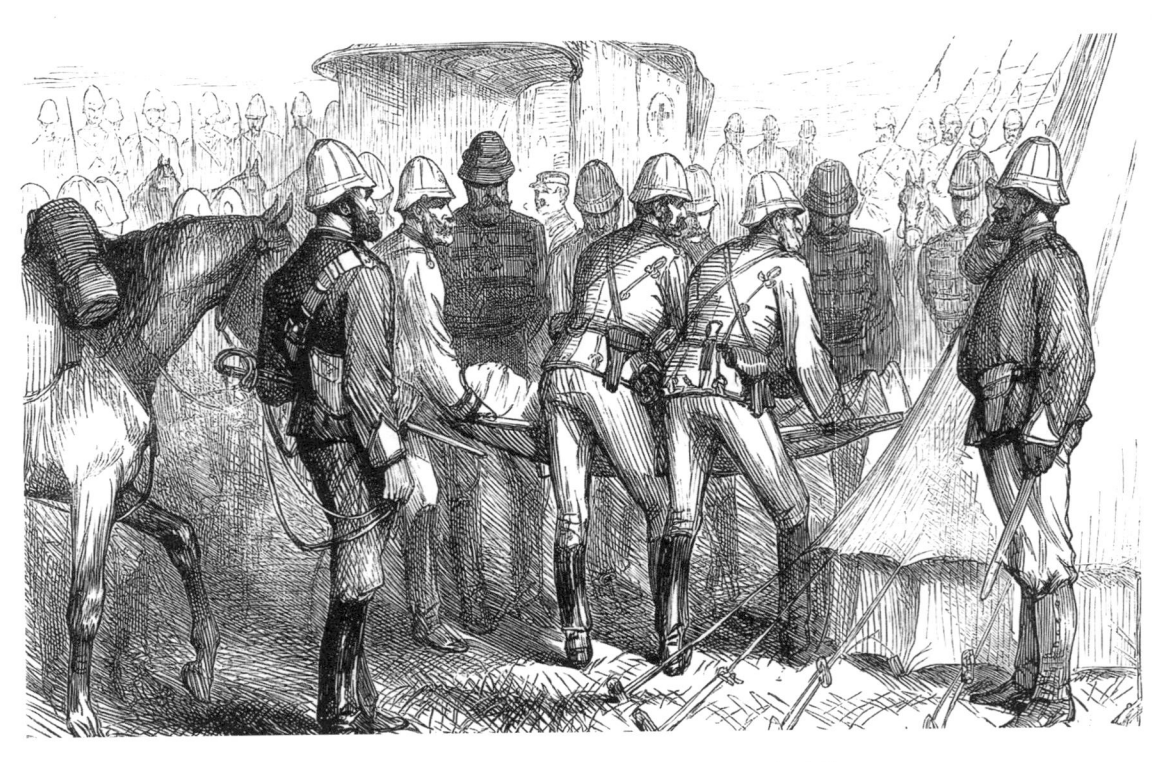

Arrival of the body of the Prince Imperial at Itelezi Camp.

We have bidden farewell as became us to Prince Louis Napoleon. We shall also minister tenderly, as becomes us, such consolation as we can to the Empress Eugénie. But we shall not join to assist in the plans, whatever they may be of the Bonapartist Family. While the tears are still in our eyes, we honestly give our hands to the French Republic, and, so long as the French people approve of it, we unfeignedly wish it "God speed".

DEATH OF THE PRINCE IMPERIAL

Our Special Artist, Mr. Melton Prior, at the head-quarters of the Army in the Zulu War, has sent us the Sketches we have this week prepared for the Illustrations of the lamentable death of the Prince Imperial, which are presented in the Number here placed before our readers.

The first is a general view of the whole locality, with the camps of General Newdigate and of Brigadier-General Wood in the distance, and with particular indications of the Zulu Kraal near the river, where the Prince and his party unsaddled their horses and lay down to rest; also of the precise spot where the unfortunate young Prince's body was found next morning, and where the two slain troopers of Bettington's Volunteer Horse were found. Another Sketch represents the kraal and the mealie-ground or field of maize, with the wall and six native huts, exactly as described in the statements of the soldiers and of subsequent visitors to the spot, which we have already published.

The arrival of the Prince's body at the camp, on June 2, the day after his death, having been found by the reconnoitring party which General Marshall led out for that purpose, has also been related circumstantially in former reports of this sad affair. But our Special Artist's sketches will have undiminished interest for all in England who have just been called upon to renew, upon the occasion of the funeral last Saturday, their sympathy with the widowed Empress, and their expressions of regret for the untimely death of her son.

The kraal where the Prince and his party off-saddled and were fired at.
The White Cross indicates where the Prince was standing when first attacked.

FUNERAL OF THE PRINCE IMPERIAL

A portion of the impression of last week's Number of this Journal, made up on Thursday afternoon, contained the announcement of the arrival of H.M.S. Orontes in the British Channel, bringing from the Cape of Good Hope the lamented Prince Imperial's body, in charge of Colonel Pemberton, of the 60th Rifles. The Orontes, which is one of the finest troop-ships belonging to the military transport service, under the command of Captain Kinahan, received the body on the 15th ult., in Simon's Bay, the eastward harbour of the Cape, from H.M.S. Boadicea, which had brought it from Port Natal.

Her approach to England was known by the telegraph from Madeira, and she lay to off Plymouth, on Wednesday of last week, to receive orders from shore, which directed her to go to Spithead, the anchorage off Portsmouth, and there to meet the Admiralty yacht Enchantress, commanded by Captain Hills. This smaller and lighter vessel, which had been fitted up for the occasion, was to convey the Prince's body from Portsmouth to Woolwich.

The Orontes accordingly reached Spithead early next morning (Thursday), and was there met by the Admiralty yacht, to which the coffin was transferred with the least possible delay. It was still in charge of Colonel Pemberton, and was received by several friends of the Empress and connections of the House of Bonaparte on board the Enchantress. That vessel arrived at Woolwich on Friday afternoon about two o'clock, and lay at the T Pier of the Royal Arsenal.

The procession at the T Pier, Woolwich Arsenal.

A distinguished company, both French and English, was there assembled to receive the Prince's body, for which elaborate preparations had been made. On the part of the members and friends of the Bonaparte family and of the late French Imperial Government, there were Prince Lucien Bonaparte, Prince Charles Bonaparte, the Duc de Bassano, General Count Fleury, M. Rouher, formerly Minister of State, M. Paul de Cassagnac, and many others. Their Royal Highnesses the Prince of Wales, the Duke of Edinburgh, and the Duke of Connaught were present to show their kindly regard for the late Prince Imperial and for the Empress, but did not mix with the phalanx of Bonapartist courtiers and partisans. The Duke of Cambridge arrived soon afterwards. A number of British officers of rank, including General Sir John Adye, General Sir Lintorn Simmons, Major-General Turner, holding special authority at Woolwich, were there in full uniform.

The coffin was borne ashore by sailors of the Admiralty yacht, while M. Rouher, General Fleury, and another French General, with Major-General Turner, walked beside it, and the Roman Catholic clergy intoned their Latin prayers. It was followed by several hundred persons to a small domed building in the Arsenal, which had been fitted up as a temporary mortuary. Here the bier was visited by the principal personages of the company; after which the medical men, Baron Clary, Baron Corvisart, and

Mr. T. Evans, the dentist, had the coffin opened and inspected the body, for the purpose of identification.

The corpse was then placed in a new shell, a leaden, and an oaken coffin, which was put on one of the guns of the Royal Horse Artillery, covered with the British flag. It was escorted from Woolwich to Chiselhurst, by way of the Common, Shooter's Hill, and Eltham, by a troop of the Royal Artillery and Horse Artillery, and by a procession on foot, which reached Camden Place, the residence of the Empress, about nine o'clock in the evening.

The temporary mortuary, Woolwich Arsenal, where the official identification took place.

The final ceremony at Chiselhurst on Saturday was quite a soldier's funeral, as befitted one who, in the words of the Princess of Wales, written by her own hand on the card which accompanied her wreath of violets, "died a soldier's death, fighting for our cause." The whole of the inscription on this wreath is well worth quotation, since it indicates the spirit in which the Royal House of England did such ungrudging honour to the memory of a cherished and lamented guest of this country.

But first the words of the Queen, thoughtfully written in French by her Majesty and attached to the wreath of golden laurel-leaves which she had laid upon the coffin, should be given. Written in the Queen's own hand, the words are:-
"Souvenir de vive affection, d'estime, et de profonds regrets de la part de Victoria Reg."

The Princess of Wales wrote:-
"A token of affection and regard for him who lived the most spotless of lives, and died a soldier's death, fighting for our cause in Zululand.
From Albert Edward and Alexandra, July 12, 1879."

When the coffin containing the remains of her son, with which was placed a crucifix blessed by Pius IX. and brought from Rome two years ago by her Chaplain, Monsignor Goddard, was brought to Camden

Place on Friday night, the Empress was anxiously awaiting it. We dare not attempt to inquire how it was received by the widowed mother. All that night, with but slight intermission, the Empress passed beside the body of her son.

Very early in the morning, at about four or five, when the tall candles burning beneath a silver cross in the little white chapel had not long paled in the light of the dawn, the Empress heard mass. It was said before her there, and before the dead, by Monsignor Goddard, who had kept the vigil with Monsignor Las Casas, Bishop of Constantine, and two of the aides-de-camp of the Prince. Afterwards the Empress retired to her room, which she did not leave during the day. At nine the white hangings with the letter "N." were affixed by the Pompes Funèbres to the outer gate, and many mourners were then arriving.

By the Queen's repeatedly expressed desire, great care had been taken in preparing the mind of the Empress for the funeral ceremony, of which she could not but be conscious, although she took no part in it. The Queen left Windsor South-Western Station at nine o'clock, accompanied by Princess Beatrice, and attended by the Hon. Horatia Stopford and the Hon. Frances Drummond, and by Lieutenant-General Sir Henry Ponsonby, K.C.B., and Colonel Du Plat, her Majesty's Equerry, of the Royal Artillery, the arm of the service with which the young Prince, following in the footsteps of the founder of his family, had associated himself. The military pageant of Saturday had strictly the character of an Artillery, or rather of a Woolwich celebration. All the troops engaged came from the Woolwich garrison, of which the Prince had been a member, and many of the Princes wore Artillery uniforms.

The Queen arrived at Chiselhurst Station, and immediately drove to Camden Place. Lord Sydney, Lord Lieutenant of the county, and Lady Sydney were present at the station on the Queen's arrival. The Queen was conducted by the Duc de Bassano, Grand Chamberlain of the exiled Court, to the *chapelle ardente*, where her Majesty knelt for a little while near the kneeling priests, and then placed upon the coffin her wreath of laurels in gold. Princess Beatrice placed a cross of violet porcelain flowers upon the coffin. Many flowers and wreaths had already been deposited in that sacred place.

The Queen gathered two or three flowers in her hand. In the reception-hall Prince Napoleon with his two sons, Prince Victor and Prince Louis Bonaparte, advanced to do her Majesty homage. The Queen was received also by Princess Mathilde, Prince Napoleon Charles Bonaparte, Prince Murat, Princess Eugénie Murat, the Duchesse de Mouchy (Princess Anne Murat), the Duc de Bassano, and M. Pietri.

The Prince of Wales' special train left Charing-cross soon after ten, and arrived at Chiselhurst at 10.30, five minutes after the Queen's train. It carried the Prince and Princess of Wales and a very brilliant company of Royal personages, members of the Diplomatic Body, and officers. On the previous day, at Woolwich, the Prince of Wales and his illustrious relatives had been dressed as civilians, but now the Prince of Wales wore an Artillery uniform with spiked busby (the uniform of the Prince of Wales's Own Norfolk Artillery, of which his Royal Highness is hon. Colonel) and the Grand Cross of the Legion of Honour, with the French military order founded by the late Emperor, and other orders on his breast.

Similar uniforms and decorations were worn by the other Princes, the Duke of Edinburgh, the Duke of Connaught, and the Duke of Teck. Prince Leopold wore the Windsor dress. The Duke of Cambridge and Prince Edward of Saxe-Weimar were in scarlet, against which the bars of crape on the arm which, like all the officers, they wore, showed more distinctly. The Crown Prince of Sweden was conspicuous in his handsome light buff cavalry dress; Prince Leiningen was in naval uniform. There were also in the train Prince Christian, the Hereditary Grand Duke of Baden, Prince Louis of Battenberg, and Count Gleichen.

Among the officers who came were:- Colonel F.A. Stanley (Secretary of State for War), Field-Marshal Lord Strathnairn, General Lord Napier of Magdala, Lieutenant-General Sir Dighton Probyn, General Sir Charles Ellice, General Stephenson (commanding the Home District), and, in short, almost every general officer of distinction who is in England at this time, and was able to attend. We believe that every regiment at Aldershot, and all arms of the service, were represented by Colonels or some of their officers.

The cadets of the Royal Military Academy, Woolwich, commanded by Major Van Straubenzee, about 200 in number, were stationed under the tall trees at the end of the avenue nearest Camden House, and presented arms as the Queen and the Princes arrived. Beyond them, on the left of the principal

Funeral of the Prince Imperial : The procession from Camden Place to the church at Chiselhurst.

entrance, the officers and the other mourners massed themselves. The gun-carriage on which the coffin was to be placed was drawn up before the door. The Queen took up a position on the gravel walk at the side of the House nearest the lodge till the ten young Captains and Lieutenants of the Royal Artillery, to whom the like duty had been confided on the precious day, had borne the coffin from the chapel to the bier.

The drums beat with a muffled sound, the first minute gun was heard, and the bearers carried their burden to the gun. It was now ten minutes past eleven. The Queen, followed by the Princess and the Ladies in Waiting, was conducted by the Marquis de Castelbajac, in attendance upon her Majesty, along a path marked out by black cloth to the raised black-draped pavilion from which she saw the passage of the funeral procession across the common to the church. The Princess of Wales had already driven to the church with the Comtesse d'Otrante and Lord Suffield, way being made for this improvised movement by the personal exertions of Captain Baynes.

A battery of artillery just without the lower gates fired the first of a series of mourning guns, and the gentlemen cadets stepped slowly off with arms reversed, while the Royal Artillery band played the Dead March in "Saul," which is always heard at a soldier's funeral. The drummers beat a monotonous funereal roll upon drums bound with black crape. The cross was borne before the gun by an Alsatian Curé. The Abbé Kœnig, Vicar of St. Eustache, followed, with the Abbé Laine, almoner to the Emperor; the Abbé Métairie, Canon of St. Denis; the learned Bishop of Constantine, Monsignor Las Casas, wearing his golden mitre.

The gun was drawn by six dark-brown horses, beside each pair of which rode a mounted artilleryman, one on the right, one on the left. The coffin above the gun was rolled in the English Union Jack and the French Tricolour. The sword of the Prince, his belt, and his sabretache were placed above.

On a cushion were the great cross, the plaque, and ribbon of the Legion of Honour, founded by the Emperor. The dismounted men carried the largest of the wreaths. By the side of the coffin walked the pall-bearers, the Duke of Connaught, the Duke of Cambridge, the Crown Prince of Sweden and Norway, with M. Rouher, on the left; the Duke of Edinburgh, Prince Leopold, and the Prince of Wales, with the Duc de Bassano, on the right.

The Princes and Princesses came to lay their wreaths upon the coffin in the chapel, and as they passed into the saloon reserved for the Queen and the Princes of the various Royal Houses, they had each received a few violets or other flowers from the chapel. The Princes who walked as pall-bearers still carried in their hands the flowers they had received. At the side of the pall-bearers walked the Ambassadors. Behind the coffin came the Prince's brown horse Stag, caparisoned in white and silver starred trappings of Imperial state, led by Mr. Gamble, the faithful retainer who attended the baptism of the Prince and now followed his funeral.

This also was the place reserved for the English soldiers, Lomas and Brown, who served as groom and valet to the Prince, and Uhlmann, his own body servant. Next came the chief mourners, Prince Napoleon and his sons Prince Victor and Prince Louis, Prince Lucien Bonaparte, Prince Joachim Murat, Prince Napoleon Charles Bonaparte, and Prince Louis Murat. These Princes of the Imperial house were followed by other personages of princely rank but not all related by kindred – the Duke of Teck, Prince Christian of Schleswig-Holstein, Prince Edward of Saxe-Weimar, the Hereditary Grand Duke of Baden, the Duc de Rivas (representing personally the King of Spain), the Prince of Monaco, the Duc d'Albe, the Duc de d'Huescar, the Marquis de Roccagiovine, Comte Primoli, Duc de Tamames, Duc de Mouchy, Duc d'Albufera, Duc de Feltre, and Duc de Marino.

Next came the great officers of the Imperial Crown, many of them bearing wreaths. Here were General Comte Fleury, the Prince de la Moscova, General de Béville, General Favé, General Castelnau, General Canu, Comte Davillier, Baron Bourgoing, M. Raimbaud, and the three aides-de-camp of the Prince, General Despeuilles, Admiral Duperré, and Colonel de Ligneville.

Here also were Marquis de Bassano, the Comte Louis de Turenne, M. Bachon; M. Franceschini Pietri, executor of the Prince; General Sir Lintorn Simmons, formerly Governor of the Royal Military Academy, with the sons of the chiefs; M.M. Conneau, Espinasse, and Bizot, the legatees; Adrien Fleury, Pierre de Bourgoing, and Scipion Corvisart, and M. Filou, tutor of the Prince. Dr. le Baron Corvisart remained near the Empress, but Dr. le Baron Larry, followed in the cortége. A place was here reserved for Mr. Strode, the owner of Camden House. There followed also Colonel Brady, Prince Poniatowski, the Comte du Bourg, the Marquis de Massa, M. Cyprian Corvisart, Comte de Labedoyère, M. Busso-Billaut, Duc de Cornegliano, Baron T. Lambert, Duc de Prévise, Baron Tascher de la Pagerie, Baron de Montbrun, Baron d'Azugon, Baron Corberon, Comte Galloni d'Istria, Dr. Evans, Comte et Vicomte Aguado, and Comte de la Poèze.

The gentlemen nearest after the chief mourners bore wreaths in their hands, the violet wreath with the Princess of Wales's card, which she had placed with her own hands on the coffin; a wreath of white roses from "Albert Edward, Prince of Wales," a white wreath from "Louisa, Victoria, and Maud of Wales," and one from "Edward and George of Wales," sent by the young Princes to the friend whose daring and skill in manly exercises were specially calculated to attract boyish admiration. Prince Leopold's offering was an immortelle with the words written by him on the card – "Hommage d'affection et d'estime de la part de Leopold."

The congregation of French mourners included many active political partisans, members of the present or former Legislative bodies. Delegations came from the manufacturing towns of Roubaix, Cambrai, and Tourcoing; from the students of Paris, the workmen of Paris (among whom marched Didion and Bradier); from old soldiers living in Paris, the Society La Jeunesse. Other deputations came from the departments of Giers, La Creuse, Tarn-et-Garonne, Allier, Seine Inférieure (Rouen).

Draped eagles, wreaths, and tricolours set with golden bees were borne aloft by the deputations; an immense and confused concourse of French mourners followed. All, even the Princess of the Imperial house, were in ordinary French mourning (evening dress), not in uniform, as so many of the English mourners were. As the several portions of the procession reached the park gates a change was made in its composition. A troop of the Royal Irish Lancers from Woolwich, with pennons flying on their lances bound with crape, and with green plumes nodding as they rode, placed themselves at the head, coming out from their station under the trees by the side of the common. Captain Paley was here in command.

When the mourners had passed on, the dull rattle of the guns of the Royal Artillery, wheeling into the line of the cortége, was also heard behind. The whole of the military display was under the command of General Turner, commanding at Woolwich, with his Staff. Colonel Markham, Colonel Wrottesley, and Captain Loraine. The riding establishment of the Royal Horse Artillery, under Major Ward-Ashton, who had formed the escort the previous day, placed themselves again in the rear of the procession. There were two batteries of the Royal Horse Artillery, under colonel Andrews, and three of Field Artillery, under Colonel Rowley.

The whole of the 5th Lancers were on the ground, under Colonel Browne. The battery on the north-east of the common, which fired minute guns, was commanded by Major Blackwell. This battery remained at its post, but the other troops joined in the procession, and so prolonged it that it formed a line stretching all the way from the park to the church. So mournful a ceremony was not looked at from the point of view of a spectacle, and the dull sky was rather unfavourable to military display. There was no sun to flash back from the helmets of the Lancers or linger on the gold of the splendidly mounted Horse Artillery. But it was a most unusual and impressive sight to see that strangely and variously composed line of soldiers on horseback, and priests and mourners on foot, moving slowly along the serpentine road across the great uneven plain of the common, with thousands of spectators stationary on each hand.

To those who thought of the childless Empress in her lonely house, and knew that the chief mourners were Princes, and that the Queen was watching the procession from her black tribune, unless she had left it to console the sorrowing mother, the sight was much more than impressive.

The head of the procession moved slowly on to the mournfully swelling and diminishing cadences of the Funeral March in A flat from the 11th sonata of Beethoven. The common was thickly lined with silent rows of spectators standing on the grass or in carriages. Many stands had been erected and were partially occupied. At the old church the 1st Kent Administrative Battalion Rifle Volunteers, 380 strong, under Major Bristowe, were formed up and presented arms. Most of the ladies who attended the service had gone beforehand to the church; but half-way across the common M. Henri Chevreau brought Madame Ferdinand de Lesseps, who is nearly related to the Empress, to join the mourners and enter with them.

Chiselhurst, 1879 : Requiescat in Pace.

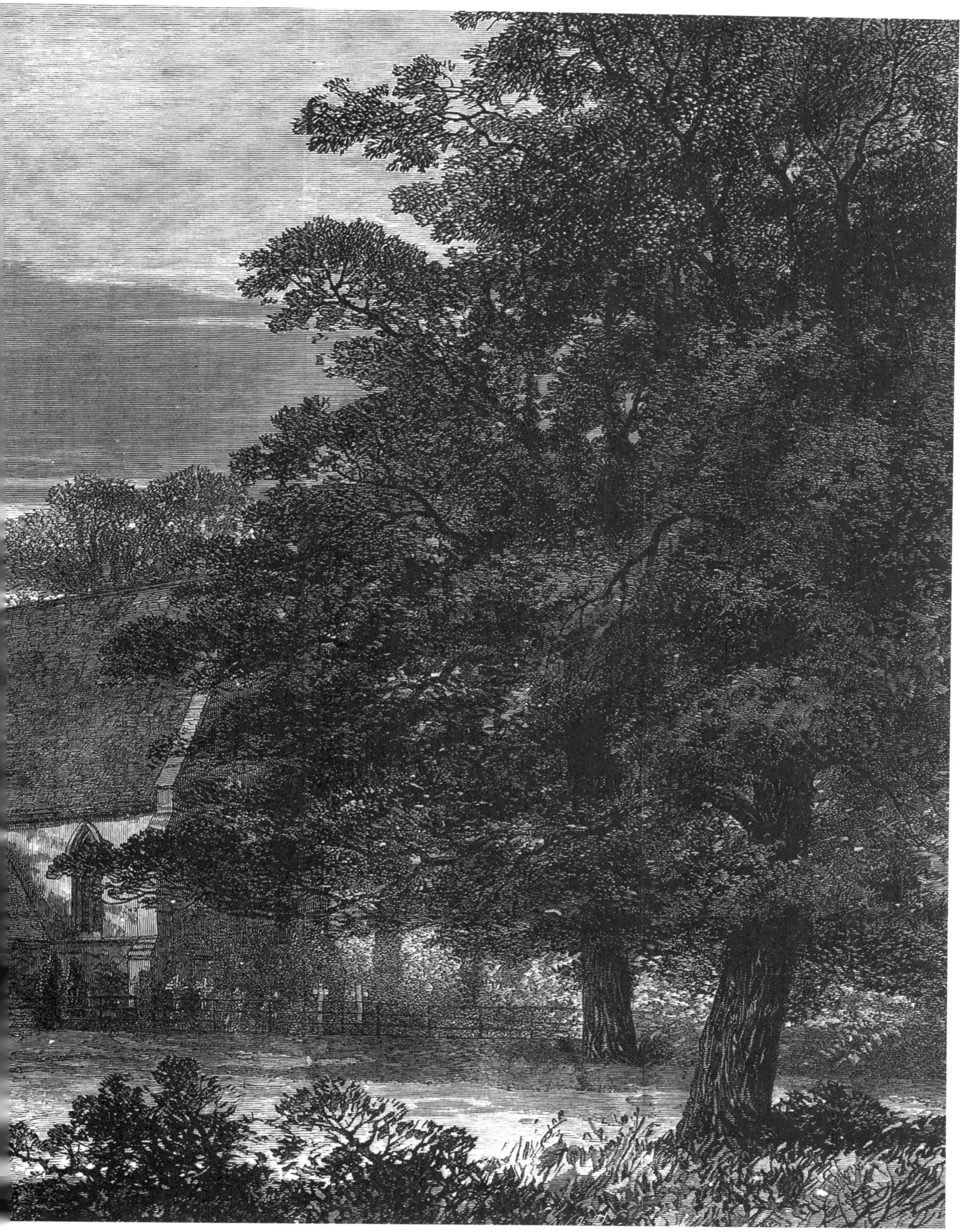

Abreast of the Catholic schools a lady tottered forward with a wreath, which she handed to the nearest person in the procession, begging him to lay it on the coffin. It was twelve o'clock, nearly an hour after leaving the house, when St. Mary's Church was reached and the gun wheeled round to allow the officers to raise its load. The cadets formed in rows each side of the way to permit the coffin to pass between them. The little bell of St. Mary's Church tolling for the soul of the departed was answered by the deeper note of the bell from the steeple of the Anglican church.

The priests came out to meet the dead. The Bishop of Southwark, in full pontificals, was preceded by Monsignor Goddard, in violet robes, and the rest of the clergy. The officers placed the coffin on their shoulders. The Bishop sprinkled the coffin with holy water and recited the *De Profundis*, and then, preceded by the cross-bearer, who had come from Camden Place, and by the whole of the clergy, he led the way for the bearers into the church. The officers placed the body on the catafalque before the sanctuary. The mourners passed in. The high mass proceeded.

When the eyes grew accustomed to the gloom of the darkened little church, hung throughout with sable cloth, on which the Imperial "N." in gold glistened, while the cross and the figures of the Virgin stood out in bold relief, it became possible to see how it was tenanted. The English Princes who had borne the pall sat to right and left of the coffin; the Imperial Princes on the left. The Princess of Wales was in the gloom on the right, Princess Mathilde sat beside her brother and nephews on the left. The only daylight came through the Napoleon Chapel.

The Ambassadors of Germany, Italy, Austria, Turkey, Denmark, Sweden, Belgium, Holland, Spain, and other foreign States, accompanied by ladies of their respective families, and the wives of several French Marshals or Generals, including those of Marshals Lebœuf and Conrobert and the Duke of Malakoff, were in the seats reserved for distinguished foreigners. This congregation now waited for the commencement of the religious ceremony.

Within the sanctuary stood the mitred Bishop of Southwark, the Right Rev. Dr. Danell, who sang the solemn requiem mass, assisted by Canon Bamber, with Father Reeks as deacon and Father Delaney as sub-deacon. Monsignor Goddard read an English prayer at the end, after the Bishop had finished the one absolution, The Rev. Father Crook was master of the ceremonial, with Mr. Louis Clovis assisting. "Napoleonis Ludovici Eugenii anima" was the soul prayed for in the Latin of the ritual. The Baronne de Caters-Lablache sang a beautiful "Ave Maria," by M. Saint-Saëns, the French composer, who has written the new cantata for the Birmingham Musical Festival. She also sang "Pie Jesu," by Faure. Other solos were sung by Dr. Crookall, Mr. Doyle, and a young French chorister. The chant was plain Gregorian.

M. Serpette accompanied the Baroness Caters-Labache. Miss Danvers, the usual organist, accompanied most efficiently the remaining part of the service. Monsignor de Las Casas, the former Bishop of Constantine, was present, together with Canons Crookall, Bamber, Doyle, O'Halloran, Wenham and North. The last words of the English prayer, said by Monsignor Goddard, were:-"To Thee, O Lord, we commend the soul of Thy Servant Napoleon, that, being dead to this world, he may live to Thee; and whatever sins he has committed in this life through human frailty do Thou in Thy merciful goodness forgive, through our Lord Jesus Christ."

The beautiful words of the introit, "Requiem æternam dona et Domine," were many times repeated. The triple peel of the bell above the church told the great crowd of mourners, who were perforce excluded from the little building and stood in the churchyard, of the elevation of the Host and chalice, and the worshippers within heard, with a sudden shock, the cadets fire their three volleys to the memory of their comrade.

After the mass, which lasted till one, the procession did not return to the house. Many remained at the church, and the public flocked in to walk round the corpse, to sprinkle it with holy water, and to add wreaths to the many upon it. It was visited by several thousands in the course of the day, and so great was the pressure that at one time the palings and the police were nearly swept away together by those anxious to enter.

The coffin, meanwhile, was vigilantly guarded by a watch of four gentlemen at a time, who relieved each other from hour to hour. From twelve to one the aides-de-camp to the Prince and M. Bachon were appointed to be on guard. At one the duty began of the Marquis de Bassano, Comte Louis de Turenne, Marquis de Castelbajac, and Colonel Brady. From two to three Capitaine Bizet, Lieutenant l'Espinasse, Sous-Lieutenant Conneau, and Sous-Lieutenant Fleury held their watch; and next came the turn of the Marquis de Massa, the Baron de Bourgoing, Pierre de Bourgoing, and Cyprian Corvisat. They were succeeded by the Comte de Labédoyère, M. Busso Billaut, Duc de Conegliano, Baron Tristan Laubert. The last and longest duty fell at five to the Duc de Trévise, the Comte du Bourg, the Baron Tascher de la Pagerie, and the Comte de la Poèze.

At seven the Princes of the Imperial house arrived again with M. Pietri. A brief service was held by the clergy, headed by Monsignor Goddard, and the coffin was removed from the catafalque to the ante-sacristy in which the Emperor's body lay for a year, till the side chapel was built for his remains. In the ante-sacristy it now lies, with the Queen's wreath and those of the Prince and Princess of Wales and Prince Leopold and Princess Beatrice's cross upon it.

The Queen returned at twelve, and the Prince of Wales at 11.5. About 1400 police were in attendance, under the direction of the Chief Commissioner, Sir Edmund Henderson, who was assisted by Colonel Labalmondière, and by Captain Baynes, District Superintendent. Mr Gernon, Mr. Butt, and other experienced officers were also on duty. The South-Eastern Railway ran thirty-two special trains to Chiselhurst, and nearly as many back. It conveyed by these and the ordinary trains, 11,000 passengers to Chiselhurst and carried from Chiselhurst 12,500.

It was variously estimated by some of the police authorities that between 35,000 and 40,000 persons were present. Photographs were given away to those who entered Camden Park early, chiefly French visitors who had obtained cards at Willis's Rooms or the station. Two thousand photographs were speedily exhausted. Rain falling in the afternoon greatly reduced the crowd at Chiselhurst. In the afternoon the mortuary built at Camden Place, in which the coffin had been deposited for a night, was visited by very many people, and large quantities of flowers were presented to the visitors as souvenirs by the graceful act of the Imperial family.

This little chapel in the vestibule was filled with beautiful wreaths. They came from Corsica and Chambéry, from the Lycée Bonaparte, from Princess Metternich, and a little one from the child whom the Prince last kissed before he left England. Some 500 or 600 wreaths were sent, and many hours were devoted on Friday night to unpacking them. Father Rooney, the priest who accompanied the remains of the Prince to England, performed the proper religious rites so far as was possible in the circumstances on shipboard.

As a proof of this confidence, Father Rooney was desired on Sunday to celebrate mass in the presence of the Empress at Camden House, in the bed-room of the Prince, where there now lie on the bed the faded violets which Lady Frere put on the coffin of the Prince, the bouquets, cross, and inscription in everlasting flowers, and all that came in the little chapel of the Orontes from Simon's Bay. The mass was said at half-past ten, and was heard throughout by the Empress, though she was at the beginning much affected.

Mass was said at Chiselhurst Catholic Church on Sunday at eleven by the Bishop of Southwark in the presence of the Imperial family and a numerous congregation, and the Cardinal Archbishop of Westminster, who has just been deprived by death of his own favourite nephew, Monsignor Manning, preached from the top of the steps of the sanctuary a most pathetic sermon. As his text the Cardinal took the verse from the Gospel of St. John – "What I do thou knowest not now but thou shalt know hereafter."

After the service the congregation came forward to see the coffin through the iron bars of the temporary sepulchre, where it lies surrounded by wreaths of white eucharis, roses, stephanotis, violets, and lilies. Princess Mary, Duchess of Teck, arrived in the afternoon, with the Duke of Teck, visited Camden House, and placed a wreath within the ante-sacristy of St. Mary's Church. The Grand Duchess of Mecklenburg-Strelitz and the Princess Frederica of Hanover paid similar tribute to the family and the dead.

Our Illustrations presented in this Number of the Illustrated London News comprise those of the procession from the landing-pier at Woolwich Arsenal to the temporary mortuary, in which the body of the Prince Imperial was first placed for surgical inspection and personal identification; the funeral procession next day, at Chiselhurst, from Camden Place to St. Mary's Roman Catholic Church; and the soldiers paying their final tribute, in military fashion, of homage to the gallant young soldier then laid in the tomb. A View of the Church, with the appropriate motto "Requiescat in Pace," is given as our Extra Supplement.

THE ILLUSTRATED LONDON NEWS

July 26, 1879

The news from South Africa indicates the approaching close of the disastrous Zulu War. A great battle was fought on the 4th inst., and the victory was gained by Lord Chelmsford, within a few miles of Ulundi, the principal military kraal of the Sovereign. Things, therefore, are drawing near to a supreme crisis in that part of the world, and it is far from improbable that before Parliament rises tidings will have reached it of the termination of the contest. It is reported, indeed, that an army of 20,000 men was lost to Cetewayo in the neighbourhood of Ulundi. But it remains still uncertain whether the looked-for peace will have been secured by the late engagement. At any rate, there would appear to be strong likelihood that by this time our quarrel with the Zulu nation has been practically settled.

Sir Garnet Wolseley, having been prevented by the raging surf from landing on the coast of Zululand, has returned to Natal, intending to join the army, now appointed to be under his command, by a tedious land journey. He will not take long in completing both the military and political task before him. There will remain only to pay the bill; and we fear it is too much to hope that it will not be a grievously heavy one. There is really nothing satisfactory to show for it. Neither the interest nor the honour of England called for the war, and it has been attended by a succession of misfortunes. Good, however, may eventually come out of what we all admit to be an evil. Still, the affair is one which the British public would fain forget, and which it will be glad to see closed. There seems, at last, to be a promising prospect that such may be the case, and we may express our earnest expectation that it will be speedily realised.

THE ZULU WAR

Arrival of news at Fort Pearson.

A great battle has been fought by Lord Chelmsford at Ulundi, the capital of the Zulu kingdom; and it is to be hoped that the easy victory he has gained, with the small loss of ten killed – one of them an officer – and fifty-three wounded on our side, may put an end to this hitherto disastrous and inglorious, as well as needless and profitless war. The following is Lord Chelmsford's despatch, forwarded by Major-General the Hon. H. Clifford to the Secretary of State for War:-

"July 4. – Cetewayo not having complied with my demands by noon yesterday, July 3, and having fired heavily on the troops at water, I returned the 114 cattle he had sent in, and ordered a reconnaissance to be made by the mounted force under Colonel Baker. This was effectually made, and caused the Zulu army to advance, and show itself. This morning a force, under my command, consisting of the 2nd Division under Major-General Newdigate, numbering 1870 Europeans, 530 natives, and eight guns, and the flying column under Brigadier-General Wood, numbering 2192 Europeans and 573 natives, four guns, and two Gatlings, crossed the Umvolosi river at 6.15, and marching in a hollow square with the ammunition and intrenching tool carts, and bearer company in its centre, reached an excellent position between Enadweng and Ulundi, about half-past eight.

This had been observed by Colonel Buller the day before. Our fortified camp on the right bank of the Umvolosi was left with a garrison of about 9000 Europeans, 250 natives, and one Gatling gun, under Colonel Bellairs. Soon after half-past seven the Zulu army was seen leaving its bivouacs and advancing on every side. The engagement was shortly after commenced by the mounted men. By nine o'clock the attack was fully developed; at half-past nine the enemy wavered. The 17th Lancers, followed by the remainder of the mounted men, attacked them, and a general rout ensued.

The prisoners state Cetewayo was personally commanding, and had made all the arrangements himself, and that he witnessed the fight from Lickazi Kraal, and that twelve regiments took part in it. If so, 20,000 men attacked us. It is impossible to estimate with any correctness the loss of the enemy, owing to the extent of the country over which they attacked and retreated, but it could not have been less, I consider, than 1000 killed. At noon Ulundi was in flames, and during the day all military kraals of the Zulu army and in the valley of the Umvolusi were destroyed.

"At two p.m. the return march to the camp of the column commenced. The behaviour of the troops under my command was extremely satisfactory. Their steadiness under a complete belt of fire was remarkable. The dash and enterprise of the mounted branches were all that could be wished, and the fire of the artillery very good.

"A portion of the Zulu forces approached our fortified camp, and at one time threatened to attack it."

MR ARCHIBALD FORBES'S REPORT OF THE BATTLE

Mr Archibald Forbes (who, as stated in Sir Bartle Frere's despatch, rode with the news in fifteen hours to Landsman's Drift) sent to the *Daily News* the following graphic telegrams describing the reconnaissance on July 3 and the decisive repulse of the Zulus on the following day:-

Camp, Umvoloosi River, July 3
The Zulus took no advantage of the grace granted to them until midday to-day. We until then remained supine on the hither bank. Soon after midday Colonel Buller took out his Irregular Horse on a reconnaissance, to support which guns were moved out in front of the camp. All the morning Zulu stragglers from the rocky hillock on the opposite side of the river were firing at us. One man was wounded. This hillock was shelled while Buller's men crossed to its right, lower down the stream, bent to the left, took the hillock in reverse, and chased the Zulus, who ran into a military kraal named Delanyo, shooting several.

Sweeping round to the left of this kraal, and leaving a detachment to cover the retreat by holding the hillock in the rear, the horsemen galloped across the open towards a larger kraal named Nondjueno, about 200 Zulus retiring before them. No more were visible, and an easy success seemed awaiting Buller as he galloped by the Nondjueno kraal and headed straight on Ulundi, but a deep hollow intervened. The body he was pursuing was merely a decoy. Suddenly from a hollow sprang up a long line of

Zulus, 2000 strong, confronting him in front and flank. He held back, but frequently turned at bay.

Meanwhile the whole plain had suddenly sprung into life. Quite 10,000 Zulus closed on his lines of retreat, intent upon cutting him off. He made good his retreat fighting all but hand to hand, with a loss of three wounded. Lord William Beresford greatly distinguished himself, killing the Zulus with his sabre in single combat, and rescuing a wounded sergeant from under a heavy fire. I understand that Lord William Beresford will be recommended for the Victoria Cross. The Zulus were much elated by Buller's retreat. The whole force crosses the river to-morrow, intent upon penetrating to Ulundi. The 24th Regiment remains to garrison the laager. We shall probably fight our way in and out of Ulundi.

A Zulu scout.

July, 4

At daybreak this morning the whole force was waiting for the order to advance again. Buller's Horse, to the front, crossed above and below the hillock, gained it, and found the country abandoned. The whole force passed the drift and through the bush clear of the Delanyo kraal. The formation consisted of a great square. The 80th formed the front; the 90th and 94th the left face; the 94th the rear; the 58th and 13th the right face. Inside, ready for action, were the Artillery, the Engineers, the Natives, &c. We had passed the Nondjueno kraal, and all was quiet as yet. The enemy was visible in one considerable straggling column moving parallel with us. Another was crowning and descending the eminence on the left rear, towards Nondjueno. Another was visible fitfully in various directions on our left. A fourth great mass was moving down on the right from Ulundi.

Consulting the map of Zululand.

It was impossible to tell how many lay in the dongas on and about the direct front. Buller was continually stirring them up, and a brisk fire was exchanged. The Zulus began to close on us on all sides. The guns were moved out on their flanks and into action. Buller's Horse resisted as long as possible, and then galloped back into square. In a short space of time the guns alone were in action; but, the Zulus coming on swiftly, the Infantry opened fire first, the closest on our right front. The artillery practice was beautiful, but it failed to daunt the Zulus, who rushed into the Nondjueno kraal, which had not been burnt, utilising the cover.

Thence men with white shields streamed with great daring against the right and rear of the square, where were two companies of the 21st, and two nine-pounders. The Zulus dashed with great bravery into close quarters amidst the deadly hail of the Martini bullets and volleys of canister, and stubbornly assailed us on all four faces of our square, which stood like a rock. The whole affair was in a small compass, which made it seem more animated. The Zulus fired half Martini and half round and jagged bullets, which rent the air above our soldiers, who observed a stern purposeful silence.

At the first shell fired, at 9.30, there rose a mighty cheer from the right flank and rear, the enemy giving way. A responding cheer came from the left; and then the front square opened to emit the Lancers and Buller's Horsemen, who burst like a torrent upon the broken enemy. The Lancers dashed towards the rear, caught a number of men in the long grass, and cut them down with their sabres and lances. Several officers of the Lancers killed four Zulus each. Two received assegai wounds. Captain Wyatt Edgell was killed, and two officers were slightly wounded. The British cavalry effectually vindicated its reputation.

The enemy were driven widely distant. Their dead lay thick all round the square, most of them facing the 21st. I estimate that 400 Zulus lay dead. After a slight halt, the cavalry moved to the front and burnt Ulundi and the neighbouring military kraals. The whole force advanced close to Ulundi, and halted to eat. About two o'clock the force marched back to laager. The success of the day is unquestionable. Its bearing on the conclusion of peace is not clear. It is estimated that about 10,000 Zulus were engaged. Our loss was ten killed and about fifty wounded, exclusive of natives.

THE KILLED

Lord Chelmsford's telegram concluded with the lists of killed and wounded, the former of which we subjoin:-

Second Division: Captain Wyatt-Edgell; Farrier-Sergeant Taylor, 17th Lancers; Corporal Tompkinson; Private Coates, 58th Regiment; Private Kent, 94th Regiment; Trooper Silona, Shepstone's Horse. Flying Column: Corporal Carter, R.A.; Bugler J. Burnes; Private W. Dirdley, 13th Regiment; Private Floyd, 80th Regiment; Trooper Jones, K.N. (sic) Horse.

The Zulu War : New trestle and pontoon bridge over the Tugela River.

ILLUSTRATIONS OF THE ZULU WAR

We present several Illustrations – one of which, drawn by Mr. Melton Prior, our Special Artist, represents the funeral parade at the Itelezi Ridge Camp on June 2, with Lieutenant-General Lord Chelmsford and his staff officers walking behind the gun carriage which served for the bier of the Prince Imperial, whose body had been found that morning. The Roman Catholic priest, the Rev. Father Bellow, follows the bier closely. The body is covered with the tricolour flag. Besides Lord Chelmsford and his staff, as mourners, walks a Frenchman, M. Deléage, correspondent of the Paris Figaro. General Newdigate, commanding the 2nd Division of the Army in South Africa, with the officers of his staff, is seen on horseback, in the background, saluting the funeral procession.

The Zulu War : Lord Chelmsford following the body of the Prince Imperial at Itelezi Camp.

The Zulu War : On the road to Ulundi.

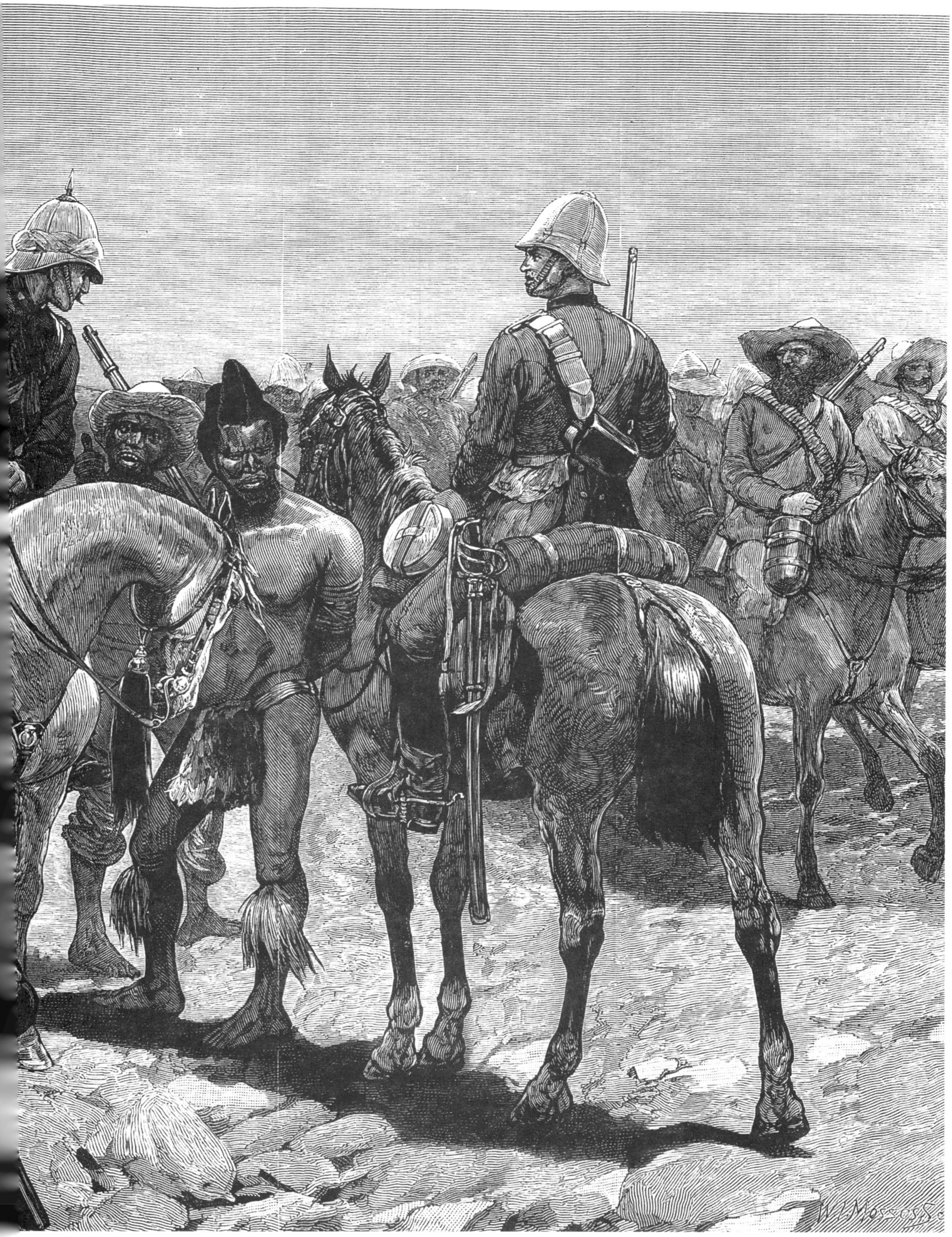
W.I.Mosses Sc

We have been reminded of an accidental mistake in the first hasty account of the Prince Imperial's death. It is to be observed that Lieutenant Carey and Colonel Harrison, respectively the Deputy Assistant and the Assistant-Quartermaster General, belonged to the Head-quarters Staff of the Commander-in-Chief – not to General Newdigate's Divisional Staff.

Our Correspondent on the Lower Tugela, writing on June 3, gives the following account of a ride into the enemy's country, and a visit to the battle-field of Gingihlovo:- "The main road from Fort Pearson to Fort Crealock is perfectly free from the enemy. Fort Crealock lies thirteen miles from the Lower Tugela, and overlooks the banks of the Amatikulu. A short ride from there takes you to the battle-field of Gingihlovo. This lies to the left of the main road going in the direction of Fort Chelmsford.

One of Lonsdale's Horse volunteered to accompany me, but was refused permission, as strict orders had been given that nobody was to be allowed to be further than a mile from camp. Luckily, an officer of the 91st Highlanders was going for a ride in the afternoon, and we started on our expedition to the battle-field. Of course we kept our eyes open as we jogged along, especially as only the week before this same officer was stalked by two Zulus, who glided like panthers through the long grass, and came unpleasantly near before they were seen. Some men of the Native Contingent, who were luckily not far off, thoroughly scoured the bush, where they were again sighted, but managed to escape. Just as we came to the road which turns off from the main track we overtook two of the Native Horse, and they volunteered to accompany us.

"A sharp canter of ten minutes brought us to the Laager, which is still covered with débris. A great many Zulu shields are scattered about the field; any heap which gives the slightest covering is a sure find. The tombstones of Lieutenant Johnstone and some men of the 99th, and that of Colonel Northey, which lies close to them, were rapidly sketched. These were in a good state of preservation; the wooden fencing around Colonel Northey's tomb has a rustic aspect, and the gravestone looks solemn and impressive, standing alone in the centre of this dreary plain. No dead bodies were to be seen, but I was told that they were lying in the surrounding bush. Luckily, no Zulus made their appearance; they swarm in the hills opposite, but perhaps our numbers were not sufficient to tempt them from their lurking-place. At any rate, a sharp trot would soon have brought us out of their reach.

"On our return to Fort Crealock we heard the alarm sounded. My friend leaped off his horse and rushed into the fort. In less than five minutes all the four faces of the fort were lined with men, two deep. The Native Contingent seemed perfectly happy, thus protected, squatting in the centre of the fort. A perfect stillness reigned during fifteen minutes. It had a peculiar effect to see so many men, with not a whisper to be heard among them. The setting of the sun heightened the picture still more. When the tattoo was sounded, a sudden transformation took place. What had seemed statues, were now animated with life and motion. The natives, as they marched to their own huts, uttered unearthly sounds.

"A neighbouring hill, a mile and a quarter distant, on which a vidette is stationed, is connected with the fort by a telephone. It is the first time that instrument has been used in warfare. It is of the greatest service, as voices are easily recognised by the sound. The telegraph has been laid between Fort Pearson and Fort Crealock, and the posts for it have been fixed nearly up to Fort Chelmsford.

"The movement of the 1st Division will be a slow one; the first steps will be to cover the landing-point at Port Durnford, and to build a pontoon bridge across the Umhlatosi river. These will of necessity be slow operations, but it is well to take such steps that another disaster may practically be impossible. This 'haphazard' war is a slow and tedious one, disliked both by officers and men. The general desire is for a successful termination of it this year, as the outcome of our vast preparations.

"There are eight hundred men *hors de combat* from the 1st Division. This is a big number, out of a total force of less than six thousand. If the present rate of sickness continues there will be no field offices left at the disposal of the General. Brigadier Clark is now laid up with fever. Yellow jaundice has lately appeared among the troops. A great deal of the sickness may be ascribed to the effluvia which arises from the carcases of oxen in different stages of decomposition. These lie on the road where the troopers have to escort the convoys, and at every hundred yards this horrible atmosphere has to be breathed. If detachments of mounted men could have been told off to drag the carcases a reasonable distance from the road, this would have greatly lessened the evil.

"The rain which has been long expected has at last come down. The grass, lately burnt up, will now soon change its arid aspect. Already green shoots are appearing. The three-days' rain did not flood the rivers to any extent; at present they are easily fordable on horseback. The huts at Fort Pearson, for the reception of the sick, are being rapidly run up. Four are already completed; they are built of reeds, and will be whitewashed inside. These huts will be a great boon to the sick; they have the advantage of being more comfortable and healthy than canvas tents.

"While the Engineers were cutting reeds from a lonely swamp, Mr Dickens, the proprietor, came up and said that he would send in a claim against the British Government for damage. He has already asked for compensation for loss of personal convenience. But he totally ignores that, if it were not for our troops, the Zulus would cross the river and burn his house, taking with them his cattle and all his moveable property. In pleasant contrast to such behaviour is the kindness of Mr and Mrs Cooley, in attending to the wants of the patients at Hirwin Hospital. They have devoted themselves entirely to the charitable work, and they deserve the thanks of every British soldier.

"Two months' provisions have now been accumulated at Fort Chelmsford, and a movement in advance will take place at the beginning of next week. The inaction has caused great complaints among the men, but the transport difficulty alone stops the onward march of the British soldier.

"The two Zulu emissaries, who made their appearance at Fort Chelmsford, did not come direct from Cetewayo, but only with his sanction. The chiefs had brought pressure upon the King to allow them to make overtures for peace. Shortly after, Usumquinto joined them, sent from the King himself.

"He was instructed to tell the white men that the King was willing to accede to any terms, if the white men would only retire across the Tugela, and the agreement should be made on the banks of that river. John Dunn was sent by the Major-General with a message asking, if the King wanted peace, why was he gathering an impi to fight against General Wood? He was told that, in future, he must send his peace messengers to Lord Chelmsford, as the Major-General was there only to fight."

We have engraved one of this correspondent's sketches. It shows a section of the trestle-and-pontoon bridge recently constructed by the Royal Engineers over the Lower Tugela, being conveyed by a team of eight horses, with an escort of soldiers, to the place on the river-banks where it will be launched for an additional component part of the structure across the water. The Lower Tugela, as most of our readers are aware, is the frontier stream dividing the British territory of Natal from Cetewayo's Kingdom of Zululand.

The other Illustrations presented in this Number are mostly contributed by Mr. Melton Prior in his sojourn at the different stations and head-quarters of the Army during this campaign. Such incidents as the arrival of news at a camp, or the study of topography in maps spread before the consulting party of officers, must often have come before his observation. The scene on the march to Ulundi, where the General and his staff draw rein and stop for a minute, while some of the natives are questioned about the route to be pursued, forms an effective subject for our larger Engraving.

The Zulu War : Death of Lieutenant Frith in skirmish at Erzungahan Hill.
From a sketch by our Special Artist Mr. Melton Prior.

The victory at Ulundi, achieved by the division of our troops under the direct command of Lord Chelmsford, news of which reached us last week, suggests more than one topic of satisfaction to the British public. It gives something approaching to definiteness to the previously hazy prospect of bringing the war in Zululand to a speedy conclusion.

Cetewayo must now be alive to the fact that, as a belligerent, he is overmatched. His chief Kraal, the centre, we may call it, of his Sovereignty, has been taken and burned to the ground. Though, perhaps, a larger portion of his army has been withdrawn to a more inaccessible and therefore a stronger position than that which they lately failed in defending; though the season in South Africa for campaigning has just come to an end; and though, if Cetewayo saw fit to do so, he might protract for some time to come the warfare which has been undertaken against him, it does not seem likely that he or his chiefs can longer indulge in visionary expectations, which the late event has done so much to destroy.

Sir Garnet Wolseley, it may be hoped, will propose terms of submission which, whilst they assure safety to the contiguous colonies, will, at the same time, consult, as far as may be, the susceptibilities of a gallant but savage foe. Such appears to be the intention uppermost in his mind. By the orders he has given, subsequently to the announcement to him of Lord Chelmsford's victory, he has made it tolerably clear, we think, that he does not contemplate a second campaign. Perhaps, even before these sheets can see the light, further tidings may reach our shores containing an announcement that, in all substantial respects, the Zulu war is over.

Another matter for congratulation may be found in the conduct of our troops. On no occasion have they exhibited greater steadiness in action. Young though the great majority of them may be, and therefore unseasoned against panic in the face of visible and appalling danger, they stood their ground with all the coolness and undaunted determination of veteran soldiers. The battle, it is true, was well and scientifically planned by Lord Chelmsford, who in person set the example of unflinching bravery, clear presence of mind, and unwavering confidence. But it might have had a different result.

It was not impossible that, confronted, as our soldiers were, with vastly superior numbers of raging foes, careless of and even courting death, they might at some point or other have given way, and have thus occasioned a pell-mell encounter. In which discipline loses its hold upon troops and science ceases to be effective. Happily, this formidable danger was obviated, or there might have been another Isandula. The description of the battle by Mr. A. Forbes, the Special Correspondent of the Daily News, presents as vivid a picture of the conflict as the pen of man can describe, and his appreciation of the conduct of the men engaged in it is emphatic.

We take the satisfaction which his assurance, corroborated by that of Lord Chelmsford, is calculated to give; but one cannot avoid the inference that, although successful in the instance before us, the immature age at which so considerable a proportion of our fighting army was hurried off to South Africa, cannot be repeated without enormous peril, and reveals some serious defect of our present Army organisation at home.

The public will be pleased, moreover, that Lord Chelmsford has rehabilitated his reputation as a soldier. He has been much and severely criticised, nor can it be denied that much of the criticism inflicted upon him appears to have been well founded. He was rash where he ought to have been especially cautious; he was hesitating where it was, above all things, important that he should have been resolute. But the difficulties of his position were, undoubtedly, great. His sense of responsibility could not have been otherwise than extremely onerous, and probably he had less confidence in his strategical skill than is indispensable in a great Commander.

When the whole truth comes to be known with regard to the material obstacles he had to surmount in moving his forces and in keeping open his communications with his base, it may be found that, although he possessed not the genius of a great warrior, he had no small share of the patience which should accompany it. It has been found, in fact, that, in front of the enemy, he knew both when and how to strike. The public will not grudge him the honour which he has redeemed, but is glad that the main object for which he so assiduously and, for a while, fruitlessly laboured, was achieved at last, not by another, nor by means of another, but by himself.

It would be folly to pretend that this victory at Ulundi is one of a character the recollection of which our country will cherish with a glow of patriotic pride. The war which, it is hoped, it will bring to a

The Zulu War : Ambassadors from King Cetewayo to sue for peace.
From a sketch by our Special Artist, Mr. Melton Prior.

close has never been one in which the people of Great Britain have taken an approving interest. It was initiated without consulting their wishes. The policy of it, however it may please the Cape Colonists, never commended itself to the authorities or to the people of the United Kingdom. It will never leave behind it any historical land mark to which posterity will revert with reverential feeling. It has not been popular even in the Army; and, although assented to by a Parliamentary vote, it has met with but few words of eulogium in Parliamentary speeches.

We have reason, perhaps, to be glad that it has not been more successful than it has. The country, having been dragged into it, could not, of course, put an end to the War, in the face of the disasters it has sustained, until it had sufficiently demonstrated its power of ascendancy. This it has now done, and it may be pretty confidently said that the best incident of the Zulu War is that which opens a way out of it.

It will, we hope, exhibit a useful warning of future High Commissioners, and it may read a lesson of some value to Governments who appoint them with so large a measure of discretionary control. Beyond this, we are afraid it will prove unproductive. It opens a way nowhere. It may place in safety colonies which need never to have been endangered. It does not even force an outlet for an expansion of trade, and it will scarcely increase the power of Christian influences among the races which it has affected.

Lastly, it may be a source of great dissatisfaction between the Colonies of South Africa and the Mother Country; for it cannot be supposed that we shall be content to let them prescribe the results of victories which, to a large extent, they leave us to achieve for them. Grave questions have still to be brought to an issue in the Colonial Office and in the Imperial Parliament, and the settlement of them, we fear, has not been forwarded by the haste with which the country was hurried into the Zulu War.

ZULU WAR ILLUSTRATIONS

The concluding act of the war has perhaps been opened by Lord Chelmsford's important victory on the 4th ult., at Ulundi, the capital of Cetewayo's kingdom. Our Special Artist, Mr. Melton Prior, has furnished some interesting Sketches for the present Number.

The Zulu War : Head-quarters of General Chelmsford, Erzungayan Camp.
From a sketch by our Special Artist, Mr. Melton Prior.

The Zulu War : General Newdigate interrogating a Zulu spy at his head-quarters, Landman's Drift.. From a sketch by our Special Artist, Mr. Melton Prior.

The interior of Major-General Newdigate's Camp at Erzungayan, with Lord Chelmsford's head-quarters there on June 16, is a business-like scene of the camping in Zululand. The Commander-in-Chief, with Major-Generals Newdigate and Marshall, stands listening to the report of a scout, one of the mounted colonial volunteer troopers, who has just come in from a ride around the outskirts of the Camp. It was in a skirmish near this place, on June 5, that the young Adjutant of the 17th Lancers, Frederick Cokayne Frith, was killed by a shot, as is shown in our front-page Illustration, falling from his horse, between Colonel Drury Lowe, who was at his right hand, and Mr. Francis, Special Correspondent of the *Times*, who rode on his left. He was not twenty-one years of age, and was a son of Major Cokayne Frith, of Dover.

The Zulu Ambassadors sent by Cetewayo to sue for peace were detained some days at Inodwengu Camp for the General's reply to their message. Our Artist had an opportunity of sketching the seated figures of these native dignitaries, Indunas or Councillors of State, and rulers of tribes or districts, folding themselves in their blankets, as they will do in presence of white men, though accustomed to be nearly naked among their own people. The almost nude figure squatting behind the nearest chief is only a servant. Their head-rings of stiffened and moulded hair betoken the respectable condition of husbands, each probably of several wives, and fathers of many children.

Natives in a farmhouse making bread for the British troops at Estcourt.
From a sketch by our Special Artist, Mr. Melton Prior.

Lord Chelmsford refused to hear of peace till the guns captured by the Zulus at Isandhlwana should be restored. On June 28, therefore, Cetewayo's messengers were sent back to him, with an intimation that the British force would advance to the river Umvolosi, a few miles from Ulundi, but would not cross that river till July 3, in order to give time for the guns to arrive, either with a Zulu regiment to lay down its arms, or with a thousand rifles to be given up. This was not done, and on the 4th, at six o'clock in the morning, the 2nd Division, under Major-General Newdigate, with the flying column of Brigadier-General Sir Evelyn Wood, crossed the river and occupied a position between Inodwengu and Ulundi.

Here it was attacked by a large Zulu army, which it resisted in the formation of a hollow square, with cavalry in the centre; till, the enemy giving way after half an hour's fruitless assault, the square opened and let out the cavalry, who charged the Zulu host in every direction, completely routing that large

The Zulu War: View of the spot where the Prince Imperial was killed, looking west. From a sketch by our Special Artist, Mr. Melton Prior.

The Zulu War : View of the spot where the Prince Imperial was killed, looking east.
From a sketch by our Special Artist, Mr. Melton Prior.

multitude of foes. An account of this battle was given in our last week's publication. The *Daily Telegraph* special correspondent, Dr. W.H. Russell, sends the following particulars:-

"The battle began at ten minutes to nine o'clock, the Zulus advancing silently and steadily from all sides. Our men were four deep, with the front rank kneeling, and the rear rank in reserve. The 90th, on the left flank of the square, were ordered to throw up shelter, which they did under fire, though not so effectively as was wished. At nine the firing became general. The noise was deafening; and the men behaved admirably. The artillery practice was excellent, and to this mainly is attributed the enemy's repulse. Gunner Morshead though wounded in the leg, crawled to the Gatling battery, and insisted on helping the Sergeant to fill the cartridge drums.

As an instance of the intrepid manner in which the Zulus came to the attack, we counted only twenty-eight paces from the front square to the nearest dead. One Zulu came within thirty yards of the Gatling gun, and when retiring was shot. The King's regiment suffered heavily. Four regiments of the Amatongas took part in the action. The Zulus were commanded by Dabulamanzi on our right, and by Sirayo on our left. Dabulamanzi was under fire for a considerable time. Our staff was much exposed during the action, which lasted for forty minutes. The Lancers, whilst pursuing the enemy, did great execution with their lances; but the horses could not compete with the little ponies.

James, of the Lancers, had a narrow escape. He charged two Zulus, and both turned upon him. One of his assailants threw an assegai and struck James's cross-belt, penetrated it, and inflicted a slight wound. After the pursuit, the mounted men were sent to burn the kraals at Ulundi. Lord William Beresford was the first in, and has been gazetted in the force as 'Ulundi Beresford'. The King's kraal consists of a round belt of huts eight deep. The house is a thatched building, consisting of four rooms and a verandah. Nothing was found but some empty gin, beer, and champagne bottles, and four prisoners.

It is stated that the King was present on a distant hill, with a regiment and a half. He believed that our men could not meet the Zulus in the open ground. The estimated Zulu loss is fifteen hundred."

The scene in camp at Landman's Drift, where General Newdigate, sitting in a camp-chair, with his lame right leg supported by a stool, interrogates a captured Zulu spy, brought in by Major Bengough's scouts, was sketched by our Special Artist at the time. He contributes also two additional Illustrations of the lamented death of the French Imperial.

These are a pair of accurately-planned views – one looking west, the other looking east – of the place where Lieutenant Carey and the unfortunate Prince, with the six troopers and one native guide, dismounted, to rest beside the stream, surrounded by the tall growth of "mealies" or native corn. The burning kraal, or hamlet of six huts, is shown at a little distance, and the donga, or dry ditch, towards which they fled when attacked by the Zulus, and in which the body of the Prince was found next morning.

A certain interest belongs also to the Sketch, furnished by Captain H.B. Laurence, of the 4th Regiment, showing a few cottages and huts at Utrecht, in the neighbouring district of the Transvaal. One of the farm-houses, indicated by a reference number, was the quarters of Colonel Bray, of the 4th, and contains the room occupied some days by the Prince Imperial. Another is the house which was occupied by Lord Chelmsford and his staff while at Utrecht. The house of the late Mr. Piet Uys, a well-known Dutch citizen and commandant of volunteers, who served with Brigadier-General Wood's force at Kambula Hill, and was killed on March 28, at the Zlobane mountain, is indicated in this view of Utrecht.

At Estcourt, in Natal, on his way from Maritzburg to the frontier, our Special Artist stopped at a farm-house which was converted into an inn, and there he saw three or four native servants employed in making bread for the 17th Lancers, who were expected next day. The farmer's wife and children, with an Indian coolie girl, nursing the baby, were looking on at the work of kneading the dough in large tubs. An officer stood by, whip in hand, but not with any intention of compelling the natives to industry by an application of the lash.

Our Extra Supplement next week is to be a large Engraving, drawn by our Special Artist, giving an extended view of the British troops, occupying a Zulu military kraal, on their march to Ulundi.

1. Residence of the late Prince Imperial.   2. Officers' Mess-Quarters.   3. House of the late Mr P. Uys

A sketch at Utrecht, showing where the Prince Imperial lived.
From a sketch by Captain H.B. Laurence, 4th Regiment.

THE ILLUSTRATED LONDON NEWS

August 9, 1879

ZULU WAR ILLUSTRATIONS

The bold, unwearied, dauntless, solitary horseman, "bloody with spurring, fiery red with haste," who is represented in our front-page Engraving, is the renowned Special Correspondent of the *Daily News*, Mr. Archibald Forbes.

This gentleman, who has served in a cavalry regiment, is equally distinguished, among those who follow military campaigns in the service of journalism, for his practical knowledge of warfare, his literary powers of description and spirited narrative, and his extraordinary feats of rapid travelling, through the roughest country and braving the most obvious personal dangers, to send off his letters or telegrams at the earliest possible moment.

After the battle of Ulundi, which was fought, between eight and nine o'clock in the morning, on the 4th ult., Mr. Forbes volunteered to convey Lord Chelmsford's despatch, for Major-General the Hon. H. Clifford at Maritzburg, announcing the victory, the news of which was to be instantly sent to England. The nearest telegraph station for the purpose of this important communication was at Landman's Drift, on the Buffalo River, the boundary which separates Natal from the Utrecht district of the Transvaal, a place situated nearly due west of Ulundi, and not less than a hundred and ten miles distant from it. Mr. Forbes had to go there as quickly as he could in order to dispatch his own report of the battle to the *Daily News*, and Lord Chelmsford was glad to avail himself of so good a messenger for the conveyance of the official despatch to be forwarded by General Clifford to the War Office.

It was a ride of the distance we have mentioned in fourteen hours, entirely alone, over a rugged and mountainous country without any proper roads, and with no small risk of being cut off by the straggling bands of the enemy dispersed all over Zululand after the rout of their main army, or probably still lurking about the British rear, and along the route of its communications, for the plunder of occasional convoys.

"Bloody with spurring, fiery red with haste."
The Zulu War : Mr Archibald Forbes's ride from Ulundi.

Mr. Forbes rode on all through the night, which was dark, with a thick fog, and he twice lost his way. He performed this valuable public service with such intrepid courage and so much personal address that we trust he will receive from her Majesty the Queen a suitable honorary distinction, at the request of the Secretary of State for War. If he cannot have the Victoria Cross, being a non-combatant, let him have the Order of St. Michael and St. George, which is usually bestowed on civilians for services rendered in any of the British colonies or foreign possessions.

The Extra Supplement given with this Number of our Journal is a large Engraving, drawn from the Sketches furnished by our Special Artist, which represents the army of Lord Chelmsford, in its advance to Ulundi, occupying a Zulu military kraal. The General and one of the officers of his Staff, on horseback, are in the centre of the ground; the troops have just come up behind, a regiment of infantry led by its mounted officers; while the half-naked men of the Native Contingent, with some Zulu women and children, who have sought refuge in camp, lie carelessly about the foreground. Officers of the Native Contingent are speaking to these people and ordering them to keep the place clear.

To the right hand are seen many of the round dome-shaped huts, built of poles and boughs, with a thatched grass roof, belonging to the Zulu soldiers, for whom the kraal was constructed by the command of King Cetewayo. Unsaddled horses, also packhorses, and waggons drawn by several pairs of yoked oxen, are brought forward to the left hand. In the distance are more waggons approaching the camp, with their guards of detached companies of soldiery, and one or two batteries of field artillery are coming up. The scene is very characteristic of South African campaigning business on the largest scale and in an open country. [The engraving described above was equal to eight pages of the original Journal, and we regret that it was so large that it was impractical to reproduce it and include it herein].

Our Correspondent with the division of the British Army which advanced from the Lower Tugela lately described, in a letter published two or three weeks ago, his visit to the battlefield of Gingihlovo. The state in which he found the graves of Lieut. Colonel Northey, of the 60th Rifles, Lieutenant G.C. Johnson, of the 99th Regiment, and others killed in that action, which took place on April 2, preparatory to relieving Colonel Pearson and the besieged garrison of Ekhowe, was particularly set forth in that letter. An Illustration of the place of sepulture, with its simple monuments hastily erected by the comrades of the slain soldiers, appears in our Supplement of this week.

The Zulu War : Graves at Gingihlovo.

We have news from the Cape to the 15th ult., with despatches from Sir Garnet Wolseley, who states that Cetewayo is now a fugitive, with his wives and a few of his personal followers, in the Ngoma Mountains. Sirayo, his brother, one of the principal Zulu chiefs, is still with the King, but Dabulamanzi, another of his brothers, who commanded the Zulu army at Isandhlwana, has surrendered himself to the British General. Lord Chelmsford has resigned his command, and is about to return to England.

The division of General Crealock, from the Lower Tugela, has joined the main army. Sir Garnet Wolseley has summoned all the Zulu chiefs to meet him, on the 19th, and to lay down their arms. He promises that their country shall not be annexed, or the ordinary customs of their nation interfered with, but only the military system of the Zulu kingdom is to be abolished. A chain of forts is to be erected across the country; and Zululand, it is said, will be divided into four separate principalities, each ruled by a native prince owing allegiance to the British Government.

The late Captain Hon. E. Wyatt-Edgell, 17th Lancers
Killed at Ulundi.

The late Lieutenant F.C. Frith, 17th Lancers
Killed at Erzungayan Hill.

THE LATE CAPTAIN WYATT-EDGELL

The only British officer killed in the battle of Ulundi, on the 4th ult., was the Hon. Edmund Verney Wyatt-Edgell, Captain of the 17th Lancers.

He was in the thirty-fourth year of his age, having been born Aug. 16, 1845. He was eldest son of the Rev. Edgell Wyatt-Edgell, formerly Rector of North Cray, and Henrietta, Baroness Braye in her own right.

The late Captain Wyatt-Edgell was heir to the peerage, and joint-owner with his mother of the Stanford Hall estate, in Leicestershire and Northamptonshire. But he thought more of his professional duty than of these brilliant prospects offered by a large property and an ancient title.

After being educated at Eton, and at Christ Church, Oxford, he entered the Army in 1866, joining the 17th Lancers, in which he attained the rank of Lieutenant in 1868, and that of Captain in 1873. He studied and passed a successful examination for the Staff College, Aldershot; but, after a few days' residence there, was summoned to active service with his regiment in the Zulu War.

His loss will be much felt by his comrades in the regiment. Captain Wyatt-Edgell was in 1877 a Liberal candidate for the representation of North Northamptonshire. He is the third of his family, bearing the same Christian name, Edmund, who has met a soldier's death. The second Lord Braye died of wounds he received at the battle of St. Quintin, in the reign of Queen Mary.

At the battle of Edge Hill, in 1642, another ancestor, Sir Edmund Verney, who was standard-bearer to King Charles I, fell grasping the Royal standard. On the paternal side, being grandson of Mr. Wyatt-Edgell, formerly of Milton Park, Egham, and of Great Missenden, Bucks, Captain Wyatt-Edgell belonged to the Verney and Hampden families, as well as to that of Wyatt of Nynehead, Somerset. The heir to the title of Baron Braye will now be his younger brother, the Hon. Alfred Thomas Wyatt-Edgell.

The Portrait is from a photograph by Messrs. Elliott and Fry, of Baker-street.

THE LATE LIEUTENANT FRITH

The death of this young officer, who was killed in a skirmish with the Zulus at Erzungayan Hill on June 5, has been noticed with much regret.

A Sketch of the incident, by our Special Artist, Mr. Melton Prior, was presented last week in our front page Engraving. It showed the unfortunate young man, struck by a shot, falling from his horse between Colonel Drury Lowe and Mr. Francis, the Times' Special Correspondent. Frederick J. Cokayne Frith was second son of Major Cokayne Frith, of Buckland House, Dover. He was in the twenty-first year of his age. He was educated at Haileybury, and, passing twelfth in the competitive examination of December, 1875, for commissions in the Army, entered Sandhurst College, from which he passed with a first-class certificate.

He was gazetted sub-lieutenant in the 17th Lancers in February, 1877; but on succeeding to a lieutenancy in the following year, his commission was ante-dated two years, in consequence of having obtained the first-class certificate at Sandhurst. In May, 1878, he joined the School of Musketry at Hythe, where he obtained a first-class certificate. He was a general favourite in his regiment, and diligent in attention to duty.

At the moment when the shot struck him he was leaning forward to take an order from the Colonel. He was buried the same evening in the camp. The funeral service was read by the Rev. G. Smith, in the presence of Lord Chelmsford, General Newdigate, the staff and other officers.

The portrait is from a photograph by Mr. Fall, of Baker-street.

THE ILLUSTRATED LONDON NEWS

August 16, 1879

THE ZULU WAR

Our Special Artist, Mr. Melton Prior, has apparently had a narrow escape of his life. It is mentioned by the *Times*' correspondent, in a letter of the 17th ult., that Mr. Prior, while sketching in the King's Kraal at Ulundi, after the battle and destruction of the Zulu capital, was chased by some lurking enemies. But they did not catch him or hit him; and, though he has met with a few rough experiences in this campaign, as in previous African and European wars, we hope soon to welcome his safe return to England.

The Zulu War : Brigadier-General Wood's division passing General Newdigate's camp on its way to the front.
From a sketch by our Special Artist.

He contributes to this Number of our Journal the sketch of Brigadier-General Sir Evelyn Wood's flying column, on its way to the front at Ipoka camp, passing the encampment of General Newdigate's division; also, that in which Lord Chelmsford, General Newdigate, and General Marshall are shown with their telescopes or field-glasses, all standing together and looking out across the country for the expected approach of Cetewayo's messengers or ambassadors of peace. These ambassadors had visited the camp some days before, and had been sent back to the Zulu King with precise information of the terms which would be accepted, and with an intimation that the army would, on July 3, cross the river on its advance to Ulundi, if no intimation were received of Cetewayo's submitting to those terms.

Hence the evident importance of their possible return to the Camp, as the time drew near, and the anxiety with which they were awaited by the three English Generals – Lord Chelmsford, attired in drab breeches, boots, and short dark coat or jacket, resting his telescope upon the tarpaulin covering of a dray or waggon, is shown in our Artist's Sketch as the one standing close to the wheel; at his right hand is General Newdigate, while General Marshall, with a smaller field-glass stands a few paces behind them; another officer lies sprawling on the top of the waggon, but not less intently scanning the distant horizon.

The same page contains an Engraving, from a Sketch by an officer of the 99th (Duke of Edinburgh's) Regiment, which formed part of General Hope Crealock's division advancing from the Tugela into Zululand. It represents the crossing of the river Amatikulu by the rear-guard of that regiment, and by the waggon-trains under their convoy.

Rear-Guard of the 99th Regiment crossing the Amatikulu River.

Our news from South Africa is to the date of the 22nd ult., but there are no fresh military events of importance. Lord Chelmsford and Sir Garnet Wolseley met at St. Paul's on the 18th, after which Lord Chelmsford went to Durban, where he was received with honours. He would return to England by way of Capetown, very shortly.

It is not expected that Sir Bartle Frere will resign. Generals Hope Crealock, Newdigate, and Marshall, Brigadier Wood, and Colonel Redvers Buller are coming home on account of health. The 17th Lancers and several other regiments will be sent home at once. Sir Garnet Wolseley had a conference with a number of the Zulu chiefs on the 18th, and received their submission. He has gone back to Natal for a few days, and was to be at Pietermaritzburg on the 21st, but would soon return to the army in Zululand.

Our three Generals watching for the return of the Zulu Ambassadors.
From a sketch by Mr. Melton Prior, our Special Artist.

Ulundi, which Lord Chelmsford had evacuated, is to be re-occupied by Brigadier Clarke with two regiments, as a fortified post. Cetewayo has retired, with six or seven thousand men, to the north-east portion of Zululand.

We learn further from a second edition of Thursday's Times that Cetewayo had on July 22 made another effort to know whether his liberty would be granted him. He said he was completely deserted by his warriors. A brigade under General Harrison, 2500 strong, one squadron of regular cavalry, and the second battery of artillery, move up to the Transvaal.

CAPTAIN CAREY

We present the portrait of this unfortunate officer, whose general character and services have been exceedingly meritorious, but whose professional career has been severely checked by the incident of the Prince Imperial's death in Zululand, and the subsequent court-martial.

He is the son of the Rev. Adolphus Carey, Vicar of Brixham, in South Devon, but his family, we believe, came from Jersey. His maternal grandfather was Admiral Sir Jahleel Brenton, who greatly distinguished himself in the naval warfare, under Nelson and others, at the beginning of this century, being First Lieutenant of H.M.S. Cæsar, and afterwards Commander of the Spartan frigate.

Jahleel Brenton Carey, the subject of this notice, was educated at a French Lycée Impériale, and at the Military Staff College, Sandhurst, where he obtained a free commission. He entered the service in 1865, in the late 3rd West India (negro) Regiment, and was placed in command of the fort at Accra, on the Gold Coast.

Having returned with his regiment to Jamaica, he served in the expedition on the Mosquito Coast, or in Honduras, and was favourably mentioned in despatches. When his regiment was disbanded he came to

England on half-pay, and went through the Hythe course of musketry instruction, for which he gained a first class certificate.

He volunteered in 1870 to serve with the English ambulance in the war between France and Germany, and received special thanks, with a cross and ribbon, for his conduct in the relief of the French wounded. He afterwards studied in the Staff College, which he left with high testimonials, and volunteered this year for the Zulu war. He was appointed to a Lieutenancy in the 98th, or Prince of Wales's Regiment of infantry, and went out in the transport Clyde, which was wrecked in Simon's Bay.

Captain J.B. Carey

Lieutenant Carey was specially commended for his conduct on board that vessel, which conveyed military reinforcements. Having arrived in Natal, he was employed in surveying the route for the troops, and in the selection of camping-grounds, all the way up the country. He was placed on Lord Chelmsford's staff with the appointment of Deputy-Assistant-Quartermaster-General, and rendered much useful service.

We are indebted to the London Stereoscopic Company for the photograph of Captain Carey, who is still awaiting the decision of the Commander-in-Chief upon the verdict of the late court-martial.

THE LATE COMMANDANT PIET UYS

Mr Piet Uys, an influential Dutchman of the Transvaal, was among those killed in the fight of March 28 on the Zlobane Mountain, while in command of a corps of volunteer horsemen. His death is much regretted by the English officers with Brigadier-General Sir Evelyn Wood's column, and by none more than Lieutenant-Colonel Redvers Buller. He had been of the greatest service to the English force during the campaign on the Transvaal border of Zululand. Mr Uys was followed into the field by his two sons, both in their teens – indeed, the youngest, if in England would, have been intent only on cricket and football; but in South Africa the development is quicker, and in these stirring times no son of Piet Uys could stay at home in laager with the women, old men, and children.

Brigadier-General Wood's despatch telling of the affair of March 28, thus speaks of him:- "Mr Piet Uys gave on the 28th a fine example to his men, as he always did, remaining behind to see them safe down the mountain. He was surrounded and assegaied." No one of the colonists of South Africa better deserves to have his memory kept alive, and we trust that the Government will show to his poor orphan children how we appreciate in England such men, English or Dutch fellow-subjects.

The drawing of Mr Piet Uys on horseback, with two mounted native followers, is contributed by Colonel J. North Crealock, Military Secretary to Lord Chelmsford. The mountain behind is that called Piet Uys Kop, at the foot of which he lived; but his children now reside near Utrecht.

The late Commandant Piet Uys, Transvaal Mounted Volunteers, killed in the Zulu War.

THE ILLUSTRATED LONDON NEWS
August 23, 1879

OFFICERS KILLED IN THE ZULU WAR

The portraits of two more officers of our Army who have lost their lives in the Zulu war appear in this Number of our Journal.

Lieutenant James Henry Scott Douglas, of the 21st Regiment (the Royal Scots Fusiliers) was eldest son of Sir George Scott Douglas, Bart., of Springwood Park, Kelso, M.P. for Roxburghshire. He was twenty-six years of age, and received his commission as Lieutenant in November, 1875. In his own neighbourhood he was much esteemed, and not less so in the regiment. While at home, cultivating his taste for historical, literary, and scientific studies, he occasionally lectured for the Kelso Institution at the Townhall. The subject of a lecture which he delivered last winter in that place was "The Beginnings of European Commerce." Upon some occasions in London also he made a successful appearance as a public speaker.

He went out to South Africa with his regiment in the spring of this year. His scientific attainments were soon recognised by his superiors in command, and he was appointed field telegraphist to General Newdigate's division, with which were the head-quarters of Lord Chelmsford. Within a few days of the battle of Ulundi, while employed in this special service, Lieutenant Scott Douglas, with Corporal Cotter, of the 17th Lancers, were missing. They may have lost their way, and some party of Zulus may have attacked them, in the same manner as what befell the Prince Imperial. On July 9, when Lord Chelmsford, with a column of the troops, was moving back from Ulundi, the dead bodies of Lieutenant Scott Douglas and the Corporal of Lancers were found at Kwanagwasa. They were properly buried on the spot next day.

Lieutenant George Rowley John Evelyn, of the 3rd (East Kent) Buffs, died of fever at the Fort of Ekowe, on March 30, being one of the garrison under Colonel Pearson, there shut up and beleaguered during two months by the enemy, till the advance of Lord Chelmsford and the battle of Gingihlovo brought relief. This promising young officer was but twenty-one years of age, and entered the service, as Second Lieutenant, in November, 1877. He was a son of Colonel G.P. Evelyn, of Hartley Manor, Dartford.

The portrait of Lieutenant Scott Douglas is from a photograph by Mr Mackintosh, of Kelso, and that of Lieutenant Evelyn from one by Messrs W. and D. Downey, of Eburystreet, and of Newcastle-on-Tyne.

Lieutenant Scott Douglas, 21st Regiment.
Killed in Zululand.

Lieutenant Evelyn, 3rd Buffs.
Died of fever at Ekowe.

ZULU WAR ILLUSTRATIONS

Our Special Artist, Mr Melton Prior, who has arrived in England, sent us before he left South Africa many Sketches of the Zulu War. The two large Engravings, which fill respectively the two middle pages of the Number and of the Supplement this week, represent the Battle of Ulundi, fought on July 4, and the Burning of Ulundi later on the same day. The Burning of King Cetewayo's House at Ulundi is the subject of another Engraving, which appears on our front page. The return, on June 28, of the Zulu Ambassadors, whom Lord Chelmsford had sent back to Cetewayo the day before, and who now brought a fresh message in reply to his offered terms of peace, is shown in one of the Illustrations. These are from our Special Artist's Sketches.

The army of Lord Chelmsford had advanced upon Ulundi from the west, along the ridge of the Babinanga hills, on the south side of the valley of the White Umvolosi. It consisted of General Newdigate's division, and what had been the flying column of Brigadier-General Sir Evelyn Wood, entering from the Transvaal frontier of Zululand. The Commander-in-Chief had massed the 13th Light Infantry, the 80th Foot, the 90th Light Infantry, Buller's Horse, and Tremlett's battery into one brigade, which was intrusted with the post of honour in the advance. The second division, under General Newdigate, consisted of the second battalion 21st Fusiliers, the 58th and 94th Regiments, with Major Le Grice's battery of Artillery, and details of the King's Dragoon Guards, 17th Lancers, and Colonial troops.

The Zulu War : Ulundi in flames – burning of Cetewayo's house.
Sketch by our Special Artist, Mr. Melton Prior.

The total number of troops at Lord Chelmsford's disposal after crossing the Umvolosi river amounted to 4062 British, 1000 natives, and fourteen guns, the remainder of the second division, consisting of the 4th Foot, and both battalions of the 24th, together with strong detachments of all other corps, amounting in the aggregate to more than 4000 men, had necessarily been left in the rear to guard our frontier line and keep open the line of communication.

On June 26 Cetewayo sent messengers asking, on various pretexts, that certain kraals or villages on the route of advance should not be burnt.

This request was disregarded, and a party was sent on to burn them; but the kraals were abandoned by the Zulus, who themselves set fire to them. On the next day Cetewayo sent in a number of the bullocks taken by the Zulus at Isandhlwana by the messengers returning to the camp, with a present of two elephants' tusks, and a letter in English, written by a sick trader in Ulundi, stating that the rest of the cattle and the two 7-pounders would follow. What he now sent proved his desire for peace. He expected that the British would now quit the country. He had been unable to call in any of the rifles taken at Isandlwana, so could not send them.

The Zulu War : General Newdigate addressing the Lancers before the battle of Ulundi.
Sketch by our Special Artist, Mr. Melton Prior.

The messengers stated that no Induna of consideration would consent to come as Ambassador, and that no regiment would consent to lay down its arms, which had been the stipulation. They acknowledged the existence of a strong force at Ulundi. The messengers were sent back next day. The ivory was returned. The cattle would be retained for a few days, awaiting events. The laying down of their arms by a thousand of the men now at Ulundi would be accepted instead of the previously stipulated submission of a complete regiment. Their safety would be guaranteed.

The Zulu messengers, as they came into the camp the second time, escorted by some of our Lancers, with the two tusks of ivory carried by the men behind, are shown in our Artist's Sketch. One of them held a cleft stick, in which was stuck the letter written by an unknown European for Cetewayo, addressed "To Lord Chelmsford, Esq." It was inclosed in an old English official envelope, which had been that of a letter sent to the Zulu King by Colonel North Crealock, Military Secretary, from Fort Newdigate, some time before. This envelope was afterwards given as a curiosity to our Special Artist, who sent it to the *Illustrated London News'* office, and a facsimile of the very document is here engraved.

The British Commander-in-Chief, as we have stated, dismissed the Zulu messengers, desiring them to tell Cetewayo that if by noon on July 3 the stipulations had not been complied with the advance would

The Zulu War : Return of the Ambassadors from Cetewayo to Lord Chelmsford.
A sketch by our Special Artist, Mr. Melton Prior.

recommence. The 3rd came and went, yet no sign of submission; so at daybreak on the 4th inst., leaving the 1st battalion 24th Foot, with some guns, under Colonel Bellairs, in laager on the banks of the White Umvolosi, Lord Chelmsford crossed the river and moved on the King's kraal over ground which had been carefully reconnoitred previously by Colonel Buller, V.C., C.B.

The Zulu War : Facsimile of envelope inclosing letter from Ketchwayo (Cetewayo).

Several accounts of the battle of Ulundi, written by Mr Archibald Forbes, by Dr W.H. Russell, by Mr Francis, and other special correspondents of the London daily papers, have already been quoted in this Journal. A further description is given by the *Natal Witness*. Its correspondent, in the course of his letter, says:- "Forming up in a hollow parallelogram, the 80th Regiment and the Gatling battery were on the front, the 90th and part of the 94th on the left flank, the 13th and 58th on the right flank, the 2nd, 4th, and remainder of the 94th forming the rear, while a battery of artillery was at each corner.

Keeping this formation, the column marched on to the second ridge beyond the drift without opposition, halting, in rear of a ruined mission station, and on the site selected the previous day by Colonel Buller. The advantages of the position were at once apparent. In front was a broad open country, with high grass sloping down to a spruit. In rear again the country was open, with little cover save a few bushes. On the left flank the slope was fully open up to the Nodwengu kraal, which was distant about 1000 yards. The Zulus were seen approaching in force both from the direction of Ulundi and from the bush on the right.

At half-past eight the mounted men under Buller were thrown out on the rear, left, and front, meeting the enemy and keeping them in check. Owing, however, to some mistake, the right was left uncovered by cavalry, and the mounted Basutos under Cochrane were accordingly sent out on that side with orders to draw the Zulus under fire. As the Basutos retired before the advancing enemy, the right face of the square came into action, commencing its fire fully five minutes before the rest of the force was engaged. At ten minutes to nine, or thereabouts, firing became general, all four sides of the square being simultaneously engaged, the Zulus after their manner throwing forward the horns of their army to surround the British force.

Coming on steadily and in complete silence, the Zulus advanced with the same intrepidity they showed at Ginghilovo and Kambula, and continued to advance until they had reached a spot not more than seventy yards from the faces of the square. The British infantry were formed in four ranks, the front rank kneeling, the rear rank reversed, facing inwards, while inside the square were all the necessary arrangements for keeping up a constant supply of ammunition. It was impossible for any force long to face the deadly storms of lead poured in among them at such a short distance. A few now and then made an attempt to advance further. One man rushed up to within thirty yards of the Gatling battery, and was shot as he was turning to retire. Another body was afterwards found twenty-eight yards from the line of square.

But it was no use. The main body wavered and paused. The moment was a decisive one. It was not the hail from the Martini-Henrys alone; there was the artillery continually at work sending shell after shell through the dark masses, breaking up every partial attempt of the Zulus to concentrate their strength for

1. The 90th Regiment.   2. Companies of 80th Regiment.   3. Two guns.   4. Brigadier-General Sir Evelyn Wood.
5. The Lancers waiting.   6. Two Gatling guns.   7. The 13th Regiment.   8. A horse just shot, which jumped 2ft. in the air.
9. Ammunition-cart.   10. Staff officer giving instructions.   11. Hospital water-cart.   12. Hospital, with surgeons at work.

The Zulu War : The Battle of Ulundi :

13. Lord Chelmsford and staff.   14. Ammunition-cart.   15. Dragoons kneeling, holding their horses.   16. Wounded man brought in, surgeon beside him.   17. Dragoon and horse just killed.   18. Bengough's Natives, kneeling or lying about.   19. Wounded officer assisted to the centre, or to the hospital.   20. Carrying ammunition to 21st Regiment.   21. Dragoons.   22. Bullock in ammunition-cart just killed.   23. Ulundi.

Inside the Square.
From a Sketch by our Special Artist, Mr. Melton Prior.

a rush. Then it was time for the Lancers to let loose. Riding down with their lances levelled, the British horsemen came upon the hesitating enemy, and in an instant their lines were broken through. The sabre was at work as well as the lance; and soon the Zulus, their ranks torn asunder, and their coherency as an army destroyed, were flying before the advancing cavalry.

And still, whenever there was a chance, the artillery thundered after them, and still the dull rattle from the faces of the square told how steadily the rain of death was supplementing the sweep of the broadsword and the thrust of the lance. But the Zulu does not fly without an effort to resist. Before the Lancers had gone 300 yards Captain Edgell was shot dead. Among the officers wounded were Lieutenant Phipps and Lieutenant Liedenbrood, of the 58th, and Major Bond, of the same regiment. Besides Captain Edgell nine men were killed, and the wounded, including the officers above named, numbered about seventy-five.

As a rule, the men behaved with great steadiness, and were completely under the control of their officers. The artillery were particularly conspicuous for their cool conduct. At one moment an artilleryman fell dead over the limber of a gun, but no pause was made to pick him up. A gunner of the name of Moorhead attracted special notice. He was wounded in the leg and rendered incapable of remaining at his gun. He was, however, determined not to remain idle, for when safe inside the square he crawled to where the drums of the Gatling battery were being filled with cartridges, and insisted on helping the sergeant to charge them. The Gatlings, by the way, were disappointing, having to cease firing six times during the action. Dabulamanzi was in command of the Zulus on the British left, and Sirayo on the right, the former being frequently under fire, while the staff on the outside were much exposed. It is stated, too, that four regiments of Amatongas were engaged on the Zulu side.

The battle over, and the enemy in full retreat, a short rest was allowed to the men, and a move was then made towards Ulundi by the mounted force, Lord W. Beresford being the first to enter the kraal. The place was wholly deserted, nothing except empty bottles being found in the King's house, a thatched building with four rooms and a verandah."

Our Special Artist's Illustration of the battle shows the various groups of figures and incidents of the day's work seen within the hollow square formed by the British troops, ranged in the order which has been described.

The Zulu War : Sir Garnet Wolseley's attempt to land at Port Durnford.

Besides the Illustrations supplied by our Special Artist, we have received from Lieutenant Crawford Caffin, R.N., of the Hind transport, two sketches of the seacoast of Zululand at Port Durnford, with the tremendous surf and swell of the sea on July 3, which prevented Sir Garnet Wolseley and his staff landing from H.M.S. Shah, and compelled them to return in that ship to Durban. The steam-tug Koodoo, commanded by Captain Twiss, the harbour-master, had taken Sir Garnet and several other officers from the Shah and met the surf-boat, as is shown in one of these Sketches; but repeated attempts to get them alongside of each other, so as to transfer the passengers to the surf-boat, were destined to end in failure. Sir Garnet was therefore obliged to go back to Natal, and to enter Zululand by the land route, losing several days before he could actually take command of the army.

The Zulu War : Signal station at Port Durnford.

RIDES IN ZULULAND

We have received the following letters from our Correspondent with General Hope Crealock's division of the army, which advanced by the coast route from the Tugela into Zululand:-

"Port Durnford, July 4

Yesterday, at three in the morning, the cavalry, consisting of the Natal Guides, the mounted infantry, Cook's Horse and four troops of Lonsdale's Horse, and two hundred of John Dunn's scouts, with several mounted Basutos, started for the camp. The first kraal we reached was eight miles beyond the river Umhlatosi. It was carefully approached, but was found deserted. At four o'clock we off-saddled for an hour, not far from Emangwene, where a military kraal, the head-quarters of a young regiment, was situated. At half-past five we reached the hill overlooking the kraal. A plan of attack was formed; two flanks were thrown out, and the centre advanced, in which were the mounted Basutos. These galloped up to the kraal, but found it was deserted.

There were three or four hundred huts, placed around that of the chief in regular form. Two of the huts had doors and windows, and all the comfort of an English cottage. The chief's hut was surrounded with an intricate palisade, which would have been serviceable against the assault of a savage foe. At half-past six the kraal was set on fire, while the cavalry, at a hand-gallop, scoured the country around for

The Zulu War : The burning of Ulundi.
From a sketch by our Special Artist, Mr. Melton Prior.

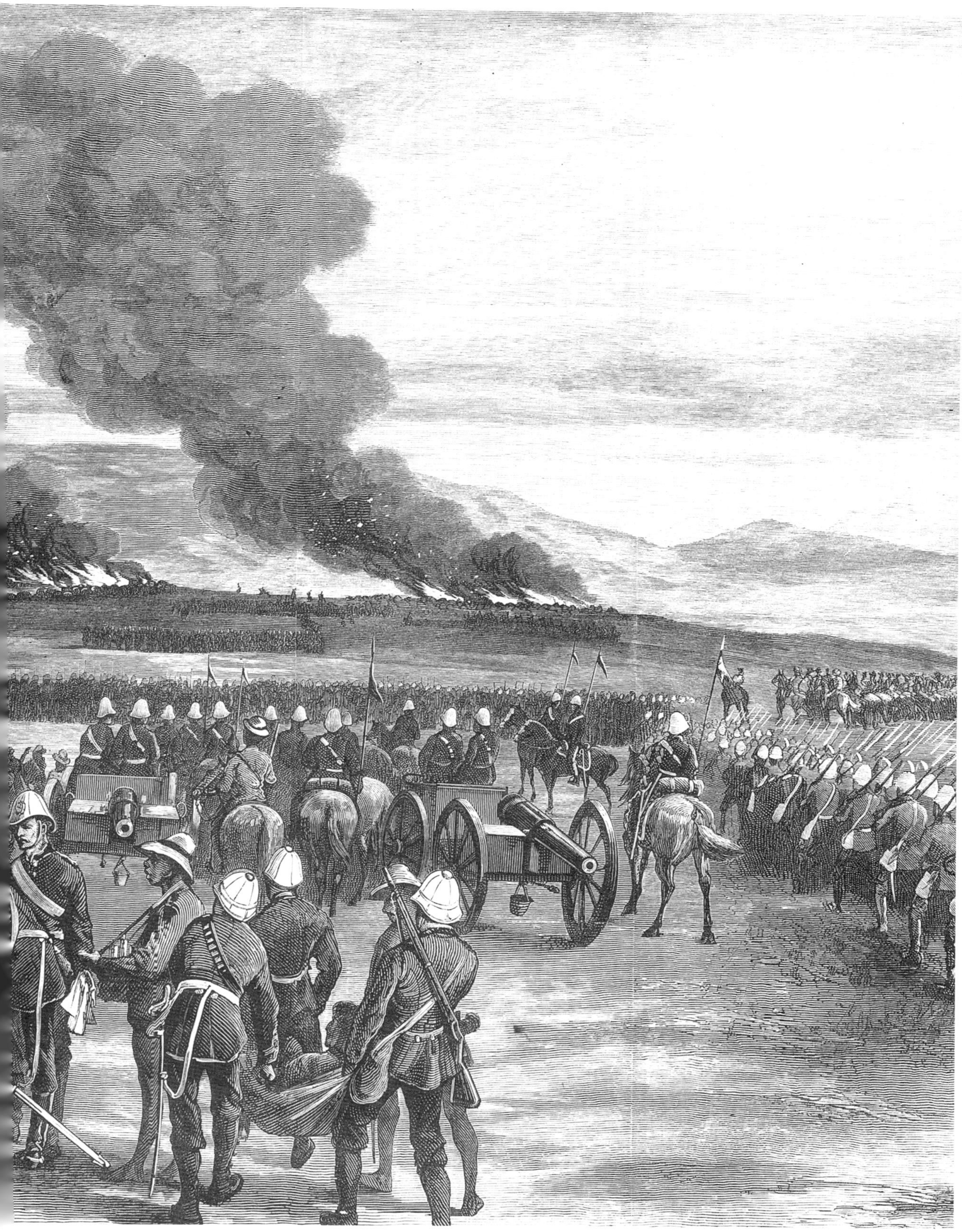

cattle. A kraal, situated about one mile from Emangwene, was surrounded. Two or three Zulus were getting ready their breakfast there. They were hauled out, and sullenly laid down their arms. Some mounted Basutos appearing, these Zulus were greatly alarmed. They have more dread of men of their own colour, who would, they know, give them no quarter.

A little further on two hundred Zulus fled in dismay at our approach. The spoils of the day were six or seven hundred cattle, eleven asses bred by Cetewayo, and about thirty goats. Major Barrow, who commands the cavalry, was apprehensive that the Zulus might assemble and endeavour to recapture the cattle. But they did not make the slightest attempt to oppose us. As usual, some Zulu women and children were brought in. It was strange to see a Kaffir woman in tears. Most likely, she had had her home burnt, and all that she cared for was scattered.

"A Zulu chief, with two hundred warriors, and a very large number of women and children, came to the camp here. The men surrendered and gave up their arms. Our troops, mustering about five hundred, were paraded, with flags unfurled, which made an imposing appearance. Only twenty-five old guns and two hundred assegais were delivered up by the Zulus. Such arms, indeed, are but a poor defence against the modern breechloaders. There is but little fight left among the Zulus now. Our vast preparations have terrified them, and their summer crops cannot be sown this year. The only fear is that Cetewayo has retreated into the bush; and, so long as he remains free, he will be a standing menace to Natal.

"The 91st Highlanders had a large bonfire on Wednesday, while the pipers played some lively strains, and several of the men sang excellent songs. During the evening, two or three officers danced a highland reel. It must have appeared a strange sight to the natives."

"July 8

"Unusual activity has been shown lately, in the way of reconnaissances by the cavalry. These were formerly kept in camp, employed in stuffing saddles or other work. At the drift of the Umhlazi, especially, where a few Zulus appeared at a respectful distance, the orders given were not to go out and test the courage of the foe. But now it is different. The Zulus evidently see that they are overpowered, and have made but a feeble resistance, firing only few shots at long ranges at our mounted men, who have driven off their cattle.

"Since it was made known to Zulus what favourable terms of surrender would be allowed, district after district has made its submission, preferring to keep their cattle rather than support a tottering King. The Zulus have been no losers by this campaign. The greater number of their kraals are left intact, and the same remark applies to their cattle. They care little for losing their men in battle. But since the battle of Gingihlovo not one man has fallen in fighting in this column of our army. Meantime, death by disease, though not by the hands of the enemy in the field, has made sad havoc with our troops.

"On Friday evening, July 4, the General started from the camp with sixty mounted infantry, three troops of Lonsdale's corps, Cook's Horse, the mounted Basutos, and the invaluable scouts of John Dunn. Previously, the 91st Highlanders and part of the Naval Brigade had marched as far as the river Umhlatosi, to give support to the cavalry if needed. On the march to this river, two troops of Lonsdale's lost sight of the main body, and soon afterwards missed each other. The country was open, but with scattered clumps of palm-trees, so that a body of men might be within fifty yards of another and still be unaware of each other's proximity. Luckily, some mounted natives appeared, who soon again found the beaten track.

"At midnight we got to the hastily intrenched camp of the 91st near the Umhlatosi. No delay took place here; the cavalry crossed the river, and we followed the well-beaten track which leads towards the Tonga country. We went nearly as far as the King's kraal at Emangwene, which was burnt two days before. Then turning sharply to the left, we went on at a foot pace until half-past two in the morning. The command was now given to off-saddle, the cavalry were ordered to form a large square, and two hours' rest was allowed. After this the order to start was again given; but the General returned to camp, as our night guide had taken us four miles out of our way. The command then devolved upon Major Barrow.

"No halt was made until we reached Undini, at half-past ten o'clock. Indeed, this long ride was too much for the horses; four of them had to be left behind; one horse actually fell down from fatigue before reaching Undini. We had to recross the Umhlatosi, and then a ride of three miles through a thick bush; but afterwards the country was comparatively open. Undini itself is situated on the top of a hill without any cover. It could not have offered any resistance to an attack. This place had evidently been deserted for some weeks. The store-house there contained ingredients for making gunpowder, some Eley's cartridges, and some of Sharp's gunpowder was found there. Before we left it the kraal, which consisted of 600 huts, was burnt. Zulu warriors came in and reported a great victory over the Zulus by Lord Chelmsford. This was the first intelligence we had of the fall of Ulundi.

"We had had a severe night's ride. At half-past twelve we again started; but, as John Dunn's scouts were to return to camp by twos and threes, taking the shortest route, two of them offered to be my escort through the Engoya forest.

"Shortly after leaving Undini we reached a deep clear pool, overhung by rocks, at the bottom of a hill. It was a tempting place for a halt, and my horse sadly wanted rest; but the scouts signified that we mush push on further before an 'off-saddle' could be allowed. A long distance had to be covered to reach the kraal at the other side of the Engoya. We came to a running stream, where three scouts had already arrived before us. They were undressed, or perhaps it would be more correct to say, they had taken off their red coats, and were enjoying the luxury of bathing, after their long journey of over thirty miles. One of them had a piece of soap, which speaks well for the cleanliness of the natives; but, unhappily, they can never get rid of the peculiar smell which all Kaffirs have. These scouts are Zulus, who have come over to our cause, together with John Dunn, their chief.

"After an off-saddle of more than an hour, a move was again made. At two in the afternoon we reached the top of the hill which overlooks the immense forest of the Engoya, which is the property of John Dunn. Here range after range of mountains could be seen stretching as far as the eye could reach, until the most distant one seemed to lose itself in the sky-line. Undini, Cetewayo's old kraal, was still blazing in the distance and sending up volumes of smoke.

"The ascent to this hill had told upon my horse. The indefatigable scouts now carried the blanket, which had previously been strapped to the saddle. After a short rest at the top of the hill, and a last gaze at the burning kraal, once the pride of Cetewayo, now to become only a heap of ashes, we entered the narrow Kaffir footpath which traverses this forest.

"It was a great relief here to get protection from the sun. Trees of various kinds grew thickly on each side. Some had fallen across the pathway, and often the scout in front had to clear away branches so as to allow my horse to pass. Nothing escaped the notice of these men. An imprint of a foot was carefully scrutinised; even a blade of grass trodden down was noticed. The scout, still leading, kept all the time a vigilant look-out on each side, moving his head rapidly this way and that. He was keen to espy any hidden danger; and, no doubt, there were numbers of Zulus in the forest. But they had made up their minds to surrender, and it did not enter into their heads to attack the white man now. Their kraals at the other side of the Engoya were left untouched, as they had been wise enough to surrender in time to save both their homes and cattle.

"The roots of the trees at each side of the forest path often entwined themselves into fantastic shapes, rising up above the ground, which lent a wild and weird aspect to this lonely scene. Two hours' ride brought us to a stream, which was clear and pure, and delightfully cool. As we neared the other side, which is towards the sea, the path became more difficult. It was frequently obstructed by rocks imbedded in the earth. At last, in one of the most picturesque spots I have seen in South Africa, the path seemed to end. Here a trickling stream had formed a pool, the water of which, tumbling over a ledge of rocks, lost itself among the tall trees which skirted both its banks. African oak, lignum vitæ, and other trees indigenous to this soil grew here in profusion.

"The pathway seemed never ending, but at last we reached a grassy slope, a pleasant relief after the three hours' ride through this forest. A young Zulu warrior quietly met us here. He was on his way to surrender himself. He seemed perfectly at ease, so perhaps he had known the scouts before the war broke out, as they belonged to this very district. Just as darkness set in we reached the open, where only eight days ago the cavalry had made a patrol in force, and had been fired on by Zulus hidden in the forest, who had driven their cattle in for shelter before our eyes. It would have been impossible to have dislodged them without great loss of life, so they were left masters of the situation.

"John Dunn's house could be seen distinctly on the right – poplar-trees grew on either side. The roof appearing untouched gave one the idea that the Zulus had spared this cottage; but it had been sacked, and the furniture was destroyed. A china basin had been recovered from one of the kraals after a raid and brought back to the owner. A kraal, temporarily formed by sheets of corrugated iron roofing, was fixed as the resting-place for the night. This formed good protection against the wind and rain.

"Next morning was wretchedly wet and miserable. We now went through plains scattered with palm-trees and a few bushes. Here the Zulus abounded, seeking shelter under every available bush. Some were busily thatching the half-burnt kraals. Others were minding their cattle. The women were carrying wood. The scene was a peaceful one. Two Zulus who were minding their cattle suddenly sprung up from the long grass, and as quickly hid themselves again. This was to show that they were friends.

"My two guides shouted their war song in bravado as we neared the kraals which were inhabited. Zulu men, women, and children came creeping from their shelter to look on the face of a white man. They seemed to have no vindictive feeling. It was simply from curiosity that they braved the rain to look upon the solitary horseman. No doubt they were happy and well pleased at the thought of being again at peace with their powerful foe. The Zulus who slept at the kraal I noticed were treated with the utmost kindness by the scouts, who gave them food and allowed them to share the warmth of the fire. A breakfast of mealies roasted over a fire was not a very nourishing breakfast, and glad I was to get to camp in time for the midday meal."

THE ILLUSTRATED LONDON NEWS
August 30, 1879

THE ZULU WAR

Lieutenant Lysons handing the Prince Imperial's sword to Lord Chelmsford.

The Illustration which occupies the two middle pages of this Number is furnished by a Sketch from the hand of our Special Artist, Mr Melton Prior, representing the distant view before Lord Chelmsford's army in the advance upon Ulundi, on July 3, with the British encampment and fortified position in the middle foreground. The King's principal Kraal or town of Ulundi, in a circular inclosure, is seen afar off; also that of Nodwengu, which was the capital of his father, King Panda, or Umpanda, and several other places which have been mentioned in the account of recent military operations. The river called the White Umvolosi pursues its course through the low-lying valley, on the left-hand of this view, which looks northward from a hill rising on the bank of that river.

Ulundi is about five miles east of Nodwengu; and ten miles below Ulundi is the confluence of the White and the Black Umvolosi, where Cetewayo had built a most formidable military kraal, with strong natural defences. Another of our Special Artist's Sketches is that showing the incident of Lord Chelmsford receiving from Lieutenant Lysons, an aide-de-camp, the Prince Imperial's sword, taken by the Zulus when he was killed, and lately sent back to the British Commander-in-Chief by their King, with his tardy overtures of peace. The view of St. Paul's Mission Station, in Zululand, situated thirty miles south of Ulundi, being the place where Sir Garnet Wolseley met Lord Chelmsford, is contributed by our Correspondent, who has accompanied Major-General Crealock's division of the army from the Lower Tugela along the route near the seacoast.

Lord Chelmsford, with Brigadier-General Sir Evelyn Wood, V.C., Colonel Redvers Buller, V.C., C.B., and other distinguished officers, arrived in England last Tuesday, landing at Plymouth from the Union Company's mail-steamer German. They were invited on board the Royal yacht Osborne to meet the Prince of Wales.

Lord Chelmsford's camp at St. Paul's.

Captain J.B. Carey, better known as Lieutenant Carey, the rank he bore at the time of the Prince Imperial's death, has been fairly acquitted by the final judgment of the Field-Marshall Commanding-in-Chief at the Horse Guards. An official letter has been written by the direction of the Duke of Cambridge to the General Commanding the Forces in South Africa announcing that her Majesty has been advised not to confirm the proceedings of the court-martial upon Lieutenant Carey. His Royal Highness proceeds to comment upon the events of June 1, having "received her Majesty's commands" to do so.

River Umvolosi   Umlambongwemya   1,2,3 Nodwengu: Kraal of late King Umpanda

The Zulu War : Advance of the British troops on Ulundi – The King's Kraal in the distance
From a sketch by our Special Artist, Mr. Melton Prior.

4. Qikazi.   5. Ndabakaombi.   6. Ulundi: Cetewayo's Chief Kraal.   7. Our Fort.   8. Our Encampment

The Field-Marshall Commanding-in-Chief approves all that Lord Chelmsford did for the reception and occupation of the Prince Imperial; but Lieutenant-Colonel Harrison mistook Lord Chelmsford's instructions to himself, and gave orders to Lieutenant Carey not sufficiently explicit, while he failed to impress upon the Prince the duty of deferring to the military orders of the officer who accompanied him. Lieutenant Carey formed a wrong conception of his position, and if his instructions were defective, his professional knowledge might have prompted him as to his duty. In conclusion, the Duke of Cambridge says he feels that he is speaking with the voice of the Army when he remarks that the "survivors of this fatal expedition withdrew from the scene of disaster without the full assurance that all efforts on their part were not abandoned until the fate of their comrades had been sealed."

Captain Carey arrived at Portsmouth yesterday week by the troop-ship Jumna, which also brought back the battalion of Royal Marines, who have not been required to fight in the Zulu War.

There is intelligence from the Cape to the 5th inst., forwarded by special telegram viâ Madeira. A successful Zulu raid is reported from Utrecht, and counter-raids on a large scale are projected under Colonel Villiers. The Pondos had attacked a native tribe under our protection, and it was feared that a war would ensue. Sir Garnet Wolseley, who reached Rorke's Drift on the 3rd inst., on his way to Ulundi, states in a telegram to the War Office that Cetewayo is still reported to be north of the Black Umvolosi with a few chiefs and a very small following. Five thousand Swazies were ready to attack him, and there would probably be 10,000 before crossing the Pongolo.

The Illustrations given in our last of the signal station at Port Durnford and the attempted landing of Sir Garnet Wolseley were from sketches by Captain H.M.G. Brunker, not by Lieutenant Crawford Caffin, as stated. In the brief memoir of Lieutenant G.R.J. Evelyn, of the 3rd Buffs, who died of fever at Ekowe, it should have been said that he was eldest son of Colonel G.P. Evelyn, commandant of the 1st Royal Surrey Militia, and grandson of the late George Evelyn, Esq., of Wotton, Surrey. Several of his family have been killed in the service of their country.

Lieutenant George Astell Pardoe, of the 13th Light Infantry, who has died of wounds received at the battle of Ulundi, was second son of the late Edward Pardoe, Esq., of Amberwood, Christchurch, Hampshire, formerly a Captain in the 15th Regiment, and a grandson of the late John Pardoe, Esq., of Leyton, Essex. Lieutenant Pardoe was born Sept. 5, 1855, and was consequently in his twenty-fourth year.

THE ILLUSTRATED LONDON NEWS
September 6, 1879

THE ZULU WAR

The battle of Ulundi, fought by Lord Chelmsford on July 4, is the subject of our large Engraving, filling a whole sheet of paper, and equal in size to eight pages of this Journal, which forms the Extra Supplement of the present week. This Engraving is furnished by a drawing from the skilful pencil of Mr. Melton Prior, our Special Artist lately with Lord Chelmsford's army in Zululand. It represents, in the foreground, the final rush of the Zulus, viewed from behind their position, near the encampment which had been occupied by our troops shortly before, and at which the spectator is supposed to remain beholding their attack on the troops, now drawn up in a closed square formation, as seen in the background some hundreds of yards distant. [The engraving described above was equal to eight pages of the original Journal, and we regret that it was so large that it was impractical to reproduce it and include it herein].

The Zulus behaved with amazing courage, repeatedly attempting to charge, though mown down by hundreds under the ceaseless fire of Martini-Henry rifles, with shells from the artillery; so that they were not able to come, in any numbers, within sixty yards of the sides of that terrible square. Their own firearms made a great deal of noise and smoke, and sent a heavy rain of bullets over the heads of our soldiers, but, for want of skill in musketry practice, failed to do much execution. Only a dozen men were killed on our side, while less than a hundred, including natives, were even wounded, but few of them very severely.

Lord William Bereford's encounter with a Zulu in the reconnaissance across the Umvolosi, July 3.
From a sketch by our Special Artist.

On the other hand, it is estimated that fifteen hundred of the Zulus were killed in this desperate conflict on their side, which did not last an hour. The force engaged was composed of Major-General Newdigate's division and Brigadier-General Sir Evelyn Wood's column, together mustering about 4000 European regulars, 1000 Native troops, twelve guns of the Royal Artillery, and two Gatling guns. After the repulse of the last Zulu attack, the square of British troops opened, and let out the 17th Lancers and Colonel Buller's irregular cavalry, which pursued the retreating enemy, inflicting much additional slaughter upon them.

An incident which took place on the day before, July 3, in the reconnaissance that was made across the River Umvolosi, is delineated by Mr Prior in his Sketch presented on our front page. It is that of a hand-to-hand single combat between Lord William Beresford and one of the Zulu warriors, who was killed, in the manner shown in the Sketch, being run through with the sword piercing his shield and his naked body. Mr Prior's other Sketches published this week are those of Lord Chelmsford and his staff, on a spur of the Ibabanango range, looking out for Ulundi; and a scene in camp on the night before the battle, with several officers discussing the chances of a fight next day; also, the Colonial Volunteers with captured cattle; and a view of the fatal crossing-place on the Buffalo River, known as "Fugitives' Drift," with the stone to which Lieutenant Melvill vainly attempted to cling when he had borne off the colours of the 24th Regiment from Isandhlwana.

The Zulu War : Investiture of Major Chard, R.E., with the Victoria Cross.

The military ceremony of General Sir Garnet Wolseley investing Major Chard, R.E., with the Victoria Cross, in the presence of Lord Chelmsford and the Staff, is the subject of another Illustration. This is from a sketch by Lieutenant N. Newnham Davis, of the 3rd Buffs, belonging to the special force of Mounted Infantry. Sir Garnet, who was on horseback, called Major Chard forward, his company of Engineers being a little in front of the line of troops. Major Chard saluted, and then held his sword at the "carry," while the General briefly addressed him with due congratulations, afterwards pinning the cross to his breast and shaking hands with him. Lord Chelmsford, also on horseback, appears to the left hand; to the right is Colonel Colley, Chief of the Staff, who read the official notification of the honour conferred on Major Chard.

The latest news from Sir Garnet Wolseley, who is at Ulundi, appears in a despatch dated the 18th ult. He states that, since the 13th, troops under Colonel Barrow and Lord Gifford had been in pursuit of Cetewayo, who had but a small number of followers. His Prime Minster, Mnyamana, and another important chief, Usingwayo, surrendered on the 14th, with three of the King's brothers. The new military kraal, Amanakanzi, at the confluence of the Black and White Umvolosi, was destroyed on the previous day. Sir Garnet Wolseley was to be at Pretoria on the 10th inst., to settle the affairs of the Transvaal. The Pondos and Basutos seem to be getting into a more pacific condition.

The Zulu War : Lancers returning from burning kraals.

THE MANCE HELIOGRAPH

The Mance heliograph, of which a description and an Engraving appeared in our Journal of April 26, showing its employment by Lord Chelmsford to flash messages to Colonel Pearson when shut up in Ekowe, continues to do good service in South Africa. Sir Garnet Wolseley, in his rapid advance to the theatre of war, was enabled by its agency, on reaching the capital of Natal, to take over the active control of the forces operating far away in Zululand. His Excellency arrived on June 28 at Pietermaritzburg, whence, a few hours later, he could report, "have placed Lord Chelmsford in command of the Second Division and of Wood's forces until I can reach them. Have no difficulty in flashing orders to him."

In a subsequent despatch, detailing his arrangements after the fall of Ulundi, Sir Garnet Wolseley states that "Heliographs are working perfectly. Stations at Altezeli, Marshall, Evelyn Wood, and Kwamagwasa, and one being established at St Paul's." Many other startling proofs of the usefulness of Mr Mance's invention have been afforded during the Afghan and Zulu wars, and have excited much attention at home. A few days ago, Mr S. Goode had the honour of showing the heliograph to their Royal Highnesses the Prince and Princess of Wales, on board the Royal yacht Osborne, and explaining its application to naval purposes. Princes Edward and George were present and showed much interest in the adaptation of sun-signalling to the dot and dash system, with which their Royal Highnesses were familiar.

Shortly before the prorogation of Parliament, the members of the House of Commons were afforded an opportunity of witnessing the working of the heliograph, Mr Goode having attended in one of the anterooms of the House on two evenings with that object.

Lord Chelmsford and staff looking for Ulundi.

The Royal warrant empowering the Commissioners of the Patriotic Fund to receive and distribute the Zulu War Funds enacts that "the Isandhlwana and Rorke's Drift Fund," and the "Zulu War General Fund," both raised by the Military Committee, and the moneys subsequently raised at the Mansion House, be kept separate and distinct, and that each account shall bear the expense of its own administration by the Commissioners.

The Zulu War: Volunteers burning kraals and driving away cattle.

The Zulu War : Fugitives' Drift, Buffalo River, with the stone to which Lieutenant Melvill clung.

Head-quarters, six miles from Ulundi, July 3 : "Shall we have a fight tomorrow?"

THE ILLUSTRATED LONDON NEWS

September 13, 1879

THE ZULU WAR

Three further Illustrations of this subject, from sketches by our Special Artist, have been engraved for the present number of our Journal. One of them is an interior view of the old post at Rorke's Drift, which was hastily converted into a fort by Major Chard, R.E., V.C., and Major Gonville Bromhead, V.C., of the 24th Regiment, then simply Lieutenants, on the night of Jan. 22, and which they held, with scarcely a hundred men under their command, during twelve hours and through that terrible night, against not less than three thousand Zulus, emboldened to the attack by their recent destruction of the British force at Isandhlwana.

The new fort on the same site, which has been constructed by the Royal Engineers and other troops forming its garrison, contains a particular quarter named "Bromhead's Post," to commemorate the place where that brave officer took his stand on Jan. 22, while engaged in directing the little garrison to repel the frequent assaults of that overwhelming multitude of foes. Not far distant from the ford over the Buffalo river, which is called Rorke's Drift, another fort has been erected, which bears the name of Lieutenant Teignmouth Melvill, the young officer who carried off the regimental colours of the 24th from Isandhlwana, and who was intercepted and slain by the enemy near this place.

"All's well!" – Sketch in Bromhead's Post, New Fort, Rorke's Drift.

Scene in the new Fort Melvill, Rorke's Drift.

Interior of old Rorke's Drift Post.

THE ILLUSTRATED LONDON NEWS   September 20, 1879

THE ZULU WAR

A sketch by Mr. Melton Prior, our Special Artist late with the army in Zululand, represents one of the native guides, accompanying a party in a reconnaissance, in the attitude of listening with his ear close to the ground, for distant sounds of movements of the enemy.

There is little fresh intelligence of the military operations under the direction of Sir Garnet Wolseley, which have been almost confined to the pursuit of the fugitive Cetewayo. His capture or surrender on the 28th ult., is reported. This news reached London on Wednesday last, by telegram which was forwarded to the Colonial Office by Mr. Pender, Chairman of the Telegraph Construction and Maintenance Company.

It is stated that the Zulu King was captured "on the north-east of Zululand on Aug.28th." We trust he will be kindly and honourably treated as a prisoner of war or prisoner of State, for he is neither a rebel nor in any way a criminal, and has bravely defended his own country, as he had a right to do, against a foreign invasion. There is now an end of the war; and Sir Garnet Wolseley can proceed with his plan of dividing Zululand into six or seven provinces, each to be ruled by a native chief responsible to the British Government.

Her Majesty the Queen, who last week received Sir Evelyn Wood and Colonel Redvers Buller as her guests at Balmoral, and personally decorated them with the Victoria Cross, for their services in the Zulu War, has also bestowed the Victoria Cross upon several other gallant officers and one private soldier, for signal acts of bravery in the same campaign. Among these are Lord William Beresford, Captain in the 9th Lancers, and Major William Knox Leet, of the 13th Light Infantry.

Lord William Beresford is thus distinguished for his gallant conduct in having, at great personal risk, during the retirement of the reconnoitring party across the White Umvolosi River on July 3 last, turned to assist Sergeant Fitzmaurice, 1st Battalion 24th Foot (whose horse had fallen with him), mounted him behind him on his horse, and brought him away in safety under the close fire of the Zulus, who were in great force, and coming on quickly. Lord William Beresford's position was rendered most dangerous from the fact that Sergeant Fitzmaurice twice nearly pulled him from his horse.

Major William Knox Leet, V.C., 13th Light Infantry, who has likewise earned the Victoria Cross by his gallant conduct in the Zulu campaign, is a son of the late Rev. E.S. Leet, Rector of Dalkey, Ireland, and the youngest of five brothers, all of whom have served, or are now serving, in Her Majesty's Army or Navy, and have received medals for war services, his brother, Captain H. Knox Leet, of the Royal Navy, being the fortunate possessor of six, including the Legion of Honour and the Medjidie.

Major Leet has been for upwards of twenty-four years in the Army, having been gazetted to the 13th Light Infantry on July 5, 1855. He served with distinction through the Indian Mutiny campaign, and was frequently mentioned in despatches for gallantry in the field. For six years he was adjutant of his regiment, and subsequently Instructor of Musketry to the 10th Dépôt Battalion, Captain Instructor on the Staff at Hythe, and D.A. Adjutant and Quartermaster-General at Cork from June 1872, until September 1877, when he proceeded to join his regiment in the Transvaal.

He served through the campaign against Sekukuni, and subsequently joined Wood's "fighting column" before it crossed the Blood River. He was then appointed Corps Commandant of the two battalions of "Wood's Irregulars," and Oham's warriors were also placed under his command. The corps was engaged in many dangerous expeditions with the Irregular Cavalry, under Colonel Buller, and that distinguished soldier reported in the strongest terms on the gallant conduct of its Commandant.

In the retreat from the Zlobane Mountain Major Leet's horse was shot under him, and his led horse was also killed. He then mounted a pack-horse, and in descending the mountain with two other officers became separated from the rest of the force, and the Zulus, seeing this, rushed after them. The mountain was very steep and rocky, with occasional precipices; and the little party suddenly found themselves over one of these, with no chance of escape, except by trying back in the direction of their pursuers.

This course they promptly adopted; but by the time they cleared the side of the precipice the Zulus were almost on them, firing and throwing their assegais. One of the three, Lieutenant Duncombe, was here struck down, and another, Lieutenant Smith, of the Frontier Light Horse, was so exhausted that he was unable to go on, and would inevitably have been assegaied had not Major Leet waited for him, and, making him hold on by the pack-saddle of his horse, thus helped him along; but in a short time,

Zulu guide listening for sounds of the enemy.

finding himself incapable of further effort, he generously told Major Leet to save himself as he could go no further.

Then, his gallant comrade, with the noble self-sacrifice of a true British soldier, refused to desert him, and, by a great effort, succeeded in dragging him up behind him, though there were no stirrups to the pack-saddle, and Lieutenant Smith was almost helpless from exhaustion. The horse was also much exhausted; but the ground was now less difficult, and at last they succeeded in escaping from the bullets and assegais of their pursuers. For this noble act Major Leet has been awarded the Cross of Valour by the Queen.

Next day, in the battle of Kambula, he commanded the fort which, with wise forethought, had been constructed by Sir Evelyn Wood in front of the position, and which contributed so materially to the overthrow of the King's Army. Soon after this battle Major Leet was obliged, on account of a severe injury to his knee which he suffered in the retreat from Zlobane, to resign the command of "Wood's Irregulars" and retire from active service, and ultimately it became necessary to invalid him to England.

The Victoria Cross has also been conferred upon those mentioned below:-

Surgeon-Major James Henry Reynolds, Army Medical Department, for the conspicuous bravery during the attack at Rorke's Drift, on Jan.22 and 23, 1879, which he exhibited in his constant attention to the wounded under fire, and by his voluntarily conveying ammunition from the store to the defenders of the hospital, whereby he exposed himself to a cross fire from the enemy both in going and returning.

Lieutenant Edward S. Browne, first battalion 24th Regiment, for his gallant conduct on March 29, 1879, when the mounted infantry were being driven in by the enemy at Inhlobane, in galloping back and twice assisting on his horse (under heavy fire and within a few yards of the enemy) one of the mounted men, who must otherwise have fallen into the enemy's hands.

Private Wassall, 80th Regiment, for his gallant conduct in having, at the imminent risk of his own life, saved that of Private Westwood, of the same regiment. On Jan 22, 1879, when the camp at Isandhlwana was taken by the enemy, Private Wassall retreated towards the Buffalo River, in which he saw a comrade struggling and apparently drowning, He rode to the bank, dismounted, leaving his horse on the Zulu side, rescued the man from the stream, and again mounted his horse, dragging Private Westwood across the river under a heavy shower of bullets.

THE ILLUSTRATED LONDON NEWS

September 27, 1879

Memorial stone on the spot where the Prince Imperial was killed.
From a sketch by Major Marter.

THE PRINCE IMPERIAL'S DEATH IN ZULULAND

We are favoured by Colonel Davies, of the Grenadier Guards, commanding at Fort Newdigate, in Zululand, with a Sketch drawn at his request by Major Marter, of the King's Dragoon Guards (the officer who has captured King Cetewayo), showing the simple memorial constructed by Corporal Sully and a few soldiers under his orders, to mark the spot where the French Prince Imperial was killed, or where his body was found next morning.

It is about six miles from Fort Newdigate, in the valley of the Ityotyosi; and views of the place, from Sketches by Mr. Melton Prior, our Special Artist, have already appeared in this Journal. The stones composing this monument, which in form resembles one of the ordinary flat gravestones in an English churchyard, were shaped by the men in garrison at Fort Newdigate, and were carried to the spot in an ox-waggon.

The headstone and those forming the cross and the letter "N" are white, the others of a dark colour. The length of the tomb, if it may be so called, is about 8 ft., the breadth, 3 ft; and the height of the banks on each side about 7 ft. To the left of the sketch is shown an easy way through the donga towards the kraal near which the party was when fired upon. Major Marter says, "Having seen the body myself lying in the donga and marked the spot, I know that the work is correctly placed." We give a portrait of this officer on another page.

THE CAPTURE OF CETEWAYO

We announced last week, that the defeated and deposed King of the Zulus had been taken prisoner, or had surrendered, in the Ngome forest, in the north-east part of Zululand. Some ten days before, on the 18th ult., a force under Lord Gifford having been dispatched by Sir Garnet Wolseley in pursuit of the King, his speedy capture was predicted.

A week later the pursuers ascertained that Cetewayo was hiding in the kraal of his Prime Minister, having become a fugitive from the time of the defeat of his army at Ulundi. Meanwhile Lord Gifford had kept up a hot pursuit, and, having on Aug. 21 captured a native, he was promised information as to Cetewayo's hiding-place in the Umvolosi bush. Acting on this statement, Lord Gifford detailed Colonel Clarke, with 300 men, to surround this locality, while the pursuing party was divided into several detachments.

Major Richard Marter, the capturer of Cetewayo.

One was commanded by Major R.J.C. Marter, of the 1st King's Dragoon Guards. These parties traversed the country in all directions. Major Marter, who came into camp with a troop on Aug. 22, had to report that he had lost during his march three horses, which had been killed by lions. Soon after this date the Major again started in quest of the defeated monarch, and on Thursday, the 28th ult., when in the north-east of Zululand, he overtook and secured the fugitive.

Major Marter entered the King's Dragoon Guards in January, 1851, and has served with considerable distinction abroad. He was at one time Assistant-Quartermaster-General in Ireland. We give the portrait of this officer, who was accompanied by a detachment of his own regiment and a troop of Lonsdale's colonial volunteer horsemen. The following account of the manner of the King's capture has been published:-

"The kraal in which the King was captured lies eighteen miles north of Brigadier Clarke's camp on the Black Umvolosi. Lord Gifford marched from near there through Tuesday night, arriving within four miles of the kraal at daybreak with the white cavalry and natives. They lay in ambush, fearing to advance across the open ground, and waiting for the night to make the attack, lest the King should see and escape into the bush, which borders the kraal within a hundred yards on the north side. Lord Gifford was on the south-east side.

In the mean time Major Marter, with his force, appeared on the north-east and was seen by the King, but was not feared, the King thinking the cavalry in the bad ground could not approach quietly or without warning. Major Marter, however, had stripped the saddles and left the scabbards behind. Disappearing from view, he stole up noiselessly through the bush. The Native Contingent, whom he had concealed, were put in advance, and were able to move more rapidly than the horses. These men dashed out of the bush and surrounded the kraal, saying, 'The white man is coming; you are caught.'

Major Marter then rode up and dismounted, entered the kraal, and coming straight to the hut in which the King was, called on him to come forth and surrender. The King feared, and said, 'No, you come in, to me;' but Marter was inflexible, and the King, creeping out, stood up among the soldiers with stately composure.

One of them sought to lay his hands upon him, but he waved the man back disdainfully, saying, 'White soldier, let me be.' He then asked to be shot. Lord Gifford's dismounted men, posted in concealment to watch the kraal, had seen Major Marter's ruse, and ran with the news to Lord Gifford, who then galloped in. The King's bearing on the march, and passing between the lines of the 60th Regiment into his tent, was dignified and calm. Wearing a red blanket over his breast in the manner of a Roman toga, he stepped slowly, looking round with head thrown back and haughty gaze at the soldiers around him.

When captured, he asked the rank of the officer who had taken him. He treated the Native Contingent contemptuously. The King's servant fired one shot. The King seems to have suffered his capture partly through weariness and exhaustion, partly because he felt himself hemmed in, and partly through one of the fits of morose and sullen resignation which have lately come upon him at intervals."

Cetewayo was brought a prisoner to the head-quarters of General Sir Garnet Wolseley at Ulundi on the 31st, with a guard of the King's Dragoon Guards, the 60th Rifles, and the Native Contingent. Eleven of his people escaped from custody during the two days' march, and five of them were shot because they would not allow themselves to be recaptured. The fallen King was to be sent down to the coast, and to be removed by sea. It was not yet known what place of residence would be assigned to him, but he was to be brought to Capetown for the present, to await further instructions from the Imperial Government.

There is no reason to apprehend that he will be harshly treated by those acting under the direct authority of her Majesty's Government in South Africa.

But we regret to observe that grossly mistaken notions of the past conduct of Cetewayo, as King of the Zulus, have become current, and that much undeserved obloquy has been cast upon him. Even a leading article in the *Times* of last Tuesday contains summary accusations which, though repeatedly put forward, in general terms, by Sir Bartle Frere and other officials seeking to justify the late war, remain utterly devoid of proof; and it is reasonable to believe that, if they had been founded in fact, some evidence of a substantial kind would ere this have been produced to support them.

It is alleged, without stating when or where, or by what agency, or under what circumstances, that Cetewayo used to send out his "impis" or bands of soldiery, "to kill Zulus suspected of conversion to Christianity;" that old men were killed by his orders because they would not attend his Court; and that girls were killed because they would not marry old men. "These facts," says the writer in the *Times*, "are well authenticated and beyond dispute."

We will undertake to deny the authenticity and veracity of such assertions, if they are supposed to stand or fall by any evidence to be founded in the documents hitherto printed for the information of Parliament. No distinct evidence has yet been furnished, and neither Sir Bartle Frere nor any other official person has claimed to be in possession of reserved evidence, fixing these charges of extreme cruelty upon the deposed Zulu King.

Neither by Sir Theophilus Shepstone, nor by Mr. Dunn, who are personally acquainted with Cetewayo and his kingdom, have these charges been expressly confirmed; while Bishop Colenso, having had constant and intimate communication with the Zulus during a quarter of a century, indignantly repels such charges as malicious fictions.

With regard, more particularly, to the rumoured massacre of some girls and young women, in 1876, for refusing to marry the soldiers of certain regiments, the whole story has no other foundation than what may be found in the Parliamentary Bluebook C – 1748, at pages 198 and 216. It comes only to this, that the magistrate resident at Newcastle, in Natal, a long way from the frontier of Zululand, chanced to hear this horrible rumour from some of the natives about him, and mentioned it, unofficially, in a private letter.

This reached the Lieutenant-Governor of Natal, who thereupon did not make any proper inquiry into the facts, but having got the same story, in a vague and uncertain manner, from mere hearsay of two other native informants, forthwith sent a message of remonstrance to Cetewayo. The messengers sent upon this occasion were Zulus, who were personally obnoxious to the King. We have only their report of the interview, at which nobody else was present; and it may well be doubted whether Cetewayo understood the precise nature of the charges brought against him, or had any opportunity of denying their truth.

It was upon this occasion that Cetewayo is reported to have said that he must and would "go on killing;" and "my people will not listen to me unless they are killed;" which seems to have been merely his way of claiming the judicial power to inflict capital punishment. It has never been shown that such punishment was inflicted by him with greater frequency, or with less regard to the formalities of a legal trial, than by other native rulers in South Africa.

No missionary in Zululand appears to have ever been molested by order of Cetewayo or any convert put to death for embracing Christianity, though several converts have been killed or ill-treated by the local chiefs on account of other transactions.

It is true that many persons, from time to time, have been made victims of the heathen superstition concerning witchcraft or sorcery. They have been "smelt out" by the professional witch-doctors, or denounced by malicious neighbours, and have then been put to death, without the King's order, by the people of their own district or village. This dreadful system prevails in most parts of Africa under native rule.

It will be found, on reference to Sir T. Shepstone's report of the coronation of the Zulu King in 1873, that Cetewayo's Councillors of State then expressly told him it would be necessary to reserve the case of witch-craft. But Cetewayo has denied that he put to death any of his subjects except those convicted of treason and other grave crimes. In a list of twenty-five homicides or murders, supplied by the Rev. R. Robertson, occurring in a period of some years, there is not one case brought home to the King's order or consent.

The reader who cares further to investigate this question may refer to *Macmillan's Magazine* of August, 1877, for the report of a Christian Zulu whom Bishop Colenso sent into Zululand. The appendix to Captain T.J. Lucas' volume, "The Zulus and the British Frontiers," also contains an examination of the subject. It is of some importance, now that Cetewayo has become a captive in our hands, to disabuse the popular imagination of false ideas concerning his character and the former acts of his reign. He is an ignorant barbarian, with all the mental and moral disadvantages of his race, but

The Zulu War: In search of Cetewayo. "Are those Zulus there?"

vindictive, or perfidious; and his good qualities were attested, in happier times, by Sir T. Shepstone and others, who had serious dealings with him.

The famous boastful phrase of "washing his spears," which only signified going to war, as a European in the age of chivalry might talk of "fleshing his sword," never bore reference to hostilities against his colonial neighbours of Natal, but against the Swazies, who are savages by far more turbulent and ferocious than the Zulus. In short, whatever may be thought of the policy of the late war, and whatever benefits may be hoped from Sir Garnet Wolseley's scheme for the subdivision of Zululand, with twelve dependent rulers, under the supervision of British Residents, Cetewayo is not to be held personally responsible for the great social evils that existed under his reign.

"These are," says Captain Lucas, "chiefly the universal military conscription, the custom of polygamy, with the buying and selling of women, and the hideous superstition of witchcraft, to which hundreds of lives are yearly sacrificed." It was long before the time of Cetewayo that these deplorable evils came into existence, and it is scarcely his fault that they could only be terminated by a revolution, consequent upon the intervention of British power.

With regard, likewise, to the alleged hostile designs of Cetewayo against the British colonial provinces, Sir Henry Bulwer, the Lieutenant-Governor of Natal, in his memorandum dated Jan. 9, two days before our actual invasion of Zululand, in pursuance of Sir Bartle Frere's policy, shows that there were no signs of an impending attack by the Zulus. On the contrary, the Zulus along the frontier had been disquieted only by Lord Chelmsford's military preparations, since the arrival of Sir Bartle Frere in September, as they feared we were about to attack them.

It is Sir Henry Bulwer, at the outbreak of the war, who makes this statement, which is entirely borne out, if we peruse all the official correspondence, by the detailed reports of civil officials on the Natal and Transvaal borders. The Earl of Pembroke has this week sent to the Aborigines Protection Society a letter which has been addressed to him, by Mr. C.F. Barker, of Little Umhlanga, Natal. The following extract from it conclusively shows how grossly Cetewayo was calumniated at the time when the public, both in South Africa and in this country, were led to believe that he meditated an attack on the colony of Natal. Mr. Barker writes:-

"When Sir Bartle Frere visited Natal, I happened to be in Zululand, and was at the Royal kraal, accompanied by two traders, whose waggon I was more or less occupying. At that time fearful reports were circulated about the doings in Zululand. Colonists said that it was unsafe for any white man to go into the country – death would be sure to be the consequence. I went in at that time and made a walking tour, accompanied by a black servant to the Emhlabalini (Ulundi), the Royal kraal. I was treated very kindly at each and every kraal I passed. I could not speak the Zulu language, but understood a little. When I arrived at the King's, I was still more hospitably treated. Everything was as peaceful as could be, while all the warlike preparations were going on in Natal.

Cetewayo could not understand the movements of the English. He inquired what they meant, who they were going to fight with, and was told that he was not to feel uneasy, as our stationing troops all round him was for no purpose of war. It was done in order to make the colonists feel themselves secure.

Then came the ultimatum, and greater indignity could not have been offered than was offered to Cetewayo's great men. They were spoken to like dogs and insulted by the colonists present. About this time a shell was fired from the fort on this side of the Tugela into Zululand. The King was informed of this, and said that, 'had one of his young men, even in a boyish way, fired his gun across the Tugela, the Colonial Government would have required a very heavy fine from him' (the King); but, added he, 'they want to force me into war. I do not want to fight, and my people shall certainly not strike the first blow or give the first shot.' A day before the ultimatum was up the troops fired shells several times across at some unoffending Zulus, who had come near the river either to watch, or look at their mealie-gardens. By this little act our troops killed one Kaffir. I was present and saw it all."

THE ILLUSTRATED LONDON NEWS

October 4, 1879

THE ZULU WAR

Two remaining Illustrations of the late war in South Africa, from Sketches by our Special Artist, find place in this week's publication. We have news from Capetown to the 9th ult., but it seems of little importance.

Cetewayo had been brought there by sea, and was to be lodged in the Castle, with two or three wives and a few servants. Sir Garnet Wolseley had left Zululand, and was at Utrecht on the 7th, on his way to Pretoria, for the settlement of the Transvaal.

The remaining hostile Zulu chiefs had surrendered, and those appointed to rule the twelve new districts had signed the requisite stipulations, promising obedience to the British Residents in North and South Zululand, and not to keep up an army or put their people to death, for witchcraft or upon other pretences, without due sentence of law. No white settlers, except missionaries, are to be allowed to hold lands in the Zulu country.

The arrangements for the disposal of the large infantry force under Sir Garnet Wolseley consequent upon the termination of hostilities in South Africa have now been made. The force consisted of fifteen battalions, of which one, the 1st Battalion 13th, has arrived, and another, the 1st Battalion 24th, may be daily expected in England.

The five battalions that left home after the news of the Isandhlwana disaster – viz., the 2nd Battalion 21st, 58th, 3rd Battalion 60th Rifles, 91st, and 94th, are to be retained in South Africa. Two more, the 88th and 90th, are embarking for India. The 80th, which has been abroad nearly eight years, will be ordered home soon. The 2nd Battalion of the 4th will go to Malta, the 2nd Battalion 24th and 57th to Gibraltar, the latter in place of the 71st, coming home; the 2nd Battalion of the Buffs to the Straits Settlements, allowing the 74th to come home; while the 99th will take the place at Bermuda of the 46th, which has been for three years at that station.

End of the Zulu War : Shelling kraals across the Umvolosi River.

GENERAL SIR EVELYN WOOD, V.C., ON THE ZULU CAMPAIGN

Brigadier-General Sir Evelyn Wood was on Tuesday evening entertained at a banquet by the Fishmongers' Company, together with his uncle, Lord Hatherley, Colonel Pearson, C.B., Major Leet, V.C., Lieutenant Lysons, and other distinguished personages – Mr. Blewitt, Prime Warden, in the chair.

We quote the eloquent speech made by Sir Evelyn Wood in answer to the toast of his health:-

"Mr. Prime Warden, my Lords, and Gentlemen, - I thank you heartily for the honour you do me to-night, and I thank you not only for myself but in the names of the comrades whom you honour in honouring me. As a soldier – and I prefer that title to any other – it would be as improper for me to praise my late gallant chief, Lord Chelmsford, as it would be to criticise his military operations. I may, however, speak of him as a friend, and, therefore, I say that the successes which you so generously appreciate were due in the first instance to the confidence Lord Chelmsford reposed in me, to the support he ever accorded me, and to his staunch friendship, which nothing has been able to shake.

"There is nothing selfish in Lord Chelmsford. Self in him is entirely subordinate to his zeal for the public service; and, as you approve of my services, you should credit him with the perspicuity which utilised them, and you should sympathise with my gratitude to him for having had the courage of his confidence at a period when a smaller mind might have hesitated to allow such large discretionary powers as I possessed to one who was, professionally speaking, a young General. Lord Chelmsford was frequently absent from Maritzburg when employed in visiting the lower frontier between Zululand and Natal; and at such times I was in constant communication with the greatest High Commissioner South Africa has yet possessed – the greatest not only in his experience of barbarian peoples, but in unflinching courage and rectitude of purpose.

"To Sir Bartle Frere I owe much. The trust he placed in me was the means not only of winning over some valuable allies, but of neutralising many colonists of Dutch extraction who would have otherwise swelled the number of discontented Boers who assembled near Pretoria to protest against our rule. I remember well the sense of intense relief amongst the colonists after a period of some doubt, when it was understood Sir Bartle Frere was to remain in South Africa. It has been stated that the colonists are cruel, bloodthirsty men, more anxious to advance their own interests than to assist in civilising the natives, and that Sir Bartle Frere is supported by them because he originated a war policy which was financially profitable to the colonists. His strongest admirers are those who have had most opportunities of seeing him – the inhabitants of Cape Colony, who have reaped as much benefit by the war near Natal as the inhabitants of Paris could from a war in Aberdeenshire.

"The colonists in Natal are mostly emigrants of the first generation from our islands, our own flesh and blood, with feelings like those who honour our soldiers. These colonists are painfully sensitive to the misconception which has prevailed generally as to their conduct. The men who made money by the war can be counted on one's fingers, and, being always on the main roads, were more noticeable than the unobtrusive but more agreeable settlers in the remoter districts. Before I went out I did not know a single colonist. Now I know many – men who left lucrative professions and charming families to serve, as did Theophilus Shepstone for eight months as a Captain of Basutos, and I am proud of being termed by him a friend. I have marched over 2000 miles; I have visited farms innumerable; and I assert that the colonists as a rule treat their black servants with as much consideration as we do our domestics here.

"To be respected by such colonists, then, is in itself a marked tribute of esteem; but it is impossible for anyone to be associated with Sir Bartle Frere without being deeply impressed by his intellect and his humanity, and our sons will find in the prosperity of South Africa, a grand recompense for our losses, and a justification of the policy which inaugurated a civilised rule in place of a destructive and barbarous despotism. While gratefully acknowledging your welcome to-night, my thoughts naturally revert to the, alas! many gallant friends who have accompanied me back in memory only. Ronald Campbell, of the Coldstreams, who gave his unselfish life up for others when he dashed forward into a cavern until, touched by a Zulu's gun, he fell a voluntary sacrifice, instantly avenged by two brave boys – Lieutenant Lysons and Private Fowler, of the 90th Light Infantry – who, undaunted by Campbell's fate, ran in and slew Campbell's slayers. The united ages of these lads scarcely exceeds my own.

"So you will not wonder that I retain considerable confidence in 'our boys,' and do not believe the race has deteriorated in fighting power. I was, however, unusually fortunate in my comrades. The 13th Light Infantry, and the 80th which joined me in time for Ulundi, were composed of veteran soldiers, while the 90th Light Infantry, which corps I have yet the honour to command, is remarkable for its excellent non-commissioned officers. Such was the spirit in the corps that when, in 1877, the battalion was ordered to South Africa for the Gaika war many non-commissioned officers who were entitled to join the Reserve, and who had in several cases obtained promises of situations in private life, sought and obtained permission to remain with the colours.

"These men have been loyal and efficient assistants to those gallant officers under whom our 'short service' lads have done many long days of work. They bore privation and endured fatigue with a cheery readiness I can never forget, and when on that glorious 29th of March 24,000 Zulus measured their strength for some five hours against our 1800 men, the veteran 13th, the younger 9th, Tremlett's gunners, and Buller's horsemen, young and old, upheld equally the traditions of our arms.

"I will not dwell long on sad reflections to-night, but, while thanking you for the compliment you are paying the flying column through its leader, I must recall some who, having died in your service, deserve to live in your memory. Robert Barton, another Coldstream, who, 'brave as he was humane,' when last seen alive, was endeavouring to save a comrade from the remorseless foe; Llewellyn Lloyd, my interpreter, brave, wise, and kind, of whom I had previously reported that 'he possessed every attribute of an English gentleman,' and who was shot down at my side; Lieutenant C. Williams, of the 58th Regiment, a volunteer, who was slain when rallying Uharnu's men, in company with Charles Potter, the sole hope of his parents, a gallant and intelligent colonial officer, beloved by the natives, by whom he was known only as 'Charlie'; Nicholson, the enthusiastic yet imperturbable Lieutenant of artillery, who, scorning the shelter of the breastwork thrown up to cover his gun, was shot through the body and mortally wounded; Private Grosvenor, of the 13th Light Infantry, who, remaining behind to save a sergeant, did so at the cost of his own life; Private Uys, that grand Dutchman to whom I promised in England's name the protection of his children, of which their father's death in our service has deprived them; Sergeant McAllen, of the 90th Light Infantry who, after having his first wound dressed, hurried out to rejoin his company in an exposed position, where he fell dead; the gallant Saltmarshe, who died at the head of his company in the Gaika war; the no less gallant Corporal Hillier, who met his death in snatching his Captain's body from the Gaikas; Arthur Bright, whose lovable qualities are ever on my mind – these soldiers of my regiment, and many of other corps, in the manner of their death have emphatically contradicted the ignorant assertion that the war in South Africa was one in which no honour was to be gained.

"In remembering these spirits, and that gallant youth, the son of England's ally, whose widowed mother is now our honoured guest, and whose body gave a noble answer to the query, 'Had he his wounds in front?' I may say as Rosse says to Siward in 'Macbeth,'

> Your son, my Lord, has paid a soldier's debt.
> He only liv'd but till he was a man.
> The which no sooner had his prowess confirm'd
> In the unshrinking station where he fought,
> But like a man he died.

'Why, then,' was the response, 'God's soldier be he!' And I will add with him who said that,

> Had I as many sons as I have hairs,
> I would not wish them to a fairer death.

"My thoughts brighten when I revert to the living, and I think with pleasure of my friend here, Pearson. May he pardon me when I call him by his South African name, 'The Bulldog of Ekowe.' I think of D'Arcy, of the Frontier Light Horse, who so nearly lost his life in trying to rescue a wounded comrade; I think of Sergeant Jeff and Private Greyham, standing over their wounded Captain; I think of Sergeant Smith, who, when both his officers were lying sorely stricken and senseless, bravely commanded the company of the 90th Infantry; I think of the rank and file who marched with me many hundreds, nay, thousands of miles, who were loyal and untiring, and notwithstanding all that has been said to the contrary, withal a Christian soldiery.

"I am aware it has been said we lifted many cattle, committed much arson. I plead guilty. As regards the cattle, they are in Africa the sinews of war. Some uninformed people have not only blamed us for destroying the enemy's military kraals, but have asserted that such a proceeding was useless, as the kraals were of no practical importance. The truth is that the military kraal to the Zulu is as much a rallying point, a badge of honour to be retained, or a symbol of disgrace if lost, as the colours are for which men in Europe give and take hecatombs of lives. From the days of the Battle of the Standard to that late sorrowful hour when Coghill, leaving his vantage-point, swam back to bear company in death with Melvill, going down under the bloody waters of the Buffalo honourably encumbered with the Queen's colours, there has always been an ideal value attached to certain objects in war.

"We have been accused of inhumanity. I have denied this charge officially for my troops and for myself. I can assure you that the only Zulu I personally chastised was one who declined to help us to carry a decrepit woman from a mountain where she must have starved; and when I tell you that it was the man's mother, you will pardon this practical effort to induce the heathen to honour his parent.

"The Flying Column is broken up. Captain Woodgate, impassive as a rock under the hottest fire; the brave surgeons – Reilly, Connolly, and Browne – who, exposed to a storm of bullets, tenderly cared for our wounded; Major Hackett, one of the ablest and bravest officers, who, directing his men to take cover, himself walked erect amidst a hail of missiles, until one wounded him so cruelly; Beresford, Browne, Leet, and Buller, are now well-known names, and I am proud to claim them as comrades. You all know how they gained their crosses. In each case they carried off soldiers who must have fallen under the Zulu assegais. You probably do not know, however, that when Major Leet took up on a tired pony the double burden, he incurred a double risk for he went into the fight so crippled by a sprained knee that, once dismounted, he could not have made an effort to escape.

"You have all heard of the valour of my right-hand man; but I, perhaps, alone can realise the full value of his services. Careful of his men's lives, reckless of his own, untiring and unflinching in the performance of duty, we owed much of our success to his brilliant leadership of the mounted men. To his devoted friendship I owe more than I can express. Men learn to know each other well on active service, and I have not known a better friend nor better soldier than Redvers Buller.

"These, my comrades, are all dispersed. Some are still serving under that splendid soldier, Sir Garnet Wolseley, and they are fortunate, for no leader has ever before so succeeded in drawing under him men of promise. The story of a bloody and selfish despotism has ended with the clever capture of Cetewayo by my friend, Major Marter, and our courageous Ashantee scout, Lord Gifford. Our eighteen months' hard living, hard marching, and hard fighting is over. To you at home our thanks are due. You inspire our best actions, your blame is what we fear more than assegais. You have found men, money, and munitions; your sympathy in the Zulu war has been an electric current; your welcome repays us for the hardships and misfortunes of war.

"I am aware I owe much to your spontaneous kindness tonight, much to the fact that I am the grandson of Matthew Wood, a name synonymous with truth, justice, unswerving honour, and courage. It would be impertinent in me to praise his son and my uncle, Lord Hatherley, but I must now avow I am very proud of being his nephew, and I am sure he prizes very highly with me the honour you have done me this evening. For this I thank you, not only for myself, but in the name of those gallant soldiers, Imperial and colonial, Dutchmen and natives, who during a time of exceptional anxiety worked so harmoniously together for the good of the service, and in the interest of our great country."

Lord Hatherley proposed "The Prime Warden," who returned thanks. There were afterwards loud calls for Colonel Pearson, but the gallant officer, having risen to respond, simply expressed his sense of the honour which he had received in being invited to come there that evening with General Wood.

End of the Zulu War : Mounted infantry skirmishing with Zulus.
A sketch by our Special Artist.

THE ILLUSTRATED LONDON NEWS

October 11, 1879

COLONEL REDVERS BULLER, V.C., C.B.

Her Majesty the Queen lately received this gallant officer, with Brigadier-General Sir Evelyn Wood, as her visitors at Balmoral Castle, and invested each of them with the Victoria Cross for their acts of personal valour in the Zulu War.

The country neighbours and old friends of Colonel Buller in Devonshire last week entertained him with a "welcome home" banquet at Exeter, and it is their intention to present him with a piece of plate. The Duke of Somerset, Lord Lieutenant of the county, presided at the banquet, and among the company were the Earl of Devon, the Earl of Portsmouth, Sir T. Dyke Acland, M.P., Sir Lawrence Palk, M.P., Mr. Arthur Mills, M.P., Colonel Drewe, of The Grange, Broadhembury, and the mayor of Exeter.

Colonel Redvers Buller, V.C., C.B.

Colonel Redvers Henry Buller, of Downes, near Crediton, is eldest surviving son of the late James Wentworth Buller, Esq., formerly M.P. for Exeter, and for North Devon, who died in 1865, and who was highly esteemed as a country gentleman and magistrate. His mother was a daughter of the late Lord Molyneaux Howard. He served with the second battalion of the 60th Rifles through the campaign in China in 1860, for which he obtained a medal with two clasps; in 1870, he served in the Red River expedition, under Sir Garnet Wolseley, with the first battalion of the same regiment.

He next accompanied that commander to the Ashantee War, in 1873, being on the staff as Deputy-Assistant Adjutant-General, and Deputy-Assistant Quartermaster-General, and head of the Intelligence Department. He was slightly wounded in the fight at Ordahsu. He was several times mentioned in despatches, obtained the war medal with clasps, and was rewarded by promotion to the brevet rank of Major, and by the Companionship of the Bath.

His recent services in the Zulu War must be fresh in recollection; he was there in command of a force of colonial volunteer cavalry, "Frontier Light Horse," and some mounted infantry, with native troops, attached to the force of Brigadier-General Sir Evelyn Wood, entering Zululand from the Utrecht district of the Transvaal, and they afterwards joined the army of Lord Chelmsford for the final advance on Ulundi.

The following extract from the *London Gazette* specifies the particular action for which he has received the Victoria Cross:- "Captain and Brevet Lieutenant-Colonel Redvers H. Buller, C.B., 60th Rifles. – For his gallant conduct at the retreat at Inhlobane, on March 28, 1879, in having assisted, whilst hotly pursued by Zulus, in rescuing Captain C. D'Arcy, of the Frontier Light Horse, who was retiring on foot, and carrying him on his horse until he overtook the rear guard. Also for having on the same date, and under the same circumstances, conveyed Lieutenant C. Everett, of the Frontier Light Horse, whose horse had been killed under him, to a place of safety. Later on, Colonel Buller, in the same manner, saved a trooper of the Frontier Light Horse, whose horse was completely exhausted, and who otherwise would have been killed by the Zulus, who were within eighty yards of him."

The portrait of Colonel Buller is from a photograph by A. Bassano, of Old Bond-street.

MAJOR CHARD, V.C., who so gallantly distinguished himself at Rorke's Drift, arrived at Portsmouth on the 2nd inst., in the transport Egypt, from the Cape.

On the following day at Taunton he met with an enthusiastic reception at the station. An address was presented to him by the Mayor expressive of their admiration of his bravery.

Major Chard, in reply, said so many gallant deeds had been performed since the affair at Rorke's Drift that he was glad to find that what happened in January last had not been forgotten, as well it might be. He would prize the address that had been presented to him as long he lived.

Major Chard then drove through the town to North Curry on a visit to his brother-in-law, Major Barret. There were great rejoicings in North Curry, a congratulatory address being presented by the Vicar, and the place being elaborately decorated.

There was a display of fireworks in the evening. Major Chard, V.C., has received the Royal command to proceed to Balmoral in order to receive the congratulations of the Queen. – Brigadier-General Pearson, the gallant defender of Ekowe, was presented on Monday, at Yeovil, with a sword of honour by his admirers in his native county. In acknowledging the gift he spoke warmly of Lord Chelmsford as a military commander, and his belief that Sir Bartle Frere's policy was a sound one for South Africa; and he praised the self-denial and patriotism of the colonists of Natal. – The arrangements for the Essex county reception of Brigadier-General Sir Evelyn Wood, V.C. K.C.B., on the 14th inst., are making rapid progress. The sword of honour bought by public subscription will be presented to Sir Evelyn on a platform to be erected in front of the Shirehall at Chelmsford.

The company at the ball in the evening promises to be a brilliant one. Lieutenant-General Lord Chelmsford had an interview with Lord Beaconsfield on Tuesday at his Lordship's residence in Downing-street.

THE ZULU WAR

The end of this unhappy business, which does not seem to have given satisfaction to the South African colonists, while it has entailed heavy burdens upon the English taxpayer, was recorded two or three weeks ago. Several of the remaining Illustrations, from Sketches by our Special Artist, and by Lieutenant D.A. East, who was engaged in the pursuit of Cetewayo, are presented in this Number of our Journal.

They comprise a view of a kraal at which the Zulu King slept, in his flight of many days to the northeastern forest region; the finding of some of his chattels, with ammunition stores, in a rock-cut recess; and the reception of a number of Zulu warriors in Sir Garnet Wolseley's camp at Ulundi, where they gave up their arms. Two scenes of the homeward march of our troops are shown in the other Engravings.

The pursuit of Cetewayo: Kraal where the King slept.
From a sketch by Lieutenant D.A. East.

Finding some of Cetewayo's treasures.
From a sketch by Lieutenant D.A. East.

There is no further news of importance; but the deposed and captive Zulu King has been received at Capetown by Governor Sir Bartle Frere, and is lodged in the Castle there, with four of his wives and a little daughter. He is in pretty good health, and his appearance and manners, and some reported fragments of his talk with privileged visitors, have made a rather favourable impression of his mind and character.

Amidst the friendly demonstrations that are now taking place in this country, to welcome home with deserved praise and honour several distinguished soldiers lately employed in the Zulu War, there have been some incidental references to the political and moral aspects of that undertaking. This was to be remarked in the banquet at Exeter last week, in honour of Colonel Redvers Buller, V.C. and in the entertainment given on Monday, at Yeovil, to Brigadier-General Pearson, who commanded the garrison of Ekowe; as well as in Brigadier-General Sir Evelyn Wood's speech at Fishmongers' Hall, reported in our last.

Sir Garnet Wolseley's camp at Ulundi: Zulus coming in to give up their arms.
From a sketch by Lieutenant D.A. East.

It may now be needful to remind the ordinary newspaper reader that the most eminent military leaders of a campaign are scarcely the persons who are most likely to have acquainted themselves with a long series of precedent transactions, which furnished the supposed casus belli. That knowledge upon which alone a correct judgement may be formed upon the question whether Sir Bartle Frere was justified in declaring war, and at once invading the Zulu kingdom, is to be obtained from a careful study of the abundant official correspondence, printed by order of Parliament.

The personal observations of a gallant officer riding over the Border country, and sometimes talking with European settlers, cannot, therefore, be regarded as sufficient material for a decided opinion in favour of a course which has been disapproved by her Majesty's Government, and by the majority of the British people, after the publication of authentic documents.

Colonel Buller, for instance, declares with perfect truth that, shortly before the war began, he saw "along what was then our border, dozens of burnt-down and deserted farms;" and he was told, by a Dutchman who rode with him, how one farmer named Beeston, had been compelled to leave by the
Zulus driving away or killing his cattle, and threatening to take his life, and frightening his wife in his absence.

The evacuation of Zululand : The 21st Royal Scots Fusiliers on the march homewards.

But Colonel Buller was probably not aware that the land upon which those farms stood, which is the tract of Border country east of the Blood river, adjacent to the Utrecht district of the Transvaal Republic, belonged to the Zulu Kingdom; that it had been wrongfully taken from the Zulus by the Dutch Boers of the Transvaal Republic; that Cetewayo's claim for its restitution to his people had been constantly urged, during many years before, and countenanced by the British Government of Natal; that this territorial dispute had been referred, by mutual consent, to the arbitration of the English Commissioners of Inquiry appointed by Sir Henry Bulwer, the Lieutenant-Governor of Natal; that these Commissioners, who were the Attorney-General of Natal, the Natal Acting Secretary for Native Affairs, and the late Colonel Durnford, R.E., had determined, after a patient local investigation of the evidence, that the Zulus were in the right, and that the land, a valuable tract of eighty by sixty miles, was the lawful property of their nation.

It has, in fact, been formally surrendered to the Zulus by Sir Bartle Frere's own decree, accompanying, as if in mockery, the ultimatum which he put forward last December to herald the declaration of war. Colonel Buller must necessarily have been unacquainted with the above-mentioned facts, when he rode over the country; seeing that it pleased Sir Bartle Frere to withhold publication of the Natal Commissioners' inquest and award, supported by Sir Henry Bulwer's earnest, honest, and just recommendations, during many tedious and perilous months of last year, keeping Cetewayo and all the Zulus in gloomy suspense meanwhile about the fate of their country.

With regard to the local outrages complained of, they occurred towards the end of 1877; they consisted of the destruction of houses and gardens, and sometimes of cattle, but without personal violence towards the European settlers. This was a rude and insolent method of enforcing the notices to quit, which had been repeatedly communicated to each of the Border farmers. We should be disposed to agree with Sir Henry Bulwer, who says, in his Memorandum of Nov. 18, 1878, "The Zulus have long looked upon themselves as aggrieved and injured with respect to this piece of territory, and some allowance must, I think, be made for them under all the circumstances of the case; but the King ought not to have taken the law into his own hands, even assuming the Zulu claim to be a good one; and he may fairly be called upon to make some compensation for the individual losses and damage."

There was, however, another tract of Border territory, north of the Pongola, which has never been recognised by the British Government as a portion of Zululand, but to which the Zulu Kings had always laid claim since a period long before the approach of European Settlements.

It was held by their neighbours, the Swazies, who made a doubtful cession of whatever title they had in it to the Transvaal Dutch Republic; and a number of German settlers, with a few English, obtained grants of land there. In that quarter, likewise, the Zulu Border chiefs resorted to a similar process of eviction, followed up by wilful destruction of property in farms and homesteads.

This sort of misconduct, for which Cetewayo would not ultimately have refused to make an apology and to give substantial redress, but which was certainly prompted by a notion of territorial right, is all that could bear any resemblance to an invasion of the European colonies by the Zulus at any time previous to the war "they did afterwards," as Colonel Buller says, "invade the part of the country I was in;" and he speaks with becoming horror and indignation, as every Englishman would do, of "the slaughter of men, women, and children" in Swaziland by the Zulu band of Umbelini's followers.

It is impossible too greatly to deplore that outbreak of ferocity, though no British subjects were among its victims; but, far from being regarded as a cause of our war against Cetewayo, it seems more like an incidental effect of the policy adopted towards that ruler, who had preserved peace so long as he confided in the friendly purposes of the British Government.

So late as Oct.27 the Landdrost of Utrecht reports a message from Cetewayo, "that he was sorry to hear that many of the border farmers along the Blood river had trekked away, and that others contemplated leaving also, as he had never desired that the Boers should leave their farms, but they should remain and live in friendly intercourse with the Zulus located on the opposite side of the river, so that when a calf strayed across the river from either side, it would be returned to its owner in a friendly way." He added, "that the white people ought to be satisfied with that portion of Zululand which they already possessed, and not claim or covet any more of his country."

The evacuation of Zululand : The M Battery of artillery crossing adrift..

At the same date, Mr Rudolph informed the Transvaal Government that Cetewayo had summoned Umbelini before him, being "very angry with Umbelini" for his attack on the Swazies, with whom the Zulu King was then "in treaty for rain." Cetewayo had actually pulled down, at the request of the Transvaal Government, a kraal built on the north side of the Pongolo for the residence of a chief appointed to keep order among his people there, notwithstanding that he did not renounce his old claim of territorial sovereignty. Sir Henry Bulwer wished to have this claim also referred to a commission of inquiry; but Sir Bartle Frere, without such investigation, decreed that the Zulus should not have the land.

It was not to be expected that soldiers called to guard the frontier should be enabled to appreciate these circumstances, which were referred to the political administrators of the Colonies, in their relations with the Zulu Kingdom. Colonel Buller's statements are perfectly correct, as we believe, in point of fact, but his inferences from what he saw and heard must appear very questionable. The traces of savage warfare in Swaziland were very shocking, but there was no ground for apprehending "such an invasion as that to be carried into Natal."

In the entire history of Natal as a British province, no Zulu invasion has ever been attempted or threatened; no colonist or settler in Natal has ever yet been molested or annoyed by any of the Zulus. And the Lieutenant-Governor of Natal, who should know best, has invariably denied that there was any danger of a Zulu attack on that side.

These questions, it may be said, have become matters of merely historical interest, since the Zulu kingdom is now disarmed, overthrown, and to be divided into a dozen petty districts under dependent native chieftains. But the affairs of South Africa appear to be more unsettled than ever. The British army is withdrawn, and untold millions of money will have to be paid by England; while the Cape Colony, Natal and the Transvaal are not at all more inclined than they were to accept Confederation and to provide for their own defences.

Two or three millions of the native race, with their old institutions of hereditary chieftainship, polygamy, and heathen superstition, not yet repressed by the power of "our civilisation," stand their ground in face of the broken-down policy of a South African Empire. The ability of Sir Garnet Wolseley is doubtless equal to the task of organising a good military administration, and much reliance may be placed on his sense of equity, as well as on his tact and prudence. We shall hope the best for the future, but will not forget or slur over the all but ruinous mistakes of the recent past.

THE ILLUSTRATED LONDON NEWS

October 18, 1879

THE CAPTIVITY OF CETEWAYO

We are already enabled, by a number of original sketches and photographs just received from several of our correspondents in South Africa, to present a complete series of Illustrations of the captivity of the deposed Zulu King; his removal from Zululand, by sea, on board the steam transport-vessel Natal; the arrangements for his safe custody and personal accommodation, with his wives and other native attendants; his arrival and landing at Capetown, and his present abode in the Castle there. These subjects occupy eight of the Engravings given in our publication of this week. They form an interesting sequel to the abundant Sketches of the Zulu War furnished during the past six months by our Special Artist.

The termination of that extraordinary contest, in a military point of view, though its political results are by no means clear, has been formally announced by Sir Garnet Wolseley in despatches to her Majesty's Government. Our attention may now be turned for a brief space to the remarkable situation and character of the fallen native Sovereign, who now finds himself (to compare small affairs with great) in a position similar to that of Napoleon III. At Wilhelmshöhe, after the battle of Sedan; a prisoner of war, and likely to be kept a prisoner of State, while the country over which he lately reigned is undergoing a total change of government.

There has been much difference of opinion concerning the personal merits or faults of King Cetewayo. Before the late declaration of war against him the only direct testimonies we had from Europeans holding responsible offices, who had actually met and conversed with him, were rather favourable. Sir Theophilus Shepstone, the long-experienced Natal Secretary for Native Affairs, who assisted at his coronation in 1873, says that "he is a man of considerable ability, much force of character, and has a dignified manner. In all my conversations with him he was remarkably frank and straightforward, and he ranks, in every respect, far above any Native Chief I have ever had to do with. I do not think his disposition is very warlike."

Mr Rudolph, the Landdrost of Utrecht, who was confidentially employed by the British as well as by the former Dutch Government of the Transvaal, bears witness to the same effect. "I have met the Zulu King," says he, "four or five times, and know him well. He is a very straightforward man, and says out what he thinks. He is not like most of his people. He is very acute, and sees the meaning of anything very quickly. I have never believed in his attacking Natal."

These estimates of Cetewayo's character are fully borne out, in our judgment, by a perusal of all the official reports, from 1875 to 1878 inclusive, of messages that passed between him and the Natal Government. His behaviour was invariably straightforward; and it was friendly and even submissive, except upon one occasion, that of his alleged refusal, in October, 1876, to listen to the native messengers sent to remonstrate against the supposed killing of women and girls. There is every reason to believe that he then neither understood the charge brought against him, nor got the language of his answer fairly reported to Sir Henry Bulwer.

In every other instance, before and afterwards, he showed a willing docility to the English Government, and especially a childlike confidence and reverence towards the person whom he called "my father Somtseu," which was not lost till that person had become the advocate of wrongful Dutch encroachments in Zululand. There are no reports of an authentic and well accredited kind showing the real state of the case with regard to Cetewayo's acts in the administration of his rule over his own people. The statements of the Rev. R. Robertson and other missionaries exhibit a list of incidental and local outrages, such as might be collected anywhere in Turkey, nowise proved to have been done by the King's order.

In the opinion of the Bishop of Natal, who has long been in constant, intimate communication with the Zulus of various ranks and tribes, Cetewayo's government was not so monstrous. The Bishop published, in *Macmillan's Magazine* of June, 1877, the report of a credible informant whom he had commissioned to visit the Zulu capital, to inspect the condition of the people, and to make particular inquiries of the King. No such trouble was taken to get at the truth by direct investigations in Zululand before Sir Bartle Frere and Mr Brownlee drew up their indictment against Cetewayo, the former having but recently arrived in Natal, and the other gentleman belonging to the Cape Colony.

There is much ground for the belief that Cetewayo, like his father Panda, was always averse to bloodshed, and that he inflicted death only on those who were regarded as heinous criminals by Zulu law. The dreadful superstition of witchcraft and sorcery, under which name however, the real crime of poisoning was frequently punished, seems to account for a large number of these cases.

Cetewayo's domestic habits, while at home in his own country, were those of other Zulu and Kaffir chiefs. He had many wives, and a multitude of male and female slaves, collected in the Royal kraal or inclosure of huts, and his wealth consisted of great herds of oxen and milch cows. He was, notwithstanding his corpulence, a man of active pursuits, fond of riding, shooting, and fishing; a plentiful eater of beef and native porridge, and drinker of Zulu beer. He never drank stronger liquors, and has not been accused of intoxication. His temper was sanguine, jovial, cheerful, and boastful, somewhat haughty, but not prone to fits of violent rage. He was quite illiterate, and had never travelled out of Zululand, but was shrewd in his questions about foreign affairs.

He believed profoundly in the religious and political traditions of the Zulu nation; he venerated the memory of his deified ancestors, the heroes and conquerors of the former Zulu empire; he consulted the oracles of Zulu priesthood, the famous rain-makers, the necromancers and witch-doctors of that heathen country. It was for the imagined beneficent power of Langalibalele as a conjuror of rain that Cetewayo sought to procure his release from the British Government. And he was at one time persuaded to forego his purposed attacked on the Swazies, because they possess a noted local shrine at which prayers for rain should be offered, and the Zulu agriculturists wanted rain.

Such was King Cetewayo, who inherited, unhappily for himself, the sceptre of a realm endowed by his predecessors, forty of fifty years ago, with a rigid military constitution. The details of this system, and his administration of it, are fully explained in Captain T.J. Lucas's instructive book, "The Zulus and the British Frontiers," which also describes his coronation, and relates the origin of his dispute with his colonial neighbours. It need not here be stated how the formidable standing army of the Zulu Kingdom became an obstacle to the secure settlement of South Africa under the British High Commissioner, till the late war, commenced in January, and practically ended in July, broke up that native State, driving its King into the forest a hunted fugitive.

The capture of Cetewayo was effected by a patrol under command of Major Marter, of the Queen's Dragoon Guards, on Aug. 28, in a kraal at the edge of the Ngome forest. He had been pursued for a fortnight incessantly by Captain Lord Gifford, under the orders of Major Barrow, through the wild region north of the Black Umvolosi river. He was immediately brought, with his companions, to Brigadier-General Clarke's encampment on the banks of that river, stopping at the Ndaza Royal kraal on the way. One of the sketches we have engraved shows the outside of the hut there in which the King slept on the night of Aug. 29, with three officers, Major Marter and Captain Astley Terry, and Lieutenant Hutton, of the 60th Rifles, reposing on the ground, and with the sentinels on guard.

Another Sketch, by Lieutenant H.C. Harford, is that of the King under guard at the encampment on the Black Umvolosi. He left that place in a waggon sent to convey the Royal prisoner to Sir Garnet Wolseley's head-quarters at Ulundi. He did not, however, choose to ride much in the waggon, as he complained of its shaking him, and preferred to walk. The soldiers were not allowed to approach within thirty yards of the King. He arrived at Ulundi on the morning of Aug. 31, having slept the night before about four miles from that place. Three wives, a female servant, and a daughter were with him, besides one Chief, Umkosana, and three other men, five of his servants having escaped, or having been shot in attempting to escape. A Correspondent thus describes the arrival at Ulundi:-

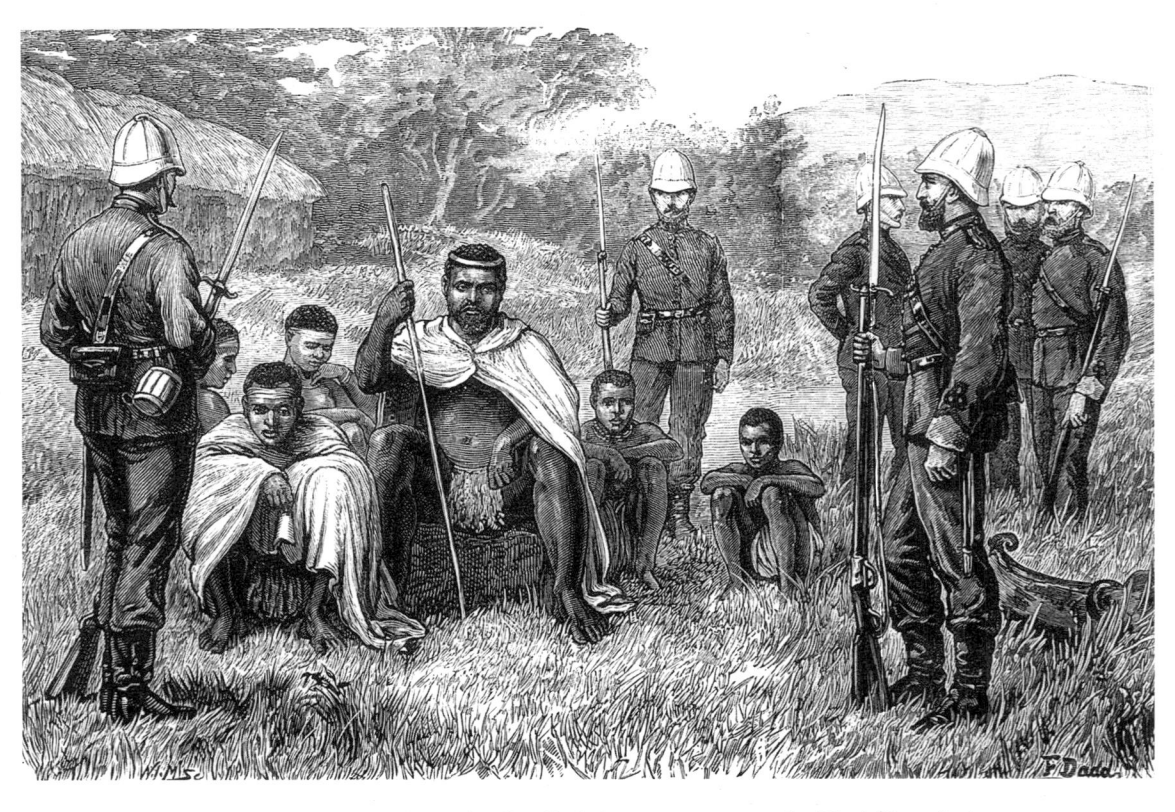

The King under guard at Brigadier Clarke's encampment on the Black Umvolosi.
From a Sketch by Lieutenant H.C. Harford, 99th Regiment.

Captain A. Terry.   Major Marter.   Lieutenant Hutton.

Guarding the King in the Ndaza Kraal during the night of August 29.
From a sketch by Captain Astley Terry, 60th Rifles.

"In front of the King's escort came some of the Dragoons and the men of Lonsdale's Horse who were present at the capture, clearing a broad path of some eighty yards wide, along the centre of which marched first some Dragoons, then a portion of the Native Contingent (Barton's), a company of the 3rd 60th, then two Dragoons, between whom stalked Cetewayo, very upright and dignified, glancing keenly from side to side, but expressing neither astonishment nor fear at his novel and humiliating position; indeed, the constant expression of his face seems one of quiet and kindly repose, and there is certainly nothing cruel or even harsh in the expression of his features.

He was wearing a bright-coloured damask table-cloth and the usual head-ring worn by all married Zulus. Directly following him came another dragoon, then some of the Native Contingent, followed by some 60th men. He was conducted straight to a tent, which he occupied by himself, while the women and men occupied respectively two others. Orders having been previously given that an escort was to be ready at two p.m. to accompany the King to Pietermaritzburg.

Cetewayo, having had some food and a rest, undisturbed, was placed, together with the four women, in one of the ambulances with Umkosana, who rode on the hind seat, while his followers were placed on another mule-waggon, which came immediately behind the ambulance. It must have been a pretty tight squeeze, as the women, like their liege, were decidedly not of a slender make. However, Cetewayo took his seat very quietly, and at ten minutes past two the party started, under the command of Captain Poole, R.A., staff officer; the escort consisting of twenty men of the Natal Horse and twenty of Lonsdale's, under Captain de Burgh, of the Natal Horse.

They had, however, proceeded no further than Fort Victoria – about ten miles from Ulundi – when an officer overtook them with orders to proceed as quickly as possible to Port Durnford, where the Natal would be in readiness to convey Cetewayo to Capetown."

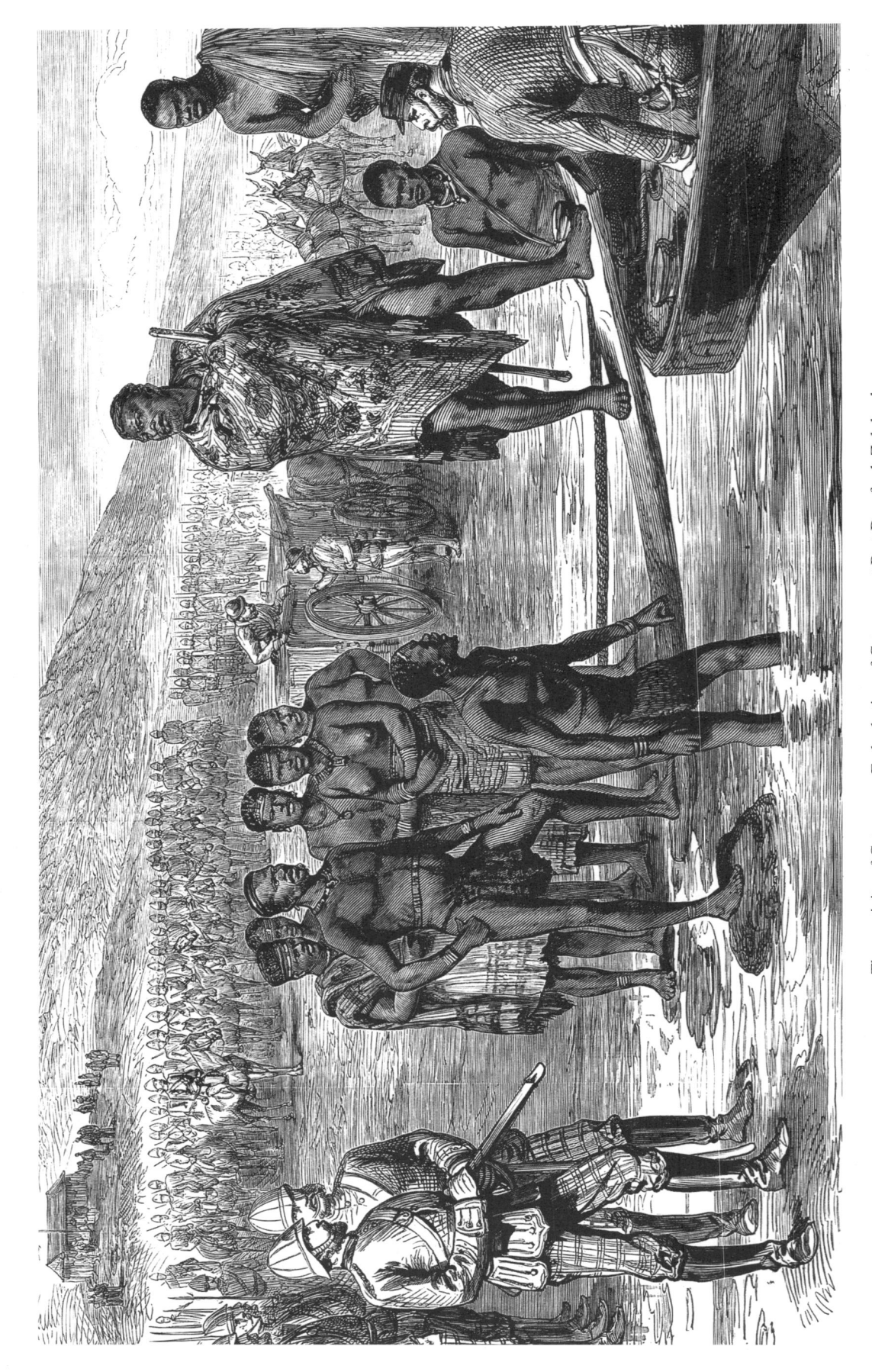

The captivity of Cetewayo : Embarkation of Cetewayo at Port Durnford, Zululand.
From a sketch by Commander Crawford Caffin, R.N.

We are indebted to Commander Crawford Caffin, R.N., for a sketch of the embarking of Cetewayo and his party, on Sept. 4, at Port Durnford, on the seacoast of Zululand. The prisoners were brought down to the seashore in a waggon drawn by ten mules, escorted by a squadron of Bettington's Horse, all in charge of Captain Ruscombe Poole, R.A. A company of the 91st Regiment was drawn up on the spot, forming line opposite to the escort, below the signal station, which had its flag flying. The waggon stood in the square between the two lines of military, with the beach at the third side, and with a surf-boat, under Commander Caffin's orders, ready to receive the distinguished voyagers. They got out of the waggon, the King, the four women and one girl, the Induna or Councillor of State, and three men-servants.

Landing operations at Port Durnford.

Cetewayo's tent on the deck of the Natal.

Cetewayo's wives and daughters, inside the tent.

From sketches by Mr W. Schröder, of Cape Town.

It was two o'clock in the afternoon. They were rowed in the surf-boat to H.M.S. Natal, steam-transport, which lay off shore with H.M.S. Forester, gun-boat, and another transport the Galatea. At five in the afternoon, the Natal sailed for Simon's Bay, with Commander Caffin on board in charge of her; Captain Poole, R.A., being still in charge of the prisoners on board. A sort of tent, constructed of tarpaulins upon a timber framework, had been erected on the poop of the vessel. In this were placed several mattrasses, one for the King, in the centre, others for his wives and the little girl. They all suffered from sea-sickness in the surf-boat, and were apparently much frightened while crossing the surf. A bridge or gangway was let down from the side of the steamer to help them to get on board.

The Natal arrived at Simon's Bay, the naval harbour eastward of the Cape promontory, on Tuesday evening, Sept. 9, but was detained there till the next Sunday evening, to await the High Commissioner's warrant for Cetewayo's reception at Capetown. During these few days, Cetewayo recovered his spirits, which had been somewhat depressed on the voyage; he had again suffered from sea-sickness, one

The captivity of Cetewayo: The King fishing over the side of the transport Natal in Simon's Bay.
From a sketch by Mr W. Schröder, of Cape Town.

rough night at sea, and had felt considerable alarm when out of sight of land. Captain Poole and Mr Longeast, the experienced interpreter from the Natal frontier of Zululand, did all they could to please and amuse him. He took to catching fish by lines cast over the ship's side in Simon's Bay, which incident is shown in our front-page Engraving, from a Sketch by Mr W. Schröder. The other person shown in this sketch was Captain (now Major) Poole, R.A., who took care of Cetewayo.

The Commodore sent him a suit of clothes, tweed coat, waistcoast, and trousers, with an ordinary black hat. These he was glad to put on, understanding that such apparel was necessary for him to make a respectable figure among Europeans. He asked for a box to keep his clothes in, and was supplied with a metal travelling trunk, in which he laid them up neatly folded at night; he also got a hat-brush and clothes-brush. The red and green table-cloth was worn as a shawl. The women were supplied with shirts, but were not always so particular about wearing them.

The King made a very tolerable figure in his English dress; he is a tall, big man, nearly six feet in height, and extremely stout, measuring about sixty inches round the chest, but not unwieldy; his thighs are very large and his knees swollen, from a disease of long standing. He is fifty-four years of age, but looks not above forty, the hair of his head being only a little grizzled. His hair at top is moulded into the stiff ring, which all married men wear among the Zulus. He has a round face, the expression of which is good natured, humorous, and smiling; he has a slight moustache, but not much beard. His colour is a light ashy brown, not like that of a negro.

The wives are lively young women, about twenty years of age, one of them rather handsome; the daughter is a girl of fourteen. The chief or induna, Umkosana, in whose kraal the Zulu King was taken, and who has voluntarily shared his captivity, is a finely-grown man, above six feet tall, well shaped and muscular. Cetewayo accepted cigarettes and a pipe, and was fond of smoking with Captain Poole.

He was taken on board H.M.S. Boadicea, where he saw the seamen and marines at their drill, and the great guns, to his evident admiration. "I am a child," he said, "I was only born yesterday; I know nothing." His behaviour, in general, was sociable and agreeable. The only dispute he had with Captain Poole was upon the demand he first made to have an ox killed and roasted every day for his dinner, which is the customary etiquette in the Zulu Royal household; but it was soon explained to him that this would not do in an English kitchen.

He did not like the company of civilians, perhaps associating them with Sir T. Shepstone and Mr Dunn, whom he now regards as his enemies; but officers, naval or military, he was always inclined to meet. No person was allowed to come near him without special permission. He consented to let his photograph be taken in several postures, though he seemed to fear that there was some baneful art-magic in the use of the lens and camera; a sketch of him was also drawn while at Simon's Bay. The portraits of the women likewise were taken.

On Monday morning, the 15th ult., the two vessels Natal and Forester having come round from Simon's Bay to Table Bay, Cetewayo and his party were landed in the Capetown Docks. They were handed ashore by Commander Caffin; our Illustration, from one of the sketches by Mr Schröder, of Capetown, gives a view of this interesting scene. The landing was effected early in the morning, so as to save the prisoner from the intrusion of a crowd; but even at that time large numbers assembled eager to get a sight of the Zulu monarch.

Accompanied by Captain Poole, the King stepped ashore dressed in European clothing, followed by four women, one little girl, and four followers. Lieutenant Shepherd, 4th King's Own, had the party conveyed in carriages, escorted by a troop of Lancers under Lieutenant Moreland, through the city to the Castle gate, where they were received by Colonel Hassard, C.B., Royal Engineers, Commandant of the Forces. Here they were at once taken to the rooms fitted up for their use, which open on to the ramparts of the castle, where the King can have daily exercise.

The captivity of Cetewayo : Embarkation of Cetewayo at Port Durnford, Zululand.
From a sketch by Commander Crawford Caffin, R.N.

At noon of the same day the ex-King was visited by Sir Bartle Frere, attended by the Hon. Mr Littleton, his private secretary; Captain Hallam Parr, military secretary; and Lieutenant Dalrymple, A.D.C. Later in the day the Premier, Mr Gordon Sprigg, and Mr Miller, Treasurer-General, visited the Royal captive's quarters to see if the arrangements for his accommodation were satisfactory. During the course of the Premier's interview Cetewayo, through Mr Longeast, the interpreter, talked with apparent frankness of many incidents of the war.

In the accounts his people had given him it seems they greatly exaggerated the English losses and magnified the Zulu successes in all the engagements which occurred. He acknowledged, however, he had done wrong in allowing his people to fight with us. "Chaka," he said, "was a child of the British Government. I was also a child and subject. My father, the Government, came to chastise me for my wrongdoing. I caught the stick with which he wished to beat me, and broke it. I did wrong to fight with him, and am punished. I am no longer a King; but the English, I find, are a great people; they do not kill those who have fought with them. I am satisfied to be in their hands. I hope the great Queen will pardon me, and allow me to return to my country, and give me a place to build myself a kraal where I may live. I am sorry I did not follow the advice of my father, Panda, on his death-bed; he told me to live at peace with the English and never make war with them."

When informed it was the wish of our Government to treat him with every consideration and supply him with all necessary comforts, he expressed his thanks, and asked that some of his favourite wives, naming ten, might be sent for to be with him, in addition to those already here. His mind was anxious about them, he said, for they had nobody to look after them now, and he felt lonely without their companionship. He further begged that his case might be put before the great Queen in as favourable a light as possible, and asked how many days it would take to send a message and receive a reply from England. He was told that two months might elapse before her Majesty's pleasure regarding him could be known. He again thanked the Premier for visiting him and the interest he had shown regarding him, and said, after what he had heard, he would sleep happier than he had hitherto done.

The Castle Gate, Cape Town.

The so-called Castle, erected by the Dutch about 1667, is a pentagonal fort; and we give a view of his ex-Majesty's present quarters, adjoining those of Colonel Hassard. The house on the left-hand side is the lodging of Cetewayo. We have also received a sketch of the castle gate, and a photograph of the exterior, taken by Messrs Bernard, of Adderly-street, Cape Town. It gives a view of the ramparts, where Cetewayo may enjoy the sea breeze from Table Bay, and contemplate the busy and picturesque streets of Cape Town.

Cetewayo's quarters in the Castle of Cape Town.

It will be for her Majesty's Government here to determine what shall be done with this remarkable State prisoner. He cannot be permitted to return to Zululand. That country has now by right of conquest fallen under the charge of the British authorities, who are responsible for its peaceable settlement, and it is their duty to exclude a person whose further presence there might encourage some future disturbances. But there is no law of nations by which the deposed Zulu king, who was neither a subject nor a vassal of our Government, could be indicted as a criminal; and there is no evidence, so far as we have been informed, that would convict him of any crime.

The Bishop of Natal, in a long epistle dated Aug. 31, pleading the cause of Cetewayo, as earnestly as he did that of Langalibalele in 1874, precisely sets forth a long series of instances, before and since the outbreak of the late war, to prove that Cetewayo was extremely anxious for peace; that he voluntarily forbore to invade Natal after the British defeat at Isandhlwana, and that he repeatedly sent pacific messages, while preparing to comply, so far as he could, with the British demands. These representations will, no doubt, have their due weight in the counsels of her Majesty's Ministers, and they will not be disposed to order a harsh or vindictive treatment of the fallen South African monarch, whose fate is watched in England with no slight degree of interest.

The Victoria Cross has been conferred upon Captain (now Commandant) Cecil D'Arcy and Sergeant Edmund O'Toole, of the Frontier Light Horse, for acts of valour before Ulundi. Mr Thomas Thompson, formerly of Cyprus, has been appointed her Majesty's Vice-Consul at Delagoa Bay. This gentleman was instrumental in rendering the colony of Natal good service, having succeeded in inducing the King of Amatonga to refuse Cetewayo a loophole of escape through his territory, or even the opportunity of finding a temporary refuge there.

ZULU WAR TESTIMONIALS

Major-General Sir Evelyn Wood, V.C., C.B., was presented by many inhabitants of the county of Essex, at a meeting held last Tuesday at the Shirehall, Chelmsford, with a sword of honour, purchased by public subscription, to commemorate his recent services in the Zulu War. This sword, of which we give an Illustration, was designed and manufactured by Messrs Hunt and Roskell, of New Bond-street, whose object appears to have been to typify modern honours by classical allusions. The scabbard is of silver decorated with repoussé plaques; the one at the point represents Apollo destroying the python. Above this is a trophy of African weapons, such as assegais, crossed by a ribbon bearing the names Kafirland, Kambula, Ulundi.

A boldly executed figure of Britannia is next in succession. Between this and the guard of the hilt is a shield bearing the arms of the county of Essex, of which Sir Evelyn Wood is a native. The guard is ornamented with branches of laurel. Where it is joined by the richly carved ivory handle, the Victoria Cross is prominently displayed. The reverse side is decorated with equal richness. It exhibits panels corresponding with those above described. The subjects are Hercules and the Hydra, a trophy of English arms traversed by a scroll with the names Crimea, India, Ashantee, a figure of Minerva, the arms of Sir Evelyn Wood, and the star of a K.C.B. Sir Evelyn Wood's initials, in monogram, are introduced as an ornament on the back of the hilt.

On the blade, which is of the finest tempered steel, is etched the following inscription:- "Presented to Major-General Sir Evelyn Wood, V.C., K.C.B., by the county of Essex, in recognition of the eminent services rendered by him to his country during the recent arduous campaign in Zululand, and the conspicuous zeal, energy, and gallantry which have distinguished his entire military career. Oct. 14, 1879." The ceremony of presentation was made a scene of great public festivity in the town of Chelmsford. Sir Evelyn Wood came from the Episcopal Palace at Danbury with the Bishop of St Albans, in a coach-and-four, escorted by the Essex Volunteers.

Sword of Honour presented to Major-General Sir Evelyn Wood, V.C., C.B., at Chelmsford.

A platform, with trophies, had been erected in front of the Shirehall. Sir Charles Du Cane, with many of the county gentlemen, stood there to receive Sir Evelyn Wood. An address was delivered by Sir Charles, to which the General replied. He was afterwards entertained at a banquet in the Royal Exchange, when he made another speech.

It was mentioned last week that Brigadier-General C.K. Pearson, C.B., had received a similar compliment, the gift of a sword, from the town of Yeovil, in Somerset. The county of Devon has subscribed for a piece of plate, a silver centrepiece, to be given to Colonel Redvers Buller, V.C., C.B. A sum of money was also subscribed by the officers and troopers of a colonial force lately under the command of Colonel Buller in Zululand; and he was desired to choose for himself some ornamental article, on which the subscribers wished to have engraved the following inscription:- "Presented to Lieutenant-Colonel Redvers Buller, V.C., C.B., by Commandant J. Baker, the officers, non-commissioned officers, and troopers of Baker's Horse, as a token of their regard and esteem for the valour and ability which he displayed while in command of the Mounted Corps Flying Column (of which they formed part) during the Zulu War of 1879."

Colonel Buller selected a dining-room clock and a pair of vases, of which the following is a description:- The base of the clock is 24in. by 18in., and consists of black marble, with bronze ornaments in pure antique Greek style and bas-reliefs, copies taken from the Parthenon. The clock is surmounted by a splendid bronze figure of Orestes, on the base of which is engraved the inscription. The whole is 39in. high. The vases are of the same style: the bases marble, with bas-reliefs from the same source, and the vases proper of bronze; the whole 24in. high. We give an illustration of these articles. They were manufactured by Le Roy et fils, of 211 and 213, Regent-street, watch and clock makers to her Majesty.

Major Chard, R.E., V.C., and Major Bromhead, V.C., have been invited to visit the Queen at Balmoral. The officer who captured Cetewayo, Major Marter, is promoted to be a Lieutenant-Colonel.

Clock and vases presented to Colonel Redvers Buller, V.C., C.B.

Our Special Artist's adventures in Zululand.

THE ILLUSTRATED LONDON NEWS

October 25, 1879

CETEWAYO IN CAPETOWN CASTLE

We have to thank Mr Cecil Woodmass, a Lieutenant attached to the 21st Royal Scots Fusiliers, for his sketch of the interview of a party of officers of the army lately in Zululand, with the captive Zulu King in the castle at Capetown. The gentlemen admitted to visit Cetewayo upon this occasion were, besides our correspondent, Lieutenant H.M. Nuthall, of the 58th Regiment, the Hon. Rupert Carington, of the Grenadier Guards, and Mr T.F. Kynnersley-Gardner, of Lonsdale's Horse. The King was accompanied by Captain Ruscombe Poole, R.A., who has the charge of him, and by Mr Longcast, the interpreter, as he knows only the Zulu language.

His Majesty was robed in a checker-patterned table-cloth, and wore a wideawake hat; he squatted or sat on the floor with his knees drawn up, and his chin resting upon one hand over the knees, which is a Zulu habit; and he seemed rather in a sulky humour. But he shook hands, and responded to the remarks that were made about his voyage and arrival at Capetown, and seemed to feel an interest in hearing that several of his visitors were at the battle of Ulundi, and that everybody admired the bravery of the Zulus in the late war. He accepted from Mr Nuthall a snuffbox, which Captain Poole showed him how to open, and he applied his nose to the snuff with an exclamation of approval.

Mr Rupert Carington also gave him some cigarettes, which were likewise accepted; and, after shaking hands again with Cetewayo, the visitors took their leave. In the sketch we have engraved Captain Poole appears seated beside Cetewayo, and Lieutenant Nuthall bends forward to speak with him, having just handed him the snuffbox.

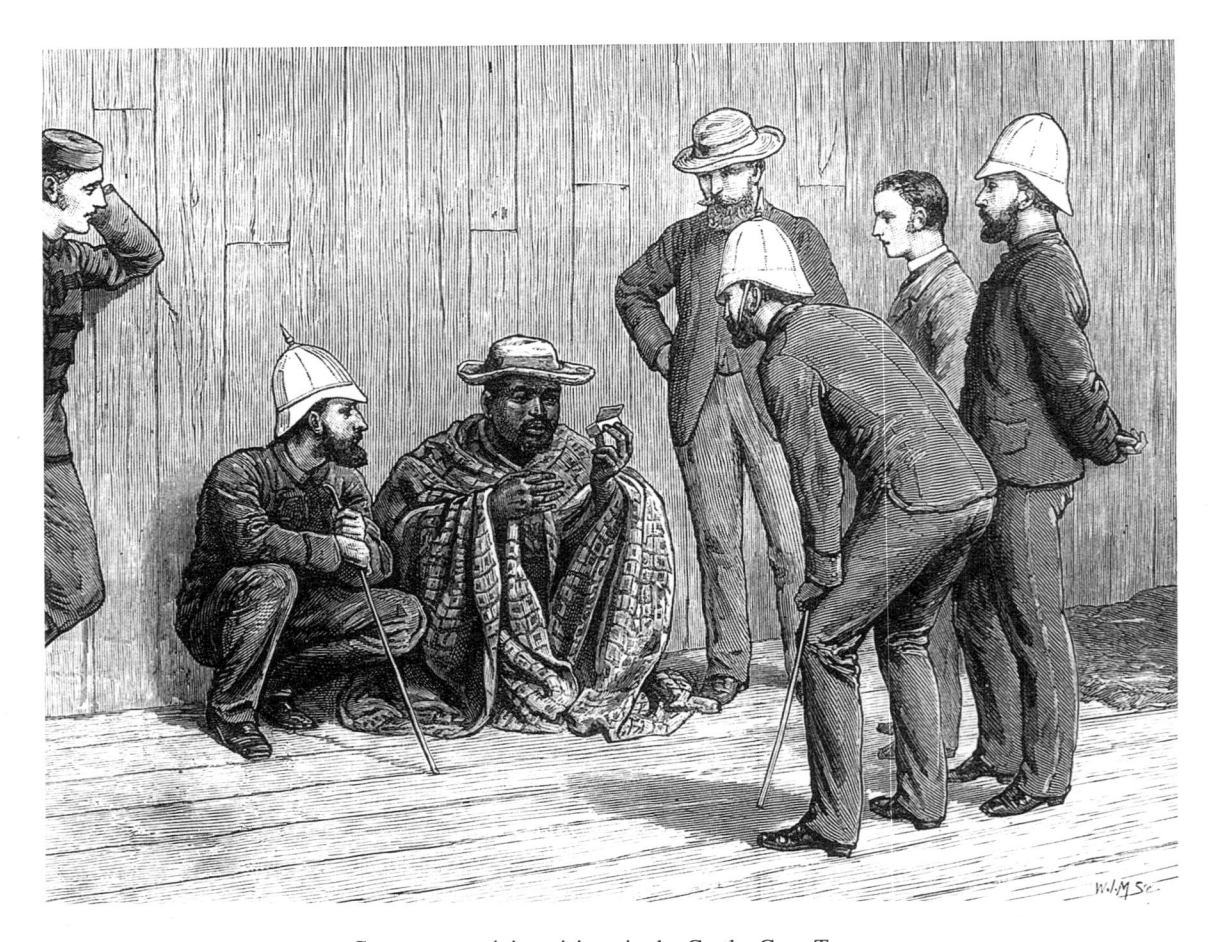

Cetewayo receiving visitors in the Castle, Cape Town.

THE EVACUATION OF ZULULAND

The very last British army corps has now quitted the country bounded by the Tugela, the Blood River, and the Pongolo, which was lately the independent Zulu Kingdom. It is to be divided into six or seven native principalities, each under a vassal chieftain owning the paramount supremacy of the British Government, with a Political Resident for North Zululand, and one for South Zululand, who will not interfere with the ordinary administration, beyond enforcing the prohibitions stipulated for by Sir Garnet Wolseley. The chiefs are not to be allowed to keep up standing armies, to put any person to death for witchcraft, or to import firearms and ammunition. They will not permit European settlers to buy land of the Zulus, and they may, if they think fit, exclude foreign traders and Christian missionaries of the white race.

One of the chiefs, who possesses a large and valuable district adjoining Natal, is Mr John Dunn. He is the son of a Scottish medical practitioner in Natal, and was fairly educated, but chose a wild, free life among the Zulus, with whom he has dwelt since his youth. Being an adopted member of the Zulu native community, and never a professing Christian, he has not scrupled to marry a plurality of wives, this condition being indispensable to a man of social respectability among the Zulus; and he obtained the rank of an Induna, with all the privileges of chieftainship, from the personal favour of Cetewayo, to whom he rendered some important services.

It has been wrongly supposed that Mr Dunn was to be appointed a British Resident, or representative of her Majesty's Government in Zululand. This is not the fact, and there seems to be no reason why he should not be recognised as a Zulu chief, on equal terms with the others who have signed the engagement imposed by Sir Garnet Wolseley. Our Illustration this week, from one of our Special Artist's Sketches during the late military campaign, shows the scene on the road in the march of a baggage-train, when some of the laden waggons, drawn by teams of twelve or even sixteen bullocks, have come to a standstill in going up a steep hill, and the soldiers are compelled to push behind, or put their shoulders to the wheel.

KAFFIR WOMEN AT PIETERMARITZBURG

The British province of Natal, which has a native African population of nearly 300,000, and scarcely 20,000 Europeans, may be considered rather as a Kaffir and Zulu protectorate, than as a colony of our own people. Its British element, though it has belonged to her Majesty's dominions thirty-three years, does not seem to grow much more considerable; and in this respect it offers a striking contrast to New Zealand, where the two races are in a reverse proportion to each other. The Zulus of Natal have lived, for an entire generation, under the rule of a civilised government; yet their social and moral condition remains just the same as that of the Zulus, about equal in number, who were subjects of Panda and Cetewayo in the adjacent kingdom.

A few converts have been made, and some hundreds of children educated, by the efforts of religious missionaries, both Church of England and Wesleyan; but heathenism still prevails, with polygamy and the slavery of the female sex, tolerated by colonial law. The native people in general, throughout the up-country districts, living in associated tribes under their own chiefs, and possessing herds of cattle with ample pasture, will not take employment from European farmers or planters. It has therefore been found necessary to import some thousands of coolies from India for the work of sugar cultivation along the coast. This produce, in 1875, amounted to no more than £100,000 in value, while that of coffee and other tropical growths was scarcely anything; and the apparent exports of Natal really consisted, in great part, of the wool, hides, ivory, and other natural products of the upland plains in the interior.

Such is the backward industrial condition of Natal and so poor its prospects of developing any independent and substantial resources of wealth that it cannot be expected to join in a South African confederation bearing its fair share of financial burdens. The Zulus, however, in and about the towns of Durban and Pietermaritzburg, are disposed to take light household and street work, though they will not toil in the fields. Mr Anthony Trollope speaks of their carrying his portmanteau, running an errand, or holding a horse for sixpence; they will scrub floors, sweep the roads, tend pigs, and the like, and the women enter domestic service. Our Special Artist lately in Natal saw Kaffir women selling pieces of sugarcane, which is greedily sucked by their own countrymen. The squatting figure of an Indian coolie, of whom the English little girl is buying fruit, appears at the left-hand corner of his sketch.

The military evacuation of Zululand : A block on the road.
From a sketch by our Special Artist.

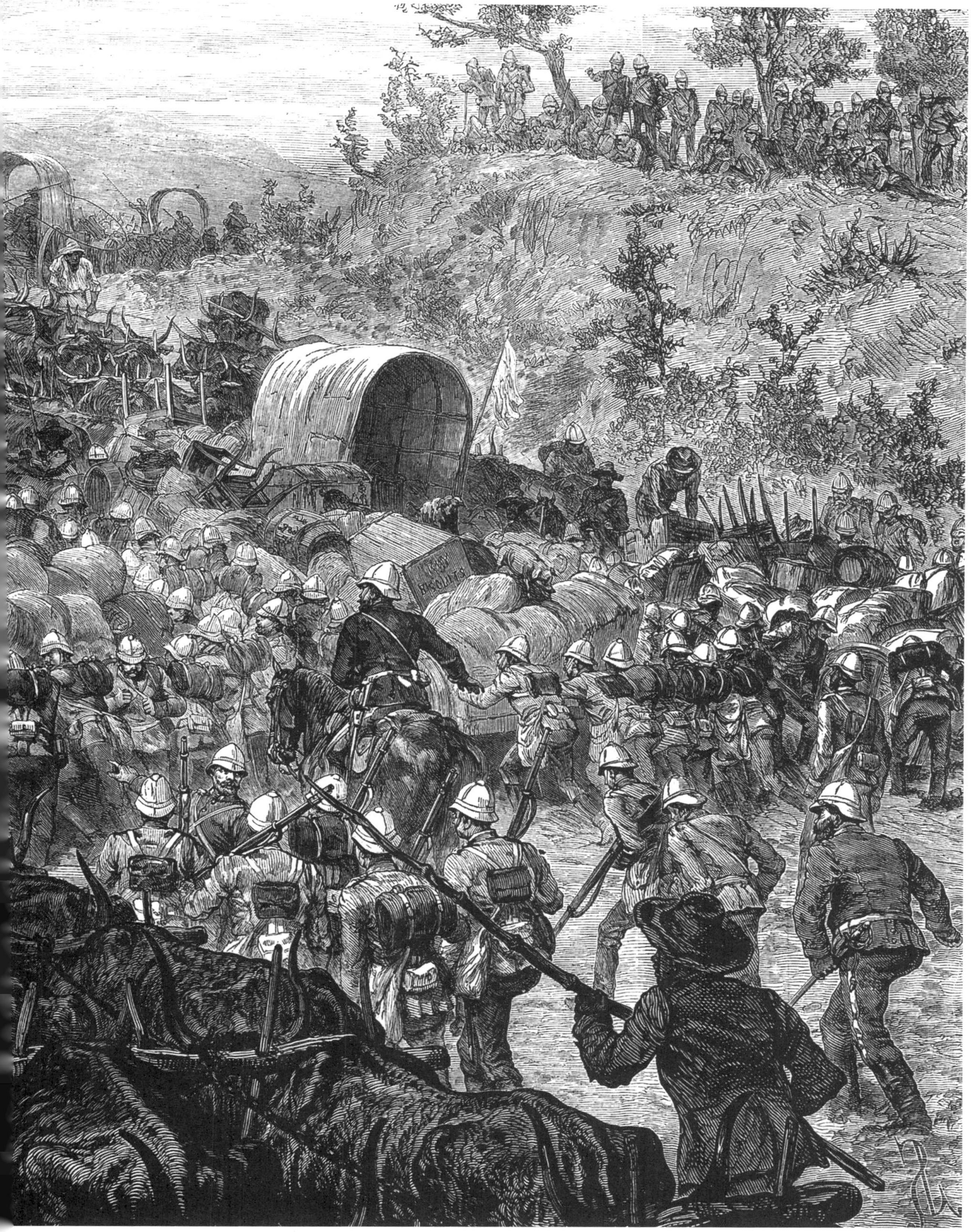

Kafir women selling sugar-cane in Pietermaritzburg.
From a sketch by our Special Artist.

THE ILLUSTRATED LONDON NEWS

November 1, 1879

CETEWAYO'S WRITING LESSON

His Majesty the ex-King of Zululand, like some of the Norman Kings of England (but not Henry Beauclerc), was unable to write his own name. But nobody has ever yet been able to spell it. Cetewayo, Cetywayo, Ketshwayo, Ketchwhyo, and several other phonetic or conventional variations have been tried in vain. We believe that the last of those given above is nearer than the others to the actual sound of the whole name, but it is not exactly right. The Zulu language has three "click" consonants of its own, or rather common to most of the Kaffir and other Bantu languages of South-East Africa.

These different "clicks" are produced by smartly thrusting the tongue against either the palate, or the roots of the front teeth, or the side teeth. In the first syllable of the King's name, there is a double click, which passes from the palatal to the dental. No letters of the European alphabet will precisely represent such sounds; but the attempt to utter "Kt," as a double consonant, makes a certain approach to this part of the name. The second portion is "whyo" or "wyo," not "wayo," according to the ordinary use of vowels in English. It is of no great consequence; but since he is now taking pains to learn how to write his name, we may as well try to speak it, barring the impossible "clicks," till he and his affairs can be safely forgotten, and there be no need to speak of him any more.

During his late voyage from Port Durnford to Capetown on board H.M.S. Natal, transport-ship, he expressed a wish to know how to write. Having recovered from sea-sickness, which he endured with patience and good-humour (only wishing he had brought his "big stick" or sceptre, to have thrown it into the sea and made a calm), the captive monarch was ready to take his first lesson. This was kindly given him by his friend Commander Crawford Caffin, R.N., who, with Captain Ruscombe Poole, R.A., had joint charge of the illustrious passenger on board. We have been favoured with facsimile copies of the writing. Commander Caffin first inscribed the King's name, spelling it as he thought fit, in printing capital letters, which the Royal pupil imitated as well as he could. The result is shown in our Engravings herewith annexed.

CETAWAYO

Copy set by Commander Caffin, R.N.

CETAWAYO

The King's handwriting, to imitate the copy.

MAJOR W. KNOX LEET, V.C.

We lately noticed an official announcement in the *London Gazette* that the Queen has been graciously pleased to confer the decoration of the Victoria Cross on this worthy officer of her Majesty's Army, whose claims were submitted for her Majesty's approval, for his gallant conduct during the recent operations in South Africa, as recorded against his name – viz., "Major William K. Leet, first battalion 13th Regiment. – For his gallant conduct on March 28, 1879, in rescuing from the Zulus Lieutenant A.M. Smith, of the Frontier Light Horse, during the retreat from the Inhlobane. Lieutenant Smith whilst on foot, his horse having been shot, was closely pursued by the Zulus, and would have been killed had not Major Leet taken him upon his horse and ridden with him, under the fire of the enemy, to a place of safety."

The testimony of Major-General Sir Evelyn Wood, V.C., C.B., in his speech at the Fishmongers' Hall banquet on Sept. 28, may also be quoted. After naming Lord William Beresford, Colonel Redvers Buller, and Major Leet, who had gained the Victoria Cross, he said, "I am proud to claim them as comrades. You all know how they got their crosses. In each case they carried off soldiers who must else have fallen under the Zulu assagais. You probably do not know, however, that when Major Leet took up, on a tired pony, a double burden, he incurred a double risk; for he went into the fight so crippled by a sprained knee that, once dismounted, he could not have made an effort to escape."

Major W. Knox Leet, V.C., 13th Light Infantry.

We published an exact narrative of this brave action in our paper of Sept. 20, and a letter from Lieutenant Smith, giving a similar account of it, and expressing his gratitude to Major Leet as his preserver, appeared in this Journal on May 31. Major Leet had previously had his own horse shot under him, and the one he then mounted was a pack-horse, or rather a pony, without bridle, riding-saddle, or stirrups. He and two other officers, Lieutenant Duncombe and Lieutenant Smith, were separated from the rest of the party retreating down the mountain, which was very steep and rocky, and they were stopped by a precipice. A numerous band of Zulus, firing and throwing assegais, rushed upon them. Lieutenant Duncombe was struck down, and Lieutenant Smith, who was on foot, became utterly exhausted.

The situation was certainly much worse than that of Lieutenant Carey and the Prince Imperial, with their party of horsemen, on June 1. But Major Leet, alone as he was with the helpless comrade exposed to instant death, had a noble spirit of self-devotion. He halted in riding off along the edge of the precipice, and, by an effort of main strength, lifted up the breathless man clinging to the pony's pack-saddle, took him up behind, and carried him safely away. On the very next day, in the defence of General Evelyn

Wood's fortified camp at Kambula Hill, the most obstinately fought battle of the Zulu war, Major Leet held command and performed the most important services, which were duly acknowledged in that General's despatches.

This exemplary officer is a son of the late Rev. E.S. Leet, Rector of Dalkey, Ireland, and is the youngest of five brothers, all of whom have served in the Army or Navy, and have received medals for war services. He entered the Army in July, 1855, and was with the 13th Light Infantry through the Indian Mutiny campaign, where he showed distinguished gallantry in the field. He was six years Adjutant to his regiment, and subsequently an Instructor of Musketry, Captain Instructor of the Staff at Hythe, and five years Deputy-Assistant-Adjutant-General and Quartermaster-General at Cork. In South Africa, after serving with his regiment against Secocoeni in the Transvaal, he was appointed to command the two battalions of irregular troops, with native auxiliaries, forming part of Brigadier-General Wood's movable column. No one did better service throughout the Zulu War, or is more deserving of substantial promotion in the ranks of the Army.

The portrait of Major Leet is from a photograph by Robinson and Sons, Grafton-street, Dublin.

THE ILLUSTRATED LONDON NEWS
November 22, 1879

MAJOR CHARD, V.C., R.E.

This gallant officer, whose defence, jointly with Major Gonville Bromhead, of the beleaguered post at Rorke's Drift, through the long night of desperate fighting on Jan.22, has gained him so much renown, was on Monday last presented with a sword and chronometer by his fellow-townsmen at Plymouth. The Earl of Mount-Edgcumbe took part in the proceedings, at the Guildhall of that town.

Our Illustration shows the design of the sword, which has been manufactured by Messrs. Hunt and Roskell. The scabbard, of silver, is ornamented with panels in repoussé, representing – 1, the mission-house at Rorke's Drift; 2, shields bearing the arms of Plymouth, and England; 3, "Vulcan forging the armour of Achilles," in allusion to the generally defensive character of the operations of the Royal Engineers. The lower part of this panel shows the thunderbolts, which form one of the devices of the Royal Engineers; 4, a trophy of broken Zulu weapons; 5, an allegorical device of lion and elephant, symbolising the pursuit and defeat of the enemy, and the triumph of the British arms in Africa.

The opposite side has corresponding panels, shewing – 1, the Victoria Cross; 2, shields with arms of Major Chard and the Royal Engineers; 3, Britannia; 4, trophy of Engineers' tools crowned with laurel by Fame; 5; St. George of England vanquishing the dragon. The guard is of silver, pierced and richly carved with the rose, shamrock, and thistle, surrounded by oak leaves. The blade, of finest-tempered steel, bears on one side the motto, "Strong to defend the right – swift to avenge the wrong;" and on the other a record of the presentation of the sword, "in recognition of his gallant defence of Rorke's Drift."

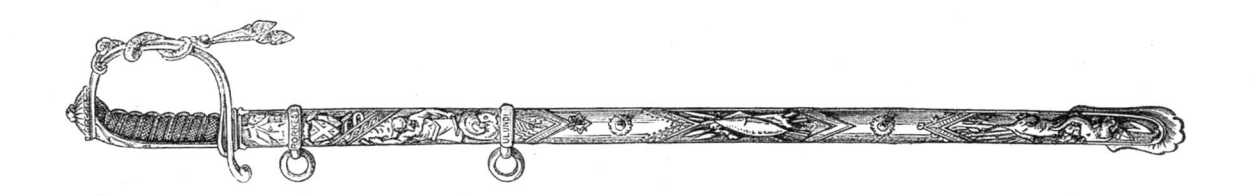

Sword presented to Major Chard, V.C., R.E., by the people of Plymouth.

The Grocers' Company entertained Major-General Lord Chelmsford and other distinguished guests in their hall, Prince's-street, Bank, on the 13th inst. The chair was occupied by the Master, Mr. John Drake. Prior to the dinner the Court of Assistants had admitted Lord Chelmsford to the honorary freedom of the company, "in recognition of his public services in the Crimea, in India, and Abyssinia; and of the energy, endurance, and skill with which he brought the recent war in Zululand to a successful issue."

THE ILLUSTRATED LONDON NEWS

November 29, 1879

THE CAPTIVE KING CETEWAYO

The deposed King of Zululand continues to reside in the Castle at Capetown, where he is for the present kept in custody, till her Majesty's Government shall have sent out definitive instructions regarding him; and he is gradually becoming acquainted with many British and Colonial fashions or habits of life. Though, before leaving his native country he saw perhaps more than he liked of some of our military corps, it was but lately, at Capetown, that he was personally introduced to the gallant 91st Regiment, Princess Louise's Argyllshire Highlanders, who had nevertheless done good service in the war.

An officer of that regiment, Lieutenant H.A. Schank, Instructor of Musketry, who had the opportunity of visiting King Cetewayo at the Castle, on the 21st ult., invited him to hear the martial music of the Highland pipers, with which the Zulu monarch was very much pleased, taking off his Kilmarnock cap and waving it as an applauding salute, while expressing in his native language, thanks and approval of the treat they afforded to his ears. We are indebted to Lieutenant Schank for a Sketch of this interesting scene. There used to be a piper in the Transvaal, who was temporarily attached to the suite of "The Gunn of Gunn," in the days of the Lydenburg Company of Volunteers; and of whose performances an amusing story is told by Dr Rowland Atcherley in his "Trip to Boerland."

The captivity of Cetewayo: The ex-King appreciates the Highland bagpipes.

But that musician, if he ever crossed the Zulu frontier, had no opportunity of proving his skill in the Royal presence of Cetewayo; and it never occurred to Sir Bartle Frere, probably, to try the effect of such a "concord of sweet sounds," by way of conciliating the formidable potentate with whom we have taken so much trouble in our recent most costly war.

THE ILLUSTRATED LONDON NEWS

December 13, 1879

COLONEL W.P. COLLINGWOOD

Among the officers who have earned fresh honours in the Zulu War is Colonel William Pole Collingwood, of the 21st Regiment (Royal Scots Fusiliers), whose portrait is engraved for this publication. He is the second son of the late Henry J.V. Collingwood, Esq., of Lilburn Tower and Cornhill House, Northumberland; his mother being a daughter of Sir T. Haggerstone, Bart., of Ellingham, in the same county. He entered the Army in 1847, as an Ensign in the 37th Regiment, with which he served in suppressing the Ceylon rebellion next year. In the Crimean War, being then a Captain of the 21st Fusiliers, he served at the siege of Sebastopol, and in the Kinburn expedition.

Colonel W.P. Collingwood, 21st Regiment.

Sub-Assistant Commissary J.L. Dalton, V.C.
Paper dated December 6, 1879

He commanded a battalion of the Land Transport Corps in the Crimea, for a twelvemonth; and when the Spartan was wrecked on the coast of Africa, in July, 1856, he was in command of the troops on board. For his conduct upon that occasion, Captain Collingwood, with the officers and men under him, received the high approbation, strongly expressed in general orders, of H.R.H. the Commander-in-Chief, as well as of Lord Panmure, the Secretary of State for War, and of Colonel M'Murdo, Director-General of the Land Transport Corps. "The courage and discipline which animated all ranks on that fearful night" were specially commended. Captain Collingwood was then rewarded with the brevet rank of Major; he attained substantial promotion to that grade in 1867, was made Brevet Lieutenant-Colonel next year, and in May, 1874, became full Lieutenant-Colonel, and Colonel in October, 1877.

He went out to South Africa, in command of the 21st Fusiliers, on board the City of Paris, when the reinforcements were sent to Lord Chelmsford after the disaster of Isandhlwana. That ship was in imminent danger of being lost at the entrance to Simon's Bay on March 21, when Colonel Collingwood's spirit and ability in command, as on the former occasion in 1856, helped to save the lives of troops and crew. In the campaign that ensued in Zululand, he was placed in command of the second brigade of

Major-General Newdigate's division; and, when that brigade was broken up, Colonel Collingwood, with his staff, was appointed Commandant of Fort Marshall and Fort Newdigate, keeping open the communications between the front and rear and the Rorke's Drift post, and guarding the district around, to the end of the war. His five years' command having expired, Colonel Collingwood has now been placed on half pay.

The portrait is from a photograph by G. West and Son, of Gosport.

THE ILLUSTRATED LONDON NEWS

December 20, 1879

Her Majesty the Queen decorating officers engaged in the Afghan and Zulu Wars, at Windsor Castle.

There is news, too, of fighting in Natal another quarter of the globe. Things are not yet settled in South Africa, though, for the present, Zululand remains quiet. Moirosi's Mountain stronghold has been captured by the Colonial Forces under Colonel Bayley. The chief himself was killed and about seventy of his followers. The loss on our side was, happily, small, and, as a result of the affair (which appears to have been skilfully conducted, but the difficulties of which seem also to have been greatly exaggerated), is spoken of in South Africa as bringing to a close "Frontier Native Disturbances." This may be true, so far as the Cape Colony is concerned. But the Transvaal is still agitated by the repugnance of the Boers to British Rule, and Secocoeni awaits upon the Frontier the operations of Sir Garnet Wolseley, which are likely enough to find a similar termination to those of the Colonial Troops against Moirosi.

THE ILLUSTRATED LONDON NEWS
December 27, 1879

ZULU WAR OFFICERS

An Illustration was given last week of the ceremony performed by the Queen at Windsor Castle, in personally decorating with the insignia of her Order of the Bath a number of military officers and others who have recently served with distinction in the Afghan and Zulu Wars. The portraits of many of those gentlemen have appeared in our Journal, with short memoirs of their careers, during the past twelve-month. We now present those of Sir Edward Strickland, K.C.B., Commissary-General; Major-General Newdigate, C.B.; Lieutenant-Colonel J. North Crealock, C.B.; Lieutenant-Colonel Drury Lowe, C.B.; Mr E.W.H. Webb, C.B., Commissary; and Surgeon-Major Cuffe, C.B., all of whom have distinguished themselves in South Africa.

Major-General E. Newdigate, C.B.   Commissary-General Sir E. Strickland, K.C.B.

Sir Edward Strickland was born in 1821, third son of the late Gerard Edward Strickland, of the ancient knightly family, Strickland of Sizergh Castle, Westmorland, one of whom bore the banner of St. George at the battle of Agincourt. After being educated at Stonyhurst College, he entered, in 1840, the Commissariat branch of the service, and thus served in Canada, Australia and Tasmania, New Zealand, Malta, and the Ionian Islands. He was sent to Turkey on special service in 1853, at the outbreak of the war with Russia, and was senior Commissariat officer with the division of the army in the Crimea which was commanded by the Duke of Cambridge. He had charge also of this department of the British force in occupation of Greece from 1855 to March, 1857, when he was appointed one of the joint Commission ordered by the three protecting Powers to examine the financial state of Greece.

In 1867, he was nominated a C.B. for distinguished services in the field during the New Zealand war of three years previous. His successful efforts to overcome the huge difficulties of transport and supply of provisions to the army in Zululand excited general admiration. Sir Edward has been twice married; and his present wife, daughter of General Tatton Brown Grieve, C.B., of Orde House, Northumberland, accompanied him through the recent wars in South Africa.

Major-General Edward Newdigate was one of the four general officers who were sent out to assist Lord Chelmsford, with the large reinforcements of troops dispatched from England immediately after the news of the disaster of Isandhlwana. An account of his previous services, which were highly meritorious, appeared at that time, since which there has been frequent occasion to notice his command of one division of the army in Zululand, that which was usually accompanied by the head-quarters of the Commander-in-Chief, and his conduct of most important operations in the late war.

Lieutenant-Colonel J. North Crealock, C.B.
95th Regiment

Surgeon-Major Cuffe, C.P.

Lieutenant-Colonel John North Crealock, of the 95th Regiment, entered the Army in 1854, and served in the Indian Mutiny campaign of 1858, at the siege and capture of Kotah, the battle of Kota ke Serai, where he was wounded, the general action resulting in the capture of Gwalior, the siege and capture of Pourie, and surprise of the enemy's camp at Kunrye; for which he received the medal with clasps, and was twice mentioned in despatches. He served as Military Secretary to Lord Chelmsford, without a day's intermission, from beginning to end of the Zulu War.

Surgeon-Major Charles MacDonogh Cuffe, who entered the medical department of the Army in 1863, serving in India and Arabia, was appointed Assistant-Surgeon to the 11th Hussars, and served with his regiment above seven years. He was promoted to the rank of Surgeon-Major in April, 1876, and proceeded to the Cape of Good Hope in October, 1877, arriving in that command just at the commencement of hostilities against the Galekas. He served as principal medical officer of the Transkeian Field Force under Colonel Glyn, C.B., throughout the campaign, and at its conclusion received the thanks of the Director-General of the Army Medical Department.

He then proceeded to the Transvaal, and joined the force then being organised under Brigadier-General Wood, V.C. He acted as principal medical officer of the flying column throughout the Zulu campaign, and was favourably mentioned in despatches. He again received the thanks of the Director-General. We are informed that Surgeon-Major Cuffe was educated at the Catholic University of Ireland, during the rectorship of the Rev. Dr Newman (now Cardinal Newman), and received his professional education at the Catholic University Medical School, and at the Richmond Hospital, Dublin. As a student he won several prizes in literature, science, and medicine. His brother, Surgeon G.M. Cuffe, also serves her Majesty in the Naval Medical Service.

Lieutenant-Colonel Drury Lowe, C.B.
17th Lancers

Commissary E.W.H. Webb, C.B.

Lieutenant-Colonel Drury Lowe, of the 17th Lancers, one of the regiments sent out in March to reinforce the army in Zululand, has gained renown as a most active and skilful leader of light cavalry, and the usefulness of his services has been repeatedly acknowledged.

Commissary E.W.H. Webb received his first commission in October, 1858, and served in the Military Train, with the rank of Captain, but was promoted in February, 1870, to his present rank; and his exertions during the late war to forward the supplies from Natal, and to organise the dépôts of provisions for the different advancing columns, have earned high official commendation.

* * * * * * * * *

ABRIDGED INDEX
(SPELLINGS, RANKS, ABBREVIATIONS AS GIVEN IN THE ORIGINAL TEXT)

A
Ababamengo, 178
Abbott, Lt., 95
Abyssinia, 9, 19, 298
Afghanistan, 32, 80, 84
Amakandah, 149
Amatikulu, 84, 91, 130, 208, 225
Amatongas, 98, 218, 236
Amaxosa race, 8
Anstey, Lt. E.O., 4, 5, 49
Ashantee, 9, 104, 122, 138, 179, 267, 269, 287
Asiatic, Union steamship, 17
Atkinson, Lt. Charles John, 4, 5, 56
Austin, Lt., 4
Aylett, Pte., 86

B
Babinanga (Babanango) Hills, 229
Baker, Comdt. J., 201, 288
Ballard, Rev. Father, 174
Balley, Pte., 87
Balte's Spruit, 130
Bamber, Canon, 175, 198
Banister, Lt. G.S., 5
Barker, Mr C.F., 263
Barrow, Capt., 3, 85, 114, 178
Barrow, Col., 249
Barrow, Maj., 85, 86, 147, 240, 278
Barton, Capt., 25, 88, 114, 124, 178, 266, 279
Bashee Valley, 134, 138, 179
Bassano, Duc de, 162, 163, 190, 192, 194
Bayley, Col., 301
Baynes, Capt., 194, 199
Beaconsfield, Lord, 270
Begbie, Capt., 83
Bellairs, Col., 201, 233
Bennett, Lt. L.H., 5
Beresford, Lord W., 157, 202, 218, 236, 248, 256, 267, 296
Black Umvaloosi (Umvelosi, Umvolosi), 9, 96, 97, 123, 201, 215, 230, 243, 246-249, 260, 278
Black, Maj. W., 5, 23, 40, 42, 60, 61, 72, 78, 135
Blackwell, Maj., 195
Blackwell, Pte., 87
Blaine, Lt., 128, 157
Bloomfield, QM, 4, 5
Bluff, 60, 61
Bond, Major, 236
Brackenbury, Commander, 95, 111
Brackfontein, 53
Brady, Col., 195, 199
Brander, Capt. W.M., 5
Bray, Col., 61, 218
Brecher, Adjt., 128
Brednard, Pte., 87

Brenton, Adml. Sir Jahleel, 176, 177 226
Brickhill, Mr., 60
Brigan, Pte., 87
Bright, Sub-Lt. Arthur Tyndal, 88, 110, 136, 137, 266

British Imperial and Colonial Forces
Naval Brigade
Royal Navy, 86
Active, HMS, 49
Boadicea, HMS, 114, 175, 283
Caesar, HMS, 226
Forester, HMS, 146, 282
Natal, HMS, 282
Orontes, HM Troop Ship, 171, 189
Tenedos, HMS, 49, 84
Royal Marines, 62, 95
Shah's (HMS) Naval Brigade, 62
British Regiments
Cavalry
1st King's Dragoon Guards, 4, 27, 229
4th Light Dragoons, 115
5th Lancers, 174, 175, 195
6th Inniskilling Dragoons, 120
12th Lancers, 26, 96
17th Lancers, 4, 27, 32, 36, 38, 51, 159, 165, 178, 179, 201, 204, 215, 218, 222, 223, 225, 228, 229, 247, 303,
19th Hussars, 3, 85
Barrow's Mounted Infantry, 178
Royal Artillery, 4, 27, 178
Tremlett's Battery, 178
Royal Engineers, 4, 27, 15, 283
Infantry
Grenadier Guards, 105, 259
Coldstream Guards, 88
3rd Regiment, 26, 44, 84, 229, 246, 264
4th (King's Own) Regiment, 104, 283
13th Light Infantry, 3, 39, 51,63, 88, 99, 110,125, 128, 148, 178, 204,229, 233, 234,246, 249,256, 264, 266, 296, 297,298
21st Regiment, 4, 27, 99, 123, 148, 165, 166, 203, 228, 229, 235, 264, 273, 290, 299
24th Regiment, 3, 4, 5, 12, 16, 18, 22, 23, 25-27, 35, 37, 38, 40, 42-44, 48, 49, 56-61, 63, 72, 76, 78, 85, 88, 105, 123, 134-136, 138, 139, 148, 150, 165, 166, 177-179, 181, 184, 202, 230, 233, 248, 253, 256, 258, 264
57th Regiment, 4, 27, 62, 63, 78, 84, 85, 86, 104, 111, 123, 178, 264
58th Regiment, 4, 27, 63, 99, 114, 123, 125, 148, 165, 166, 178, 203, 204, 229, 233, 236, 264, 266, 290

60th Rifles, 4, 27, 28, 32, 63, 67, 84, 85, 96, 104, 111, 114, 137, 138, 148, 189, 221, 260, 264, 269, 270, 278, 279
70th Regiment, 88
71st Regiment, 264
80th Regiment, 3, 63, 76, 77, 78, 96, 97, 99, 102, 123, 125, 128, 178, 203, 204, 229, 233, 234, 258, 264, 266
87th Royal Irish Fusiliers, 120
88th Regiment, 3, 13, 51, 62, 63, 78, 87, 88, 123, 178, 264
89th Regiment, 32
90th Light Infantry, 3, 39, 51,63, 87, 88, 99, 102, 104, 110, 115, 123, 136, 137, 178, 203, 218, 229, 233, 234, 264, 265, 266
91st Regiment, 88, 93
94th Regiment, 4, 27, 63, 99, 123, 134, 148, 157, 165, 166, 178, 203, 204, 229, 233, 264
95th Regiment, 8, 13, 19, 37, 57, 59, 111, 302
98th Regiment, 158, 166, 176, 227
99th Regiment, 62, 63, 64, 71, 72, 78, 84, 85, 86, 87, 91, 104, 111, 114, 120, 123, 137, 148, 165, 166, 178, 208, 221, 225, 264, 278
Kent Administrative Battalion Rifle Volunteers, 195
<u>Army Service Corps</u>, 4, 13, 27, 123
<u>Colonial</u>
Alexandra Mounted Rifles, 3
Beatson's Irregular Horse, 102
Berrington's (Bettington's) Horse, 158, 159, 166, 189, 281
Buffalo Border Guards, 3, 23
Crook's Horse, 123
Dunn's Scouts, 85, 237, 241
Durban Mounted Volunteers, 12, 13, 27
Durham (Durban) Mounted Rifles, 3
Frontier Light Horse, 3, 51, 96, 99, 104, 108, 111, 123, 124, 125, 128, 157, 158, 257, 266, 269, 270, 287, 296
Kaffir Mounted Rifles, 96
Lonsdale's Colonial Horse, 123, 165, 178, 208, 237, 260, 279, 290
Lydenburg Company of Volunteers, 53, 298
Natal Carbineers, 3, 57, 179, 181
Natal Hussars, 3
Natal Mounted Police, 3, 7, 13, 23, 37, 39
Natal Mounted Volunteer Corps, 3, 40
Natal Native Contingent, 23, 25, 26, 37, 61, 114, 145,
Natal Native Sappers, 63
Nettleton's Native Contingent, 178
Newcastle Mounted Rifles, 3
Raaf's Corps (Raaff's Rangers), 96
Shepstone's Horse, 166, 204
Sikali's Horse, 23
Stanger Mounted Rifles, 3, 49

Swazi Levies, 3
Transvaal Mounted Volunteers, 228
Transvaal Rangers, 123, 128
Victoria Mounted Rifles, 3
Weatherley's Horse, 88, 96
Wood's Irregulars, 123, 128

Bromhead, Lt. G., 5, 18, 22, 25, 26, 27, 37, 40, 44, 54, 72, 136,
Brooks, Henry, 52
Brown, Mr., 194
Browne, Lt. E.S., 5, 258
Browne, Sir Samuel, 32
Browne, Surgeon, 267
Brownlee, Mr, 2, 277
Bruce, Maj., 95
Brunker, Capt. H.M.G., 3, 246
Buckingham, Fort, 3
Buffalo River, 3, 9, 38, 40, 41, 44, 48, 49, 52, 57, 59, 60, 72, 134, 135, 148, 165, 177, 219, 248, 252, 253, 258, 267
Bulger, Seaman, 87
Buller, Lt. Col. Redvers, 51, 88, 96, 99, 102, 104, 110, 115, 124, 125, 128, 134, 157, 158, 159, 169, 201, 202, 203, 225, 227, 233, 243, 247, 256, 266, 267, 269, 270, 272, 274, 276, 287, 288, 296
Bulwer, Sir Henry, 121, 157, 263, 274, 276, 277
Burnes, Bugler J., 204
Burrows, Capt., 95, 111
Byrne, Assist. Commissary L.A., 26, 56, 57

C
Caffin, Lt. Crawford, 237, 246, 280, 281, 282, 283, 284, 295
Caldwell, Capt. J.F., 5
Cambridge, Duke of, 32, 51, 108, 142, 156, 157, 161, 172, 174, 190, 192, 194, 243, 246, 301
Campbell, A, 104
Campbell, Capt. Hon. R.G.E., 2, 88, 102, 114,115, 124, 265
Campbell, Col., 163
Campbell, Commander, R.N., 64
Cane, Lt., 84
Carey, Lt. J. Brenton, 158, 159, 166, 167, 169, 170, 176, 177, 208, 218, 226, 227, 243, 246, 296
Carey, Rev. Adolphus, 226
Carington, Hon. Rupert, 290
Carrington, Capt. F., 5, 51
Carter, Cpl. R.A., 204
Cavaye, Lt. C.W., 4, 5, 49
Cetewayo (Ketchwayo, Seketwayo, Ketchwhyo, Cetywayo, Ketshwayo), 1, 6, 8, 9, 13, 19, 25, 26, 34, 37, 51, 53, 67-69, 71, 78, 88, 91, 96, 98, 121-124, 130, 131, 133, 134, 147, 149, 165, 178, 200, 201, 209, 211-213, 215, 221, 222, 225, 226, 229-233, 240, 241, 243, 245, 246, 249, 256, 259,

260-264, 267, 270, 271, 274, 276-288, 290, 291, 295, 298, 299
Chamberlin, Capt. W.R.B., 5
Chard, Lt. R.E., 4, 12, 18, 22, 25, 27, 37, 40, 44, 54, 57, 72, 136, 248, 249, 253, 270, 288, 297
Chatham, 4, 27
Cheery, Capt., 124
Chelmsford, Lt-Gen. The Hon. Lord (Frederic Augustus Thesiger) C.B., 1, 4, 5, 9, 12, 13, 19, 20, 22, 23, 26, 27, 32, 34, 37-39, 41-44, 47, 49-52, 56, 57, 61-63, 65, 67, 69, 76, 79, 80, 84, 85, 90, 91, 93, 95, 98-100, 103, 104, 111, 114, 121, 123, 124, 130, 133, 134, 136, 139, 142, 147-149, 156-158, 161, 165, 176-178, 184, 200, 201, 204, 205, 208, 209, 211, 213, 215, 218, 219, 221-223, 225-233, 235, 241-243, 246, 248-250, 263, 265, 269, 270, 287, 298, 299, 302
Cherry, Fort, 122, 124, 145
Chillianwallah, 5
Chiselhurst, 150, 153, 161-164, 170-175, 184, 191-193, 196, 199, 200
Church, Capt. H.B., 5
Clarke, Brig., 84, 208, 226, 260, 278
Clary, Baron, 190
Claughton, Bishop, 115
Clements, Lt. R.A.P., 5
Clifford, Gen. the Hon. H., 98, 134, 177, 201, 219
Coates, Pte., 204
Cobbin, Surgeon, 76, 99
Cochrane, Capt., 167, 233
Cockerell, Captain, 157
Codrington, Admiral Sr., Henry, 80
Coghill, Lt. M.J.A., 4, 5, 25-27, 48, 61, 72, 135, 267
Colby, Col. R.E., 81
Colenso, 3
Colenso, Bishop, 261
Coleworth, Lt., R.N., 148
Colley, Col. Pomeroy C.B., 122, 137, 138, 249
Collingwood, Lt.-Col. W. Pole, 166, 299, 300
Conference Hill, 130, 135, 139, 145, 148, 157, 158, 165
Connolly, Surgeon, 267
Conway Castle, 69
Coode, Sir John, 61
Cordy, Seaman, 87
Corvisart, Baron, 161, 162, 190, 194, 195
Courtenay, Lt., 111
Cox, Capt., 110
Coxwell, Capt., 76
Craigie, Lt. R.N., 49
Crampton, Sgt., 128
Crealock, Fort, 130, 208
Crealock, Maj-Gen. Hope, C.B., 8, 13, 37, 42, 43, 46, 47, 61, 78, 98, 111, 118, 123, 130, 133, 134, 146-148, 177, 178, 222, 225, 228, 231, 237, 243, 301, 302

Croneys, Lt., 88
Crookall, Rev. Dr., 175, 198
Cuffe, Surgeon-Maj. Charles MacDonogh, C.B., 301, 302, 303
Cunynghame, Gen. Sir Arthur, 19, 52, 53, 120
Curll. 2nd Lt. C.E., 5
Curteis, Lt. E.W., 5

D

Dabulamanzi, 68, 71, 72, 84, 85, 130, 133, 218, 222, 236,
Dallard, Sgt., 86
Dalmain's Farm, 122, 124
Dalrymple, Lt. A.D.C., 285
Dalton, Sub-Asst. Commissary J.L., V.C., 299
Daly, Lt. J.P., 4, 5
Danell, Right Rev. Dr., 198
D'Arcy, Capt., 287
Dartnell, Maj., 3, 7, 12, 37, 39,
Davies, Col., 259
Davis, Col., 105
Davis, Lt. Newnham, 44, 51, 57, 95, 249
De Burgh, Capt., 279
Deacon, Pte., 86
Degacher, Capt. W., 4, 5
Degacher, Lt-Col. H.J., 3, 5, 23, 135
Delagoa Bay, 2, 8, 61, 91, 98, 99, 287
Derby, 76, 77, 78, 96, 99, 102, 161
Dirdley, Pte., W., 204
Dobree, 2nd Lt. L.G.L., 5
Doornberg (Dornberg), 98, 99, 123, 145
Douglas, Lt. James Henry Scott, 228, 299
Downe, Lord, 139
Doyle, Canon, 175, 198
Doyle, Gen. Sr. Hastings, 161
Drew, Pte., 87
Drewe, Col., 269
Drinkwater, Canon, 175
Drummond, Hon. Frances, 166, 192
Drummond, Lt., 95
Du Cane, Sir Charles, 287
Du Plat, Col., 192
Dublin Castle, 22, 27, 32, 67
Duffy, Trp., 128
Dunbar, Maj. W.M., 5
Duncombe, Lt., 128, 257, 296
Dunn, John, 85, 89, 91, 133, 209, 237, 240, 241, 242, 261, 283, 291
Durnford, Col. R.E., 3, 4, 9, 17, 23, 25, 27, 32, 37, 40, 44, 57, 58, 123, 139, 146, 181, 208, 236, 237, 246, 274, 279-281, 284, 295
Dyer, Lt. H.J., 4, 5, 49
Dyer's Island, 88, 108, 109
Dyson, 2nd Lt. E.H., 4, 5, 49

E

East, Lt. D.A., 270, 271, 272
Edgell, Capt. Wyatt, 203, 204, 222, 223, 236
Edinburgh, Duke of, 161, 190, 192, 194, 225
Eland's Nek, 39, 49, 51

Ellice, Gen. Sir Charles, 192
Ellis, Sgt., 128
Emangwene, 237, 240
Emhlabalini (Ulundi), 263
Eshowe (Ekowe, Etchowe), 12, 13, 26, 32, 54, 61-63, 69, 76, 78-80, 84-86, 89-91, 93, 95-99, 104, 106, 111, 130, 133, 136, 229, 246, 249, 266, 270, 272
Estcourt, 3, 145, 215, 218
Eugénie, Empress, 142, 150, 151, 153, 160-163, 172, 175, 184, 185, 188-192, 194, 195, 199
Euphorbia Hill, 63, 147
Evans, Dr., 195
Evelyn, Col., G.P., 246
Evelyn, Lt., George Rowley John, 229, 246
Everett, Lt. C., 270

F
Fannin, Mr JE., 67, 68
Farquhar, Capt. H.R., 5
Farrar, Mr J.A., 130
Fitzmaurice, Sgt., 256
Flannery, Pte., 86
Floyd, Pte., 204
Forbes, Mr Archibald, 201, 211, 219-21, 233
Fowler, Pvt, 115, 265
Franey, Pte., 86
Franklin, 2nd Lt. A.W., 5
Frere, Lady, 76, 157, 161, 176, 199
Frere, Sir Bartle. 1, 5, 8, 34, 53, 54, 67, 69, 98, 121, 135, 142, 157, 176, 201, 225, 260, 261, 263, 265, 270, 272, 274, 276, 277, 285, 299
Frith, Adj. Frederick Cokayne, 210, 215, 222, 223
Fynn, Mr H.F., 2
Fynney, Mr., 147

G
Gaika War, 266
Gaikas, 7, 8, 52, 266
Gatewood, Capt., 88, 104
Gilbert, Col., 88
Gillespie, Pte., 86
Gingihlovo (Gingindlovu), 84, 85, 91, 95, 96, 137,
208, 221, 229, 240
Glennie, Capt. F., 5
Glyn, Col. R.T., 3-5, 9, 22, 23, 25, 26, 37, 38-40, 48, 51, 57, 61, 72, 98, 139, 184, 302
Goddard, Monsignor, 162, 175, 191, 192, 198, 199
Godwin-Austen, Capt. A.G., 5
Godwin-Austen, Lt. F., 5
Gordon, Deputy-Commissary W.G., 148
Graves, Maj., 2, 3
Gravesend, 27
Grey Town, 3, 26
Greyham, Pte., 266
Griffiths, Maj. Arthur, 14
Griffiths, Sub-Lt. T.L.G., 5
Griqualand, 121

Grosvenor, Pte., 266
Grubb, Cpl., 167, 169, 170

H
Hackett, Maj. R.H., 88, 102, 104, 110, 137, 267
Haines, Pte., 86
Halliday, Lt. S.T., 5
Hamilton, Capt., 88
Hamilton, Sub-Lt., 95
Hankey, General, 162
Hankey, Lady Emily, 162
Harbour, Mr., 61, 72
Hardinge, Lt-Gen. the Hon. A.E. C.B., 174
Harford, Lt. H.C., 71, 72, 278
Harley, Brig.-Gen., 177
Harrison, Capt. H.A., 5
Harrison, Lt-Col., 134, 165, 166, 176, 208, 246
Harrison, Gen., 226
Hartley, Pte., 87
Harvey, Capt. J.J., 5
Harward, Lt., 78, 99
Hasley, Asst-Commissary-Gen., 148
Hassard, Col, C.B., 26, 176, 283, 286
Hatherley, Lord, 265, 267
Heath, Maj-Gen., 19
Heaton, Lt. W., 5
Helpmakaar, 3, 7, 9, 13, 25, 26, 27, 37, 40, 48, 56-58, 61, 69, 72, 76, 95, 98, 99
Henchley, Seaman, 87
Henderson, Col. Sir E.Y., 175
Henderson, Lt., 95, 157
Hewitt, Trp., 128
Hicks-Beach, Sir Michael, 121, 161
Hillier, Cpl., 266
Hinchingbrook, Viscount, 161
Hinxman, Capt., 85, 86
Hlobane (Tlobane, Zlobane, Inhlobane, Mhlobani) Mountain, 88, 102, 110, 114, 115, 124, 125, 149, 218, 227, 256, 258, 270, 296
Hodson, Lt. G.F.J., 4, 5, 27
Hutton, Lt., 148, 278, 279

I
Ibabanango (Babanango), 148, 178, 248
Imbanani River, 167
Intombi Drift, 76, 78, 97, 99, 102, 128
Inyezane, Battle of, 136
Inyoni, 84, 91
Isandlwana (Insandusuna, Isandula, Insanhlwana, Isandhlwana), 22, 23, 25-27, 32, 34, 35, 37, 38, 40-42, 44, 51, 54-57, 59, 61, 65-69, 71, 72, 76, 78, 84, 85, 88, 95, 134, 135, 136, 138, 145, 146, 158, 177-180, 182, 184, 211, 215, 222, 231, 248, 250, 253, 258, 264, 286, 299, 302
Itelezi Hill, 148, 158, 159, 166, 170, 176, 188, 204, 205,
Ityotyosi, 259

J

James, Pte., 218
Jeff, Sgt., 266
Johnson, Lt-Col. Noble, 120
Johnson, Lt. G.C.J., 85, 86, 99, 111, 120, 221
Jolled, Pte., 86
Jones, Trp. K.N., 204

K

Kambula, 88, 99, 102, 104, 105, 110, 114, 116, 123-125, 130, 134, 137, 139, 178, 218, 233, 258, 287, 297
Kent, Pte., 204
Kerr, Lt., 111
Kinahan, Capt. G.R., 174, 189
King Panda, 91, 243, 244, 277, 285, 291
King William's Town, 13, 51, 52, 139
Kingscote, Col. M.P., 161
Kingscote, Lt., 63, 111
Koppie Allein, 148, 178
Kranzkop, 145
Kwanagwasa, 229

L

Ladysmith, 3, 130, 145, 149
Laine, Abbé, 194
Lambert, Baron T., 195
Landsill, Trp., 128
Langalibalele, 277, 286
Lanyon, Col., 121, 134
Laurence, Capt. H.B., 76, 104, 108, 218, 219
Laye, Captain, 110
Le Grice, Maj., 229
Leet, Maj. W. Knox, 125, 128, 256-258, 265, 267, 296, 297
Legrave, Rev. W., 174
Letocq, Trp., 167, 169
Liedenbrood, Lt., 236
Lindsay, Lt., 95
Littleton, Hon. Mr., 176, 285
Lloyd, 2nd Lt. W.W., 5, 56-59, 76
Lloyd, James, 2, 13, 33, 50
Lloyd, Llewellyn, 88, 102, 114, 115, 266
Logan, Lt. H.M.K., 5
Logan, Maj. W.B., 5
Lomas, Mr., 194
Longeast (Longcast), Mr., 72, 283, 285, 290
Longfield, Dr., 85, 86
Lonsdale, Comdt. La Trobe, 3, 12, 39
Loraine, Capt., 128, 195
Lord, Capt. B, 148
Lowe, Lt-Col. Drury, C.B., 138, 159, 184, 215, 223, 301, 303
Lower Tugela, 2, 26, 33, 37, 49, 61, 62, 63, 66-68, 84, 90, 91, 123, 130, 144, 146, 147, 166, 208, 209, 221, 222, 243
Lucas, Capt. T.J., 139, 261, 263, 278
Luckhurst, Capt., 105
Luneberg, 3, 76, 77, 95, 96, 99, 102
Lydenburg, 3, 53, 298

Lysons, Lt., 115, 242, 243, 265

M

Macdonald, Lt., 4
Macgregor, Capt., 90, 91
Maclear, Capt. H.W., 13
Madeira, 13, 17, 20, 22, 32, 51, 54, 76, 78, 190, 246
Mahony, Paymaster J., 5
Mainwaring, Lt. H.G., 5
Markham, Col., 195
Marshall, Fort, 300
Marshall, Maj-Gen. Frederick, 13, 98, 122, 124, 138, 159, 165, 170, 178, 179, 184, 189, 215, 225, 243, 246
Marter, Maj. R.J.C., 258-260, 267, 278, 279, 288
Martini-Henry (Rifle), 85, 88, 95, 110, 111, 145, 147, 169, 233, 246
Martyn, Col. Mountjoy, 120
Mashue, 54
Mason, Lt., 96
Maude, Capt., 88
Mavumgwana, 67, 71
McAllen, Sgt., 266
McIntyre, Pte., 87
Mellsop, Pte., 134, 135, 136
Melvill, Lt. T., 4, 5, 25, 48, 61, 72, 135, 184, 248, 252, 253, 255, 267
Mhlazatze, 158
Mnyamana, 88, 249
Moffat, Capt. H.B., 5
Moirosi Mountain, 301
Molyneux, Capt., 111
Moodie, Mr., 149
Moreland, Lt., 283
Moriarty, Capt., 76-78, 96, 99, 102, 125, 128
Morosi, Basuto Chief, 166
Morshead (Moorhead), Gunner, 218, 236
Morshead, Lt. A.A., 5
Mostyn, Capt. W. Eccles, 4, 5, 37, 49
Much, Capt. W.T., 5
Murray, Capt., 147, 148

N

Napier, Fort, 145
Napier, Lord of Magdala, 19, 41, 172, 192
Napoleon III, Emperor, 150, 152, 153, 156, 162-164, 172, 174, 175, 192, 194, 199
Napoleon, Prince Louis, 114, 123, 134, 139, 141-143, 148, 150-154, 156-164, 166, 167, 169, 170, 172-177, 184-186, 188-190, 192-194, 199, 200, 204, 205, 208, 216-219, 226, 229, 242, 243, 246, 258, 259, 296
Natal, 2-9, 12, 13, 17, 23, 25-27, 33, 34, 37, 40, 41, 45, 48, 50-54, 58, 60, 61, 63, 67, 69, 71, 72, 76, 78, 79, 89-91, 95, 96, 98, 99, 102, 105, 114, 121-124, 130, 134, 139, 140, 144, 145, 147-149, 157, 166, 172, 175, 177, 178, 181, 189, 200, 209, 218, 219,

225, 227, 237, 240, 249, 261, 263, 265, 270, 274, 276, 277, 281, 283, 287, 291, 301, 303
Natal, Bishop of, 277, 286
Newcastle, 3, 134, 139, 145, 261
Newdigate, Fort, 259, 300
Newdigate, Maj-Gen. E., 13, 99, 123, 130, 134, 148, 158, 165, 168, 176, 178, 181, 187, 189, 201, 204, 208, 214, 215, 218, 223-225, 228, 229, 231, 247, 300-302
Ngome Forest, 278, 259
Nicholson, Lt. R.A., 88, 102, 104, 110, 266
Nkobamakosi (Zulu Regiment), 71
Nodwengu (Zulu Regiment), 71, 215, 233, 243, 244
Nokenke (Zulu Regiment), 71
North, Canon, 198
Northey, Lt-Col. Francis V., 85, 96, 111, 120, 137, 138, 208, 221
Nuthall, Lt. H.M., 290

O
Oham (Hamu, Uhamu), 68, 102, 256
Oscarburg (Oscarsburg), 41, 45, 48, 134, 136
O'Toole, Sgt. Edmund, 287

P
Palmes, Lt. G.C. , 5
Pardoe, Lt. George Astell, 246
Parnise, Bombadier, 87
Parr, Capt. Hallam, 176, 285
Pearson, Col., 3, 4, 12, 13, 26, 32, 37, 49, 50, 51, 54, 61-63, 67, 69, 78, 80, 84, 89-91, 95, 96, 98, 99, 104, 114, 136, 221, 229, 249, 265-267
Pearson, Fort, 2, 33, 49, 61, 63, 66, 99, 130, 133, 136, 137, 139, 147, 165, 166, 177, 200, 208, 209
Pearson, Mr T., 79, 90
Peel, Capt. Sir William, 102
Pemberton, Major, 84, 104
Pembroke, Earl of, 263
Penfold, Capt. MH, 28
Perkins, Pte., 86
Peyton, Capt. G. , 5
Phillips, Capt., 95
Phipps, 2nd Lt. A.B., 5, 236
Pietersen, Trp., 128
Pinetown, 124, 130, 131, 146,
Pongola, 8, 49, 51, 95
Ponsonby, Sir H., 163, 192
Poole, Captain, R.A., 279, 281, 283, 290, 295
Poole, Lt., 88
Pope, Lt. C. D'A., 4, 5, 23, 27
Port Durnford, 208, 236, 237, 246, 279-281, 284, 295
Port Natal, 60, 189
Porteous, Lt. F.P., 4, 5, 27
Porteous, Petty Officer, 87
Porter, Lt., R. da Costa, 136

Potchefstroom, 54
Pots Spruit, 3
Potter, Mr Charles, 266
Pretoria, 3, 54, 102, 120, 249, 264, 265
Prior, Melton, 10, 13, 16, 26, 67, 76, 88, 92, 93, 98, 100, 103, 104, 106, 110, 116, 122, 124, 130, 131, 133, 137, 139, 143, 144, 149, 164, 165, 172, 178-180, 182, 186, 189, 204, 209, 210, 212-217, 223, 226, 229-232, 235, 238, 243, 244, 246, 248,256, 259, 298
Probyn, Maj-Gen. Sir Dighton, 161, 192
Pulleine, Col. (Pulleyne), 4, 5, 9, 23, 25, 27, 37, 38, 40, 49, 51, 57
Pullen. QM J., 4, 5

Q
Queenstown (Cork Harbour), 13, 27

R
Raaf, Capt. (Raaff), 99, 128
Rainforth, Capt. T., 5
Raw, Capt. Charles, 60, 72, 157, 158
Reilly, Col. C.B., 165
Reilly, Surgeon, 267
Reynolds, Surgeon-Maj. James Henry, 258
Richards, Commodore, R.N., 104
Roche, Lt. the Hon. U. de R.B., 5
Rogers, Trp., 167, 169
Rorke's Drift (Rourke's Drift), 3, 4, 8, 9, 12, 13, 17, 22, 25-27, 37, 38, 40, 41, 44-49, 54, 56, 57, 60, 61, 67, 69, 71, 72, 76, 99, 102, 134-136, 138, 148, 157, 165, 177-179, 184, 246, 250, 253-255, 258, 270, 297, 300
Russell, Capt., 4, 23, 66
Russell, Lt-Col., 26, 39, 46, 47, 88, 96, 99, 110, 124, 125

S
Sandilli, 52
Sarmenter, Lt., 88
Schank, Lt. H.A., 298
Schermbrucker, Comdt., 3, 96, 99
Schreuder, Bishop, 67, 90
Scott, Lt., 57, 181
Secocoeni (Sekukhuni), 3, 53, 178, 297, 301
Shepherd, Lt., 283
Shepherd, Surgeon-Maj., 4, 5
Shepstone, Capt. W., 12, 13, 27, 139, 181
Shepstone, Mr J., 2
Sherrard, Lt., 99
Silona, Trp., 204
Simmons, Gen. Sir Lintorn, 156, 172, 190, 194
Simon's Bay, 171, 174, 175, 282, 283, 299
Sirayo, 20, 22, 23, 25, 26, 67, 134, 136, 138, 149, 158, 218, 222, 236,
Smith, Capt. Stuart R.A., 4, 23
Smith, Lt. A. Metcalfe, 88, 125, 128, 257, 258, 296
Smith, Maj., 57

Smith, Sgt., 266
Smith-Dorrien, Lt., 57, 59, 93, 95, 109, 112, 114,
Spring, Lt. W.E.D., 5
SS Clyde, 88, 105, 108, 109, 177, 227
St Lucia, 1, 2, 147
St. Vincent, 4
Stanley, Col. F.A., 33, 192
Stephenson, Gen., 192
Stewart, Maj., 159
Stewart, Vice-Adml. Sr. W.H., 162
Strathnairn, Field-Marshall Lord, 172, 192
Strong, Lt., 110
Sugden, Lt. W., 5
Sully, Cpl., 259
Sutton, Pte., 86
Swaziland, 102, 274, 276,
Sydney, Lord, 161-163, 192
Symons, Capt. W.P., 5

T
Taylor, Farrier-Sergeant, 204
Tenedos, Fort, 61-63, 69, 90, 91, 98, 99, 104, 136
Terry, Capt. Astley, 278, 279
Thring's Post, 49
Tinta's Kraal, 32
Tompkinson, Cpl. 204
Tongue, Capt. J.M.G., 5
Tremlett, Maj. R.A., 110
Trollope, Anthony, 52, 291
Trower, Lt. C.V., 5
Tucker, Maj., 78, 99
Tugela, 1-3, 8, 9, 13, 17, 34, 49-53, 61, 63, 67,
    69, 78, 80, 84, 85, 90, 91, 93, 95, 96, 98, 100,
    103, 104, 130, 133, 134, 136, 137, 144, 145,
    147, 177, 204, 209, 225, 237, 243, 263, 291
Turner, Maj-Gen., 174, 190, 195
Twiss, Capt., 237
Tyingwayo (Ntshingwayo), 71

U
Uhamu (see Oham)
Ulundi, 85, 88, 123, 130, 133, 148, 149, 177, 178,
    200-204, 206, 209, 211, 213, 215, 218-223,
    225, 226, 228-231, 233-236, 238, 241, 243-
    246, 248-250, 253, 259, 260, 263, 266, 269,
    270, 272, 278, 279, 287, 290
Umbelini, 76, 88, 95, 124, 274, 276
Umbonambi (Zulu Regiment), 71
Umcityu (Zulu Regiment), 71
Umhlatosi River, 147, 208, 237, 240, 241
Umhlatusi, 85
Umkosana, 278, 279, 283
Umsundusi River, 91
Undini, 241
Upcher, Capt. R., 5
Usingwayo, 249
Ussher, Lt. Beverley W.R., 77, 78, 97, 99
Utrecht, 3, 13, 51, 96, 98, 102, 114, 130, 133, 148,
    165, 177, 218, 219, 228, 246, 264, 269, 274,
    277
Uys, Lt. Piet, 88, 99, 102, 114, 218, 219, 227,
    228, 266

V
Van Straubenzee, Major, 192
Vaughan, Capt. H., 124
Vaughan, Maj. R.A., 88, 110
Vereker, Lord, 139
Verulam, 79, 90, 144, 145, 146
Vinnicombe, Trp., 128

W
Walker, Col, 2, 3
Ward-Ashton, Maj., 195
Wardell, Capt. G.V., 4, 5
Wardrop, Dr., 99
Wassall, Pte., 258
Watkin, Sir Edward, 163
Weallens, 2nd Lt. W., 5
Weatherley, Lt-Col., 88, 96, 99, 102, 114, 115,
    124, 125
Webb, Mr E.W.H., C.B., 301, 303
Wedenas, Pte., 86
Westwood, Pte., 258
White Umvolosi (Umvelosi, Imvolosi), 9, 32, 130,
    229, 233, 243, 249, 256
White, Capt. Loraine, 128
White, Maj. Francis F., 4, 5, 38, 48
Whitecross, Trp., 128
Williams Lt. Charles Ellis, 102, 114, 125, 266
Williams Capt. G., 124, 125, 128
Williams, Lt. H.M., 5
Willis, Sgt., 167, 169, 170, 199
Wilson, Lt., 128
Witt, Rev, 41, 46, 47, 71, 72,
Wolseley, Sir Garnet, 41, 104, 121, 137, 138, 177,
    200, 211, 222, 225, 236, 237, 243, 246, 249,
    250, 256, 259, 260, 263, 264, 267, 269, 270,
    272, 276, 278, 291, 301
Wood, Brig-Gen. Evelyn, 3, 9, 13, 22, 26, 32, 51,
    54, 66-69, 79, 88, 96, 97-99, 102, 104, 105,
    108, 110, 114, 115, 120, 123-125, 128, 130,
    134, 136, 137, 145, 148, 149, 158, 159, 165,
    167, 169, 178, 186, 189, 201, 209, 215, 218,
    224, 225, 227, 229, 234, 243, 247, 249, 250,
    256, 258, 265, 267, 269, 270, 272, 287, 296,
    297, 302
Woodgate, Capt., 104, 110, 267
Woolwich, 27, 51, 104, 105, 142, 150, 152, 153,
    156, 157, 164, 172, 174, 175, 190, 191, 192,
    195, 200
Wrottesley, Col., 195
Wynne, Capt. Warren R.C., 136, 137

Y
Younghusband, Capt. R., 4, 5
Younghusband, Major-General, 174